The SCERTS™ Model

*A Comprehensive
Educational Approach
for Children with
Autism Spectrum Disorders*

Volume I

Assessment

The SCERTS™ Model

A Comprehensive
Educational Approach
for Children with
Autism Spectrum Disorders

Volume I
Assessment

by

Barry M. Prizant, Ph.D., Amy M. Wetherby, Ph.D., Emily Rubin, M.S.,
Amy C. Laurent, Ed.M., OTR/L, and Patrick J. Rydell, Ed.D.

·P·A·U·L·H·
BROOKES
PUBLISHING Cº ®

Baltimore • London • Sydney

Paul H. Brookes Publishing Co.
Post Office Box 10624
Baltimore, Maryland 21285-0624

www.brookespublishing.com

Typeset by Integrated Publishing Solutions, Grand Rapids, Michigan.
Manufactured in the United States of America by
Sheridan Books, Chelsea, Michigan.

Library of Congress Cataloging-in-Publication Data
The SCERTS model : a comprehensive educational approach for children with autism
   spectrum disorders / by Barry M. Prizant ... [et al.].
     v.   cm.
   Includes bibliographical references and index.
   Contents: v. 1. Assessment—v. 2. Program planning and intervention
   ISBN-13: 978-1-55766-689-5 (v. 1) — ISBN-13: 978-1-55766-809-7 (v. 2)
   ISBN-10: 1-55766-689-X (v. 1) — ISBN-10: 1-55766-809-4 (v. 2)
   1. Autistic children—Education.   2. Autism in children—Treatment.
   I. Prizant, Barry M.   II. Title.
   LC4717.S28 2006
   371.94—dc22   2005026703

British Library Cataloguing in Publication data are available from the British Library.

Contents
Volume I

Contents
Volume II

About the Authors

Barry M. Prizant, Ph.D., CCC-SLP, Director, Childhood Communication Services, 2024 Broad Street, Cranston, Rhode Island, 02904; Adjunct Professor, Center for the Study of Human Development, Brown University, 133 Waterman Street, Box 1831, Providence, Rhode Island

Barry M. Prizant has more than 30 years of experience as a clinical scholar, researcher, and consultant to young children with autism spectrum disorders (ASD) and related communication and developmental disabilities and their families. Dr. Prizant has published more than 90 articles and chapters on ASD and pediatric communication disabilities, serves on the advisory board of six professional journals, and has presented more than 500 seminars and numerous keynote addresses at national and international conferences. Dr. Prizant also served on the Committee on Screening and Diagnosis of Autism Spectrum Disorders at the National Institutes of Health and co-authored the Practice Parameters published by the committee. He is co-editor (with Amy M. Wetherby) of the book *Autism Spectrum Disorders: A Developmental, Transactional Perspective* (Paul H. Brookes Publishing Co., 2000), a volume in the *Communication and Language Intervention Series*. Dr. Prizant is a Fellow of the American Speech-Language-Hearing Association and has received numerous awards as well as widespread recognition for his clinical and scholarly work.

Amy M. Wetherby, Ph.D., CCC-SLP, Laurel Schendel Professor, Department of Communication Disorders, and Executive Director, Center for Autism and Related Disabilities, Florida State University, Tallahassee, Florida 32306

Amy M. Wetherby has more than 20 years of clinical experience and is a Fellow of the American Speech-Language-Hearing Association. Dr. Wetherby has published extensively and presents regularly at national conventions on social and communicative profiles of children with autism spectrum disorders (ASD) and early identification of communication disorders in infants and toddlers. She served on the National Academy of Sciences Committee for Educational Interventions for Children with Autism. Dr. Wetherby is the Project Director of the FIRST WORDS Project (http://firstwords.fsu.edu), which is funded by a U.S. Department of Education Field-Initiated Research Grant on improving early identification of young children at risk for ASD, a Model Demonstration Grant on early intervention for very young children with ASD and their families, and a Doctoral Leadership Training Grant specializing in autism.

Emily Rubin, M.S., CCC-SLP, Lecturer, Yale University School of Medicine; Director, Communication Crossroads, Post Office Box 222171, Carmel, California 93922

Emily Rubin is Director of Communication Crossroads, a private practice in Carmel, California. She is a speech-language pathologist specializing in autism, Asperger syndrome, and related social learning disabilities. As an adjunct faculty member and lecturer at Yale University, she has served as a member of its Autism and Developmental

Disabilities Clinic. She has also served as an instructor for the Communication Sciences and Disorders Department of Emerson College in Boston, Massachusetts, where she has developed courses to prepare graduate-level students to address the needs of children with autism and their families. Her publications have focused on early identification of autism, contemporary intervention models, and programming guidelines for high-functioning autism and Asperger syndrome. She has participated as a member of the American Speech-Language-Hearing Association's Ad Hoc Committee on Autism Spectrum Disorders (ASD), a committee charged with developing guidelines related to the role of speech-language pathologists in the diagnosis, assessment, and treatment of ASD. She lectures internationally and provides consultation to educational programs serving children and adolescents with autism and related developmental disorders.

Amy C. Laurent, Ed.M., OTR/L, Occupational Therapist, Private Practice, North Kingstown, Rhode Island

Amy C. Laurent is a pediatric occupational therapist who holds a master's degree in special education. Currently in private practice, she is a New England affiliate of Communication Crossroads and of Childhood Communication Services. Ms. Laurent specializes in the education of children with autism spectrum disorders (ASD) and related developmental disabilities. Through her practice, she provides comprehensive evaluations, direct therapeutic services, and consultations to educational programs for children with ASD. She also provides extensive educational and emotional support to families of children with ASD. Ms. Laurent has co-authored several journal articles and frequently lectures throughout the United States on topics related to therapeutic and educational intervention for children with ASD. Her areas of clinical interest include therapeutic intervention as it relates to the development of self-regulation and social-adaptive functioning across contexts (e.g., school, home, and community settings).

Patrick J. Rydell, Ed.D., Director, Rocky Mountain Autism Center, Post Office Box 620578, Littleton, Colorado 80162

Dr. Rydell has been in the field of autism and communication disorders for more than 24 years in public school, hospital, university, administration, and private practice settings. Dr. Rydell is the owner and director of Rocky Mountain Autism Center, a private center dedicated solely to working with children with autism spectrum disorders and their families. The center provides comprehensive center-, community-, and home-based assessments, programs, interventions, and training to individuals with autism, their families, and professionals. Dr. Rydell earned his doctoral and master's degrees in the field of communication disorders and special education, with a primary program emphasis in autism and early childhood education. Dr. Rydell is a Fulbright Senior Specialist grant recipient (2005) and has previously co-authored five book chapters and numerous research articles on autism and unconventional verbal behaviors. In addition, he frequently speaks at international, national, and state levels on topics related to autism.

For the Reader

The SCERTS™ Model: A Comprehensive Educational Approach for Children with Autism Spectrum Disorders is a two-volume manual. Volume I, *Assessment,* describes the three domains of the SCERTS Model—Social Communication, Emotional Regulation, and Transactional Support—with detailed information about developmental sequences and priorities for each domain. The SCERTS Model is also discussed in the context of the array of educational options for children with autism spectrum disorders (ASD). Volume I also describes in detail the SCERTS Assessment Process (SAP) and provides specific assessment criteria at three stages of communication development: Social Partner, Language Partner, and Conversational Partner. Appendix A contains a number of photocopiable forms for collecting information and monitoring progress for a child during the SAP.

Volume II, *Program Planning and Intervention,* addresses the how-to of implementing the SCERTS Model across home, school, and community settings. It describes how to prioritize goals and implement practices that fall under the Transactional Support domain, including how to link Transactional Support goals with Social Communication and Emotional Regulation goals. Volume II also presents in-depth vignettes about several children and their families at the three major developmental stages in the model. These vignettes include examples of completed forms used during the SAP. An appendix at the end of Volume II contains quality indicator rating scales that can be used to address program-level assessment and planning.

A glossary appears as Appendix B of Volume I. This glossary is placed in Volume I because most of the key terms defined in it are first presented in Volume I.

The index at the end of each volume is identical. It serves both books together, containing page references to both volumes.

Acknowledgments

The SCERTS Model and the manual *The SCERTS™ Model: A Comprehensive Educational Approach for Children with Autism Spectrum Disorders* have resulted from support we have received over many years and from many different sources. The SCERTS Model collaborators would like to acknowledge those who have provided the "transactional support" that has made this manual possible.

First and foremost, we would like to thank the children and older individuals with autism spectrum disorders (ASD) and their families who have and who continue to teach us about their courage and humanity every day. We consider it a privilege that they have allowed us to be a part of their lives and their ongoing journeys. Their generous sharing of their spirit and wisdom provides the fuel that drives us in our life's work and helps us to strive to do our very best.

We would like to thank our families and friends, whose support and understanding helped to create the opportunities and space in our lives to do the painstaking and seemingly never-ending work during the years of developing the SCERTS Model and this manual. We hope their sacrifices are counterbalanced by the potential positive impact the SCERTS Model will have in the lives of individuals with ASD and their families.

We would like to thank our academic, clinical, and research mentors, who have instilled the values and beliefs that have guided our life's work and that are infused throughout the SCERTS Model. These values and beliefs are grounded in 1) an understanding that each child and family should be treated with respect and integrity, in recognition of the unique relationships we establish with them in our work, 2) that each individual, regardless of the challenges in his or her life, has interests and strengths that must be understood and enhanced, and 3) that an understanding of the complexities of human development is the most respectful guide to working effectively with children and families.

Finally we would like to acknowledge the staff of Paul H. Brookes Publishing Co., who have enthusiastically supported our efforts in developing and sharing the SCERTS Model. Their insistence on clarity and quality and their expertise at all levels of this project have contributed to a final product that we are proud to share.

With all of the support we have received, it is our sincere hope that this manual, in turn, will support the efforts of educators, therapists, family members, and other caregivers in promoting the most positive quality of life for individuals with ASD and related disabilities.

Chapter 1

Introduction

The SCERTS Model is a comprehensive, multidisciplinary approach to enhancing communication and social-emotional abilities of individuals with ASD and related disabilities (Prizant, Wetherby, Rubin, & Laurent, 2003). The acronym SCERTS refers to Social Communication, Emotional Regulation, and Transactional Support, which we believe should be the primary developmental dimensions targeted in a program designed to support the development of individuals with ASD and their families.

This innovative educational model is based on an integration of research and clinical practice published by us since the mid-1970s. In this collaborative effort, we have attempted to honor the complexities of child development as well as the challenges faced by children with autism spectrum disorders (ASD) by striking a balance between sound research and theory and practical application to improve the quality of life of children with ASD and their families.

In the SCERTS Model, it is recognized that most learning in childhood occurs in the social context of daily activities and experiences. Therefore, efforts to support a child's development within the model occur with caregivers and familiar partners in everyday routines in a variety of social situations, not primarily through work with a child in isolation. The SCERTS framework has been designed to target priority goals in social communication and emotional regulation through implementation of transactional supports (e.g., interpersonal support, learning supports) throughout a child's daily activities and across partners to facilitate competence within these identified goal areas. When a child's development in social communication and emotional regulation is supported, with the strategic implementation of transactional supports, there is great potential for comprehensive, long-term positive effects on a child's development in educational environments and everyday activities.

We believe that an effective program for a child with ASD requires the expertise of a team of professionals working in a careful, coordinated manner in partnership with parents and family members. Therefore, the SCERTS Model is best implemented as a multidisciplinary team approach that respects, draws from, and infuses expertise from a variety of disciplines, including general and special education, speech-language pathology, occupational therapy, child psychology and psychiatry, and social work. In this chapter, we provide a brief overview of the domains of the SCERTS Model; discuss what the SCERTS Model is and is not; and discuss the philosophical foundations, core values, and guiding principles of the model.

We have made every effort to make this manual user-friendly and accessible for professionals, paraprofessionals, and parents. However, we also believe the reader must make an investment in understanding the rich theoretical and research foundations of the model to apply it effectively. Although we have infused the manual with helpful examples and creative activities, the strength of the SCERTS Model is in the integration of understanding a child in the context of his or her family and daily activities and the transactional impact of people and learning supports that become critical influences on the child's development in everyday experiences.

By design, the SCERTS Model is comprehensive, in that it can be applied across different settings and partners in a child's life. The model works best as a team approach, as the expertise of professionals from different disciplines in partnership with the family is the best way to support a child's development. The manual addresses the need for professionals to be accountable in educational practices, as it includes data-based systems for assessing a child and family's strengths and needs and for tracking progress and determining the next logical steps in a child's program. It is our hope that the SCERTS Model will contribute to all of our efforts to support children with ASD and their families. We also believe that ultimately, the children and their families will be the ones who continue to educate us about what to focus on in applying the SCERTS Model in the most relevant manner to improve their quality of life.

The SCERTS Model is a life-span model, as we believe it is applicable to people with ASD and related disabilities of all ages. This belief is based on the fact that the model is derived from research and literature on human development, and that challenges in social communication and emotional regulation and the need for transactional support are ongoing issues highlighted in research on people with ASD of all ages and developmental capacities. However, this manual focuses more specifically on children in the preschool and elementary school years, and the examples given throughout the manual are of individuals with ASD within this age range. This is because educational curricular issues may shift dramatically as a child moves into adolescence and beyond (e.g., to a vocational and community skills focus for many students) and then again in the transition from school issues to issues relevant for adults who are no longer served in school programs. However, it is our experience that in practice, the SCERTS Model is applicable for most older students and adults, with appropriate modifications and adaptations for addressing their more specific needs. It is our intention to continue to develop specific resources based on the SCERTS Model to address issues for older students and adults in a more specific manner.

The structure of this two-volume manual is designed to provide a rich understanding of the model and its theoretical and research underpinnings, with progressive movement into the specific assessment and educational practices that define the model in practice. In Chapter 1 of this volume, we present an overview of the model, discuss why we focus on the Social Communication, Emotional Regulation, and Transactional Support domains of the model, and discuss tenets of recommended practice underlying the model. Chapters 2, 3, and 4 describe in detail the rich developmental and research foundations of the Social Communication, Emotional Regulation, and Transactional Support domains of the model, which are the source of the specific assessment practices and educational goals. Chapter 5 specifies the priorities for the Social Communication, Emotional Regulation, and Transactional Support domains and lists the challenges faced by children with ASD and their families. It also provides a detailed listing of developmental milestones that contribute to the specific frameworks presented for assessment and intervention in later chapters. Chapter 6 discusses the SCERTS Model within the context of the landscape of educational options for children with ASD. Given that the SCERTS Model is not an exclusive model, similarities and differences with other models are discussed along a variety of dimensions of educational programming. That is, relevant educational strategies and treatment practices from other models may be infused when implementing the SCERTS Model. Chapter 7 and 8 present detailed considerations of assessment practices in the SCERTS Model, including the SCERTS Assessment Process, or SAP, for collecting information and monitoring progress in the domains of Social Communication and Emotional Regulation for a child and Transactional Supports for his or her partners. Appendix A presents the blank, photocopiable forms for use in the SAP, and Appendix B is a glossary of key terms.

Chapters 1 and 2 in Volume II are the gateway chapters for the remainder of Volume II, which focuses on implementing educational practices following the SCERTS Model. These two chapters provide specific information about how to prioritize goals in and implement the first two components of the Transactional Support domain—Interpersonal Support, which includes teaching practices, interpersonal style, and issues related to inclusion and learning with and from peers, and Learning Support, which include the design of functional and meaningful activities, use of visual supports, and curriculum modification. Chapter 3 in the second volume provides a discussion and specific practices in implementing the two final components of Transactional Support—*support to families* and *support among professionals.* Chapter 4 highlights the integrative nature of the model by demonstrating how the Social Communication, Emotional Regulation, and Transactional Support domains must be linked in program planning. Finally, Chapters 5, 6, and 7 of Volume II provide spotlights, in-depth vignettes on a variety of children and their families, to illustrate implementation of the model and the identification of practices to address specific goals for children at the three major developmental stages in the model: the Social Partner, Language Partner, and Conversational Partner stages. An appendix to Volume II presents quality indicator rating scales for use in program-level assessment and planning.

It is our sincere hope that a journey through this manual will reap rewards for you, whether you are a professional, a parent, or another caregiver concerned with supporting the development of a child with ASD. Of course, the SCERTS Model was developed with the primary motivation that it will ultimately benefit individuals with ASD and their families.

CORE DOMAINS OF THE SCERTS MODEL

Our discussion begins with an overview of the core domains of the SCERTS Model: Social Communication, Emotional Regulation, and Transactional Support. Throughout the remaining chapters of this manual, we describe these domains in much greater detail in reference to 1) the research, educational, and clinical basis for focusing on these domains and 2) the practical application of the model in assessment and educational efforts for children with a range of abilities from early intervention through the primary school years. By its very nature, the SCERTS Model can be applied in educational and clinical settings and in everyday activities at home and in the community. For ease of communication, we use the term *educational* throughout of this manual to refer to all efforts to support the development of children with ASD, with the understanding that such efforts are not limited to educational settings and that educational professionals are not the only facilitators of positive change.

Social Communication

The Social Communication domain of the SCERTS Model addresses the overriding goals of helping a child to be an increasingly competent, confident, and active participant in social activities. This includes communicating and playing with others in everyday activities and sharing joy and pleasure in social relationships. To do so, children must acquire capacities in two major areas of functioning: *joint attention* and *symbol use.* These two foundations of social communication underlie functional abilities in a variety of ways. First, children must learn to share attention and emotion with a partner, as well as to express intentions across communicative partners. One aspect of symbol use is *how* children communicate, also referred to as *communicative means.* Communicative means may be presymbolic, such as gestures or use of objects, or symbolic, including signs, picture symbol systems, and/or speech. Although the ultimate goal for a child is to develop and use effective and efficient means to communicate in one primary modality, multimodal communication is valued and targeted in educational efforts. That is, it is most desirable for a child to have a variety of ways to communicate so that if one strategy does not work (e.g., speech), the child may shift to another (e.g., pictures, gestures). In fact, a high level of communicative competence is defined by flexibility in the means a child has available to communicate.

Capacities in joint attention enable children to attend to and respond to the social overtures of others and, ultimately, become a partner in the complex dance of reciprocal social communication. In addition, it is recognized that children are more competent communicators when they are able to communicate for a variety of purposes or functions in everyday activities, such as expressing needs, sharing observations and experiences, expressing emotions, and engaging others in social interactions. With increasing abilities in social communication, a child is better able to participate with shared attention in emotionally satisfying social interactions, which are the foundation for developing relationships with children and caregivers. Research as well as clinical experience also has demonstrated that with increased social-communicative abilities, behavioral difficulties may be prevented or lessened. Put simply, if a child has socially acceptable nonverbal or verbal means to make choices, to protest, and to get attention, there is less of a need for the child to express strong emotions or attempt to exert social control through socially unacceptable means.

Social communication and language abilities also are essential for learning in educational settings and everyday activities and have broad-ranging effects on a child's social and cognitive understanding of daily experiences and growing sense of competence and self-esteem. The great majority of opportunities for learning in childhood are mediated by symbolic activities such as language use and pretend play, as well as nonverbal communication; therefore, the more competent a child is in language and communication abilities and symbolic play, the more opportunities that child will have for benefiting from learning experiences. The ultimate goal of the Social Communication domain of the model is to support children in developing the foundational abilities in joint attention and symbol use that support communicative and social competence. With these abilities, a child is more likely to find satisfaction and even great joy in being with, relating to, and learning from family members and from other children and caregivers, thereby further increasing the child's social motivation to seek out learning opportunities with others in the future.

Emotional Regulation

The Emotional Regulation domain of the SCERTS Model focuses on supporting a child's ability to regulate emotional arousal. Emotional regulation is an essential and core underlying capacity that supports a child's availability for learning. A child is most available for learning when he or she is better able to

1. Attend to the most relevant information in an activity or setting

2. Remain socially engaged with others

3. Process verbal and nonverbal information

4. Initiate interactions using higher level abilities, including language

5. Respond to others in reciprocal interaction

6. Actively participate in everyday activities

For a child to be optimally available, he or she must have the emotional regulatory capacities and skills to

1. Seek assistance and/or respond to others' attempts to provide support for emotional regulation when faced with stressful, overly stimulating, or emotionally dysregulating circumstances (referred to as *mutual regulation*)

2. Remain organized and well-regulated in the face of potentially stressful circumstances (referred to as *self-regulation*)

3. Recover from being "pushed over the edge" or "under the carpet" into states of extreme emotional dysregulation or shutdown, through mutual- and/or self-regulatory strategies (referred to as *recovery from extreme dysregulation*)

Enhancing capacities for emotional regulation goes hand in hand with helping a child to more effectively maintain optimal arousal, or at the very least, a well-regulated state, so that the child is not experiencing predominant patterns of arousal of being too high or too low with regard to the demands of the social and physical environment and so that the child is not shifting too frequently between such extreme states of arousal. Children who experience such extremes, especially frequent high states of arousal, are often at the mercy of overwhelming reactions such as anxiety, fear, distress, or even dysregulating positive emotional states of elation and giddiness. These children may also withdraw or shut down to attempt to cope with disorganizing or overly stimulating experiences, especially when qualities of environmental stimulation (e.g., loudness of noise, intensity of visual input, a history of negative emotional experience associated with an activity or place), social interaction demands, and /or violations of expectations contribute to emotional dysregulation. In contrast, children who are consistently in a low state of arousal often have difficulty attending to the salient features of their environment and sustaining attention for social interactions and educational activities. These children often appear passive, disengaged, and inattentive. Therefore, the ultimate goal of the Emotional Regulation domain of the SCERTS Model is to support a child in adapting to and coping with the inevitable and uniquely individual daily challenges that he or she will face in maintaining a well-regulated state of arousal most conducive to learning and relating to others.

Transactional Support

Transactional Support is the third and final core domain of the SCERTS Model. Because learning occurs within the social context of everyday activities, transactional support needs to be infused across activities and partners. Transactional support includes

1. *Interpersonal supports:* These include the adjustments made by communicative partners in language use, emotional expression, and interactive style that are effective in helping a child with ASD process language, participate in social interaction, experience social activities as emotionally satisfying, and maintain well-regulated states. Interpersonal support also includes peer support, which provides a child with positive experiences with children who are responsive partners and who provide good language, social, and play models, leading to the development of positive relationships and friendships.

2. *Learning supports:* These include environmental arrangement, or the ways typical settings and activities are set up or modified to foster social communication and emotional regulation; visual supports for social communication and emotional regulation, which may be implemented in educational settings as well as in everyday activities; and educational curriculum modifications and adaptations to support success in learning.

3. *Support to families:* These include educational support such as the sharing of helpful information and resources or direct instruction in facilitating a child's social communication, emotional regulation, and daily living skills and implementation of learning supports for the child. When appropriate, emotional support also is provided to family members to enhance their skills for coping and adaptation to the challenges of raising a child with ASD.

4. *Support among professionals and other service providers:* This includes informal and planned opportunities for enhancing educational and therapeutic skills and for providing emotional support, whenever necessary, to cope with the challenges of working with children with ASD and to prevent burnout.

The term *transactional* comes from a contemporary model of child and family development, referred to as the *Transactional Model of Development,* first introduced by psychologist Arnold Sameroff (1987). This term is used in reference to a few defining characteristics of the SCERTS Model that have been strongly influenced by the transactional model:

- First, a child is viewed as an active learner, and true learning best occurs when the child is challenged to problem solve, to think creatively and flexibly (rather than to simply learn rote skills in an inflexible manner), and to seek and respond to social engagement as learning opportunities. When learning supports (e.g., visual supports) are used, the goal is for a child to actively use such supports in meaningful ways that best match that particular child's abilities, interests, and needs.

- Second, all aspects of development are seen as interrelated. For example, social-communicative abilities support emotional regulation; increased competence in fine and gross motor skills supports active problem solving and academic learning; increased competence in imaginative play is strongly influenced by language abilities, which, in turn, has a positive influence on social relationships; and so forth. Training "skills" in an isolated manner and in contrived repetitive practice in unnatural activities may not address these interrelationships.

- Third, interactions with children without special needs and children who could provide good social and language models in more natural activities and routines are viewed as an essential part of supporting communication and emotional regulation for children with ASD. This is due to the flexibility and opportunities for problem solving and negotiating inherent in these more natural activities and experiences. These opportunities may also help children without ASD to become more sensitive and supportive partners by developing a greater understanding of children who have developmental differences, thus having a mutually interdependent, transactional benefit for children with ASD as well as for children without ASD.

- Finally, in the SCERTS Model, it is recognized that when professionals and paraprofessionals begin to work with a child with ASD, they enter into dynamic, transactional relationships with the child and his or her parents and other caregivers. Important qualities of these relationships that must be nurtured include trust, respect, and empowerment for the child and family to be competent and independent. Furthermore, these relationships must change and evolve over time, as children grow and develop, and as parents become more knowledgeable about ASD, more confident in supporting their child's development, and more clear about their priorities for both the child and the family. As parents change and family needs change, professionals must be flexible and responsive to such changes and respectful of family decisions.

In summary, the ultimate goals of the Transactional Support domain of the SCERTS Model are for professionals to 1) develop and provide the necessary learning supports for a child; 2) coordinate efforts among all of the child's partners in using interpersonal supports most conducive to social communication and emotional regulation; 3) provide learning experiences with children who provide good language and social models leading to the development of meaningful peer relationships; and 4) support families with educational resources, direct strategies, and emotional support.

The Whole Is Greater than the Sum of the Parts

Although we just have discussed social communication, emotional regulation, and transactional support as separate entities, they are by no means mutually exclusive in theory, development, or educational practice. Unlike the typical separation of developmental domains in an individualized education program (IEP), one of the unique characteristics of the SCERTS Model is recognition of and respect for interdependencies among various aspects of development in children. Here are but a few brief examples we have observed repeatedly:

1. Increased abilities in social communication prevent or lessen behavioral difficulties. This occurs because social-communicative abilities allow children to seek assistance from others (e.g., requesting help), to express emotions (e.g., communicating anger or fear), and to have social control in socially acceptable ways (e.g., choosing or refusing activities). Thus, when a child communicates in these ways, the child's emotional regulation is supported.

2. When communicative partners sensitively adjust levels of language and social stimulation (interpersonal transactional support) or use visual supports in daily activities (learning transactional support), a child's ability to process and respond to language (social communication) and to stay engaged in a social activity with focused attention (emotional regulation) is enhanced.

3. If a student is given opportunities to engage in organizing and calming movement activities (emotional regulation) and is provided with a visual schedule following the transition from a school bus to the classroom in the morning (transactional support: learning supports), the student is more likely to be able to participate successfully in cooperative learning activities (social communication) rather than needing more time to settle in at the beginning of the school day.

SOME QUESTIONS AND ANSWERS ABOUT THE SCERTS MODEL

We now address questions regarding the motivation for developing the SCERTS Model. We also review the basic tenets, core values, and guding principles underlying the model.

Why Focus on Social Communication, Emotional Regulation, and Transactional Support?

One may ask "What is the justification for focusing on these particular areas in the SCERTS Model?" This is a reasonable and important question to consider. In fact, there have been ongoing debates for many decades about what is most important to teach and prioritize and what are the most effective methodologies for teaching children with ASD. Such differences of opinion are reflected in a myriad of different educational approaches currently available and have been passionately debated in published literature and at conferences. (We return to this issue in Chapter 6 in a more in-depth discussion of how the SCERTS Model compares with other educational approaches.) For example, some approaches consider eye contact, matching skills, imitation, and compliance to directions as the essential readiness skills that must be the focus of educational efforts. Such skills are typically taught in a highly structured, repetitive, drill-like teaching format, especially in early stages of treatment. Other approaches emphasize reciprocal social engagement as the primary goal, whereas others strive to teach children to work independently following a sequence of visual, organizational supports, with less attention paid to social communication. Implicit in focusing on any of these priorities is the belief that the skills being worked on will have the greatest positive impact on the lives of children. It is noteworthy, however, that following a review of 2 decades of research on educational interventions for children with autism, an expert panel appointed by the National Academy of Sciences (National Research Council [NRC], 2001) concluded that there is no evidence that any one approach is more effective than other approaches and that in studies that report long-term outcomes of different approaches, only about half of the children have very positive outcomes regardless of the approach. It is also noteworthy (and somewhat discouraging) that results of the most positive outcome studies, claiming a close to 50% "recovery" rate, have not been replicated as of 2005, despite nearly a decade of attempts to do so. Finally, the NRC expert panel addressed the very controversial concept of "recovery" from autism and concluded that there is no simple relationship between "recovery" from autism and any particular intervention approach.

Most important, the committee argued for the development of innovative educational models based on a number of educational priorities (NRC, 2001). The priorities include functional spontaneous communication, development of social relationships and play skills with peers, and acquisition of functional abilities in meaningful activities, which are fully consistent with the priorities of the SCERTS Model.

The SCERTS Model reflects our conviction that by prioritizing social communication, emotional regulation, and transactional support, educators, parents, and clinicians are better able to have a positive impact on a child's development and quality of life. We believe that the focus on these domains of the SCERTS Model is best supported by research on core challenges in ASD, as well as priorities and concerns identified by parents and experts in the field. Furthermore, despite the fact that there is a great need for continued research on the factors that best predict positive outcomes in children with ASD, available research and years of clinical experience indicate that abilities in social communication and emotional regulation, with implementation of transactional supports, are likely the primary factors that are very closely related to positive outcomes in children.

Social Communication as a Core Challenge

For many years, researchers and clinicians have engaged in debates about the very nature of the underlying deficits in ASD. Although diagnostic schemes have evolved and changed over the years since Leo Kanner's first description of "infantile autism" in 1943, two criteria for diagnosis have remained constant: ASD is virtually defined by difficulties in 1) the development of social-communicative abilities and 2) the development of social relationships (Koenig, Rubin, Klin, & Volkmar, 2000). These essential criteria are relevant for all subcategories of ASD. Furthermore, when researchers have examined the abilities that are most essential for individuals with autism to lead independent and productive lives, social-communicative abilities are inevitably at the top of the list. Finally, parents of children with ASD have identified their children's lack of social-communicative abilities as among the most significant stresses they experience when their children are in their preschool and school years.

Emotional Regulation as a Core Challenge

The challenges faced by children and adults with ASD in emotional regulation are readily apparent in the experiences of families and caregivers, have been described vividly in firsthand accounts of adults with ASD who have written about and who speak about their lives at conferences, and have been documented in years of empirical research. In fact, challenges in emotional regulation are so pervasive and striking that in the past, ASD was described primarily as a behavior disorder or a serious emotional disturbance. This unfortunate belief was eventually abandoned with an increasing understanding that ASD is primarily a developmental disability and that difficulties in emotional regulation were a secondary consequence of a range of factors. Such factors may include problems in developing effective, socially conventional means to communicate, sensory processing disturbances resulting in unusual reactions to various forms of sensory stimulation, motor planning difficulties resulting in limited or unintelligible speech as well as problems in coordinating and executing skilled action, and confusion and anxiety caused by problems in social understanding. Furthermore, in our experience, emotional regulation may be compromised when partners are unable to read a child's signals of dysregulation, misinterpret signals, or are insensitive to such signals such that they may not respond in ways that support a child. This may be due to the child's limited ability to produce conventional signals or signals that are easily understood by others. Thus, difficulties are most often not solely in the child or with the partner alone. Difficulties experienced by both the child and the partner contribute to compromised social experiences. Given these challenges, the development of social relationships and learning in general may be significantly compromised unless partners are able to support a child's emotional regulation in response to the child's signals of dysregulation or requests for support (mutual regulation) and the child demonstrates some independent emotional regulatory capacities (self-regulation).

The Ongoing Need for Transactional Support

It is widely known and accepted that the great majority of children with ASD and their families benefit from a broad range of supports. As noted previously, learning occurs within everyday activities; therefore, transactional support must be implemented across settings, activities, and partners. Due to pervasive problems in processing complex oral language as well as the nonverbal behavior of partners (e.g., emotional expressions), multisensory teaching approaches, especially those which rely on visual supports, have been shown to be beneficial and necessary for most children with ASD. In fact, in our experience, the demands and challenges inherent in processing spoken language may actually contribute to emotional dysregulation by causing anxiety and uncertainty regarding expectations.

Parents and family members of children with ASD experience many challenges and considerable stress related to the everyday difficulties that they and their children encounter, as well as to the long-term uncertainty in planning for the future of the family. Families who do well and even grow in positive ways due to the experience of having a family member with ASD are those who can rely on and draw strength from a number of formal and informal supports. Formal supports may include responsive professionals who are sensitive to a family's as well as a child's needs, and informal supports may include social and emotional support from relatives, neighbors, and/or members of a religious community, who may help to mitigate the stresses and daily challenges of raising a child with ASD.

In addition to evidence from research with children with ASD supporting the need for an educational focus on social communication, emotional regulation, and transactional support, we now consider additional sources from outside of the ASD literature that support this focus. Furthermore, our experience as educators and clinicians during decades of educational and clinical experience with children with and without disabilities also underscores the need for these priorities.

Social Communication and Emotional Regulation Are Core Capacities Underlying Learning and Social Engagement for All Children

Close to 30 years of research on the development of children with and without disabilities has demonstrated that the earliest development of specific abilities in social communication and emotional regulation are essential capacities for optimal communication and social-emotional development in the first year of life and throughout childhood. As noted, most learning in childhood occurs in the social context of everyday activities with caregivers and familiar partners. Limitations in social communication and emotional regulation prevent a child from fully participating and benefiting from rich opportunities for active learning that are embedded in activities as simple as sharing meals; participating in joyful, emotionally charged social games; and interacting in meaningful shared experiences that occur innumerable times every day. Although it is important for children with ASD to learn functional skills, such skills must be built on and emerge from a foundation of social communication and emotional regulation that will result in self-sufficiency and active learning.

Social Communication, Emotional Regulation, and Transactional Support Are Life-Span Abilities

The SCERTS Model, as discussed in this manual, focuses primarily on children in the preschool and elementary school years. However, professionals and parents to whom we provide consultation services or who have attended seminars or trainings on the SCERTS Model have provided feedback that it is not just a model for children, but that it is a life-span model, relevant for individuals from childhood through adulthood. In fact, after attending a seminar, a mother of a 43-year-old son with ASD stated, "This approach would be as helpful for my son as it is for the little ones you show on videotape!" Certainly, this contention would need to be validated by successful application of the SCERTS Model with older individuals. However, we believe that the relevance of the model throughout the life-span is a logical assumption, considering that abilities in social communication, emotional regulation, and the use of transactional supports are factors that enhance human development and quality of life for people of all ages. To bring this point home, we need only to step back and reflect on each of our own lives, and the considerable influence that capacities in social communication, emotional regulation, and transactional support have on a daily basis on our emotional well-being and quality of life.

Priorities for Families

Based on research and our experiences, families' major concerns about their children appear to be related primarily to issues of social communication and emotional regulation. For example, in a seminal study in the 1980s, Marie Bristol and Eric Schopler (1984) interviewed hundreds of parents to explore the family experience of raising a child with ASD. They found that parents reported that in the preschool and school years, a number of specific difficulties related to their child's disability caused the greatest stress on the family. Major sources of stress included the children's lack of effective communication, problems in developing relationships with family members and lack of response to family members, and behavior management problems and family members' embarrassment in public due to their children's behavior. As can easily be seen, all of these difficulties can be directly attributed to limitations in social communication and emotional regulation.

Our Experience as Clinicians and Consultants in the Field

Our many years of experience in consulting for and working directly with children with ASD also have validated the primacy of social communication and emotional regulation and the need for transactional support when working with young children with ASD and their families. In routine consultations for schools and families focused on supporting children's development, as well as in crises, the problems that invariably arise are related to a youngster's difficulties in communicating basic needs; exerting social control in socially acceptable ways; and in staying well-regulated and organized and keeping attention focused in the face of overly stimulating, frustrating, and stressful circumstances. Such difficulties affect professionals' and caregivers' relationships with a child and their ability to support positive behavior and to provide emotionally satisfying learning experiences. In the following chapters, we elaborate on these difficulties through many examples and vignettes demonstrating both challenges faced by children and caregivers and practical approaches to address these challenges.

In summary, we believe that multiple sources of information support the need for an educational model that focuses on social communication and emotional regulation, with the strategic implementation of transactional support. We also believe that competence and confidence in communicating and in developing positive relationships is best supported in everyday social activities with caring and responsive partners who are able to enhance capacities for social communication and emotional regulation. In addition, the very process of enhancing social-communicative abilities is an essential part of connecting with a child, which leads to long-term trusting relationships. Establishing such relationships, in turn, may prevent behavioral difficulties or problem behaviors caused by frustration, a lack of trust in others, and limited success in social interaction.

What the SCERTS Model Is and Is Not

We have noted a great deal of confusion as to what defines the available educational models or approaches for children with ASD. In other words, what are the essential characteristics that a make specific model or approach different from others? We have proposed in previous writings that it may be more helpful to think of the range of educational approaches as falling along a continuum as opposed to being mutually exclusive (this topic is discussed in greater detail in Chapter 6). Nevertheless, due to this current state of confusion and in the interest of clarity, we now address what the SCERTS is and is not.

The SCERTS Model <u>*is not*</u> *a prescription. It is systematic and semistructured, but it is also flexible.* Some educational approaches for children with ASD are highly prescriptive. That is, they are characterized by teaching practices that follow a specific sequence of teaching steps, with little room for variation, flexibility, or spontaneity on the part of the instructor or the child. Some approaches may also involve adherence to a lock-step sequence of goals in particular skill areas, with training in readiness or prerequisite skills necessary before work is begun on other abilities that are believed to be more sophisticated or advanced. In many cases, such approaches rely primarily on adult-led directive teaching strategies, with the primary focus being on teaching children to comply with requests and to produce "correct" responses. Consistent with this focus, progress is assessed primarily in terms of percentage of correct responses in predetermined teaching programs. The often-stated justification for highly structured directive approaches is that very young children with ASD or those with less ability who may be older cannot learn in less structured settings and without an instructional approach focused on a high degree of repetitive practice. Furthermore, it is believed that these children are not able to learn from other children in social settings due to the nature of their disability and therefore require primarily one-to-one tutorial instruction. There is no doubt that the high degree of structure in prescriptive programs provides clear expectations and a highly predictable format. It is our experience, however, that an overreliance on prescriptive teaching practices perpetuates social and cognitive inflexibility, which is such a challenge for many children with ASD who are predisposed to interacting, learning, and behaving in inflexible ways due to the learning style observed in ASD and the very nature of the disability.

In contrast to adult-directed prescriptive approaches, other approaches base their goals and teaching practices primarily on following a child's preferences and motivations and accepting the child's behavioral responses through imitation or positive emotional reactions. For these approaches, which have been referred to as *facilitative teaching approaches,* the goals tend to be more focused on building social relationships and trust, rather than on providing any direct instruction in specific social-communicative, cognitive, or self-help skills. We certainly agree that by acknowledging a child's motivations and focus of attention and interacting with a high degree of emotional responsivity, the parent or teacher is more able to build relationships conducive to the development of trust and a learning partnership. However, we also believe that most children with ASD benefit from some degree of external structure (i.e., consistency and predictability) provided by partners to entice and motivate communication and social engagement and to support emotional regulation. Furthermore, by infusing learning opportunities in motivating meaningful activities that are functional in everyday routines, skills can be directly targeted and acquired in a more flexible manner.

Thus, in contrast to either adult-directed prescriptive approaches or facilitative approaches that follow the child's lead, the SCERTS Model attempts to work in the middle ground, in that it is systematic and semistructured but also flexible, with a hierarchy of goals in social communication and emotional regulation informed by research and based on each child's needs and parental priorities. Activities are designed to be consistent and predictable, with a priority on social communication, social and emotional reciprocity, and creative problem solving fostered in the context of meaningful activities, shared enjoyable experience, and shared control. Shared control involves two or more partners having opportunities for turn taking and choice making, with the ultimate goal of each partner developing the capacity to follow the other partner's agenda, a critical ability that underlies cooperative learning. In this manner, the model is flexible and responsive, allowing partners to capitalize on a child's motivation, spontaneous communication, and teachable moments.

basis of emotional regulation and the focus on self-determination, rather than external management (this issue is discussed in greater detail in Chapter 6).

- *An educational approach for young children with ASD should be based on current knowledge of child development, which places learning within the context of natural environments and is both child and family centered.* The SCERTS Model at its very core is a developmental model. Goals and teaching strategies are derived from research and literature on the development of children with and without disabilities. A child's needs and a family's priorities guide the selection of both specific goals and the learning contexts most conducive to developing a child's abilities. The roles of family members in supporting a child's development are also considered from a family systems perspective and as part of a collaborative process with professional input. Family members are not directed by professionals as to what their role is or should be in the educational process. The model incorporates a strong preference toward using more natural activities and routines for children with ASD, to foster motivation for active participation, conceptual understanding, and generalization of acquired abilities and skills.

- *An educational approach should be individualized to match a child's current developmental level and his or her profile of learning strengths and weaknesses.* Due to the developmental foundation of the SCERTS Model, individualized goals and learning differences are naturally addressed and incorporated in efforts to support a child's development. Children with ASD clearly demonstrate variability in their profile of strengths and needs. In fact, in terms of strengths and needs, one child with ASD may be more like a typically developing child or a child with a different developmental disability such as a developmental language disorder than like another child with ASD. Therefore, the results of a comprehensive assessment of a child's strengths and needs is directly linked to educational goals and approaches for that particular child. This linkage of assessment and educational programming is in contrast to approaches in which there is a discontinuity between assessment and education. Approaches that use standardized, uniform curricula for all children, by definition, ignore or give too little attention to individual differences in children. Furthermore, the SCERTS Model takes into account *learning style* differences and makes the most of a child's strengths, unlike approaches that are skewed primarily toward remediating a child's weaknesses or "deficits." It is well documented that children with ASD typically have peaks and valleys in their learning abilities, and these must be addressed in educational programming.

- *An educational approach should demonstrate a logical consistency between its long-term goals and teaching strategies to achieve those goals.* The continuum of goals in social communication and emotional regulation in the SCERTS Model follows a logical sequence guided by developmental research, with earlier abilities providing a foundation for more developmentally sophisticated abilities. For example, if an overriding goal in social communication is for a child to be competent and confident reciprocal communicators, an early foundation for this goal is supporting the child's ability to remain engaged and to initiate communication with a variety of partners and for a variety of purposes, whether the child is a preverbal or verbal communicator. Some approaches that focus on compliance training in early stages of treatment demonstrate an inconsistency with the long-term priorities of supporting social independence and self-determination for children with

ASD. Approaches that rely too heavily on behavior management goals with excessive external adult prompting and direction are inconsistent with the long-term priority of helping a child develop self-regulatory strategies to support emotional regulation. In our direct work with children and in our consulting, we often have to recommend strategies to undo the effects of approaches that result in a child's being too passive due to the teaching strategies that primarily taught the child to respond to external prompting for communication or emotional regulation.

- *An educational approach should be derived from a range of sources.* In the SCERTS Model, it is recognized that there are many sources of information that may contribute to and guide the development of a program for a child. These include the following: 1) *theory* (e.g., developmental theory, learning theory, family systems theory), 2) *clinical and educational data* (i.e., documented results of practice in everyday contexts and learning environments), 3) *knowledge of recommended practices* (i.e., cumulative knowledge based on clinical and educational experiences), 4) *social values* (i.e., practices and goals based on societal and/or personal values), and 5) *empirical data* (i.e., results of experimental research typically conducted with a minimal required level of experimental control) (Shonkoff, 1996).

  The SCERTS Model draws from a convergence of findings from developmental theory and research, clinical and educational data, curriculum based assessment, family-centered research, and contemporary behavioral literature emphasizing functional assessment of challenging behavior and positive behavioral supports. Furthermore, for children with ASD, documenting progress and efficacy of teaching strategies in meaningful ways is an essential criterion to determine if a program is effective for a particular child.

- *An educational approach should develop and apply meaningful measures of progress and outcome.* We have argued previously that educational research on children with ASD has been negligent in documenting a range of meaningful outcome measures. For example, one must question the meaningfulness of often-used short-term measures of progress such as mastery of isolated skills taught out of context of meaningful activities (mastery is often defined as 80%–90% correct responding in teaching sessions). For example, progress in receptive language training programs is typically measured by frequency counts of correct responses in pointing to pictures or following commands, without careful consideration of whether such skills truly make a difference in a child's life in everyday activities. Regarding long-term outcomes, the most common outcome measures used have been changes in IQ scores and school placement, both of which are of questionable validity and have major limitations (NRC, 2001). Such measures may not be ecologically valid because they do not measure changes in adaptive functioning and self-determination within natural environments and do not address the core deficits in ASD.

  In demonstrating a child's progress and the effectiveness of an educational approach, it is important to go beyond traditional static measures, such as improvement on standardized tests or school placement. Examples of broader and more dynamic measures include degree of participation and success in everyday communicative exchanges; related dimensions of emotional expression and regulation; social-communicative motivation; social competence; peer relationships; competence and active participation in natural activities and environments; and, ultimately, the ability to make important short- and long-term decisions about one's life. We address this in the SCERTS Model by measuring ongoing progress in eight Social-Emotional Growth Indicators, which are derived from the specific objectives we use in measuring progress in social communication, emotional regulation, and transactional support: 1) Happiness, 2) Sense of Self, 3) Sense of Other, 4) Active Learning and Organization, 5) Flexibility and Resilience, 6) Cooperation and Appropriateness of Behavior, 7) Independence, and 8) Social Membership and Friendships. These indicators were developed to reflect the typical priorities and concerns expressed by parents and professionals in everyday discussions about a child's progress in a program and in activities outside of school.

Furthermore, assessment can not be limited to the evaluation of child variables only; it should be extended to variables that relate to how partners, environments, and activities, which we refer to as transactional supports, either support or inhibit a child's developmental progress. Service providers need to gather meaningful measures of a child's abilities to guide educational decisions and to determine whether positive educational effects are being achieved. As priorities, such measures should include 1) gains in initiation of spontaneous communication in functional activities; 2) ability to remain well regulated in the face of challenges to emotional regulation; and 3) generalization of newly acquired skills and across activities, partners, and environments.

In other words, enhancing communication and social-emotional abilities for children with ASD entails not only increasing specific communicative skills but also increasing many of the dynamic aspects of social communication, social relationships, and emotional regulation that are targeted as high priorities in the SCERTS Model, as well as modifying partner behavior and designing facilitative activities and learning environments. The ultimate goal is for children to be able to participate more successfully in developmentally appropriate activities with adult partners and peers in a variety of settings. In this manual, we present and discuss many more specific high-priority goals for children at different levels of ability and for their partners, as well as strategies to achieve these goals. In addition, we provide approaches and strategies to measure progress and meaningful change in *ecologically valid* ways as part of the comprehensive SCERTS Assessment Process (SAP).

The SCERTS Model Is a Values-Based Model

Unlike other educational models used with children with ASD, the SCERTS Model is grounded in explicitly stated core values and principles that guide educational and treatment efforts. It is our belief that without such core values and guiding principles, there is the risk of teaching skills to a child that may be thought of as important (based on the bias of the developers of a program or approach), when in reality, such skills have a minimal impact on a child's and family's quality of life and independence and may not be highly valued by family members. Furthermore, we believe that it is essential that an educational approach be respectful of a child and family.

The core values and guiding principles of the SCERTS Model are based, in part, on the most common issues raised by parents. For example, when parents are asked "What are you most concerned about?" or "What do you hope to get from our services?" typical responses are "I want my child to communicate more effectively and learn to talk," "I want my child to have friends," and "I want my child to be happy and not get upset so easily." We believe that by explicitly stating the values and principles underlying implementation of the SCERTS Model, we can ensure that when this model is applied, practices will be focused on the most functional and meaningful goals for a child and will be respectful of children and families. Each of these values and principles will be illustrated through practical examples and elaborated on throughout the remainder of this manual.

SCERTS Model Core Values and Guiding Principles

1. The development of spontaneous, functional communication abilities and emotional regulatory capacities, which support all aspects of development and independence, are of the highest priority in educational and treatment efforts.

2. Principles and research on child development frame assessment and educational and treatment efforts. Goals and activities are developmentally appropriate and functional, relative to a child's adaptive abilities and the necessary skills for maximizing enjoyment, success, and independence in daily experiences.

3. All domains of a child's development (e.g., communicative, social-emotional, cognitive, sensory, motor) are interrelated and interdependent. Assessment and educational efforts must address these relationships.

4. All behavior is viewed as purposeful. Functions of behavior may include communication, emotional regulation, and engagement in adaptive skills. For children who display unconventional and/or problem behaviors, there is an emphasis on determining the functions of the behaviors and supporting the children's development of more appropriate ways to accomplish those functions, within the context of enhancing emotional regulatory capacities.

5. A child's unique learning profile of strengths and weaknesses plays a critical role in determining appropriate accommodations (i.e., transactional supports) for facilitating competence in the domains of social communication and emotional regulation.

6. Natural routines across home, school, and community environments provide the educational and treatment contexts for learning and for the development of positive relationships. Progress is measured in reference to increasing competence and active participation in daily experiences and routines.

7. It is the primary responsibility of professionals to establish positive relationships with children and with family members. All children and family members are treated with dignity and respect.

8. Family members are considered experts about their child. Assessment and educational efforts are viewed as collaborative processes with family members, and principles of family-centered practice are advocated to build consensus with the family and enhance the collaborative process.

We strongly encourage you to take these core values and principles to heart as you use the SCERTS manual. We are excited to introduce the SCERTS Model as a vehicle for helping to move education of children with ASD forward in a more comprehensive and meaningful manner and hope you will be motivated as well as you proceed in your journey through the remainder of the manual.

Chapter 2

Social Communication

It is now well documented that positive long-term outcomes for children with ASD are strongly correlated with the achievement of *communicative competence* (Garfin & Lord, 1986; Koegel, Koegel, Shoshan, & McNerney, 1999; NRC, 2001; Venter, Lord, & Schopler, 1992). In other words, higher level abilities in social communication and language are two of the major factors that are related to children having better outcomes.

In this chapter, we review in some depth the developmental underpinnings of the Social Communication domain of the SCERTS Model and will highlight the challenges faced by children with ASD in the developmental domain of social communication. We strongly recommend that readers who are not familiar with or who are only generally familiar with this knowledge base review this chapter carefully, as it will provide the information necessary to implement the SCERTS Model with the greatest level of understanding and confidence.

The most detailed, research-based accounts that document the development of communicative competence come from studies on the development of children without disabilities. Therefore, to better understand and address the communication challenges of children with ASD, the SCERTS Model is grounded in the extensive knowledge base on typical development and incorporates this knowledge in developing effective approaches to enhance communication abilities. The SCERTS Model is predicated on the belief that research on the development of communicative competence of typical children provides the richest foundation for, the greatest insights on, and the most specific guidance on how to facilitate the development of communicative competence of a child with ASD and measure progress in the most meaningful ways.

Given that the child development literature has examined the development of communicative competence in the greatest detail and therefore has significant and direct implications for supporting the development of children with ASD, we now consider the critical developmental capacities that have been identified in this research. For children with ASD, the most critical capacities that need to be directly addressed include 1) the ability to feel effective and engage successfully in reciprocal interaction and conversation, 2) the ability to find social-communicative interactions with a variety of partners emotionally satisfying, and 3) the ability to communicate shared meaning for more social functions of communication (e.g., sharing information and experiences with others). In fact, children with ASD who display a greater capacity to engage in reciprocal interaction and to communicate shared meanings, which requires the capacity to establish and follow the attentional focus of communicative partners, are most likely to develop more sophisticated communicative abilities. These include the ability 1) to initiate spontaneous communication for a variety of functions; 2) to follow turns and topics in conversation; 3) to use more sophisticated nonverbal communication and symbolic language; 4) to recognize and repair communicative breakdowns;

and 5) to respond to contextual and nonverbal cues reflective of a partner's attentional focus, knowledge, and preferences (Carpenter & Tomasello, 2000; Wetherby, Prizant, & Hutchinson, 1998).

As these developmental capacities emerge, children become more active participants in everyday social activities, thereby increasing their sense of competence and confidence as social partners, which leads to increased opportunities for learning and growth in social situations with partners. Moreover, these early capacities are strongly related to the ability to interpret and share emotional states and intentions and to consider another person's prior experiences and perspective in relation to events or conversational topics at more advanced language stages; these factors contribute to more effective and mutually satisfying social exchanges. In other words, a youngster who communicates more effectively experiences greater success and satisfaction within social interactions and becomes increasingly motivated to independently seek out others for social engagement. Likewise, the potential partners of a youngster with ASD typically respond reciprocally and favorably when the child initiates more social bids and does so in a socially appropriate manner. Acceptance within a peer network further increases a child's opportunities to practice and learn the rules and subtleties of social interaction and provides the foundation for the development of positive relationships.

Social-communicative disabilities are transactional in nature in that the child and all partners are affected. Thus, the SCERTS Model recognizes that direct instruction focused on the child in socially isolated teaching programs does not necessarily ensure positive social-communicative exchanges and development of relationships across a number of different partners. To ensure social success, supports must be fostered across all partners and settings within a child's life, including family members at home, peers and teachers at school, and individuals within the community. Partners must also learn to be self-reflective and to accommodate and modify their interactive style to facilitate the child's social-communicative competence. Social-communicative success is a partnership, with each partner bearing some degree of responsibility. Therefore, the SCERTS Model recognizes not only the need to foster a child's developmental capacities but also the need to increase the frequency and efficacy of a child's social experiences across contexts and people.

OVERVIEW OF THE THREE STAGES OF SOCIAL COMMUNICATION DEVELOPMENT IN THE SCERTS MODEL

The Social Communication domain of the SCERTS Model is derived from knowledge of how typical children take on an active learning role and achieve social-communicative competence. This knowledge base provides the framework for prioritizing educational goals and implementing appropriate learning supports for children with ASD across partners and settings. As a result, the core challenges in social communication faced by children with ASD are directly addressed by supporting a child's movement along a three-stage developmental continuum. The first stage is the *Social Partner* stage, in which children communicate intentionally before language emerges through gestures and vocalizations. The second stage is the *Language Partner* stage, in which children acquire and begin to use symbolic means to communicate shared meanings, such as oral language, sign language, picture symbols, and so forth. The third stage is the *Conversational Partner* stage, in which children acquire more advanced language abilities and social awareness of others, which allows for extended sequences of communicative exchange, and greater sensitivity to others' perspectives and emotions.

CORE CHALLENGES IN SOCIAL COMMUNICATION

Despite the individual differences observed across the three stages and across children with ASD, research since the 1980s has identified core social-communicative challenges that compromise the developmental processes involved in the achievement of communicative competence. These challenges affect two significant developmental capacities. The first is the *capacity for joint attention,* which underlies a child's ability to engage in reciprocal social interactions with a variety of partners and across a variety of social contexts, as expressed through 1) the sharing of attention, 2) the sharing of emotion, and 3) the sharing of intentions. The second is the *capacity for symbol use,* which underlies a child's understanding of shared meanings, as expressed through 1) the conventional use and interpretation of *nonverbal* communicative forms, such as gestures, facial expressions, and vocalizations; 2) the acquisition of single words, word combinations, and more advanced linguistic forms; 3) the ability to engage in the appropriate use of objects, which leads to imaginative play (Wetherby, Prizant, & Schuler, 2000); and 4) an awareness of the conventions of appropriate social and communicative behavior in conversation across different social contexts. Thus, the Social Communication domain of the SCERTS Model prioritizes educational goals in both joint attention and symbol use to enhance these core developmental capacities and foster a child's communicative competence when engaged with a variety of partners across a variety of home, school, and community settings.

In the SCERTS Model, the term *joint attention* is used in two different ways. The first is the broader use of Joint Attention as a component of the Social Communication domain. This broader use of joint attention refers to the developmental capacity that underlies a child's ability to engage in reciprocal social interactions with a variety of partners and across a variety of social contexts, as expressed through 1) the sharing of attention, 2) the sharing of emotion, and 3) the sharing of intentions. The second is a more specific use of *joint attention* to refer to one of the goals in the domain of Social Communication (*JA6 Shares intentions for joint attention*). When used in this manner, joint attention is a specific function or intention of communication, where the child's goal is to bring another person's attention to an interesting object or event, by commenting, requesting information, or providing information. In this more narrow sense, communicating for joint attention is a goal category subsumed under the broader component of Joint Attention.

CHARACTERISTICS OF AND TRANSITIONS IN THE THREE STAGES OF SOCIAL COMMUNICATION

In the SCERTS Model, the literature on typical communication development forms the basis for understanding and addressing limitations in *joint attention* and *symbolic behavior* in children with ASD. As noted, the first developmental stage of the Social Communication domain is the Social Partner stage. This stage encompasses two major transitions that enable a child to be an active partner: 1) the transition to communicating with purpose or intent and 2) the transition to the acquisition and use of conventional gestures and vocalizations. These developmental transitions typically occur from 6 to 12 months of age.

It is now widely accepted that communication development and language learning are active processes in which children construct knowledge and use gestures and words that have shared meanings. That is, as part of the developmental process, children and caregivers come to have the same meanings (i.e., they share the meanings) for gestures and words because the development of these meanings is based on shared interactions in everyday experiences (Bates, 1979; Bloom, 1993; Lifter & Bloom, 1998).

Therefore, the communication of young children is easily "read" and easily understood by others as they acquire and use the very same conventional means to communicate that they observe others using. By the end of the first year, most children are not yet producing true words but are nonetheless using active learning strategies and are able to communicate intentionally or deliberately with conventional gestures and vocalizations that have shared meanings with caregivers (Bates, O'Connell, & Shore, 1987).

The second developmental stage of the SCERTS Model is the Language Partner stage, which encompasses two transitions to symbolic communication that typically occurs between 1 and 2 years of age. The first is the transition to *first words,* which is usually slow and gradual from 12 to 18 months of age, and the second is the transition to *word combinations,* which usually occurs when children go through a burst in vocabulary growth at about 19 months of age, at which time they usually begin combining words.

Between 1 and 2 years of age, a child's behavior shows growing evidence of intentionality, as the child becomes more persistent in communicating for specific social goals (e.g., requesting comfort) as well as relatively nonsocial goals (e.g., requesting a drink). In addition, children use a larger repertoire of active learning strategies to develop the capacity to use symbols, as evident in the ability to use and understand words to refer to objects and events, to imitate new behaviors, and to pretend with objects in play. By their second birthday, most children can use and understand hundreds of words and begin to construct short sentences. A young child's communication becomes much more readable and explicit, with growth in language skills and the accumulation of successful communication experiences. The dramatic changes in social-communicative abilities that occur between 1 and 2 years of age are reflected in the acquisition of language as a symbolic communication system as children understand and use words that have shared meanings.

The third developmental stage of the SCERTS Model is the Conversational Partner stage and encompasses two major transitions—the transition to sentence grammar and the transition to conversational discourse—which typically begin to develop in the preschool years and continue to develop during the school years.

The first transition, to sentence grammar, occurs when children learn to understand and use grammatical rules for combining morphemes (e.g., -*s* in *cats* to mark plurality, -*ing* in *walking* to mark ongoing action) and words to form a variety of simple and complex sentence structures. During this transition, children also are expanding their vocabulary and relational meanings, which means that the children have more information to share with others that needs to be expressed through language efficiently in longer sentences. By their third birthday, children are able to use more complex language to communicate about abstract concepts and experiences, such as past and future events and feelings. By the time they enter kindergarten, children can use thousands of words, have learned most of the grammatical rules of their language; are engaging in conversations; and are beginning to learn more complex social rules of communication, such as the need to secure others' attention before speaking and rules for being polite. The dramatic changes in language abilities that initially emerge between 2 and 5 years of age are reflected in the acquisition of a linguistic communication system, which is rule governed and generative.

The second transition is to conversational discourse, when children learn to sequence and connect sentences in a cohesive manner in conversation. This allows for communication on a topic or multiple topics to occur over many sentences about more complex and related events. For partners to follow connected discourse, sentences must

terest in exploration of the immediate environment, many opportunities are provided for adults to engage in teaching interactions involving language modeling and mutual engagement with toys. During this period, caregivers continue to respond to children's behavior as if it were intentionally communicative, and such contingent responding eventually leads to the children's intentional use of signals to affect the behavior of others (McLean & Snyder-McLean, 1978).

The ability to share intentions is the ability to direct behavioral signals to others to achieve specific goals. In this manner, a child shares intentions with a partner or with many partners. Put simply, sharing of intention is communicating with others with specific purposes in mind. A young child first develops the ability to share intentions at about 9 months of age. In this early period of development, sharing of intention involves coordinating shared attention and/or emotion with the use of gestures and vocalizations to express intentions or to communicate to another person. A child's ability to monitor the social environment through social referencing (i.e., shifting gaze) and to share emotion typically precedes and is a foundation for the developmental milestone of intentional communication. At about 9–10 months of age, a child begins to use gestures and vocalizations to communicate intentionally—that is, the child deliberately uses a particular signal or combination of signals to affect another person's behavior to accomplish a specific, preplanned goal (Bates, 1979).

Thus, intentional communication involves initiating a communicative signal (e.g., gestures and/or vocalizations); directing it toward another person with eye gaze, physical orientation, or physical contact; and monitoring the partner's reaction to the signal. Because communication involves reciprocal interaction, physically touching one's communicative partner, orienting by turning or moving toward the partner, and/or shifting one's gaze to confirm that a message has been received is crucial for the success of the social transaction. Therefore, intentional communication involves both sending a message and evaluating whether the message was received and whether the goal was achieved.

The developmental milestone of intentional communication is followed by an ever-expanding ability to express intentions across communicative partners and for a broader range of communicative functions or purposes. Likewise, during the Social Partner stage (before the acquisition of first words), most children already have learned to express a variety of intentions or communicate to accomplish a variety of goals. A child's capacity for joint attention underlies this ability to express a variety of intentions, first at preverbal and then later at verbal stages. These purposes include less social or need-based instrumental purposes (e.g., protesting or requesting by using pushing-away or giving gestures, respectively) as well as more social purposes, which are reflective of a child's emerging capacity to share experiences (e.g., commenting, sharing observations, relating basic experiences using showing or pointing gestures).

Although the terms *communicative intention* and *communicative function* are often used interchangeably, we believe it is useful to make a distinction between the two. *Communicative intention* refers to the communicative goal of the child or speaker, and *communicative function* refers to the effect on the listener. If a child's communicative attempt is effective, the function matches the intention. That is, the child's communicative behavior will function as intended as a child achieves his or her goals through communication. To illustrate this distinction, consider the following scenario: A 12-month-old sees a toy on a shelf out of his reach. He points to the toy, vocalizes with glee, and looks back (i.e., shifts gaze) to his father. He wants to play with the toy, and his intention is to have his father get it; thus, he is requesting the toy. If his father gets the toy and gives it to him, the child's communicative behavior has functioned as intended. However, if the child's father simply thinks the child is communicating to bring his father's attention to the toy, the father may comment about the toy by saying, for example, "Oh, I see the truck," but may not respond to his child's request. In this case, the child's communicative act would not have functioned as intended because the child's goal was not achieved. When faced with this circumstance, the child may persist in directing the same signal, repair by using a modified signal to his father, become frustrated and emotionally dysregulated, or do none of these and simply move on.

Bruner (1981) indicated that typically developing children communicate to express three major intentions by the end of the first year of life. These communicative intentions are initially expressed through gestural and vocal means, and later are expressed through language as words emerge:

1. *Behavior regulation,* which occurs when signals are used to regulate the behavior of another person to obtain or restrict environmental needs (e.g., requesting or protesting, rejecting or refusing an object or action). In this category, a child's goal is usually related to fulfilling immediate, tangible needs and involves getting a partner to do something or stop doing something.

2. *Social interaction,* which occurs when signals are used to attract and maintain another's attention to oneself (e.g., requesting a social game or continuation of a game, requesting comfort, greeting, calling, showing off). In this category, a child's goal is to establish social attention and engagement, which may result in getting a partner to look at or notice, or directly interact with the child.

3. *Joint attention,* which occurs when signals are used to direct another's attention to an object or event for purposes of sharing observations or experiences (e.g., commenting on an object or event, requesting information). In this category, a child's goal is to get the partner to look at or notice something that the child is focused on or has observed, or to share information or have the partner share information that the child desires.

It is the combination of achievements in capacities to share attention, share emotion, and share intentions that provides the developing child with the broader capacity to share experiences with a partner. At the Social Partner stage of development, the child is learning that he or she has a distinct and unique mind that embodies a sense of self, as manifest in particular likes, dislikes, and opinions; cumulative experiences on which he or she draws; relationships with others; and emotions and emotional memories. The child also begins to understand that other people have their own distinct and unique minds and that thoughts and feelings, the subject matter of any one person's mind, can be shared with others through communication.

This understanding has been referred to as *intersubjectivity,* or the sharing of subjective experience, which underlies a child's deliberate and spontaneous attempts to share experiences with caregivers with the expectation that caregivers will share experiences with them (Stern, 1985; Trevarthen & Hubley, 1978). Intersubjectivity requires a shared framework of meaning and means of communication, including gestures; facial expressions; intonation; and ultimately, words (Stern, 1985; Trevarthen, Aitken,

Papoudi, & Robarts, 1998). This newly emerging capacity to share experiences underlies reciprocal social interaction or social reciprocity in that the child's behavior becomes more finely attuned to the behavior and goals of the communicative partner. The caregiver and child co-create social dialogues by taking turns both initiating and responding to each other's communicative bids in an ongoing transactional manner. In other words, they are building or co-constructing shared meanings grounded in a shared focus of attention over sequences of reciprocal turns or exchanges in social interaction. Thus, at the Social Partner stage in the SCERTS Model, we use the term *capacity for joint attention* to refer to the combination of processes that are involved in sharing attention, emotion, intention, and experiences.

Developmental Challenges in Joint Attention at the Social Partner Stage

Children with ASD have been found to experience difficulties in the significant aspects of joint attention at the Social Partner stage, including challenges with the sharing of attention, sharing of emotion, and sharing of intention. Research has found that young children with ASD do not differ significantly in the frequency of gaze to their caregivers' face or overall frequency of displays of positive emotion compared with typical children, but these children show significantly less positive emotion shared with caregivers or directed to caregivers and coordinated with eye gaze (Dawson, Hill, Spencer, Galpert, & Watson, 1990). Children with ASD have also been found to be less likely than typical children to respond to their mothers' smile. Wetherby, Prizant, and Hutchinson (1998) found limitations in gaze shifting and sharing of emotion in young children with ASD as compared with that of children with developmental language disorders. Thus, children with ASD demonstrate limitations in sharing and attuning to others' emotional states, abilities that are first evident at the Social Partner stage. These children's capacity to consider what another person may be trying to communicate or what another person may be attending to often may be quite compromised.

Children with ASD also have been found to be delayed in learning to use intentional communicative signals and may show a low rate of communication compared with children with other developmental delays at the same developmental stage, a reflection of difficulties coordinating the developmental achievements of sharing attention, affect (emotion), and intentions (Wetherby et al., 2000). These challenges place a child with ASD at a disadvantage for learning symbolic language and social rules of communicating because these achievements are built on the earlier foundation of learning to communicate intentionally. In other words, the less a child initiates intentional communication, the fewer the opportunities the child has to learn from the responses and models of caregivers.

Children with ASD in the early stages of communication and language development have been found to show significant limitations and a skewed profile in the range of communicative intentions expressed. As noted, research has demonstrated that typically developing children and even children with disabilities that do not have a significant social component (e.g., some children with developmental language disorders or mental retardation) express the three communicative intentions of behavior regulation, social interaction, and joint attention before the emergence of words (Stone & Caro-Martinez, 1990; Wetherby, 1986; Wetherby & Prizant, 1993b). However, research has demonstrated that the continuum of behavioral regulation ↔ social interaction ↔ joint attention represents a hierarchy of least to most difficult for children with ASD, presumably because of the differing social underpinnings of these abilities. Due to this

Social referencing through gaze shifting and expression of emotion are important goals for children with ASD at both preverbal and verbal levels of communication.

hierarchy of difficulty, the easiest and first emerging communicative intention for children with ASD is behavioral regulation because it is the least social in terms of purpose of the three categories, whereas the most difficult is joint attention because communicating for this purpose is driven by the purely social goal of sharing observations and experiences.

Thus, given a consideration of this unique learning pattern, goals that target movement along this continuum, such as fostering the ability to move from communicating primarily for behavioral regulation, to communicating for social interaction, and eventually to communicating for joint attention are prioritized in the SCERTS Model. The overriding goal is to help children with ASD learn to communicate for more social purposes and ultimately to help them to be more desirable communicative partners. For example, for a child who communicates only for behavioral regulation by requesting objects or protesting, communication for social interaction would be the target, such as requesting social routines, greeting, or calling others, which may serve as a potential bridge toward communicating for the purpose of joint attention (i.e., commenting and requesting information).

How the Capacity for Symbol Use Supports Development at the Social Partner Stage

The capacity to use symbols is the ability to make one thing stand for or represent something else, as well as the ability to hold and manipulate that symbol in one's mind. For example, words are symbols that may represent entities such as specific people or objects, as well as more general entities or actions (e.g., classes of objects such as balls, general actions such as kicking). Play is symbolic when an action or sequence of actions stand for or represent actual events experienced by a child or imaginary events that never really happened. For example, when a child enacts an event in play, such as pretending to cook food and feed a doll, such play stands for or represents the real-life event that the child has experienced when food was prepared by a caregiver. During the Social Partner stage, children are not yet symbol users but engage in play primarily at a sensory and motor level or are at the very earliest stages of beginning to represent objects and people mentally. Over the first year of life, mental representation becomes evident in children's communication, imitation, play, problem solving, and understanding.

Shared Meaning

A prominent transition during the Social Partner stage takes place when a child shifts to using conventional means or behaviors to communicate intentions. Use of conventional means refers to a child's emerging capacity to communicate purposefully using gestures and vocalizations that have shared meanings with partners. Before using words, young children acquire a repertoire of conventional sounds and gestures that express communicative intentions and that reflect their growing knowledge of shared meanings (Bates, 1979). For example, a 9-month-old may use a very exaggerated open–close hand reach with large hand movements repeated several times to request a desired object out of reach, and by 12 months the child may use a very abbreviated open–close hand reach. This ritualization of the gesture reflects an understanding of the communicative effect of this signal with the caregiver. Conventional communication initially includes the ritualization of functional actions, such as reaching and grasping and the imitation of new behaviors that have either generally agreed-on meanings, such as waving and pointing, or private meanings in ritualized exchanges with caregivers (Bates, 1979). Although such means are intentional and conventional, they are presymbolic forms of communication and are the foundation for the emergence of first words as a child makes the transition to symbolic communication.

The roots of receptive communication development also are apparent from birth and reflect the early evolution of symbol use. Receptive communication involves understanding the nonverbal and verbal communicative signals used by others. Early in development, infants

> Expansion of functions from less social (e.g., behavior regulation) to more social functions (e.g., joint attention) is a high priority goal in social communication for children with ASD.

orient to sounds and speech in the environment and recognize familiar voices and, by approximately 4 months, become proficient at localizing auditory stimuli. There is increasing evidence that an infant's auditory system is especially attuned to perceive acoustic features of oral language, especially intonation, that aid in recognition of familiar voices (Leonard, 1991). By 9–12 months of age, children demonstrate nonverbal comprehension strategies by responding to many nonverbal cues such as *gestural cues* (e.g., when an adult points to a ball and says, "Get the ball"; when an adult extends an outstretched hand and says, "Give it to me"), *situational cues* (e.g., when an adult stands in front of the sink and says, "Wash hands"; when an adult says, "Put in," after putting several objects in a container to clean up), and *intonation cues* (e.g., when an adult says, "Stop it," with a firm tone of voice; when an adult says, "I'm gonna get you," with a playful voice). By responding to this rich array of cues, a young child may give the appearance of fairly sophisticated comprehension of spoken language (Wetherby, Reichle, & Pierce, 1998). That is why it is common to hear caregivers of young children report, "She understands everything I say," even when referring to a young child at the Social Partner stage.

Learning Strategies and Play

The capacity to acquire conventional behaviors is triggered by young children using active learning strategies that involve exploring objects, observing others, listening to others, and learning from others (McLean & Snyder-McLean, 1978). Over the first year of life, children actively manipulate and explore properties of objects by grasping, mouthing, banging, and throwing objects and by taking them on or off or in and out of containers. A child at this age learns to take turns in social interactions, which is first evident when a caregiver takes a turn immediately after the child's turn (often by imitating the child), followed by the child repeating his or her own behavior. Usually by 6–9 months of age, the child is then able to imitate familiar actions or sounds immediately after the caregiver (i.e., immediate imitation). By 12 months, the child is able to spontaneously initiate imitation of a growing repertoire of familiar actions or sounds at a considerably later time than first observed (i.e., deferred or delayed imitation). It also is important to differentiate between spontaneous imitation, when the child imitates with no adult direction or prompting, and elicited imitation, when the adult instructs or prompts the child to imitate a particular behavior. In typical development, children readily spontaneously imitate, and therefore, caregivers have minimal need to elicit imitation. Thus, by the end of the first year of life, a child has a set of active learning strategies that allow him or her to establish shared meaning through production and comprehension of conventional signals in social exchange.

The emerging capacity to imitate and to explore objects and people in the environment also leads to the ability to use familiar objects functionally and conventionally, which is an important precursor to imaginative play. By 6–9 months of age, children are actively exploring a variety of objects using actions such as banging and dropping. By 12 months, children are able to use a variety of familiar objects conventionally, such as drinking with a bottle, eating with a spoon, and wiping with a washcloth. These acts of deferred imitation (i.e., the functional use of objects) reflect a child's awareness of another's intent when engaged with a particular object (e.g., one wipes a baby's face with a washcloth to clean him or her after eating). These conventional actions are not symbolic but reflect the child's underlying cognitive knowledge as well as social awareness of events that the child has experienced, which is part of the transition to becoming a symbol user.

Developmental Challenges in Early Precursors of Symbol Use at the Social Partner Stage

Research has demonstrated that children with ASD have difficulty acquiring conventional behaviors and shared meanings. Children with ASD have a limited range of conventional gestures and vocalizations in the early stages of communication development (Wetherby et al., 2000). Children with ASD may, in fact, communicate through the use of presymbolic motoric gestures (i.e., contact gestures of leading, pulling, or manipulating another's hand, often without eye gaze) for extended periods in lieu of using conventional gestures such as showing, waving, pointing, and shaking one's head (Prizant & Wetherby, 1987; Stone & Caro-Martinez, 1990; Wetherby, Prizant, & Hutchinson, 1998). Challenges in visually orienting to a partner contribute to the difficulties that children with ASD have when performing elicited imitation tasks both with actions of their body without objects and with actions with objects (Rogers & Bennetto, 2000). Likewise, children with ASD who are very young or nonverbal typically have very limited use of functional actions with objects as well as relative weaknesses in nonverbal comprehension (Wetherby, Prizant, & Hutchinson, 1998).

The communicative repertoire for a very young or less able child with ASD may be restricted to only reenactment strategies. Such strategies involve a child replicating an event or part of an event, which may be either immediate or delayed imitation, to request that the event happen. Reenactment strategies are based on episodic associations, as a child comes to associate specific elements of events with the events themselves but may not have a deeper conceptual understanding of how such elements relate to the meaning of the events. Reenactments are considered presymbolic representations because they are exact replications of the event or part of the event they represent. Reenactments may occur through physically directing an adult and/or using vocalizations or words associated with an event. For example, a child may bring a puzzle to a table and physically direct his or her caregiver to sit at the table as a request to start a puzzle activity. Another child may move a caregiver's hands in the position of the movements that go with "Eensy Weensy Spider" and even vocalize an approximation of "eensy" to request that social routine. When children use reenactment strategies, the communicative intention may not be easily understood if the partner does not know how the behavior relates to a previous event or if the partner is not familiar with the previous event. Furthermore, even for children who have language and who therefore are symbol users and are beyond the Social Partner stage, reenactment strategies may con-

tinue to be used through the repetition of language that is borrowed from previous events
as the event is being reenacted. In such cases,
the use of such scripted utterances, also referred to as *delayed echolalia,* become a part of
the reenactment (we return to this issue shortly, in our discussion of the Language Partner
stage).

> Movement from uncon-
> ventional communicative
> behaviors, such as re-
> enactments, to conven-
> tional communicative
> behaviors, must be
> targeted in efforts to
> enhance symbol use.

Given that reenactments are so commonly observed in children with ASD, they may
be a necessary first step as part of the transition to symbolic communication (Wetherby,
Warren, & Reichle, 1998). A child with ASD
may, in fact, need to acquire a large set of communicative behaviors at a reenactment
level before moving on to become symbol users. While these behaviors may not be
conventional or symbolic, they clearly do reflect underlying communicative intent and
are most often used as the means to achieve communicative goals.

Some children with ASD may also develop other unconventional and socially
undesirable behaviors to communicate, such as screaming, showing aggression, engaging in self-injurious behavior, having tantrums, or going limp and dropping to the
floor to avoid or escape from activities. The use of such problem behaviors for communication may be a direct consequence of limitations in acquiring conventional and
more symbolic means to communicate, as they are often used in lieu of more conventional gestures for protesting or for establishing social control. Despite the fact that at
least 50% of individuals with autism display some functional speech and language
skills (Lord & Paul, 1997), problem behaviors are often used to seek attention, to avoid
or escape from a task or situation, to protest against changes of schedule and routine,
or to regulate social interactions in a predictable manner (Fox, Dunlap, & Buschbacher,
2000). The use of problem behavior needs to be considered relative to the repertoire of
other verbal and nonverbal communicative behaviors available to a child and a child's
emotional regulatory abilities, as such behaviors may reflect limitations in symbolic
capacity.

Language Partner Stage

The second developmental stage of the SCERTS Model is the Language Partner stage
and encompasses two transitions in the acquisition of symbolic communication, the
transition to first words and the transition to word combinations, which typically
occur between 1 and 2 years of age. This section describes the major milestones that
are reached during this stage in joint attention and symbol use and how these achievements are particularly challenging for children with ASD.

How the Capacity for Joint Attention Supports Development at the Language Partner Stage

As a child makes the transition to the Language Partner stage, the capacity for joint attention facilitates the development of a more sophisticated and more explicit system of
communication. Joint attention underlies a child's mastery of the foundations for engaging in reciprocal communication, which involves the coordination of the sharing of
attention, emotion, and intention and culminates in the sharing of experiences. In this
stage, a child develops an increased awareness of his or her effectiveness in communicating intentions to partners and the need to use more explicit and sophisticated com-

> Movement from socially less desirable to more desirable communicative means and from less to more conventional communicative means must be targeted in efforts to enhance symbol use.

municative signals to be most effective. The acquisition of an initial repertoire of words, followed by a rapid expansion of vocabulary, enables a child to share a greater variety of intentions, emotions, and personal experiences (Wetherby et al., 2000). Likewise, during the Language Partner stage, the child expands his or her ability to share attention, as evidenced in an emerging capacity to infer the underlying intentions of others' verbal and nonverbal communication by noticing what they are attending to and by considering ongoing activities of others. More sophisticated joint attention capacities enable a child to use additional strategies to secure another's attention (e.g., calling out a caregiver's name), to greet a wider range of partners, to request permission, and to comment about interesting items and events (Carpenter & Tomasello, 2000).

Developmental Challenges in Joint Attention at the Language Partner Stage

Children with ASD at the Language Partner stage may have achieved some of the basic developmental milestones of intentional communication, but challenges in the capacity for joint attention continue and compromise important foundational abilities for further social-communicative growth. Research has documented limitations in the following abilities in ASD: 1) limited visual observation of partners and use of more sophisticated strategies to secure partners' attention, 2) limited monitoring of the attentional focus of partners by looking at and/or commenting on what they are paying attention to, 3) problems in interpreting others' nonverbal social cues to both infer and describe the emotional states of others, and 4) problems in communicating for a variety of social purposes (e.g., expressing emotions, commenting, and requesting permission) to maintain more extended reciprocal exchanges (i.e., requesting social games, taking turns, sharing experiences). At this stage, these limitations are particularly evident as a child with ASD begins to interact with more varied partners and in more varied contexts. Although some ability to establish joint attention may emerge for children with ASD at the Language Partner stage, this ability may be evident only with familiar partners and in familiar routines. For example, children with ASD at the Language Partner stage are more likely to demonstrate an ability to establish shared attention, share emotional expressions, and communicate their intent with a caregiver and/or a sibling at home than they are with a new teacher and/or peers within a classroom environment. Such discrepancies may also be observed in typically developing children, especially when they are first exposed to new settings or people. The degree of discrepancy, however, is usually so great and so prolonged with children with ASD that the term *situation-specific learning* often is used to describe these differences across settings or people. Ongoing difficulties in initiating bids for shared attention, responding to another's bid for shared attention, and communicating one's emotional state and intentions across contexts clearly contribute to challenges in acquiring shared meanings with respect to language and play skills, establishing peer relationships, and in emotional regulation across partners and settings.

How the Capacity for Symbol Use Supports Development at the Language Partner Stage

At the Language Partner stage, children make two major developmental transitions in acquiring symbolic communication. First, children make the transition to first words when they use words as symbols that represent objects, events, or concepts. This is followed closely by the second transition to word combinations, which usually takes place when children go through a burst in vocabulary growth that occurs after the first 20–50 words (Wetherby, Reichle, & Pierce, 1998).

Transition to First Words

A child's discovery that things have names begins to unfold at about 12–13 months of age. First-word acquisition has been described as situation specific, tied to the context, or event bound in that initially words may be used only with a narrow meaning in a highly specific context or situation (e.g., "up" only refers to being picked up out of a crib; "dog" refers only to the family pet and not other dogs). Later in development, words are used to refer to generalized concepts of actions or objects (e.g., "up" refers to any action involving movement up a vertical plane, "dog" refers to any small four-legged animal that barks). First words also are used to mark a predictable point in an episode (e.g., waving and saying "bye-bye" when closing a book; saying "uh-oh" when a tower of blocks is knocked over). Bloom (1993) described the acquisition of words as initially based on episodic associations. A child hears and remembers a word as part of an episode, and it is the episode itself that cues the use of early words. Participation in ritualized, turn-taking routines with caregivers provides essential scaffolding from which the child links words to events (Bruner, 1981; Tomasello, 1992). During early first-word acquisition, the extent to which caregivers model language that follows a child's attentional focus was found to be strongly related to the size of the child's vocabulary in later development (Carpenter & Tomasello, 2000). That is, the more a caregiver speaks about what a child is watching or doing, the greater the positive influence on early language development. This finding clearly indicates the importance of following a child's attentional focus to support language development.

> At the Language Partner stage, it is essential to provide many learning opportunities and specific goals to address the capacity for joint attention.

The earliest first words are not yet symbolic or referential because they most often appear to be tied to a specific context or event rather than referring to a more abstract and generalized class of objects or actions (Bates, 1979). When children begin using first words, preverbal communicative signals such as gestures and vocalizations continue to be the primary means for communicating, with a sprinkling of words used here and there. Early in the one-word stage, new word acquisition is very slow, averaging about one new word per week, with great variability across children. During the one-word stage, gestures are used in the vast majority of children's communicative signals, about half of these gestures are accompanied by vocalizations, and only a small proportion of vocalizations are intelligible speech (Carpenter, Mastergeorge, & Coggins, 1983; Wetherby, Reichle, & Pierce, 1998).

A word is considered a symbol when it has been decontextualized or dissociated from the occurrence of a particular event. That is, a word is being used as a symbol when the child either understands or uses that word as referring not only to a particular object, action, or location but also to similar objects, actions, or locations. The capacity to use words as symbols corresponds with the cognitive achievement of mental representation. Piaget (1971) has argued that the capacity for mental representation is derived from the child's actions with objects in the world. From this perspective, a symbol is the "representation or internal reenactment (re-presentation) of the activities originally carried out with objects or events" (Bates, 1976, p. 11). Thus, children are viewed as active learners by acting on objects and being able to think about representations of objects and events. During the late one-word stage, the event-bound use of words becomes decontextualized (Bates, 1979). That is, children learn to free up their understanding and use of words from very specific events to a wider variety of contexts by hearing the same word in different events and hearing different words in similar situations (Bloom, 1993). New word acquisition becomes associated with broader and richer concepts of objects and events. With the formation of concepts, similar or new experiences with objects or events can cue the use of words that a child has acquired. Thus, a child's evolving concepts underlie more flexible use and broader applications of words. Clearly, language development is closely tied to cognitive development.

In early language development, children typically comprehend more language than they can produce. During the transition to first words, children's receptive language development is characterized by more consistent responding to language directed to them with less need for support from situational cues. At the beginning of the Language Partner stage, consistent responses to prohibitions (i.e., "no") and simple familiar actions and social games are observed in young children. By 18 months, children can locate familiar objects, identify body parts, and follow simple directions, but comprehension is still very influenced by cues available in the immediate context and by a child's familiarity with activities and routines.

Vocabulary Burst and Transition to Word Combinations

Vocabulary increases slowly and steadily until about 18–21 months, when vocabulary growth begins to accelerate at a dramatic rate. This period of sudden acceleration in the rate of new word acquisition is known as the *vocabulary burst* (Bates et al., 1987; Bloom, 1993). The mean age at the onset of a vocabulary burst is 17–19 months, and children typically produce 50–100 different words at the vocabulary burst (Bloom, 1993; Fenson et al., 1994). At the point of the vocabulary burst, the rate of gestural communication begins to wane as children begin to discover the relative efficiency of using words (Bates et al., 1987). After the vocabulary burst, speech becomes the primary means of communicating and gestures become secondary (Carpenter et al., 1983; Wetherby, Reichle, & Pierce, 1998). As children go through the vocabulary burst and comprehension of vocabulary expands greatly based on increased symbolic growth, children are increasingly able to understand and respond to words and phrases referring to object or people not in the immediate environment.

Shortly after children go through the vocabulary burst, they begin to combine two or more words in novel combinations and truly have acquired a generative, productive language system. The transition from single words to word combinations has been documented at about 20 months (Bates et al., 1987). Another new achievement that corresponds with the onset of the vocabulary burst and the shift to multiword combinations is the ability to predicate. Predication is the ability to describe states, qualities, and relations of objects and is the essence of constructing sentences. That is, a sentence consists of a predicate (i.e., verb phrase) that provides information about a subject (i.e., noun phrase). In addition to being able to name things, children can now tell caregivers something about things by describing actions, attributes, locations, and other relations. Predication may first be evident when a child combines a gesture and word, such as saying "dada" while pointing to Daddy's shoe and later in word combinations (e.g., "dada shoe").

Children are now able to determine the focus of an adult's attention and learn the meaning of words that the adult models in directives to the child (Carpenter & Tomasello, 2000). This new ability to learn words by following the adult's attentional focus, rather than needing the adult to follow the child's attentional focus, is particu-

in play. As they make the transition to the use of word combinations, they display multiple action schemes in play.

Developmental Challenges in Symbol Use at the Language Partner Stage

A number of developmental vulnerabilities and learning style differences contribute to challenges in symbol use at the Language Partner stage for children with ASD. These include 1) difficulties with learning through social observation (which affects the development of action words and symbolic play), 2) difficulties recalling words outside of the specific contexts in which they were learned (i.e., word retrieval), 3) a reliance on gestalt language processing (i.e., echolalia), and 4) difficulties with speech production.

Difficulties with Learning Through Social Observation

A child with ASD may have difficulty establishing, maintaining, and following an adult's focus of attention and thus may demonstrate significant challenges learning through social observation, which affects symbol use. As a result, vocabulary development at the Language Partner stage often remains constrained to those word forms that are learned when the adult follows the *child's* attentional focus (e.g., nouns or object labels of preferred toys or snacks). Symbolic word forms for referents other than nouns (e.g., action words, modifiers) therefore develop later in a child with ASD, as these forms require the child to determine the focus of an adult's attention and observe the adult's actions and intents while processing language models (Carpenter & Tomasello, 2000). Likewise, the development of spontaneous make-believe and functional play, which are also learned through observation of social activities, is often quite constrained at this stage (Wetherby et al., 2000).

Difficulties with Word Retrieval or Flexible Word Use

Difficulties with word retrieval or recalling words outside of the specific contexts in which they were learned also are a result of challenges in the development of symbol use in a child with ASD. Symbol use is often compromised by a prolonged reliance on inflexible episodic associations, discussed earlier as a typically developing learning strategy observed in very young children. With a strong preference for static environmental or visual cues and/or relative strengths in rote memory, a child relying on episodic associations may hear and remember and understand a word or a chunk of language as an inherent part of a specific experience or an episode, in contrast understanding that the word or words have meaning apart from the particular experience. Thus, it is the situation-specific learning conditions of that episode, such as the visual cues in the environment, the verbal cues of a partner, or the physical cues of a specific person, that support word recall rather than true conceptual knowledge or the more abstract semantic relationships between the words and the events. For example, a child may use the word "apple" only with red apples at school and not in reference to any other apples in other places or may request a tickling game using the delayed echolalic phrase "Do you want to play tickle-tickle?" with his father but not with other people in other places.

This reliance on relatively inflexible episodic memory may compromise word retrieval when a child with ASD is using single words early in the Language Partner stage as well as when he or she is beginning to combine words later in the Language Partner stage. Once again, these difficulties are even more likely to occur with action words rather than with object labels. Action words, unlike objects, involve constantly changing episodes or conditions. For example, the word "open" can encompass many distinct and unique actions, as the action of "open" looks different with a door than with a jar of bubbles. In contrast, nouns often have nontransient referents that are defined by similarities in perceptual attributes (e.g., roundness for balls). Thus, word retrieval challenges are often more apparent as a child begins to develop action words and more abstract language.

Echolalia and Gestalt Language in Children with Autism Spectrum Disorder

Echolalia and gestalt language, commonly observed developmental patterns in children with ASD during the Language Partner stage, need to be considered in understanding the language development of children with ASD, in targeting vocabulary development, and in making decisions about communication modalities (e.g., spoken words, pictures, signs). The unique learning style of children with ASD, however, also must be taken into account. The vast majority of children with ASD who do learn to talk go through a period of using echolalia, the immediate repetition (i.e., immediate echolalia) or delayed repetition (i.e., delayed echolalia) of the speech produced by others (Prizant, Schuler, Wetherby & Rydell, 1997; Rydell & Prizant, 1995). In early stages of development, an echolalic utterance may be equivalent to a single word or a label for a situation or event. An echolalic utterance may appear to be composed of many words but is actually learned as a gestalt language form, or a single unit or chunk. This pattern is similar to patterns observed in those typical children who are gestalt language learners.

Current understanding of echolalia indicates that it may serve a variety of communicative and cognitive functions (Prizant & Rydell, 1984) and can be an effective language learning strategy for many children with ASD, not unlike imitation for typically developing children. Children who use echolalia learn to talk by imitating phrases (either immediately or in a delayed manner) associated with situations or emotional states, followed by learning the phrases' meanings by using the phrases in different social contexts and seeing how they work by observing how partners respond to them. Over time, children learn to use these gestalt forms to express communicative intentions with greater relevance and meaning in communicative interactions. With language growth and partner modeling (i.e., transactional support), children with ASD are often able to break down the echolalic chunks into smaller meaningful units corresponding to the words or constituents in each chunk. This process of segmenting echolalic utterances is critical to the process of transitioning to a rule-governed, generative language system.

In fact, there appears to be a predictable developmental progression in language development for children who use echolalia. Prizant (1983b) suggested that for many verbal children with ASD, language acquisition progresses through a number of stages:

1. The predominant use of echolalic or gestalt forms, with little evidence of comprehension or communicative intent

2. The use of echolalia in more meaningful ways for an increasing variety of communicative functions, as well as early production of creative, analytic language

3. The more frequent production of mitigated echolalia (i.e., echolalia produced with change) and a proportionate decrease in production of rigid, inflexible echolalia, both co-occurring with a more dramatic increase in creative, spontaneously generated utterances

4. Production of predominately generative, creative language, with echolalia only being used at times of confusion, fatigue, or emotional dysregulation

In Stages 2 and 3, the production of creative language is based on the acquisition of a more flexible, rule-governed linguistic system and a more analytic approach involving the segmenting of echolalic patterns, rather than primarily a rote-memory, gestalt approach to language use. Pronoun reversals, stereotypic utterances, and insistence on certain verbal routines, all common characteristics of language use of verbal children with ASD, may also reflect a gestalt strategy in acquisition and use. The prevalence of gestalt forms can thus be conceptualized as variation at the extreme end of a continuum, which apparently corresponds with differences in cognitive style (to be discussed as an important aspect of learning style in Chapter 4 in this volume, which addresses transactional support).

> **Assessment efforts should document a child's functional use of echolalia as one aspect of social communication.**

Each of the four stages of echolalia described by Prizant (1983b) corresponds with a point in the stages of language and social communication of the SCERTS Model. Although children in Stage 1 are producing utterances that appear to be word combinations, these children may be at the Social Partner stage because their phrases are chunks with little evidence of communicative intent and symbolic meaning. Exact repetitions of phrases that are triggered by specific contexts are similar to and often co-occur with the motoric reenactments described previously and are likely presymbolic. Children in Stage 2 are in the transition to first words in the Language Partner stage as they learn to use echolalic chunks and a small number of creative forms to share meanings and to express a variety of communicative intents. Children in Stage 3 are in the transition to word combinations in the Language Partner stage as they move from using primarily chunks of language to using more frequent mitigated echolalia by breaking down their chunks into smaller phrases and individual words and by making novel combinations with other words or chunks. Children in Stage 4 are in or are about to make the transition to the Conversational Partner stage, in which echolalia is minimal and they are using a rule-governed linguistic system in conversational discourse.

Thus, the emergence of echolalia represents a positive prognostic indicator for most children with ASD. Efforts should be made to determine the size and flexibility of the gestalt forms used by a child with ASD and to help the child acquire creative language by following a developmental progression of language and social-communicative abilities such as the one delineated in the stages of the SCERTS Model.

Difficulties with Speech Production

Although core challenges in the capacity for joint attention and the capacity for symbol use are the most obvious factors to consider when addressing a child's social and communicative competence at the Language Partner stage, some children with ASD also have difficulties with speech production. In fact, it is estimated that one third to one half of children and adults with ASD have significant difficulty using speech as a functional and effective means of communication. This is clearly observed in children whose speech is of limited intelligibility due to difficulties producing a variety of consonant sounds, and using more complex syllable structures such as those in multisyllabic words. Problems underlying these difficulties may include oral motor planning difficulties and/or delays in phonological development (Bryson, 1996; Lord & Paul, 1997; NRC, 2001). Difficulties in speech production clearly need to be considered when prioritizing goals and objectives for a child as well as when developing appropriate interpersonal and learning supports for a child with ASD.

Patterns and Challenges in the Development of Play

A lack of varied, spontaneous make-believe and functional play is a significant limitation documented in research on the development of children with ASD (American Psychiatric Association [APA], 2000) and is further evidence of developmental weaknesses in these children's symbolic capacity (Wetherby et al., 2000). Even for those children with ASD who develop symbolic play capacities, the quality of play may be repetitive and inflexible and these children may have considerable difficulty incorporating themes or modifications introduced by partners. Thus, play is rarely observed to be truly cooperative and co-constructed based on a social partnership.

Difficulties in speech production clearly need to be considered when prioritizing educational goals and objectives for a child with ASD.

In contrast to these limitations in functional object use and symbolic play, children with ASD perform at similar or higher levels on constructive play (e.g., using objects in combination to create a product, such as stacking blocks, nesting cups, or putting puzzles together) as compared with typically developing children or children with language delays (Wetherby & Prutting, 1984; Wetherby, Prizant, & Hutchinson, 1998). What may account for this discrepancy is that symbolic play is learned through observation in social activities and constructive play may be learned through observation of others or through trial-and-error problem solving. In addition, success in constructive play depends, largely, on visual-spatial problem solving, a relative strength of children with ASD (see Chapter 4 in this volume). The use of conventional gestures, conventional meanings for words, and conventional uses of objects can only be learned through observational learning, which entails observing and imitating others within a social context, and must be decontextualized, which involves using conventional behaviors in new contexts to develop a functional, symbolic system. Learning shared meanings, learning and using conventional means to play and communicate, and being able to decontextualize meaning from the context compose the symbolic deficits in children with ASD.

Conversational Partner Stage

The third developmental stage of the SCERTS Model is the Conversational Partner stage, which encompasses two major transitions, first the transition to sentence grammar and second the transition to conversational discourse. These transitions typically begin within the preschool years and continue to emerge during the school-age years. This section describes the major milestones that typically develop during this stage in joint attention and symbol use as well as the challenges faced by children with ASD in acquiring these core capacities.

How the Capacity for Joint Attention Supports Development at the Conversational Partner Stage

As a child makes the transition to the Conversational Partner stage, the capacity for joint attention continues to expand as language abilities blossom, resulting in a profound bidirectional developmental influence between joint attentional abilities and social experience. With increased language and cognitive abilities allowing for communication about past, future, and even imaginary events, shared attention about events and experiences now occurs on an abstract symbolic level, without the necessity of having concrete support of actual real-life events. By this developmental stage, a child also has had an extensive history of participating in a variety of social learning experiences with a range of communicative partners across a variety of settings. These cumulative social learning experiences allow the child to refer to contextual cues to consider another's perspective and to modify use and interpretation of language based on the perspectives of those involved. Thus, social-communicative competence at the Conversational Partner stage requires more sophisticated capacities for joint attention as well as increased opportunities for a child to feel successful when engaging in everyday social interactions across partners and settings.

The combination of these factors (i.e., developmental advances in joint attention and language and a child's unique social experiences) facilitates the ability to take another's perspective and the ability to adjust language use and interpret language based on the unique perspectives, perceived abilities, and social roles of communicative partners. These skills contribute to a child's growing knowledge in presupposition, or assumptions that are made about how much or how little a partner knows about or has interest in the topic, depending on whom one is talking to and what one is talking about. Accurate judgment in presupposed knowledge is essential for reciprocity in conversation. For example, children now begin to simplify language for younger children and may use a different conversational style with familiar people such as caregivers than with unfamiliar people (e.g., being less polite with familiar people but more polite with strangers).

> Assessment efforts should document symbolic and constructive play abilities, with goals directed at developing play as one aspect of symbol use.

Children develop the ability to establish and maintain joint attention in conversation by selecting appropriate topics, by staying on topic in conversations, and by repairing communicative breakdowns. With more sophisticated capacities in joint attention, a child's social awareness evolves as the child is better able to infer the perspective of new partners and consider their ever-changing intentions. This process does not terminate in the childhood years; it is ongoing as the child matures into early adolescence and adulthood. Clearly, there are vast differences among typically developing children and even adults with respect to level of social competence in any given setting.

Developmental Challenges in Joint Attention at the Conversational Partner Stage

For children with ASD, limitations in the capacity for joint attention often remain a significant challenge throughout development, even for those individuals with relatively advanced symbolic language skills. Challenges in the capacity for joint attention compromise the capacity to understand the perspective of different partners, which is also referred to as having a theory of mind (Baron-Cohen, Leslie, & Frith, 1997; Mundy & Stella, 2000; Volkmar, Klin, Schultz, Rubin, & Bronen, 2000). At the Conversational Partner stage, these limitations compromise the development of increasingly sophisticated abilities to 1) understand the communicative intentions of another (e.g., a partner's attentional focus, interests, and opinions); 2) interpret and use nonverbal communicative signals (e.g., gaze, facial expressions, body orientation, proximity, prosodic patterns) as they relate to another's attention, emotion, and intention; 3) modify topic selections and repair communicative breakdowns based on a listener's perspective (e.g., past experience with that topic, interest, emotional state); and 4) interpret more abstract, nonliteral language forms used by partners (e.g., sarcasm, humor, figurative expressions).

How the Capacity for Symbol Use Supports Development at the Conversational Partner Stage

Increasing abilities in symbol use continue to have a significant impact on language and social communication as children advance to the Conversational stage.

Sentence Grammar

The process of learning grammar is set into motion at the Conversational Partner stage, with the acquisition of the fundamentals of morphology and syntax beginning between 20 and 30 months (Bates et al., 1987). Between 24 and 36 months, children learn the basics of sentence grammar, including morphology or word organization, and syntax or sentence organization. Children move from producing utterances based on semantic meaning (i.e., early multiword utterances composed of words that carry the most information) to constructing sentences based on rules of grammar (i.e., more sophisticated grammatical utterances that include many grammatical markers). Grammatical knowl-

> Social conversational skills and perspective taking are important priority goals in joint attention at the Conversational Partner stage.

edge and forms that serve to fine tune and modulate meanings, such as plurals, possessives, and verb tenses, are now used more consistently. Due to an ever-expanding vocabulary, use of language is more precise, explicit, and descriptive. A variety of sentence constructions appear within a child's symbolic repertoire, allowing for more conventional grammatical means for asking questions and expressing negation. Communication about future and past events and about emotional states increases substantially throughout this period, and connected narrative discourse emerges as children begin to relate logical sequences of events across many utterances, such as when they recount personal experiences, tell stories, and negotiate with others. Advances in comprehension typically predate achievements in production. Children are increasingly able to understand language pertaining to past and future events and are capable of responding to a much wider range of vocabulary. Children's greater comprehension and increased ability to follow meaning in narrative discourse (e.g., stories) play a major role in their emergence as conversational partners. Language elements and sentence constructions understood and expressed by children at the Conversational Partner stage are presented in Tables 2.5 and 2.6, respectively.

Conversational Discourse

Following the development of sentence grammar, a child typically makes the transition to conversational discourse at approximately 4–5 years of age. At this developmental transition, a child has a strong mastery of early symbolic capacities in conventional gestures, language, and play. The child also has experienced a variety of social learning opportunities and has interacted with a range of communicative partners across a variety of settings. In a similar manner to how a child's capacity for joint attention develops, the combination of these core developmental capacities in symbol use and a child's unique social experiences and cultural background facilitates an awareness of the verbal conventions for social-conversational exchanges, as well as the requirements and social conventions for appropriate behavior in different social situations. In addition, an awareness of learning strategies such as instructed and collaborative learning (described in greater depth shortly) leads to the child's understanding that successful conversational exchanges are only achieved through a cooperative effort with one's partner or partners (Damico, 1985).

At the Conversational Partner stage, children begin to adhere to the conventions of pragmatic discourse. Grice's (1975) "cooperative principle" suggests that in typical development, children implicitly adhere to a set of conversational rules, primarily falling in following four categories:

1. The *Quantity Category,* which refers to the amount of information provided (i.e., providing an adequate amount without providing too much)

2. The *Quality Category,* which relates to the truth value of statement (i.e., providing information that is accurate and based on adequate evidence)

3. The *Relation Category,* which refers to the relevance of information provided and/or the question forms used given one's current partner's attentional focus, prior knowledge, preferences, and emotional state

4. The *Manner Category,* which refers to the way discourse is delivered and reciprocated (i.e., the provision of information in an organized and concise means based on the needs of one's partner)

Table 2.5. Language elements in the Conversational Partner stage

Category	Examples
ADVANCED RELATIONAL MEANINGS	
Wh- words	*what, where, who, whose, which, when, how, why*
Temporal relations	*now, later, before, after, since, then, until, in a minute, in a day, in a week, while*
Physical relations	*colors, shapes, hard/soft, big/little, heavy/light, tall/short, thick/thin*
Numerical relations	*numbers, few, some, many, more/less*
Location terms	*in, on, under, next to, behind, in back of, in front of, above, below, left/right*
Kinship terms	*mother, father, sister, brother, son, daughter, grandmother, grandfather, aunt, uncle, cousin, niece, nephew*
Causal terms	*but, so, because, if, or*
REFERENCE TO THINGS: Helping to locate the intended reference	
Pronouns	
Subject	*I/you, he/she, it, we/they*
Object	*me/you, him/her, it, us, them*
Possessive	*your/my, yours/mine, his/her, our, their*
Indefinite	*some, any, none, all, every, many, lots, something, nothing, anything, everything*
Demonstrative	*this, that, these, those*
Determiners (articles)	*the, a*
Plurals	*cats, cookies, cows, sheep*
VERB PHRASES: Helping to ground the event in time and attitude	
Main verbs	
Change of state	*open, break, stop, find, fall down, die*
Activity	*run, smile, jump, lick, draw, see, catch*
Enduring states	*to be, have, love*
Mental states	*think, know, guess, remember, wish, bet, hope, feel*
Tense markers	
Present progressive	*is walking, am going, are running*
Third person	*barks, hits, runs, goes, does, has*
Past tense	*dropped, spilled, broke, came, brought, was, were, been, had, did*
Future tense	*will, can, may, should, wanna, gonna, hafta*
Helping verbs	*has, have, had, do, does, did, am, is, are, was, were, been*
Modal verbs	
Early	*wanna, gonna, hafta, needta*
Advanced	*may, might, can, could, shall, should, will, would, must*
Negation	*no, not, won't can't, don't, doesn't, wasn't, wouldn't*

Sources: Owens, 2000; Tomasello, 2003.

Thus, children at the Conversational Partner stage develop more sophisticated social conversation including the abilities: 1) to use and understand higher level grammar and syntax (e.g., subordinate clauses and conjunctions) to be more efficient in conveying meaning and to clarify differences in meaning for one's listener; 2) to interpret and use nonverbal information (e.g., gaze, facial expressions, body orientation, proximity, prosodic patterns) and nonliteral meanings (e.g., idioms, puns) as they relate to social conventions and clarification of meaning; 3) to adhere to the conversational conventions of initiating interactions, exchanging turns in interactions, demarcating topic shifts, and terminating interactions; and 4) to adhere to the social requirements of different social settings (e.g., home, classroom, community).

Learning Strategies and Play During the Conversational Partner stage, children develop two new levels of learning strategies—instructed learning and collaborative learning (Tomasello, 1999; Tomasello, Kruger, & Ratner, 1993). Instructed learning occurs when the child is able to in-

Table 2.6.   Sentence constructions in the Conversational Partner stage

Type	Examples
Active declarative	*I need a break.*
	The boy is riding a bike.
	He has a brand new car.
Imperative	*Go outside now.*
	Pick up your toys.
	Take this home to your mom.
Negation	*I don't know.*
	I don't want any peas.
	I can't do that.
Interrogative	
Yes/no questions	*Can you help?*
	Will you open this?
	Did John kick the ball?
Wh- questions	*Who is in the house?*
	What do you think?
	Which one is right?
	When are we done?
	Why did you go home?
Embedding	
Prepositional phrases	*The bird is in the cage.*
	The dog is on the bed.
Infinitive phrases	*I wanna go outside.*
	I gotta go to the bathroom.
Object noun phrases	*I think I should go first.*
	I see you have some, too.
	Here's the toy that spins.
Subject noun phrases	*The boy who lived next door came over for dinner.*
	The man selling balloons gave one to the boy.
Conjoining	*There is a little boy and he is running home.*
	The boy is crying because he fell down.
	If I eat all my dinner, then I get dessert.
	But you said I could, so I hafta have some.
	When I am done with my work, I get to go outside.

Source: Owens, 2000.

ternalize adult (caregiver) instruction, a capacity that usually develops between 3 and 5 years of age. Children internalize a dialogue that requires coordinating two different perspectives, their own and the instructor's, and are able to recall and reflect on it in the future in similar situations. It is through instructed learning that children are able to learn specific problem-solving rules, inhibit their behavior based on social and moral rules, and monitor the social impression they are making on others. They also begin to use mental-state language (e.g., "He thinks that I think X") and acquire literacy skills, which use metalinguistic abilities requiring a focus on both language form and meaning. Collaborative learning is reciprocal between partners and occurs when a child learns from another child or person who is not an authority figure. Collaborative learning entails "co-constructing new knowledge about a task" (Tomasello et al., 1993, p. 501). Preschoolers may solve problems collaboratively, but collaborative learning is not usually evident until the primary school years. Instructed and collaborative learning are means of cultural learning in that cultural information is being shared from adult to child or child to child.

Advances in children's learning strategies are evident in both language and play development. As children move to the use of more advanced linguistic communication and sentence grammar, parallel achievements typically occur with respect to play. With the transition to sentence grammar, children's play becomes truly symbolic. Children are able to plan logical sequences in play, such as preparing and serving food, and pretend in play with miniature or abstract objects, such as using a block for a telephone. Children learn to engage in dramatic play, which involves taking on a role and collaborating with a peer in play. Dramatic play is an essential developmental milestone for facilitating the transition to conversational discourse. It is within the context of play that children symbolize real-life experiences, thus providing a context within which to practice and learn to "initiate, interpret, and respond to another's social cues to successfully extend invitations and gain entry into peer group activities (Dodge, Schlundt, Schocken, & Delugach, 1983)" (Schuler & Wolfberg, 2000, p. 254). Within the context of engaging in interactive play exchanges with one's peers, children acquire vocabulary, more complex language structures, and conversational rules (Schuler & Wolfberg, 2000). Children's ability to move from instructed learning to collaborative learning is essential for success with rule-based group recreational skills such as in organized sports.

> Enhancing the ability to be flexible and to make appropriate adjustments in social communication across different situations and partners is an important emphasis of programming at the Conversational Partner stage.

The very nature of dramatic play and recreation also requires as well as stimulates development of the capacity for joint attention, as each child needs to monitor the attentional focus of his or her peers, to follow play themes initiated by others, and to demarcate shifts in themes while maintaining engagement within the peer group. In the context of play, children develop their ability to construct stories or narratives using increasingly sophisticated sentence grammar to convey their intent; they learn to mark temporal transitions (e.g., *first, next, last*) as they chain sequences of social events; and they learn to use nonliteral language during role playing to express the intentions, emotional states, and plans of each character (Schuler & Wolfberg, 2000).

Developmental Challenges in Symbol Use at the Conversational Partner Stage

For children with ASD, pragmatic difficulties are often noted with respect to the quantity, quality, relation, and manner of the children's conversational discourse, leading to frequent communicative breakdowns based on their limited adherence to Grice's cooperative principle. These challenges limit these children's ability 1) to recognize the need to incorporate higher level grammar and syntax based on the information needed by the listener to ensure adequate comprehension, 2) to accurately gauge the amount of information that is needed without providing too much or redundant information, 3) to develop and use verbal conventions within conversational discourse, 4) to use and interpret nonverbal communicative forms that have a shared or symbolic meaning, and 5) to understand the requirements of different social situations. Factors that contribute to these challenges include but are not limited to the cumulative impact of fewer opportunities for social problem solving due to limited social opportunities and success with peers and the individual learning style differences that may compromise a child's ability to derive meaning from nonverbal social cues and situational cues. These factors result in

> Play is an essential context for fostering development in symbol use and joint attention skills for children with ASD.

difficulties that limit a child's higher level language skills as well as his or her knowledge and awareness of the expectations for appropriate participation and social behavior in a given context.

For a child with ASD, challenges in the capacity for symbol use at the Conversational Partner stage limit the ability to understand and adhere to the social rules of pragmatic discourse. Because social experiences are often limited and symbolic understanding is fragile, children with ASD struggle on a daily basis to adapt their strategies for initiating, maintaining, and terminating conversation depending on the social setting (e.g., a friendly conversation about sports during recess versus a formal presentation to the class on the history of Mesopotamia) and the status of their partner (e.g., talking to a friend versus talking to a teacher). Likewise, these challenges continue to compromise the ability to adapt conversational discourse based on the cultural or religious background of a partner, as the conventions for conversational discourse vary greatly from one family to the next. Children with ASD may have limited or no awareness of these variations in symbolic conventions and, as a result, it is not uncommon for a child to develop an adherence to a more specific and unchanging set of rules of social discourse that is applied faithfully regardless of his or her partner or setting. This extreme literalness or social inflexibility compromises the child's competence at the Conversational Partner stage, as social-communicative success at this level is built on flexibility and sensitivity to changing requirements across partners and social contexts.

For children with ASD, limitations in both the capacity for joint attention and symbolic representation affect their experiences and success in sociodramatic play. It is commonly observed that children with ASD tend to develop and adhere to relatively inflexible unchanging play schemes to cope with the ever-changing themes of their peers. This pattern restricts the ability to acquire more sophisticated sentence grammar to convey narrative discourse; to acquire the social conventions of conversational discourse; and to foster social relationships through the modality of play, which is one of the primary contexts for social activity in children's lives.

SUMMARY

In summary, close to 3 decades of research and the daily experiences of parents and professionals underscore the centrality of challenges in social communication for children with ASD of all ages and ability levels. In the SCERTS Model, these challenges are best understood and targeted by referring to the developmental research literature on the two major underpinnings of social communication, joint attention and symbol use, to guide assessment and educational programming efforts. With a simultaneous focus on these two developmental underpinnings of social communication, efforts to support the development of children with ASD therefore become well grounded and most meaningful as specific skills, as well as foundations of more advanced, emerging capacities.

Chapter 3

Emotional Regulation

In this chapter, we review the developmental foundation of the Emotional Regulation domain of the SCERTS Model and highlight the challenges faced by children with ASD in these capacities. We strongly recommend that readers who are not familiar with or who are only generally familiar with this knowledge base review this chapter carefully, as it will provide the information necessary to implement the SCERTS Model with the greatest level of understanding and confidence.

EMOTIONAL REGULATION DEFINED

Emotional regulation is a core process underlying attention and social engagement and is essential for optimal social-emotional and communication development and for the development of relationships for children with and without disabilities (Prizant & Meyer, 1993). To fully understand the concept of emotional regulation, we must first begin with a discussion of the concept of emotion. Human emotional experience has been widely discussed in recent years and has become a topic of major interest in attempts to understand human development. Emotion is an internal and complex multidimensional state experienced by a person in response to an actual, remembered, or imagined situation, event, or interaction. An emotional state may be categorized according to the nature, quality, and polarity of emotion, including positive emotions, such as excitement and joy, or negative emotions, such as anger or anxiety. An emotion may also be described using terms to specify its intensity along a continuum (e.g., happy versus ecstatic, upset versus outraged). Intensity of emotion is closely associated with the degree of emotional arousal subjectively experienced by an individual, as well as with the impact of the emotion on everyday abilities. Although emotions of lower intensity may have little effect on a person's daily functioning, more extreme and intensive emotional experience may significantly affect a person's abilities, regardless of the polarity of the emotion (positive or negative). For example, either extreme negative emotion (e.g., extreme anxiety or anger) or extreme positive emotion (e.g., great joy and excitement, giddiness) can detrimentally affect attention, communication skills, and problem solving. In these circumstances, an individual must be able to regulate emotional arousal to support adaptive behavior.

Cicchetti, Ganiban, and Barnett defined *emotional regulation* as "the intra- and extra-organismic factors by which emotional arousal is redirected, controlled, modulated, and modified to enable an individual to function adaptively" (1991, p.15). Emotional regulation has been described as having five dimensions: 1) cognitive appraisal, 2) physiological aspects of emotion (arousal), 3) emotional expression (i.e., affect display and action), 4) socialization, and 5) regulation of emotion and mood states (DeGangi, 2000; Sherrer, 1984). These dimensions are critical in helping to understand how emotional regulation develops in young children and in helping to identify areas of difficulty and breakdown for children with ASD.

The dimension of *cognitive appraisal* involves a person's abilities to reflect on his or her own emotional experience, as well as to read and understand social-emotional cues from others such as facial expression, body posture, and vocal tone. The combination of these skills allows a child to make judgments and predictions about others' emotional and behavioral reactions, as well as his or her own. *Physiological aspects of emotion* refer specifically to arousal state changes that occur during the emotional experience, which allows one to feel emotions in the body. These neurophysiological and neurochemical responses influence perceived intensity of emotion, link meaning to emotion, and help to prepare a person for action. When we use the term *physiological arousal,* we are referring to this dimension.

Emotional expression is viewed as the communicative component of emotional regulation. It involves observable expression of internal feeling states, which are also referred to as *affect displays,* which provides information about a partner's specific emotions and the intensity of those emotions. Communication of emotion occurs through involuntary as well as volitional, intentional means. Involuntary emotional expression may include changes in body posture, physical tension, muscle tone, and skin color, as well as crying, laughing, other vocalizations, facial expression, and gestures. Facial expression, body movement, gestures, vocalizations, and speech may also be used intentionally to express emotions, when such expressions are directed purposefully to others to accomplish specific goals or purposes. Examples at the Social Partner stage include smiling with pleasure at a caregiver in an effort to share an experience. At the Language Partner stage, a child may pair an angry expression with simple words to express displeasure (e.g., "no no!"). At the Conversational Partner stage, a child may use language to express more complex emotions such as gratitude (e.g., "Thank you for helping me with my homework"). Emotional expression provides a window into the partner's emotional experience as related to a situation, interaction, or event at any point in time.

Socialization refers to the process of how others react to one's emotional expression and whether such expression is viewed as socially acceptable relative to culturally determined standards of behavior. Partners may selectively encourage or discourage forms of emotional expression based on cultural values and norms, which vary according to different social contexts and the behaviors used to communicate emotions. For example, it is more acceptable for a child to express intense anger to a friend or a parent in a private context than it would be to do the same in the presence of relative strangers in public. In public, it would be more acceptable for the child to state his or her anger through the tempered use of words (e.g., "That makes me really mad!") as opposed to through the use of obscene gestures and screaming. As part of the socialization process, parents or familiar partners provide verbal and/or nonverbal feedback to a child regarding the acceptability of his or her emotional expression. Although socialization is an ongoing developmental process, corrective feedback from caregivers typically occurs during the more advanced Language and Conversational Partner stages of development, when children are more able to benefit from direct instruction.

The final element of emotional regulation involves *regulation of emotional and mood states,* specifically the ability to modulate emotional reactions and to adjust or modify one's emotional response relative to constitutional (internal) variables and the demands of the physical and social environment. It also involves the ability to recover from extreme emotional reactions and dysregulating experiences and to maintain active engagement in goal-directed activities (Tronick, 1989). In the SCERTS Model, we refer to this last component as *recovery from dysregulation.* This is viewed as a critical component of social and emotional development and is essential for adaptive functioning across varied social contexts.

Clearly, the process of emotional regulation significantly influences a child's perception of experiences, his or her capacity to learn, and his or her performance of adaptive and functional skills in daily activities involving other people. Emotions guide thoughts; influence attention, organization, problem-solving abilities, and actions; and affect motivation. Research has found that children who learn to manage (i.e., regulate) their emotions have an easier time relating to others, forming peer relations, and engaging in positive social interactions (Shonkoff & Phillips, 2000). For children with ASD, the development of emotional regulatory capacities is often hindered by a number of factors, including but not limited to social-communicative and sensory processing difficulties (unusual responses to sensory stimuli), as well as inflexible learning styles.

Levels of Development of Emotional Regulatory Capacities

Emotional regulatory abilities may also be considered relative to their level of developmental sophistication. In the SCERTS Model, we consider three different levels of emotional regulatory strategies. *Behavioral strategies* develop initially during the Social Partner stage of development and are simple motor actions or sensory-motor strategies that the child engages in to regulate his or her arousal level, remain alert, and/or self-soothe. Examples easily observed in a child's behavior include vocalizing; focusing attention on oneself for self-soothing or distraction (e.g., looking at one's hands, seeking oral sensory input); and engaging in repetitive motor actions, such as rocking, spinning, or finger tapping. The purpose of such activity may be to shift attention away from dysregulating events to neutral or more organizing events or to provide sensory or motor input that in and of itself has a regulating impact. The use of behavioral strategies for the purpose of regulation persists throughout the course of a child's development and therefore is observable at the Language Partner and Conversational Partner stages, as well as at the Social Partner stage.

The second level of regulatory strategies in the SCERTS Model, *language strategies,* are more sophisticated strategies and develop as a child becomes a symbolic communicator during his or her transition into the Language Partner stage. Language strategies are words or other symbols (e.g., signs, pictures) that the child uses that regulate his or her arousal level, evidenced by changes in the child's level of attention, alertness, activity level, emotion, and engagement. Such strategies may include a child's creative or imitative use of symbols (e.g., words, signs, pictures) to engage in audible or observable self-talk, as well as in inner language (e.g., thinking in symbols or images). A child at the Language Partner or Conversational Partner stage may employ these strategies in an effort to organize actions, express emotional state, or to self-calm when too highly aroused. Examples of language strategies include a child repeatedly saying or signing "okay" after falling down; a child selecting the picture icon for "mad" from his or her communication book during play; and a child stating, "Don't worry," when afraid.

The final level of regulatory strategies recognized in the SCERTS Model, *metacognitive strategies,* involves a child's abilities to reflect on and talk about cognitive processes that support organization, decrease anxiety, and regulate attention and arousal to guide behavior. These strategies typically emerge as a child makes the transition to the Conversational Partner stage and develop in complexity throughout Conversational Partner stage. The ability to use sophisticated symbolic strategies and increasing social awareness, achievements associated with the Conversational Partner stage of development, supports a child's abilities to recognize another's perspective, to reflect on social conventions for appropriate behavior in different social situations, and to consider one's own actions in relation to others and in relation to accepted social standards.

Therefore, metacognitive strategies involve the process of internalizing a dialogue that requires coordinating different perspectives, which allows for greater social problem solving; inhibiting behavior based on social and moral rules; and using reflective problem solving (e.g., "If _____ happens, I can always do _____"). An example of a metacognitive strategy is a child's reflecting on his or her own abilities in relation to the demands of an activity, as well as his or her own regulatory strategies, and then using this information to successfully engage in an activity (Zeidner, Boekaerts, & Pintrich, 2000). For example, a child who is faced with a challenging activity might consider his or her ability to succeed in the activity and to remain well regulated and subsequently might formulate a plan for completing the activity. The plan might include specific self-regulatory strategies, such as knowing that help can be requested from the teacher if needed. Cognitive-linguistic growth and transactional support and guidance from caregivers are viewed as key elements in the development of these metacognitive emotional regulatory strategies.

The Relationship Between Emotional Regulation and Arousal

Each of us has an inner drive to attain and maintain a steady, internal state, which promotes adaptive functioning, learning, and active social engagement. *Homeostasis* is a term used to refer to this concept of emotional and physiological stability. The autonomic nervous system (ANS) plays a significant role in this unconscious process and either increases or decreases arousal state in reaction to emotional changes, body movements and positional changes, environmental conditions, internal physiological variables, and/or cognitive processes. The attainment of physiological homeostasis is one of the first developmental achievements for a young child and usually occurs within the first 6 months of life. It is evidenced by a child's greater consistency in basic capacities such as sleeping, eating, and digestion, as well in higher level capacities such as attention to people and nonsocial stimuli. Therefore, the attainment of homeostasis is directly correlated with a child's increasing ability to be available for active participation in a variety of learning interactions.

It is through the process of emotional regulation, involving volitional regulatory strategies and ANS function, that children actively strive to attain homeostasis and to maintain an *optimal state of arousal,* allowing them to respond adaptively to the social and physical demands of everyday activities (DeGangi, 2000). *Arousal* has been defined as a continuum of physiological states or biobehavioral states ranging from deep sleep to wakeful and alert to highly agitated (Brazelton & Cramer, 1991; Lester, Freier, & LaGasse, 1995). Volitional emotional regulatory skills (i.e., behavioral strategies, language strategies, and metacognitive strategies) in combination with the process of *modulation* enable children to make transitions along this continuum to promote adaptive function. Modulation refers to the unconscious process controlled by the ANS of increasing or decreasing arousal state based on perception of internal sensation and external stimulation.

To illustrate how this interplay between volitional strategies and the unconscious process of modulation supports emotional regulation, let us consider a child at the Language Partner stage who is playing quietly in a preschool classroom and suddenly hears the fire alarm. The child's modulation abilities will likely cause a pronounced increase in arousal due to this intense, unanticipated stimulation. In reaction, the child may employ behavioral strategies and language strategies for self-regulation to counter this increase in arousal and maintain a well-regulated state that supports an adaptive response. For instance, the child may cover his ears, a behavioral strategy, and repeat to himself a familiar phrase previously modeled by a caregiver (e.g., "It's okay, it's just the fire alarm"), a language strategy. In addition, he may also recall previous fire drills and the sequence of steps involved to decrease anxiety, also a symbolic or language strategy. In this example, both the unconscious ANS response and the conscious regulatory response facilitate the child's transition to an active alert state and prepare the child to participate in the fire drill. As previously indicated, factors influencing the ability to make transitions along the continuum of arousal states include but are not limited to environmental characteristics (e.g., types and intensity of environmental stimulation), social context (e.g., availability of familiar routines and communicative partners), internal or constitutional variables (e.g., illness, level of fatigue, pain), and emotional regulatory capacities.

Pert (1997), a renowned neuroscientist, argued that physiological state and emotional state are interdependent: "Every change in the physiological state is accompanied by an appropriate change in the mental emotional state, and every change in the mental emotional state (conscious or unconscious) is accompanied by a change in the physiological state." Therefore, physiological arousal, emotional arousal, and emotional regulatory abilities have a cumulative impact on a child's attention, availability for learning, and ability to engage in social activities.

DEVELOPMENT AND MUTUAL AND SELF-REGULATORY CAPACITIES

From a developmental perspective, Tronick (1989) distinguished between emotional *mutual regulatory* capacities and *self-regulatory* capacities, both of which serve to aid in regulating emotional arousal. Mutual regulatory strategies occur in the context of social interaction and involve a child's ability to request and/or respond to assistance from others in helping to maintain a state of optimal arousal, whereas self-regulatory strategies are self-initiated and self-directed.

As noted previously, the achievement of homeostasis in infancy, in turn, supports a child's ability to maintain an optimal state of arousal, a well-regulated state in which he or she can meet the sensory, motor, and social challenges inherent in everyday activities and that promotes interaction, exploration, and engagement. The achievement of this goal, which is dependent on both mutual and self-regulatory strategies, is of primary importance because optimal arousal promotes further regulatory skill development (e.g., conventional behavioral strategies, language strategies, and metacognitive strategies), emotional responsivity, and regulation of attention.

Also as discussed previously, the interdependent emotional/physiological state also influences a child's development and use of mutual and self-regulatory strategies. Therefore, it must be considered in addition to arousal state when reflecting on the mutual and self-regulatory strategies that a child uses. Similar to arousal state, a child's emotional/physiological state biases or colors the child's perception of experiences and, in turn, his or her response to challenges embedded in those experiences. For example, a child who is in a high state of arousal and who is hyperreactive to tactile input may feel threatened when touched without warning. This sense of feeling threatened in combination with his or her heightened arousal state may color the child's perception of the innocent behavior of another child as being aggressive and therefore as a threat to his well-being. The tactilely defensive child may then run from and subsequently avoid a child who inadvertently bumped into him or her, a self-regulatory behavioral strategy intended to protect him- or herself from the perceived threat. The same child, however, may not react as defensively if he or she were in a lower state of arousal before being bumped, even though he or she would still be likely to perceive the bump as distressing.

Thus, a child's emotional regulatory capacities may be viewed as critical factors supporting social and emotional development because the effective employment of these capacities maximizes the amount of time that the child is in an optimal arousal state, is well regulated emotionally, and is actively engaged. This state is best achieved through a combination of caregiver support (mutual regulation) and a child's independent efforts (self-regulation).

Mutual Regulation

Child development is a transactional process involving active participation in social transaction between the child and all partners (McLean, 1990; Sameroff & Fiese, 1990). Mutual regulation, or emotional regulation that occurs in the context of social engagement between a caregiver and a young child, is a clear example of the ongoing influences among children, caregivers, and environments that result in the achievement of developmental milestones and positive developmental outcomes. The process of mutual regulation begins when caregivers respond sensitively to a child's signals within the first few moments of life.

How the Capacity for Mutual Regulation Supports Development During the Social Partner Stage

Throughout the first 6 months of life, infants demonstrate highly variable fluctuations in arousal state largely due to the immaturity of their nervous systems; therefore, parents and other caregivers play a critical role in supporting the newborn child's ability to maintain a regulated state. In these early stages of mutual regulation, caregivers coordinate their activity level and respond to an infant based on behavioral signals indicating the infant's arousal state and comfort level (Prizant & Meyer, 1993; Tronick, 1989). To do so, caregivers must carefully read and respond to an infant's preintentional and often subtle behaviors, which are not directed intentionally and purposefully to the caregiver but nonetheless signal to the caregiver the infant's emotional state and level of arousal. For instance, infants cry when their homeostasis is challenged due to internal sensations such as fatigue or hunger and in response to disturbing environmental stimulation (e.g., noise, changes in temperature). The crying that results from such internal and external sensory experiences is a reflexive reaction that is not produced with communicative intent but that is nonetheless communicative because of how it is perceived by caregivers. Preintentional nonverbal behavior may serve similar communicative functions as well, such as when an infant's facial expression or bodily tension signals discomfort or fear, to which a caregiver responds with verbal or nonverbal comfort (e.g., picking up the child, speaking softly, rocking the child). Therefore, we refer to this type of mutual regulation as *respondent mutual regulation* because partners respond to a child's signals of dysregulation even though the signals are not directed to others with purpose or intent.

In addition to relying on assistance from others for emotional regulation, infants also have self-regulatory, biologically determined protective mechanisms to help them to make transitions between states and to prevent overarousal. These mechanisms include but are not limited to falling asleep after intensive play interactions and startling during encounters with noxious stimuli such as loud noise or intense visual stimulation. By the fourth or fifth month of life, infants begin to integrate these and other protective mechanisms during social interactions, and, in turn, they exhibit a greater range of coping techniques. For example, even at this young age, infants exhibit self-regulatory capacities such as turning away from sources of stimulation (e.g., gaze aversion), and engaging in self-soothing behaviors such as thumb sucking or mouthing objects. Infants also begin to produce differentiated cries that signal different emotional states to caregivers who may then respond accordingly (respondent mutual regulation). These early developing emotional regulatory strategies and signals of dysregulation enable a child to cope with potentially disorganizing, aversive stimuli. However, although these strategies may promote a better regulated state, they do not necessarily facilitate a state of optimal arousal and engagement. For example, an infant may become extremely self-absorbed in mouthing an object to support emotional regulation but may not be able to engage with others due to this intense nonsocial focus.

By the time that a child is 6–9 months of age, caregivers commonly use respondent mutual regulation strategies, as they now respond to a wide range of subtle and not so subtle vocal and nonverbal signals displayed by the child in an effort to support the child's emotional regulation. It is through these interactions with caregivers that an infant's abilities to self-soothe during and following dysregulating experiences are facilitated and expanded. Self-soothing first occurs by behavioral means such as oral sensory exploration and repetitive movement. For instance, the multisensory (i.e., tactile, kinesthetic, visual, and auditory) properties of interactions with parents and caregivers promote an infant's early abilities to mouth objects, hold his or her feet, look at engaging sights, and/or listen to pleasant sounds. Toward the end of the first year, coping mechanisms acquired through social interactions become more flexible, sophisticated, and subtle in nature and can be observed in cyclical episodes of gaze aversion, visual reengagement, and shifting attention between object exploration and social engagement. These coping strategies allow for continued engagement even in the presence of disorganizing stimuli.

Toward the end of the first year of life, children develop greater social awareness of the effects of their behavior on others and develop more sophisticated communicative abilities; in turn, children begin to use *initiated mutual regulation strategies.* Such strategies may be used to request assistance from a caregiver to help with emotional state regulation. That is, the children not only become more aware of their own needs but also are better able to intentionally communicate their needs (e.g., for assistance, for comfort) to their caregivers through vocal and gestural signals purposefully directed to others. For example, to request comfort a child may reach up and vocalize to be held. This increased repertoire of coordinated gestures and vocal signals enables a child to request assistance when feeling threatened and in need of support to maintain an organized and engaged state.

The quality of an infant's emotional experience in the social and physical world is closely tied to arousal state (Shonkoff & Phillips, 2000; Tronick, 1989). During the first year of life, infants are developing emotional awareness and the ability to discriminate the emotions of others. As early as 3–7 months of age, infants develop the ability to discriminate and respond to changes in caregiver's facial expression associated with emotions. For instance, at 6 months, babies appear to attune to maternal expression of emotion. For example, if a mother displays a sad, depressed affect, her baby in turn will exhibit an emotional response of sadness, anger, or gaze aversion (Tronick, 1989). Thus, emotional development in the first year is intimately related to emotional regulatory capacities, and this relationship continues into the Language Partner stage during the second year and beyond.

How the Capacity for Mutual Regulation Supports Development During the Language Partner Stage

At the end of the first year of life and throughout the second year, children continue to develop increased social awareness and communicative abilities and, in turn, use initiated mutual regulation strategies to a much greater extent to request assistance from caregivers to help with state regulation. During this stage in development, as a child's awareness of his or her own needs increases, so does the ability to intentionally communicate these needs to caregivers. A child may use nonverbal means or emerging verbal means for purposes of acquiring assistance or comfort, organizing activities, and so forth. For example, to protest a distressing activity a child at the Language Partner stage may repeatedly use symbolic communication (i.e., speech, signs, or pictures) to convey "all done" in addition to using a pushing-away gesture or a head shake to augment the message of negation. Often children at this stage of development will persist in the use of these communicative strategies until their goal is achieved. This ability to coordinate gestures with symbolic communicative means, such as words, enables a child to request comfort when threatened, protest activities when distressed, seek interaction when excited, and request help when frustrated. Therefore, a toddler's use of intentional communication strategies, in addition to the display of preintentional signals (e.g., body posture, muscle tone), to convey emotional and arousal state helps to facilitate and promote the child's behavioral organization in interactions with caregivers. Caregivers' consistent responsiveness to a child's communicative bids for behavioral comfort or stimulation and/or for cognitive information increases the child's awareness that he or she is able to exert control in his or her social world, which in turn assists with development of emotional regulatory skills. Therefore, children begin to recognize that they can manage their emotions and need not be overwhelmed by them (Shonkoff & Phillips, 2000). Similarly, a child uses these same nonverbal and verbal communicative signals to share positive emotional states. Sharing of emotional state with preferred partners is one clear indicator of a young child's attachment to preferred primary caregivers.

The emotional capacities of children in the Language Partner stage of development become more advanced as the children approach the end of their second year. Children begin to view themselves as separate from others and thus begin to develop a clear and distinct "sense of self" (Stern, 1985). This differentiated sense of self from others further underlies important social-emotional capacities, including a sense of mastery motivation, as well as frustration in reference to the achievement of goals. As discussed previously, children also are able to engage in higher forms of symbolic representation as is evident by the explosion in language and imaginative play abilities. Collectively, these developments result in a dramatic increase in children's abilities and needs to cope independently with emotionally challenging situations.

As children in the Language Partner stage become more goal directed, they also become increasingly aware of barriers to achieving goals, which sometimes results in extreme protest behaviors. Such expressions of frustration and related behavioral patterns are associated with increasing self-determination, characteristic of the developmental stage referred to as the terrible twos. During toddlerhood, social referencing abilities also continue to expand, which enable a child to observe, read, and interpret another person's emotions. This is one aspect of a process known as *socialization,* which begins to shape and guide a child's emotional responses and behavior as the child begins to modify his or her actions based on events and the reactions and emotional expression of others. Caregivers often expand on these early aspects of socialization of emotion by attaching emotional meaning to a child's behavioral displays and modeling emotion words for a child during interactions in an effort to support the child's understanding of emotional concepts. As a result, children at the Language Partner stage of development begin to use emotion words such as "happy" or "sad" appropriately in conversation by 2½–3 years of age. This ability to express emotions has been identified as a major hallmark in mutual regulation (Prizant & Wetherby, 1990), as the ability to express emotions through language is considered to be an important achievement in developing mastery over one's emotions rather than being "at their mercy" (Stern, 1985).

How the Capacity for Mutual Regulation Supports Development During the Conversational Partner Stage

In the preschool and early school years, caregivers continue to facilitate greater development of emotional self-regulatory capacities by giving children at the Conversational Partner stage greater responsibility in daily experiences. For example, if a child is being challenged in an activity, a caregiver may intervene only if he or she perceives that the child's skill level is exceeded or if the child initiates a bid for support (i.e., initiated mutual regulation) by expressing frustration or requesting assistance. Typically, children at the Conversational Partner stage need less physical contact from caregivers to help maintain a well-regulated state. They now rely more heavily on instrumental dependence, such as cognitive support in problem solving in particular situations. Language and cognitive skills developing during this stage enable children to think at higher symbolic levels and plan alternative solutions to achieve goals, resulting in a greater sense of mastery and confidence. Increased confidence in problem solving and in the ability to delay gratification, in turn, result in increased tolerance for frustration, which further supports emotional regulation.

These developing skills are closely associated with metacognitive strategies. Metacognitive strategies reflect a child's awareness of his or her own abilities in relation to the demands of an activity, knowledge of which regulatory strategies to employ, and the ability to use this information to successfully engage in an activity (Zeidner et al., 2000). They also reflect a child's ability to integrate different perspectives and interpret daily events relative to previous experiences. Through the use of metacognitive strategies, children are better able to organize their behavior and adjust their emotional expression based on social-cultural norms and environmental factors. The result is better impulse control and control of emotions, which results in fewer problematic behaviors related to extreme states of dysregulation, as well as more flexible and adaptive responses to situational demands (e.g., the ability to collaborate and negotiate with peers during problem solving).

During the Conversational Partner stage, the process of socialization of emotion expands. Caregivers continue to acknowledge and provide feedback to their children about the appropriateness of their emotional reactions. Caregivers also expand the complexity of emotional vocabulary modeled for children, including advanced emotion words and words that reflect intensity of emotion. As a result, children at the Conversational Partner stage learn to map emotion words and concepts on internal states and experiences through interactions with others and therefore often demonstrate a more elaborate emotional vocabulary that reflects social-cultural understanding (e.g., guilt, embarrassment, pride) and gradation of emotion (e.g., pleased versus ecstatic). As previously stated, this ability to express emotions has been identified as a major hallmark of mutual regulation (Prizant & Wetherby, 1990).

Self-Regulation

Self-regulation involves the independent use of a variety of self-initiated strategies to regulate emotional state and physiological arousal, to regulate mood, prepare for interaction, self-calm, delay gratification, and cope with challenges such as transitions between activities and environments. It is a complex process resulting from the interaction of physiological maturation, caregiver responsiveness (e.g., respondent mutual regulation), and a child's increasing adaptation to environmental stimulation and events. Self-regulatory skills are essential for a child to respond adaptively to challenging social and emotional experiences, bids for interaction, disorganizing environmental stimulation, and violations in expectations. With the ability to self-regulate, children are more able to remain engaged and to actively participate in activities that support psychological, social, and emotional development. Children who have limited self-regulatory capacities are at greater risk for compromised development, as is often the case for children with ASD. From a developmental perspective, there is a clear progression of competence in self-regulation, which we now trace from the Social Partner through Conversational Partner stages.

How the Capacity for Self-Regulation Supports Development During the Social Partner Stage

Self-regulatory abilities first appear and become increasingly refined during the Social Partner stage. For instance, a young infant first uses self-regulatory behavioral strategies involving simple motor actions and sensory-motor activities such as sucking a thumb, averting gaze, or engaging in repetitive motor activity. These strategies to self-regulate arousal and emotional state initially develop as a result of the interplay between the infant's biologically determined protective mechanisms and his or her interactions with caregivers. Mutual and self-regulatory capacities clearly are codependent in development when one considers the essential role played by caregivers. As alluded to throughout the previous section on mutual regulation, this interdependence between mutual and self-regulatory capacities continues throughout development. In addition to early mutual regulatory interactions, the availability of environmental supports, such as comfort objects and/or organizing stimulation (e.g., music, vibration) affects a child's ability to tolerate stress, use adaptive coping strategies, and develop strategies for social engagement.

Behavioral strategies for self-regulation of emotional state and modulation of physiological arousal during the Social Partner stage are viewed as critical for successful adaptation to the environment and as the foundation for more sophisticated self-regulation skills (Prizant & Meyer, 1993). The use of these strategies enables a young infant to observe both people and objects in his or her environment, to show an interest in a variety of sensory and social experiences, and to actively seek engagement. As an infant becomes more successful in the use of behavioral strategies, during both familiar social and solitary activities, he or she is better able to maintain a well-regulated state and participate in extended interactions and activities. In turn, the infant is more available for learning and interacting. In addition to supporting interaction in familiar environments, the effective use of behavioral strategies at the Social Partner stage of development enables a child to participate in new and changing situations. New situations are activities or features of activities that are unfamiliar to the child (e.g., an activity that the child has not participated in; a new person joining a familiar activity). Changing situations are ones that vary in key features, such as sensory stimulation, activity level, activity sequence, task difficulty; that have unexpected features, including changes in the location of events or in the sequence of common routines; or that are terminated prematurely. A young child's engagement in both new situations and changing situations opens up greater opportunities for learning and engaging.

A final function for which children employ behavioral strategies at the Social Partner stage is to recover from incidences of extreme dysregulation. Extreme dysregulation is a state in which a child may experience intense emotions and is not available for engagement or learning. Examples of behavioral evidence of extreme dysregulation include expression of intense and seemingly inconsolable distress, frenetic motor activity, and/or physical disengagement for an extended period. Extreme dysregulation may be associated with arousal levels that are very high (i.e., extreme distress or excitement) or very low (i.e., extreme passivity, disengaged state) precluding social engagement.

How the Capacity for Self-Regulation Supports Development During the Language Partner Stage

As children make the transition to the Language Partner stage, their self-regulatory capacities incorporate not only behavioral strategies but also emerging language strategies. Language strategies involve the use of symbols (e.g., words, signs, pictures, images) that the child uses to self-regulate. Language strategies are dependent on the development of symbolic capacities, or mental representational capacities that result in the ability to formulate mental images, to retrieve memories more effectively, to understand and use language, and to engage in pretend play. These abilities allow for verbal mediation of thoughts and actions, which in turn promotes self-regulatory behavior through intentional, purposeful control. A child now becomes able to use inner language or self-talk to regulate arousal during an anxiety-provoking situation. For example, a toddler may repeatedly say, "I'm okay," after bumping his head during play. This use of self-talk has a regulating effect on the child's arousal level as it provides him with repeated and reassuring information.

Thus, there is a clear distinction between the emotional regulatory abilities of a presymbolic child at the Social Partner stage and those of a symbolic child at the Language Partner stage. A child at the Social Partner stage of development is limited to behavioral strategies, as a presymbolic child does not use language-based or other symbolic strategies. The abilities of a child at the Language Partner stage, however, consist of both presymbolic behavioral strategies and symbolic language strategies, as children at this stage of development can use symbols as well as sensory and motor stimulation to remain well regulated. A child's state of arousal and environmental and activity demands determine which of these specific types of strategies, or combinations of strategies the child employs.

As a child's self-awareness, autonomy, and symbolic capacities continue to develop throughout the Language Partner stage, the child's abilities to identify and express basic emotions symbolically develop as well, promoting greater self-regulatory abilities. Greater control of autonomic function due to neurological maturation, along with increased cognitive abilities, also help children to anticipate and adapt to novel and potentially stressful new and changing situations. Therefore, it is a Language Partner's collective use of behavioral strategies and language strategies that contributes to increased self-regulatory competence. Hallmarks of these expanding regulatory abilities at the Language Partner stage include a child's increasing ability to tolerate transitions, manage changes in routine, persist in tasks with reasonable demands, delay gratification, and control behavioral impulses.

How the Capacity for Self-Regulation Supports Development During the Conversational Partner Stage

A number of critical milestones in the capacity for self-regulation contribute to a child's growth within the Conversational Partner stage. These milestones support the child's expansion of effective, efficient, and socially appropriate regulation strategies that, in turn, culminate in a greater ability to achieve successful communicative exchanges with a range of partners, both adults and peers, across contexts. Early in the Conversational Partner stage, a child is likely to use a variety of behavioral strategies and language strategies as a means to self-regulate. The behavioral strategies employed by a child at this stage may either be biologically driven, such as oral sensory input (e.g., mouthing a finger or an object), or modeled by responsive partners (e.g., stomping one's feet when mad). Language strategies typically exhibited at this stage include the use of words (i.e., self-talk) or other symbols (e.g., signs, pictures, written words) that the child has learned to use for the purpose of self-regulation through various learning strategies, including imitation, instructed learning, and collaborative learning. For example, a child who is anxious about transitions may prepare for an impending change in activity by using self-talk, such as saying, "First clean up, then snack."

Later in the Conversational Partner stage, a child may begin to develop metacognitive strategies for the purpose of self-regulation. Metacognitive strategies are closely tied to a child's ability to reflect on emotional memories associated with previous experiences, people, and places. Emotional memory is the affective component of memory, involving such aspects as feelings experienced with a person (e.g., joyful or stressful), a place (e.g., familiar and safe, unfamiliar and threatening), or an activity or experience (e.g., fun and of interest, unexciting and boring). Such memories develop from birth; however, emotional memory comes to play an increasingly greater role in emotional regulation as children at the Conversational Partner stage develop greater capacities to reflect on previous experiences. In addition to immediately perceived experience, such memories become significant factors affecting a child's ability to remain well regulated. For example, a preschooler may become anxious when visiting a pediatrician's office if previous recent visits involved painful procedures, and this anxiety may require greater parental efforts to support emotional regulation. Such anxiety may be expressed by the child when approaching the physician's building or when sitting in the waiting room, even before seeing the pediatrician. Emotional memory also affects social relationships over time. Based on previous experiences, children become more selective as to the adults or children they will seek out or avoid. In general, people who are most effective in providing positive emotional experiences and who are more successful in supporting a child's emotional regulation become preferred partners.

During the Conversational Partner stage, children demonstrate distinct emotional reactions to situations and experiences. Caregivers continue to attach emotional meaning and social expectations to activities and interactions, thus increasing a child's ability to understand a wider range of emotions as well as the language of emotions. Therefore, a child's increasing emotional repertoire is socially constructed (Shonkoff & Phillips, 2000). Children rely on their memories and often recall strategies that were successful earlier in emotionally challenging situations to help them integrate and self-regulate emotional arousal in the context of social interactions. A child's emotional expression provides insight into the effectiveness of available self-regulation strategies in the face of challenging circumstances. State changes continue to affect a child's emotional experience, but social awareness and the child's interpretation of interactions and events begin to become defining factors in the child's emotional experience.

The collective use of behavioral strategies, language strategies, and metacognitive strategies contributes to a child's ability to maintain a well-regulated state for longer periods and through more challenging circumstances. Therefore, a child's ability to interact, explore, and engage in social interaction across contexts and partners is greatly enhanced. The child's current state of arousal, the demands of the social environment, and the child's previous experiences determine which of these specific strategies or combinations of strategies the child employs. Hallmarks of these expanding self-regulatory abilities at the Conversational Partner stage include a child's increasing ability 1) to use emotional memories to assist with emotional regulation, 2) to reflect on social experience to guide emotional experience and activity, 3) to plan and prepare for experiences and interactions, 4) to identify and reflect on strategies to support regulation, and 5) to use language to negotiate in difficult situations.

EMOTIONAL REGULATORY DIFFICULTIES ASSOCIATED WITH AUTISM SPECTRUM DISORDERS

It has been well documented that children with ASD have significant difficulties in emotional regulation. Such difficulties are due to neurophysiological factors, such as a hyper-reactive and/or hyporeactive biases to sensory stimuli (Anzalone & Williamson, 2000; Dawson & Lewy, 1989; DeGangi, 2000; Kientz & Dunn, 1997), social-communicative difficulties and limitations in symbolic capacities (Prizant et al., 1997), regulatory disturbances such as sleep disorders and feeding problems, and delayed motor skills and motor planning difficulties (Anzalone & Williamson, 2000). Likewise, challenges in the development of metacognitive skills and language capacities affect emotional regulatory skill development. For children with ASD, the cumulative impact of these challenges may be observed in fluctuating arousal levels, unpredictable reactions, transition difficulties, problems sustaining and shifting attention, variable responses to sensory information, and the development of problem behaviors.

Of particular interest for children with ASD is the influence of neurophysiological factors on arousal modulation and emotional regulatory abilities because arousal state biases one's perception of environments, interactions, and events. This influence may take the form of a low threshold for physiological and emotional reactivity, resulting in being at risk for experiencing heightened states of arousal and emotion (i.e., hyperreactivity), which causes anxiety, agitation, and limitation in the ability to be available for learning and interacting. In these heightened states of arousal, children at all developmental stages may exhibit fight-or-flight reactions, which are frequently misinterpreted and treated as "behavior problems." Thus, when a child exhibits these reactions, he or she may be described as being aggressive, noncompliant, or intentionally manipulative. For instance, a child who is hyperreactive to visual and auditory stimulation may attempt to escape from overly stimulating environments or activities. If an escape response is not permitted or if it does not remedy the problem of sensory overload, a child may then enter a state of shutdown as a secondary coping strategy in which the child appears to be underaroused.

For other children, persistent states of hyporeactivity (i.e., underarousal) secondary to high thresholds for physiological and emotional reactivity may result in passivity, lethargy, and a similar inability to be available for processing social and environmental experiences. These children are often described as unmotivated, self-absorbed, nonfocused, or "spacey." Some children may experience shifting states of hyper- or hypoarousal that occur cyclically (e.g., according to time of day) or unpredictably, which result in a complex and seemingly inconsistent pattern that is challenging to both families and professionals (see Anzalone & Williamson, 2000, for further discussion).

Mutual Regulation and Core Challenges in Autism Spectrum Disorders

Due to the transactional nature of development, respondent mutual regulation skills may be compromised early on if a child's cues indicating arousal and emotional state are difficult to read due to the child's social-communicative challenges. This is often the case for children with ASD, as parents and other partners consistently report difficulties in reading the children's signals, sometimes resulting in having to guess through trial and error what the child is either experiencing or is trying to communicate. Variability in arousal state, unpredictable responses to stimulation, and idiosyncratic and unconventional displays of emotional state have been documented as common patterns in children with ASD. Collectively, these challenges compromise caregivers' ability to assist a child in attaining and maintaining a well-regulated state. In turn, social interactions may be stressful for both the child and the caregiver. For instance, if a child who is at the Social Partner stage and who is hypersensitive to motion is crying, and a caregiver picks the child up in an attempt to soothe him, the child may be further stressed due to the unanticipated movement stimulation, which will likely escalate the crying, as opposed to the desired result of calming the child. The youngster's reaction may be confusing and lead the caregiver to question his or her abilities to support the child, leading to further trial and error or avoidance. Such patterns of response may further exacerbate the child's disorganized state and, in turn, affect abilities to develop effective self-regulatory behavioral strategies.

Similar challenges persist at the Language Partner stage of development. For example, at this stage a child's difficulties understanding and using conventional nonverbal cues to express a range of emotions will affect how emotion is expressed. Therefore, a child may respond to an internal state of heightened arousal with a grimace, regardless of whether the child is experiencing a positive or negative emotional state. Thus, the child's state may be misinterpreted by a caregiver or other partners and may result in the use of inappropriate respondent mutual regulatory strategies, limiting opportunities for the child to develop effective behavioral and language strategies for self-regulation through the mutual regulatory interactive process. For example, if a child responds with a tense facial expression when actually enjoying an activity and the expression is read by a partner to be one of anxiety or fear, the partner may terminate the activity prematurely, resulting in increased dysregulation.

Challenges with respondent mutual regulation may also persist into the Conversational Partner stage of development. At this stage these challenges are often associated with idiosyncratic emotional displays corresponding to periods of extreme dysregulation. For example, a child who is extremely dysregulated may be unable to efficiently request assistance from a partner, and may revert to the use of immature and less sophisticated behavioral strategies such as chewing on clothing, having a tantrum, or fleeing from the social setting. These displays may be particularly perplexing to partners, as these behaviors seem to stand in sharp contrast to the child's abilities to communicate for mutual regulation in more appropriate and sophisticated ways when in a more regulated state, such as expressing emotion through language or requesting assistance. Such inconsistency and variability in the behavior of children with ASD is a commonly observed pattern, even for children at the Conversational Partner stage.

For a child with ASD, the ability to employ initiated mutual regulation strategies may also be compromised at all three stages of development. Again, physiological aspects of emotion and modulation of emotion influence the acquisition and use of initiated mutual regulatory skills. Specific emotions often change arousal states, such as fear resulting in a sudden increase in arousal as in a fight-or-flight reaction. Likewise, arousal state biases perception of intensity of emotions. Therefore, when a child experiences a strong emotion and a corresponding extreme change in emotional state, the child's ability to respond adaptively to a situation may be compromised. For instance a child in a high state of arousal due to anxiety may have difficulty retrieving and using conventional communicative means such as words, gestures, or signs to request assistance from another, as a result of being overwhelmed and disorganized. In contrast, when in a low state of arousal, the child may have difficulty requesting assistance due to difficulties recognizing the presence of others, evaluating the problem, and/or formulating a plan to reach his or her goals by communicating to others. In either case, the very same child will be more able to socially problem solve and use conventional communicative means commensurate with his developmental level when he or she is in a more optimal arousal state. In extreme cases, the child may appear to be a different child in different arousal states, resulting in apparent inconsistency across settings and circumstances and causing great confusion for partners.

> Respondent mutual regulation, or a partner's ability to read a child's emotional signals of dysregulation and respond appropriately, must be fostered as part of a more general plan to support emotional regulation.

For children with ASD, challenges expressing emotion in a conventional manner also affect the children's ability to use initiated mutual regulatory strategies effectively, regardless of their developmental level. Restricted emotional expression due to limitations in the use of nonverbal gestures, facial expressions, and body language often associated with ASD affect a child's abilities to direct signals to and secure assistance from others. In turn, communicative partners often have a great deal of difficulty interpreting the child's emotional and arousal states, even when the child attempts to direct signals to partners to communicate these states. At other times, extreme emotional reactions, resulting from arousal biases and/or difficulties understanding and expressing emotions in a graded manner, may catch partners off guard, limiting the partners' ability to respond in a supportive manner.

In addition, other immature and unconventional patterns of emotional expression, such as crashing into others, hitting, biting, shutting down, engaging in repetitive behaviors, and dropping to the floor may not be perceived by others as bids for assistance with emotional regulation, when in fact, this may be the child's intent. A child who demonstrates such behaviors may be considered aggressive or noncompliant, whereas in reality, the child may engage in such behavior to seek physical contact or other forms of support for emotional regulation. For example, a child at the Language Partner stage of development may repeatedly use a behavioral strategy of crashing into a caregiver in an apparent attempt to request assistance, such as engaging in sensory-motor activity, to regulate arousal. Likewise, a child at the Conversational Partner stage may use socially undesirable strategies such as physically striking out at another to communicate distress to attempt to request cessation of an activity. In these unfortunate circumstances, the child's attempts at securing assistance from others may lead to further isolation and/or emotional distress, as the partner's reaction (e.g., punishing or ignoring the behaviors) may not address the child's need for support.

For children with ASD, coexisting difficulties in the dimensions of cognitive appraisal and socialization of emotional experience further limit their abilities to use initiated mutual regulation strategies and respond to assistance provided by caregivers. Children with ASD may not view a caregiver as a potential source for mutual regulation (e.g., comfort, assistance), due in part to difficulties in joint attentional capacities as well as in more general social-communicative abilities, which are considered to underlie the development of secure relationships (Stern, 1985). This further limits the strategies the children develop and employ to maintain a well-regulated emotional

The development of initiated mutual regulation strategies, which a child uses to seek out and express the need for support from others, should be emphasized in goals to support emotional regulation.

state. For example, a child may not know that another person can provide comfort through physical or verbal means and therefore may not seek others out. Even for a child with this knowledge and social awareness, mutual regulatory strategies may be significantly compromised during periods of extreme dysregulation, which are associated with both very high and very low arousal levels.

In addition to the impact of limitations in expressive communication, limitations in receptive language and communication may also detrimentally affect the capacity to maintain a well-regulated state. For example, a child's emotional reaction to problems in comprehending gestures or language due to their transient nature may cause confusion and/or frustration resulting in dysregulation. At the Conversational Partner stage, the impact of social-communicative challenges is particularly evident when a child is developing greater awareness of more complex emotions (e.g., guilt, embarrassment, pride, jealousy) that rely heavily on social norms or conventions of appropriate and desirable behavior. Because a child learns to map emotion words and concepts on internal states and experiences through interactions with others, difficulty understanding and interpreting social interactions results in difficulties comprehending and using emotional concepts that reflect complex interpersonal experiences.

Self-Regulation and Core Challenges in Autism Spectrum Disorders

Children with ASD typically show difficulties in learning to use effective and socially appropriate self-regulatory capacities, as is often observed in the behavior of children at the Social and Language Partner stages. For example, children at these stages of development often demonstrate challenges sustaining attention during social interactions, may display strong and sudden emotional reactions, and have difficulty tolerating transitions. Children at the Conversational Partner stage have similar difficulties, as observed in these children's tendencies to display strong, unpredictable emotional reactions and/or to be unavailable for learning and social engagement in everyday activities. Their challenges are further evidenced by difficulties attending to relevant information in a social setting, delaying gratification, and controlling impulses. For children in all stages, patterns of obsessive-compulsive behavior such as inflexible adherence to rituals and routines may be attempts to self-regulate in the face of a social world that is too busy and too noisy, that moves too fast, and that at times is simply too unpredictable and overwhelming.

By referring to four of the dimensions of emotional regulation outlined at the beginning of this chapter (i.e., cognitive appraisal, physiological aspect of emotions, emotional expression, and socialization), we can further understand and break down the specific self-regulatory skill difficulties frequently seen in the behavioral profiles of children with ASD. The fifth dimension, recovery from dysregulation, is discussed later, as it is associated with more intense and prolonged emotional reactions. *Physiological aspects of emotion* and modulation of emotional state often are influenced by a child's arousal biases and the child's resulting unusual responses to stimulation (e.g., hypersensitivity to sensation and stimulation such as sound or touch resulting from a bias for a high state of arousal). Thus, arousal bias influences a child's perception of situations, events, and interactions. For example, if a child is already in a high state of arousal, a relatively low level of stimulus input or a relatively low task demand will likely be perceived by the child as far more intense and less tolerable than when the child is in a lower state of arousal. In such circumstances, what appears to be a benign level of input or task challenge may be the straw that breaks the camel's back and will push the child into a dysregulated state. Recall the child we discussed previously who was inadvertently touched by a classmate while in a high state of arousal, resulting in the extremely defensive response of running from the classmate. If that child had been in a quiet but alert arousal state, it is unlikely that this protective reaction would have been triggered. Rather, the child would most likely have tolerated the touch and adjusted his or

> A child's arousal state always must be taken into account in activities and interactions, as it will affect the child's reactions and responses. Appropriate supports should be provided to maintain optimal states of arousal.

her body position to allow space for the peer. In contrast, a child in a low state of arousal may fail to register stimulation if it is not intense enough to be alerting, resulting in limited or no reaction to environmental input or task demands. This is commonly observed in children who have such a high threshold for pain due to a low arousal bias that even the intense stimulation of a significant injury is not registered and may not result in the expected physical pain reaction and emotional distress.

In addition, regardless of developmental stage, children with ASD may have difficulties perceiving physiological changes in arousal states, often times not registering state changes until an extreme fluctuation has occurred (Attwood, 1998). For instance, a child may not notice that he or she is becoming increasingly irritated by low-level background noise and in turn may not express his or her discomfort or attempt to employ a regulatory strategy to remain well regulated. However, once that child becomes overwhelmed by the cumulative effect of the stimulation and is thrust into a dysregulated state of high arousal, he or she may display a sudden extreme reaction, which may appear as an unpredictable response to an observer and disproportionate to the situation. Therefore, emotional expression in children with ASD is often equated with extreme and often unpredictable all-or-nothing reactions, which then require greater self-regulatory efforts for recovery from a dysregulated state. In such instances, partners may also be affected by such unpredictability, as they are less able to read a child's signals that are indicative of escalation into a dysregulated state and therefore are less able to respond proactively and preventatively to support the child's emotional regulation to preclude extreme dysregulation. Parents of children with ASD often comment that the only thing consistent about their children's responses is their inconsistency. It may very well be that patterns of inconsistent behavioral responses are due, in large part, to fluctuating states of arousal associated with arousal modulation difficulties. As noted, such variability in arousal state is exacerbated by limitations in emotional regulatory capacities.

Difficulties in *emotional expression* of children with ASD have also been well documented at the Social Partner stage as well as at the Language and Conversational Partner stages (Attwood, 1998; NRC, 2001; Wetherby, Prizant, & Hutchinson, 1998). Limitations in the ability to use conventional expressions of emotion, including facial expressions, gestures, and words, characterize these challenges. The source of these difficulties is complex and multidimensional. Due in part to social-communicative limitations, children with ASD often have difficulty interpreting the nonverbal emotional

> Goals in educational programming should address expression and understanding of emotions and the ability of the child and familiar partners to make judgments about the child's arousal states to support emotional regulation.

signals of others and consequently have difficulty internalizing these nonverbal signals for their own use. This is particularly true if the signals are subtler in nature and convey less intense emotional states. These same challenges are reflected in a child's ability interpret and acquire emotional vocabulary.

Social-communicative difficulties further affect the development and use of self-regulatory skills. *Socialization* (the process of modifying one's behavior and emotional expression based on feedback from others) typically experienced during the Language and Conversational Partner stages is greatly influenced by these difficulties. Due, in part, to frequent arousal level fluctuations and difficulties sustaining and shifting attention, children with ASD are often challenged by the fleeting nature of social feedback and in turn have difficulty responding in appropriate and conventional ways. In particular, challenges with socialization affect a child's ability to express changes in emotion, in a graded manner, that are readable and socially acceptable and to employ emotional regulatory strategies that have been modeled for the child. As a result, a child with ASD at the Social Partner stage often uses self-regulatory strategies that appear to be idiosyncratic; unconventional; and, in some cases, socially stigmatizing (e.g., flapping hands, walking on toes, biting, rocking, dropping to the floor, shutting down).

Challenges in the dimension of *cognitive appraisal* experienced at the Conversational Partner stage may also pose self-regulatory difficulties for a child with ASD. The process of cognitive appraisal relies heavily on metacognitive skills and directly affects a child's ability to reflect on and make judgments and predictions about the behavioral patterns of partners. This ability requires the capacity to represent events symbolically in memory and to reflect on those events. As discussed, children with ASD demonstrate difficulties with symbolic capacities. These difficulties may have a negative impact on the development of inner language. It has long been understood that inner language (Vygotsky, 1978), or the ability to represent events in memory and problem solve through inner symbolic means, serves the important cognitive functions of organizing experience and behavior, thinking about and learning from past events, and planning for future events. With limited ability to use inner language for these cognitive functions and when faced with stressful events, it is less possible for a child to reflect on past events to plan for dysregulating and potentially threatening events in a manner that supports emotional regulation. These difficulties may also contribute to the unpredictable reactions to daily events observed in many children with ASD as they are at the mercy of challenging events in the heat of the moment.

Furthermore, due to the fact that children with ASD often demonstrate relative strengths in rote associative memory, emotional memory processes may have a significant impact on emotional regulation when children have strong memories of stressful emotional experience associated with particular people, places, or events. In such circumstances, without the benefit of reflection through inner language to support emotional regulation, these children may demonstrate extreme panic reactions in an almost reflexive manner when confronted once again with those people, places, or events. For example, we have met many children who have been exposed to stressful "learning" experiences that they have come to associate with a particular person, room, or even a location in a room. When these children are brought to that person, room, or work table again, extreme avoidance reactions may be observed, such as dropping to the floor, fighting to escape, or hitting themselves, sometimes accompanied by utterances such as "No work, no work!" In one specific instance, a child received a shock from static electricity when touching the door knob of the resource room in a school, and it took many months before that child would even approach the door of the room voluntarily. Even walking within 8–10 feet of the door resulted in extreme anxiety. For some children who are hyperreactive to sound, simply seeing an infant may result in significant anxiety, due to previous experiences of hearing infants crying causing painful sensory overload. This may occur even if the infant is not crying, as the reaction is associated with the previous experience and emotional memory of seeing an infant. Finally, as noted previously, it is common for children with ASD to either seek out, or conversely, avoid other people, based on previous positive or negative emotional memories.

> An important emotional regulation goal is to support children's ability to develop meta-cognitive strategies to reflect on challenges to emotional regulation, as one way of supporting well-regulated states.

In summary, the collective challenges experienced by a child with ASD in the areas of physiological responses of emotion and modulation of emotional state, expression of emotion, socialization, and cognitive appraisal significantly affect a child's ability to develop and use self-regulatory behavioral strategies, language strategies, and metacognitive strategies. Therefore, for children with ASD who are well beyond the toddler years, partners may have to continue to support children primarily through respondent mutual regulation strategies, as the burden is on partners to monitor children's emotional regulatory status and to help them maintain a well-regulated state that allows for active engagement in everyday activities. This important issue is dealt with in detail in the Interpersonal Support component of the Transactional Support domain of the SCERTS Model (discussed in Chapter 4 of this volume).

Recovery from Dysregulation and Core Challenges of Autism Spectrum Disorders

We have highlighted many of the specific challenges encountered frequently by children with ASD with respect to the development and use of mutual and self-regulatory skills. These difficulties often contribute to intense and prolonged emotional reactions to challenges to people or events in the social and physical environment, which negatively affect children's abilities to maintain an optimal state of arousal because it is less likely that regulatory strategies can be used effectively during daily activities. In the SCERTS Model, we refer to these prolonged and intense emotional reactions as *periods of extreme dysregulation*. In addition to the core challenges faced by children with ASD in the development and use of mutual and self-regulatory capacities, additional factors influence abilities to maintain a regulated state that may contribute to periods of extreme dysregulation. Factors such as a child's physiological condition, characteristics of the environment, and motor demands associated with tasks play a role in emotional dysregulation. Table 3.1 presents factors related to emotional regulation and dysregulation for children with ASD.

Extreme emotion and/or arousal state changes associated with periods of dysregulation can significantly affect a child's functional abilities. For instance, when a child is overwhelmingly distressed, communication skills, problem-solving abilities, and attentional capacities are likely to be degraded. In turn, the ability to call on and use mu-

Table 3.1. Factors related to emotional regulation and dysregulation

Factors related to emotional regulation or dysregulation	Factors that cause emotional dysregulation (risk factors)	Factors that support emotional regulation (protective factors)
Physiological (general)	Illness, fatigue, food, sleep disorders, or food/environmental allergies	Good health, sleep, eating nutrition, and few or no allergies
Sensory (constitutional)	Vulnerable sensory profile	Few sensory challenges
Sensory (environmental)	Disorganizing environmental sensory input in any modality	Input within processing tolerance
Cognitive	Violation of expectations, such as changes in routine	Consistency and predictability
	Negative emotional memory	Positive emotional memory
Communication and language	Receptive: Input beyond processing capabilities	Receptive: Input consistent with processing capabilities
	Expressive: Limited ability to express intentions	Expressive: Ability to express intentions
Interpersonal	Directive controlling styles	Shared control
	Overstimulating input (e.g., visual, auditory)	Calibrated input
	Lack of support, or inappropriate support attempts when needed (lack of, or unsuccessful mutual regulation)	Support appropriately calibrated to needs for regulation (successful mutual regulation)
	Lack of trust in relationships	Trusting relationships
Social	Overwhelming social complexity and expectations	Good match between processing abilities and social experience
Motor	Motor demands (e.g., fine, gross, motor planning) of activity exceed motor capabilities	Good match between motor abilities and activity demands
Developmental shifts and changes	Developmental regression due to cognitive reorganization and/or asynchronous advances across developmental domains (e.g., increase in sense of self and self-determination and limited communication skills results in increased problematic protest behavior)	Developmental abilities across domains in synchrony to address new developmental challenges (e.g., language development supports self-determination and more acceptable protest behavior)
Emotional regulatory strategies	Lack of, inflexible, and/or limited range of mutual and self-regulatory strategies	Flexible and broad range of mutual and self-regulatory strategies

tual and self-regulatory strategies to help recover from states of extreme dysregulation are likely to be reduced or inaccessible. For example, a child who is in the Conversational Partner stage and who is typically able to employ language strategies and metacognitive strategies may have a difficult time using self-talk or inner language to regulate anger and to reflect on the situation when an unanticipated schedule change results in extreme confusion and dysregulation. Likewise, a child at this same stage of development who is typically able to benefit from the use of transactional supports such as Social Stories (Gray, 1994) and verbally mediated scripts when experiencing mild anxiety may shut down or react negatively when caregivers attempt to introduce these supports for mutual regulation during periods of extreme distress and anxiety. The additional social input, in addition to the distress caused by the unexpected schedule change, may simply be too much to tolerate. Similarly, a child who is at the Social Partner stage and who typically employs behavioral strategies such as jumping and hugging familiar caregivers to help regulate arousal level may have difficulty organizing and executing these motor actions when experiencing a period of dysregulation associated with extreme giddiness.

> Specific strategies and plans for supporting recovery from extreme states of dysregulation must be included as part of a comprehensive plan to support emotional regulation.

Thus, in addition to difficulties in developing emotional regulatory strategies to prevent dysregulation, children with ASD are faced with additional challenges in their efforts to recover from more extreme states of dysregulation. Furthermore, the regulatory strategies a child may have that are typically effective may be ineffective during periods of extreme dysregulation associated with heightened periods of arousal and emotional state. Therefore, when designing an educational plan for a child with ASD, it is important to target the development of a broad range of mutual and self-regulatory regulatory strategies that can be employed effectively for a range of arousal levels and emotional states and during different states of dysregulation. For instance if the child's behavioral signals indicate mild stress, such as fidgeting and looking away from a task, transactional supports such as refocusing attention with visual support and/or defining the end point of the task may be helpful (e.g., by indicating visually and verbally how many more steps to completion or how much time is remaining). However, if the child is engaged in an activity but is exhibiting signals of increasing dysregulation such as chewing on a shirt sleeve or using a loud voice with more agitated emotional expression when talking, more intensive supports may be necessary, such as providing clear written directions to follow and modifying task expectations, such as simplifying or shortening the task. Likewise, if a child's level of emotional distress escalates to a state of more extreme dysregulation, more intrusive approaches, such as providing a break from the dysregulating activity and encouraging participation in organizing behavioral activities, such as those with a sensory and motor component, may be warranted. As is evident, emotional regulation is a dynamic process; therefore, approaches to support recovery from extreme dysregulation must be flexible and dynamic as well and must be calibrated to a child's signals of dysregulation and knowledge of what best supports a child. Such flexibility in supporting emotional regulation is an important goal in the Emotional Regulation domain of the SCERTS Model and is explored in greater detail in Volume II.

The Ultimate Goal in Supporting Emotional Regulation: Fostering "Flow"

From this discussion, it is clear that in the SCERTS Model, emotional regulation is a core challenge of the highest priority for children with ASD. Therefore, emotional regulation goals are addressed in a comprehensive manner in all social contexts. The ultimate goal and rationale for supporting emotional regulation may be considered in reference to the psychological construct of "flow" or "optimal experience" (Csikszentmihalyi, 1990). Flow has been discussed as a goal that all human beings strive to achieve and may be the most significant factor affecting quality of life. Flow has been described as a state in which a person experiences focus, deep concentration, and productive engagement with a particular experience or activity (social or nonsocial) and a sense of control, motivation, and satisfaction in that experience. Flow requires that there be a good match between 1) a person's abilities and 2) demands and challenges in activities or experiences in everyday life. The more one is able to engage in activities and experiences in life in a manner that fosters a state of flow, the greater the long-term impact on learning; self-esteem; and, ultimately, quality of life. Due to challenges in emotional regulation, children with ASD are less able than most other children to achieve such optimal experience, especially in circumstances requiring social engagement and communication. Thus, in the SCERTS Model, we are highly invested in supporting the development of a broad and flexible range of emotional regulatory capacities, which have an undeniable impact on providing the foundation for and allowing for flow experiences in the lives of children with ASD.

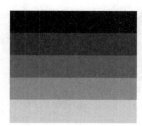

Chapter 4

Transactional Support

In this chapter, we consider Transactional Support, the domain of the SCERTS Model that is designed to address many challenges faced by children with ASD and their families by ensuring that appropriate supports are in place. As with the other domains of the model, Social Communication and Emotional Regulation, we recommend that readers who are not familiar with or who are only generally familiar with this knowledge base review this chapter carefully, as it will provide the background information necessary to implement the SCERTS Model.

Most children with ASD require a variety of supports to participate optimally in interpersonal interactions and relationships and to understand and derive enjoyment from everyday activities. This is due, in large part, to the pervasive difficulties that these children experience in social communication, social understanding, and emotional regulation, as well as to learning style differences. Supports also are needed to maximize learning in educational settings, and to reinforce families' efforts to support their child's development. Families also benefit from supports to assist them in coping with and adapting to the challenges of raising a child with ASD and in seeking the most appropriate services. Finally, service providers must also be supported in their work to be most effective with children and families.

As discussed previously, we believe that the transactional model of development is the most appropriate model for designing effective educational strategies for young children with ASD and their families (Prizant & Wetherby, 1989), as it addresses child development within the context of the family and other significant social and societal influences. This model stipulates that developmental outcomes are "the result of interplay between child and context over time, in which the state of one affects the next state of the other in a continuous dynamic process" (Sameroff, 1987, p. 274). Thus, the transactional nature of the SCERTS Model is underscored by the following principles:

1. The active role of the child in learning is of paramount significance, and partners must respond flexibly and in a supportive manner to a child's efforts in social communication, emotional regulation, and learning.

2. All people who interact and engage with children with ASD in everyday activities are considered important facilitators of development, including parents, other caregivers, brother and sisters, and peers.

3. Educators and clinicians must expand their roles from focusing primarily on enhancing a child's abilities to supporting others such as family members and colleagues in creating growth-inducing interactions and activities designed to support the child's developmental capacities.

4. Learning supports for a child, such as environmental adaptations and educational modifications (e.g., use of visual supports, curriculum modification) must be de-

signed to incorporate the learning strengths of the child to address the challenges of social communication and emotional regulation.

5. Transactional supports must be flexible and responsive to the changing needs of children and families in different social contexts and learning environments. Most important, however, is that both children and family members see supports as relevant to their daily life experiences and develop a sense of confidence and competence in using and responding to supports.

Transactional support is addressed in four major domains in the SCERTS Model:

1. Interpersonal support (from adults and peers)

2. Learning supports

3. Support to families

4. Support among professionals

It is necessary to address supports in a broad-based and comprehensive manner due to the many challenges faced by children with ASD in everyday interpersonal interactions, as well as in educational settings and other learning contexts. Family members also are faced with many varied challenges that can be addressed through a comprehensive plan of transactional support. Professionals and paraprofessionals must also be supported in their efforts in working with children with ASD. We now discuss some of the most common core challenges faced by children and their families as well as other caregivers that are addressed through transactional support in the SCERTS Model.

CORE CHALLENGES REQUIRING TRANSACTIONAL SUPPORT STRATEGIES

Children with ASD may benefit from a wide range of strategically implemented supports. For supports to be most effective and relevant, they must be based on a thorough understanding of the challenges faced by children and their families.

Core Challenges Requiring Interpersonal Support

Challenges Faced by Children

The difficulties experienced by children with ASD in engaging successfully in interpersonal interactions and developing emotionally fulfilling relationships is underscored by the daily experiences of professionals and family members (Domingue, Cutler, & McTarnaghan, 2000; Quinn, 2003), firsthand accounts of individuals with ASD (Grandin, 1995; Shore, 2001; Williams, 1992), and empirical research (Bristol & Schopler, 1984). It is now understood that these challenges are due to the core, definitive characteristics of ASD. That is, children are not choosing to be disengaged from social interaction and relationships because of a primary lack of interest or desire. Due to limitations in social-communicative, social-cognitive, and emotional regulatory capacities, children with ASD often are limited in the requisite abilities and skills to be more successful, active participants or may be incapable of coping with the language and social processing demands inherent in interpersonal interaction. These demands may include the need to simultaneously process oral language and the subtle and not-so-subtle nonverbal social cues embedded in body language and emotional expression. The presentation of this complex array of social information often is further embedded in environments with a great deal of superfluous sensory input (noise, movement), resulting in additional challenges for a child's ability to shift attention and to attend selectively to the most relevant information.

> Partners as well as children with ASD must be supported in developing skills to participate in successful and emotionally satisfying interpersonal interactions as part of an educational plan.

Finally, the rules of social-communicative interactions constantly change across settings and partners, requiring the social judgment to test, problem-solve, and reflect on feedback received from others. In other words, in the SCERTS Model, we work under the assumption that most children want to communicate and engage socially with partners; however, they just may not know how to participate and how to adjust their efforts according to different social contexts or may be unable to do so due to environmental complexities outside of their control. It is truly amazing that so many children with ASD choose to be part of social-communicative interactions to the degree that they do, given all of the concomitant confusing and anxiety-provoking scenarios. In contrast to notions of children with ASD actively choosing to be asocial, efforts to cope in social situations seem to suggest a significant degree of social motivation to remain connected to the social world, even at the expense of repeated social-communication breakdowns and unsuccessful and even stressful experiences. Unfortunately, some children who experience cumulative stressful social experiences may also have negative emotional memories of these experiences, which further reduce the children's motivation to stay engaged socially.

In addition, some partners who regularly interact with children may also be limited in the requisite knowledge and skills (whether intuitive or consciously learned) to support children's efforts, inadvertently adding to a child's perception that social interaction is just too difficult. For example, some partners may speak too quickly or too loudly, may use excessive touch, or otherwise may be insensitive to a child's specific needs to remain engaged in social interaction. Therefore, some children with ASD are at risk for developing a sense of interpersonal interaction as overwhelming, confusing, and stressful based on a history of repeated unsuccessful experiences, whereas others are at risk for limited engagement and low motivation to participate in social interactions due to language and sensory processing difficulties and/or a hyporesponsive (underaroused) bias toward interpersonal events. Caregivers also are at risk for experiencing interactions with children with ASD as challenging, especially in reference to supporting reciprocal engagement in social communication and emotional regulation. The challenges faced by caregivers are discussed in greater depth in the section on family support.

How a Child's Challenges in Language Processing Affect Partners

We live in a world in which daily events are largely mediated by oral language. For most of us, it is hard to conceive of participating in daily activities without the benefit of our abilities to process language, which helps us make meaning of everyday experiences. Yet, for many individuals with ASD, limitations in oral language processing become major barriers to full participation in activities with others, and these limitations affect partners as well.

Even at the most basic levels of competence, it is clear that some language processing abilities are essential to be a full partner in social-communicative exchanges. The reciprocity inherent in the dance of social communication is built on the capacity to both process as well as send verbal and nonverbal signals to others. Thus, for children, challenges in processing language may affect social motivation and social engagement over extended sequences of interaction.

This may easily be understood by reflecting on a very common situation most of us have experienced. Consider what is like to be in a setting where all other people are speaking a language that you do not understand or for which you only have minimal proficiency (e.g., Greek). Even if highly motivated, you may only be able to attend to other people speaking at a conversational level in Greek for a short period, as the processing load is just too great for you to maintain your attention. This same phenomenon also is observed in the development of all young children, who may either ignore or attend to everyday adult conversation for only brief periods. It is almost as if a young child understands that the conversation is not intended for him or her.

However, even in the face of oral language processing difficulties, responsive partners may react in a manner to support successful interaction. For example, with appropriate communicative style adjustments (slower pace, increased use of gestures or visual supports, increased repetition and redundancy in speech production), the person with limited abilities in processing Greek, or the very young child, will be more successful in participating in these social contexts due to the supports provided. As noted previously, we have commonly observed that some children with ASD actively avoid or remove themselves from situations in which activities are too driven by oral language. These reactions are an understandable and a natural consequence of both the intensity of auditory stimulation that occurs when there is much talking, as well as the feeling of confusion and lack of confidence that children must experience when faced with heavy language processing loads. These reactions may seem to suggest inconsistency or even lack of interest in responding but are clearly rooted in the language processing difficulties.

Even for the most able children at the Conversational Partner stage who have higher level expressive and receptive language abilities, such children with Asperger disorder or so-called high-functioning autism, the requirements to process language in busy and complex environments that demand rapid shifting of attention and selective focus on speech can be overwhelming. Furthermore, higher level language abilities, such as comprehension of nonliteral language forms (e.g., idioms, metaphors, cynicism, sarcasm), which require an integration of linguistic and social understanding relative to a social situation, provide additional challenges even for those youngsters with relatively strong language abilities. Once again, partners may be perplexed about limited responsiveness or concrete and "incorrect" responding in these youngsters who may appear so bright in other ways.

How Challenges in Understanding Emotional Cues, Gestures, and Facial Expression Affect Partners

A related challenge experienced by children with ASD is limitations in understanding others' facial expressions and gestures, which not only provide information about others' intentions but also information about others' emotional states. Difficulties in understanding emotional expressions, as well as difficulties in expressing or sharing emotional states, may be closely related to problems experienced by children with ASD in developing empathy and trusting relationships with others. To fully appreciate these difficulties, however, one must consider the complexity involved in reading emotional and social cues. One person's grimace may be another person's laughter; one person's smile may be another person's pained expression. Understanding facial expressions often requires an intimate understanding of how a partner uses facial expressions in any given context and what that means for that individual. A smile might not really be a smile—it may be a sign of nervousness. Social judgment about facial expression within and across individuals is a daunting task for a child who is struggling to participate in the dance of social interaction.

> An educational plan must be based on an understanding of a child's difficulties in processing language and nonverbal cues. Interpersonal supports must be developed to directly address such challenges.

It has been said that human communication is 30% verbal and 70% nonverbal. The pervasiveness of challenges in communication in ASD is underscored by documented limitations in understanding of both nonverbal as well as verbal signals (Prizant et al., 1997). A common observation about children with ASD is that they may misread and respond inappropriately to others' emotional expressions, which has a clear impact on partners. For example, parents and teachers may be perplexed as to why a child laughs in response to their verbal and/or facial expression of anger. A child's reactions may be misinterpreted on the part of a partner, leading to the belief that the child is mocking the other person or "pushing the partner's buttons." An alternative to this explanation more consistent with our understanding of ASD is that a child may feel that people may literally look and sound funny if that child does not understand the emotional meanings behind words, tone of voice, and facial expression. It is the responsibility of more able partners to simplify their expression and clarify the meanings behind facial expression, gestures, and tone of voice for their less able partners. It also is important for partners to understand that lack of, inconsistent, or inappropriate responses to partner's verbal and nonverbal communication and emotional expression are an inherent part of ASD and can be addressed in appropriate programming. As noted, this is a major focus of the Social Communication domain of the SCERTS Model.

How the Tendency to Shut Down or Tune Out Affects Partners

As noted previously, the transactional impact of difficulties in processing language, emotional expression, and other nonverbal signals, compounded by challenges in making meaning of everyday events, may have a secondary impact on the social motivation of children with ASD. Children may become less motivated to participate in activities in which successful participation requires processing of linguistic and nonverbal communicative information. For example, children may avoid specific activities, such as group circle activities, classroom lectures, or other activities that rely heavily on processing language and nonverbal signals, or the children may experience increasing anxiety and eventually shut down when they are in such activities.

This is most apparent when one considers the common observation that in general, children with ASD are much less likely to seek out or stay in group situations, where the complexity and level of stimulation compounds processing difficulties. Another factor is how partners respond to children. It is no wonder that some children shut down or avoid challenging interpersonal exchanges given that they may be told in many ways each day that they are not responding or acting appropriately. Society and individual partners determine interpersonal rules and boundaries, which may seem

An educational plan must be based on an understanding of a child's difficulties in sensory processing. Interpersonal supports must be developed to directly address such challenges.

so simple and intuitive to people with "intact" social abilities. To children with ASD, however, social rules and norms may appear inconsistent and illogical, as they change so frequently relative to social contexts and social partners. Continual change and realignment of interpersonal expectations may keep children off balance even as they are expected to participate in social activities which may more closely resemble a random beehive of activity than a predictable, orderly flow of interaction. Once again, partners must realize that shutting down or tuning out may be coping strategies (i.e., self-regulatory strategies) exhibited by children in the face of stressful and difficult to understand circumstances. Thus, it is necessary to determine the appropriate supports to put in to place to lessen these tendencies to disengage, rather than viewing them primarily as reflecting a child's unwillingness to respond or participate.

How Challenges in Sensory Processing Affect Partners

The well-documented difficulties in the processing of sensory information (Anzalone & Williamson, 2000), sometimes referred to in the literature as *abnormal responses to sensory experiences,* heightens the need for interpersonal support for many children. Some children may experience great difficulty in both social and nonsocial activities, due to a bias toward hyperreactive responses to sensory events across a variety of sensory modalities (e.g., auditory, visual, tactile). For example, a child with ASD may attempt to avoid an enthusiastic and familiar partner who speaks too loudly, moves too quickly, or hugs too firmly.

Specific activities or environments that present similar challenges may also become aversive to a child to the extent that patterns of anticipatory avoidance or anticipatory defensiveness may be observed even before the child actually experiences the activities or is in the environments. This is commonly observed when a child drops to the floor and refuses to go into a particular setting such as a noisy gym or cafeteria or covers one or both ears before entering such situations. Clearly, it will be far more difficult for the child to communicate with and stayed engaged with others under such circumstances. Once again, inconsistent arousal states and abnormal responses to sensory experiences may result in a highly confusing picture to partners due to inconsistent responding by a child with ASD. Partners must develop strategies to support well-regulated states in the face of such sensory challenges, and doing so is a major thrust of the Emotional Regulation domain of the SCERTS Model.

The Moral of This Story: The "Problem" Is Not Solely "Within" the Child

It is widely accepted that early interactions and family relationships set the stage for a child to experience success or difficulty in early communicative and social-affective experiences. Furthermore, a child develops a sense of self as a partner and as a competent communicator through repeated instances of communicative success or failure, initially within the family context, and eventually throughout broader social experiences. With persistent social-communicative difficulties, interactions may come to be viewed as stressful and anxiety arousing for children and partners. Conversely, success in social activities supports motivation and a sense of competence and confidence. Therefore, supporting a child's sense of self as an effective and competent social partner is crucial in motivating further communication and social interaction with partners.

At this point, it should be obvious that in the SCERTS Model, we consider it to be overly simplistic and even inaccurate to view difficulties and challenges solely "within" the child. In contrast, a child with ASD, family members, and all other partners may be affected by social-communicative and emotional regulatory difficulties in a dynamic, transactional manner. For example, not only may a child have difficulty processing communicative signals of partners, but partners may also have difficulty processing the child's subtle and unconventional communicative signals as well as difficulty monitoring the child's states of emotional arousal. Partners may become frustrated by what they perceived as a lack of responsiveness from the child with ASD. For some teaching approaches, this may be the result of a partner's predetermined decision as to how the child should respond and what the correct response should be. If the child does not respond, or if the response is minimal or unconventional, the partner may become frustrated at his or her own or the child's inability to establish or maintain a rewarding interpersonal experience. Transactional support is critical for families and professionals in these instances to avoid or minimize interpersonal breakdowns and the potential feelings of incompetence or frustration on the part of both the child and partner.

> In the SCERTS Model, it is recognized that learning is a partnership; thus, both a child and his or her adult partners bear responsibility for making interactions work and for growing and adapting over time. In practice, the behavior of both child and partners is assessed, with goals set for each partner.

Thus, family members and other partners also adopt a sense of themselves as either effective or ineffective communicative and social partners relative to a child with ASD. Family members and children who are more successful communicative partners anticipate, initiate, and actively contribute to smoother, more rewarding, and emotionally satisfying interactions with the child. Such success is highly dependent on a partner's reading the child's intentional or preintentional communicative signals, as well as signals of emotional regulation or dysregulation. Effective support for a child depends on the partner's making communicative style adjustments based on successful reading of and continuous monitoring of such signals. Family members and children who are less skilled as communicative and social partners are less likely to recognize opportunities for engagement and therefore may not successfully initiate and/or respond to the child's communicative overtures. This lack of recognition results in a greater likelihood of increased interactive breakdowns in ongoing reciprocal social and communicative interaction, which hinders the development of positive relationships. Therefore, the SCERTS Model explicitly addresses the need to enhance a child's abilities as well as support caregivers' success in social-communicative exchanges that fosters a sense of success, social motivation, and emotional reward for both the child and his or her partners.

It also is recognized that children with ASD are very much like any other children, who tend to gravitate to and even seek out those people who are most intuitive, understanding, and able to take the perspective of others. The most successful interpersonal interactions that occur with family members or professionals include partners who are able to take the time to consider, "If I were this child, how would I feel, or what would I be thinking right now?" Interpersonal interactions in which one partner dominates the other, regardless of the perspective of the partner with less power, will often fail in the long run. There is no genuine long-term incentive to remain part of the relationship. Thus, in the SCERTS Model, we recognize the need to look as much at the behavior of partners as at the behavior of the child and the need to foster positive change in partners that supports social communication, emotional regulation, and positive relationships.

Core Challenges Requiring Learning Support

In addition to the quality and characteristics of interpersonal interactions, children with ASD also experience challenges related to their pattern of learning strengths and weaknesses. Many educational innovations that have had such a great impact on services for children with ASD have been based on a greater understanding of the learning or cognitive style observed in most children with ASD. An increased understanding of learning and cognitive style issues has come from a variety of sources, including empirical research, first-person accounts of people with ASD, and educational and clinical experience. To understand this dimension of transactional support, we begin with an overview of the patterns of learning strengths and weaknesses of children with ASD, followed by a discussion of why these patterns pose challenges for these children.

Learning Strengths and Weaknesses

As a group, children with ASD demonstrate a unique pattern of learning strengths and weaknesses, which in and of itself creates special challenges (as well as opportunities) for these children and their partners. Commonly cited abilities in ASD include a relatively strong rote, associative memory (i.e., episodic memory or gestalt memory) for both visual and auditory information and proficiencies in tasks demanding visual-spatial processing and pattern recognition (Grandin, 1995; Prior, 1979; Prizant; 1983b). Specific skills related to these strengths may include precise construction of visual-spatial patterns in play (e.g., arrangements of blocks); strong abilities with puzzles, form boards, and block design tasks; and, for school-age students, competence with related tasks such as creating and understanding maps and visual design. Some children have relatively strong abilities in developing and following routines in a precise manner; recognizing and reproducing songs or melodic and rhythmic patterns; and remembering details about previous experiences and events, even when they have limited understanding of the events themselves.

Information processing research has demonstrated that children with ASD perform well on tasks that rely on spatial location and simultaneous, gestalt information processing. These children, however, have difficulty with the coding and categorization of sequential information, especially when there is a need to induce abstract rules based on conceptual understanding rather than physical characteristics (Frith, 1971; Hermelin & O'Connor, 1970; Schuler, 1995). Strengths in rote memory abilities have been documented in research that has demonstrated that children with ASD perform equally well in the recall of nonsense as opposed to meaningful series of information, when visual as well as auditory input is presented (Hermelin, 1976). This is in contrast to control groups of typical children and children with mental retardation, who did better in the recall of meaningful information. In other words, children with ASD typically rely on a rote memorization strategy that may not be aided by reference to meaning.

Furthermore, children with ASD process and recall nontransient information (i.e., visual information that remains stable over time, such as pictures) considerably better than transient information (i.e., information that is fleeting over time, such as speech) (Prizant, 1983b; Wetherby, Prizant, & Schuler, 1997). Thus, most children with ASD experience greater success and motivation when activities involve judgment of physical properties and spatial orientation of visual stimuli, rather than activities that involve conceptual understanding and judgment about others' actions, thoughts, emotions, and beliefs.

Relative weaknesses of children with ASD also include language processing (as discussed previously); the related ability to use a more flexible, language-based memory (i.e., semantic memory); and social understanding and reading of social and emotional cues. Reports of this pattern of relative strengths and weaknesses were highlighted in Kanner's very first description of "infantile autism" in 1943. Kanner noted that strengths tended to revolve around object manipulation, object knowledge, and rote memory, resulting in a picture of a sometimes remarkable but inflexible cognitive endowment. According to Kanner, apparent weaknesses were related to the development of social relationships and communicative abilities, the definitive characteristics in ASD, and inflexibility in cognitive functioning, which resulted in "an insistence on preservation of sameness" (Kanner, 1943) It may be speculated that, at least in part, specific weaknesses are noted in social-communicative domains because signals that regulate social interactions are largely transient, as are the interactions themselves. Table 4.1 summarizes frequently observed learning strengths and weaknesses in children with ASD.

Frequently cited characteristics of language and communicative behavior in ASD may also be understood in reference to similar differences in cognitive style and language acquisition styles of typically developing children. As discussed in Chapter 2 of this volume, a differentiation between gestalt and analytic language forms has been made in reference to differences in styles of language acquisition (i.e., gestalt versus analytic styles) (Peters, 1983). Gestalt language forms are multiword utterances that are memorized and produced as single units or chunks, with little analysis of their internal linguistic structure and with little or no comprehension of the utterances themselves. Analytic forms, on the other hand, are generated on the basis of the application of linguistic rules with greater comprehension of language structure and the specific meanings encoded by those utterances. Both gestalt and analytic forms of language have been noted to be used by typically developing children and appear to be of great relevance to the understanding of language acquisition strategies used by children with ASD (Prizant, 1983b; Rydell & Prizant, 1995; Schuler & Prizant, 1985).

Prizant (1983b) initially proposed that children with autism use a gestalt strategy in early language learning by immediately repeating speech, referred to as *immediate echolalia,* or memorizing and repeating unanalyzed chunks or multiword units of speech at a later time, referred to as *delayed echolalia.* Most children with ASD who acquire speech demonstrate a gestalt style of language acquisition in that early utterances

Table 4.1. Learning strengths and weaknesses in autism spectrum disorders (ASD)

Strengths	Weaknesses
Visual-spatial processing	Language processing
Rote memory	Conceptually based semantic memory
Gestalt processing	Analytic processing
Processing static information	Processing transient information
Nonsocial object knowledge	Social understanding

In the SCERTS Model, educational practices are infused with strategies based on an in-depth understanding of learning style differences of children with ASD, as well as on an individual child's profile of learning strengths and weaknesses.

are typically echolalic and early communicative functions tend to be expressed through immediate and delayed echolalia (Prizant, 1983a; Prizant & Duchan, 1981; Rydell & Prizant, 1995; Schuler & Prizant, 1985). Prizant (1983b) suggested that for most verbal children with autism, language acquisition progresses from the predominant use of echolalia with little evidence of comprehension or communicative intent, to the use of echolalia for a variety of communicative functions, which is later followed by a decrease in echolalia that co-occurs with an increase in creative, spontaneously generated utterances. In addition to immediate and delayed echolalia, other commonly observed forms of unconventional verbal behavior in ASD, including *perseverative speech* and *incessant questioning,* also reflect a gestalt strategy in acquisition and use (Rydell & Prizant, 1995). Table 4.2 provides forms and definitions of unconventional verbal behavior. The prevalence of gestalt forms and unconventional verbal behavior can thus be conceptualized as variation at one extreme end of the normal continuum, which apparently corresponds with differences in cognitive style.

In addition, *hyperlexia,* or precocious self-taught written language decoding skills (reading skills) observed in some children with ASD, is of relevance when considering learning strengths and weaknesses. A major difference between written and spoken language lies within the modalities involved—that is, written language involves nontransient visual input, whereas speech involves transient auditory signals. The intensive interest and attention to numbers and letters so commonly observed in children with ASD, and seen in its most extreme form in hyperlexia, is easily understood in reference to cognitive and processing style strengths, as the decoding of written language is not as dependent on sequential analysis of transient stimuli, as it is in processing speech.

It may thus be that the pattern of learning strengths and weaknesses, including a preference for nontransient signals, contributes to difficulties in the acquisition of rule-governed systems of linguistic and social knowledge. On the other hand, it also is conceivable that the prevalent cognitive style in ASD results from impairments in social interaction and relatedness, if early social-emotional experience is viewed as a primary determinant of the acquisition of more flexible social, linguistic, and cognitive knowledge.

Whatever the case, the SCERTS Model approach to social communication and emotional regulation addresses cognitive differences, taking into account both strengths and weaknesses and the associated gestalt style of learning and of language acquisition, to provide an educational approach of best fit, considering the distinctly different learning style of children with ASD (Grandin, 1995; Prizant & Wetherby, 1989; Schuler, 1995). Commonly cited challenges related to learning style differences include inflexibility in patterns of communication and language development, development of unconventional verbal behavior including echolalia, insistence on preservation of sameness, and an adherence and apparent need to develop and follow routines and rituals. We contend that such behavioral patterns need to be approached and understood as directly reflecting these cognitive differences and possibly functioning as coping strategies or alternative paths to adaptation and learning and should not simply be dismissed as "deviant" or "pathological" behaviors.

Even though these general patterns of learning style are often observed, it is important to note that patterns of relative strength and weaknesses must be considered

Table 4.2. Forms and definitions of unconventional verbal behavior

Form of unconventional verbal behavior	Definition	Example
Immediate echolalia	Repetition of speech that 1. Is produced either following immediately or within two turns of original production 2. Involves exact repetition (pure echolalia) or minimal structural change (mitigated immediate echolalia) 3. May serve a variety of communicative and cognitive functions	A child repeats, "Want some juice?" immediately following an adult's question. The child's nonverbal behavior (i.e., reaching toward his or her juice bottle) indicates that the child was repeating the utterance to acquire juice, serving the function of affirmation (Kanner, 1943) or "yes-answer" (Prizant & Duchan, 1981).
Delayed echolalia	Repetition of speech that 1. Is repeated at a significantly later time (i.e., at least three turns following original utterance, but more typically hours, days, or even weeks later) 2. Involves exact repetition (pure echolalia) or minimal structural change (mitigated delayed echolalia) 3. May serve a variety of communicative and cognitive functions	A child states, "Time to go for a walk," as a request to get a drink of water. The utterance is a repetition of what his teacher said to him 2 weeks earlier, before he left the room for a drink.
Perseverative speech	*Persistent* repetition of a speech pattern that 1. Consists of a word, a phrase, or a combination of utterances that are imitated (echolalia) or that are self-generated 2. Is produced in a cyclical, recurring manner 3. Is produced with or without evidence of communicative intent or expectation of a response from the partner	A child states repeatedly, "We must clean up the mess," while pacing in a corner of the classroom away from the other children and the teacher. The teacher said this to the child a month before in the same location after the child spilled some juice. In this example, the perseverative utterance is also delayed echolalia.
Incessant (repetitive) questioning	Repeated verbal inquiries that 1. Are directed toward the communicative partner 2. Are produced with communicative intent, with an expectation of a response 3. Persist either immediately following a response or after a short respite even though a response was provided	Over a 2-hour period, a child asks his mother repeatedly, "Going swimming after lunch?" despite the fact that his mother has responded three times earlier that they will go swimming at the beach in the afternoon. The questioning has continued despite the affirmative responses from his mother.

Sources: Prizant & Rydell, 1993; Rydell & Prizant, 1995.

on an individual basis. This profile of strengths and weaknesses has been established in the empirical literature and is observed on a daily basis in our own experiences with children. The learning profile of a small minority of children with ASD, however, may not reflect these general trends. For instance, some children have very significant visual processing and memory difficulties. Some children may learn to memorize a sequence of skills with one presentation, whereas other children may require a very high frequency of repeated opportunities to learn this same sequence. Some children may be incessant in their social-communicative pursuits, whereas others may remain reticent. Some children may benefit greatly from visual supports, whereas other children may not benefit to the same degree. Clearly, individual differences must always be taken into account.

The Challenge of Developmental Discontinuity

The term *developmental discontinuity* refers to patterns of peaks and valleys of developmental abilities and disabilities related to learning style issues in ASD. Developmental discontinuity has intrigued and confused caregivers as well as professionals ever since the publication of Kanner's first case studies in 1943, in which he referred to his subjects as cognitively "well endowed" based primarily on observations of isolated specific abilities. Although some of the commonly observed areas of relative ability have been dismissed as "splinter skills," the true nature of the cognitive differences and cognitive impairments continues to challenge practitioners, parents, and researchers. The often striking contradictions between apparent cognitive "islets of strength" based on observation of specific nonsocial skills, and limitations in social-cognitive, communicative, and adaptive skills, have been a source of great interest as well as frustration for those closely involved with children with ASD.

The challenge of developmental discontinuity begins very early for some families. Despite serious concerns that parents may have about their children's difficulties in relating socially and in communicating, they may be comforted by their children's relative strengths in playing with puzzles or, for some children, repeating songs or videos or learning how to recite rote sequences of letters or numbers in sequential counting. Many parents have reported to us that their first impression of their child was that he or she was a genius. Unfortunately, some professionals with a limited understanding of learning patterns in ASD may minimize the significance of social and communicative limitations when they observe higher level non–social-cognitive skills (which are most often based on learning style differences as just discussed), leading to deferred referral for more in-depth developmental assessments, which could have led to earlier services and support for families.

Challenges regarding developmental discontinuity may be perpetuated over time. For example, in the years following diagnosis, there may be an inordinate emphasis on training rote skills (counting, reciting the alphabet, labeling pictures) due to the appearance that such behaviors reflect increasing cognitive competence. Rote learning may be easy for some children due to their relative strengths in visual memorization; however, in the SCERTS Model, we ask the questions, "Why is this child learning this skill?" and "How does this skill relate to the real-life events and challenges that this child faces? In other words, what functional purpose does this rote skill serve?" For many if not most children, rotely learned skills may not contribute to true developmental progress, especially in the core areas of social communication and emotional regulation, as well as in conceptually based, flexible cognitive development. Finally, developmental discontinuity can contribute to behavioral difficulties, especially when there is too much of an emphasis on teaching children to passively respond and comply in lieu of developing specific communicative skills that lead to more appropriate means of social control and social engagement and social-communicative competence that supports emotional regulation.

Standard Academic Curricula

Due, in part, to the learning style differences noted previously, children with ASD often are extremely challenged by academic curricula typically used in schools. These challenges clearly become more pronounced as a child leaves the preschool years and moves into kindergarten and the elementary school years. Most academic curricula are very heavily language-based, a modality of clear weakness for students with ASD. Even math curricula may be taught primarily through spoken and written language and may utilize language-based problems for assessment purposes. More abstract subjects that require understanding embedded in social knowledge and nonliteral language, such as English literature, social studies, and so forth, may be particularly challenging for students with ASD, who typically deal better with concrete and factual information. These subjects require understanding and retention of information beyond that which is concrete and factual.

> Educational programming must be meaningful and motivating, and based on documentation of a child's learning strengths and weaknesses. A focus on building repertoires of rote skills most often does not result in meaningful progress.

Such learning challenges require that professionals on a child's team look carefully at what is being taught at how it is being taught, relative to the child's learning strengths and weaknesses. Modifications to standard curricula often are required, both in content and in teaching practice. For example, more abstract concepts may be taught with many visual supports and in relation to a child's own life experiences. In many cases, different curricula may be used than are used with other students. For example, for many students, a visually based math curriculum would be preferable to a math curriculum that is heavily language based.

Core Challenges Requiring Support to Families

First and foremost, family members are challenged by the difficulties in social communication and emotional regulation experienced by their child, and these issues are among the first that raise concerns for parents (Bristol & Schopler, 1984; Domingue et al., 2000). Of course, such difficulties become more apparent as children develop in the preschool years and as parents and other partners have greater expectations for their children to be able to engage socially and to communicate with increasing effectiveness. It is important to emphasize, however, that family members face additional difficulties. These challenges may be related to factors within the family, factors outside the immediate family, or in reference to systems of service delivery and interactions with professionals and other service providers.

Challenges within the Family

Finding the Balance in Family Life

Finding the balance in family life is a significant challenge for most families, especially when there are other children in addition to the child with ASD or when the parents are bearing other caregiving responsibilities, such as caring for elderly parents (Domingue et al., 2000). In addition to meeting the needs of the child with ASD, parents have many other duties to fulfill, such as becoming educated about ASD and exploring and arranging for services, which can take up the precious little time and energy available for family activities and for the other children in the family. As parents become more actively involved in their child's program, the time demands to coordinate necessary services may leave little time for other family members. For most parents, the extra cost of therapies and services not provided by schools creates an additional fiscal burden. Many parents may feel that "balancing time, energy, and finances within the family is a constant struggle" (Domingue et al., 2000).

*Family
Decision Making*

Due in part to the many difficult decisions that parents need to make, some families are at risk for experiencing additional stress related to the possibility of two parents or partners having differing opinions when they are raising a child with ASD. Difficult decisions may include the types of educational approaches to follow, techniques to use to support a child's development (including the very difficult issue of discipline for child with ASD), how to prioritize fiscal resources for additional services that may not be covered by insurance or the educational system, and if and when to challenge systems that are legally responsible for providing services when parents believe that their rights are being violated or services are not being provided in an effective manner. Furthermore, when there is an imbalance in the time actually spent with a child from day to day, such as when one parent is working full time and the other parent is not, some of these important decisions may be based on very different perceptions of the child, due to the different relationships that each caregiver may have with the child. These are important issues for parents or caregivers of all children; however, when they involve children with ASD, there likely are many more crucial and stressful decisions that need to be made typically under more difficult and urgent circumstances.

*Differences in How
Family Members
Respond to the
Disability of Autism
Spectrum Disorder*

Professionals need to be cognizant of the full range of possible responses that family members may experience in raising a child with ASD and that most often, such responses are natural, not maladaptive, abnormal, or pathological responses. Reactions may vary widely within a family and across families, which may cause further difficulties due to disagreements. On the other hand, differences in family member's reactions to ASD may be a positive factor, if a wider variety of options are discussed and considered. Whether differences of opinion are positive or negative factors depends, to a great extent, on how family members respond to such differences and if and how differences are resolved.

Some family members may have strong personal reactions such as guilt, anger, or denial, whereas others may not. Some family members may view ASD as a challenge to overcome within a specified period of time, if only the "right" treatment (educational or biomedical) could be found, as in attempting to cure a physical condition. In such cases, "recovering" the child from autism may become the family's or an individual family member's mission. In contrast, other family members or families who view ASD as a lifelong disability may come to view their child's ASD as an inseparable part of who their child is, and as the "hand the family has been dealt." Yet other family members or families may see the challenges of supporting their child's development as an opportunity for growth for all family members and for reaching out to and supporting other families affected by ASD. For example, we have known many parents or brothers and sisters who were influenced in positive and meaningful ways by the experience of having a child with ASD in the family.

*Changes to the
Family System:
Roles, Lifestyle,
and Routines*

It is now well accepted that a family system is challenged and changed in unique ways when there is a child with special needs in the family; caregiving roles, lifestyle, and everyday routines are affected as a result (Prizant & Meyer, 1993). For example, many families need to reduce leisure activities due to difficulties experienced by their child in new and unfamiliar settings, possibly related to emotional dysregulation that results in behavioral difficulties. For some children, the extreme need for predictability and consistency requires families to follow a relatively fixed schedule and may require that social visits from other people be minimized. Such changes, most often instigated by the desire to support a child's development and emotional regulation, may have a negative secondary impact of isolating the family or limiting the family's participation from everyday activities with friends or the extended family. Thus, friendships and social networks may shift as parents seek out other parents who can provide informal support and who may understand the experience of raising a child with ASD.

Brothers and Sisters

Challenges to brothers and sisters vary according to the gender, relative ages of the children, birth order, and role expectations for the children who do not have ASD. In addition, characteristics of the child with ASD, such as communication and emotional regulatory abilities, also determine the nature of challenges faced by siblings. Challenges for siblings may include difficulties in playing and developing a positive relationship with the brother or sister with ASD, feeling embarrassment in public, figuring out how to react to problem behaviors (when present), bearing extra responsibility, coping with changes in family routine and activities, and dealing with inequitable attention. Brothers and sisters may experience reactions unique to sibling relationships, such as jealousy; resentment; or a desire to play the role of protector, teacher, or surrogate parent.

These challenges are not static, but change as the children develop. For example, we have known many brothers or sisters who wished to play an active role in supporting the development of their sibling, by being a teacher and a social mediator. However, as these children approached the years in which they became far more aware of influences of their sibling's disability on their social status among their peers (which typically happens between 9 and 12 years of age), these children no longer wished to be as involved, due to reactions of friends, embarrassment in public, and so forth. In many cases, the desire to be an active support and friend to their brother or sister with ASD then returned as these individuals matured and grew into adolescence. Such changes in relationships highlight the importance of understanding how the developmental stage of the brother or sister and not simply the characteristics of the child with ASD may affect sibling relationships.

Future Uncertainty

The most common, understandable concern that a parent or family member may have has to do with how the disability of ASD will affect a child's future, and ultimately, the future of the family. Parents begin to feel these concerns at the point of receiving a diagnosis, and for many families, uncertainty about the future will become a major source of stress as decisions are made year to year and, in some cases, month to month, regarding the services to pursue and the directions to take for a child and family. Many families entertain the prospect of relocating to another town, city, or part of the country if they feel that such changes will have a positive effect for the child due to services that may not be available in their current locale. Some parents or caregivers may change jobs, leave employment, or turn down new employment possibilities because of the perceived needs of the child and family. In our experience, families with a child with ASD must consider factors and make decisions that would not need to be made otherwise. Typically, there are a narrower range of options and less freedom to choose from those options than for a family not having to plan for a child with ASD.

Challenges Related to Factors Outside the Immediate Family

Feelings of Isolation

Many families often identify an extreme feeling of isolation as one of the most difficult challenges to cope with. When families do not have opportunities to spend time with or speak to other families who have children with ASD, the feeling that no one else can understand what the family is going through can create a source of stress in addition to the daily challenges of supporting their child. Once the "word is out" that a family has a child with ASD, people once considered friends may no longer call as often or may become "too busy" to stop by. A family's shrinking social network may be a direct reflection of the discomfort felt by friends or relatives or the concern by parents that their child with ASD may not behave well or may be challenged by other people visiting. Many parents have commented that they have come to understand who their real friends are by observing friends and relatives who remain connected. In general, with fewer informal supports available to a family (e.g., friendships, extended family contacts, membership in a social network), the higher the risk that strong feelings of being isolated will cause additional stress for family members. (Professionals may also encounter feelings of isolation; however, parents cannot end their workday by leaving a child, as professionals can.)

How Family Members Interface with Their Social Community

Depending on a child's social-communicative and emotional regulatory abilities, families may limit exposure to everyday activities and social events. This is especially true when a child is young and the family is just beginning to develop strategies for dealing with difficult circumstances in public due to emotional dysregulation. However, this may also continue for many years, depending on the risk the family members may feel they are taking due to the likelihood that their child may have difficulty or due to the possible reactions of others to their child's behavior. One often-cited risk factor is embarrassment in public. As noted by Domingue et al. (2000), "The public stares, the whispers, the judgments—spoken and unspoken—constantly follow the family. Visits to restaurants and other family outings, once a source of joy, become experiences fraught with stress or embarrassment."

Understanding Autism Spectrum Disorder and Explaining it to Others

ASD is a disability that is still poorly understood, even to the extent that the very nature and core deficits defining ASD are currently being debated. It is no wonder that most families find it challenging to explain ASD to others, including relatives. Furthermore, when the pressure to explain their child's behavioral characteristics or everyday difficulties comes from other people's unfair judgmental attitudes, rather than from a true desire to understand, many parents understandably feel resentful.

Greater complications may occur with relatives than with people outside of the family, when there is a need to explain ASD or why a child behaves the way he or she does. Whereas some extended family members may be understanding and supportive, others may increase stress on families, even if their attempts at helping are well intentioned. For example, some relatives may feel compelled to provide advice liberally, ranging from suggesting the need to use strict discipline with the child, to insisting that the family try the new "breakthrough" treatment that they heard about on a television news magazine program. In some cases, relatives may insist that there is nothing wrong, even after the parents have come to some level of understanding and acceptance of their child's disability. Under such circumstances, parents may face the double bind of wanting to express appreciation to family members who truly want to help but at the same time not desiring to encourage an endless tirade of ill-advised recommendations. Extended family members of friends may then feel put off if their advice is not followed. As noted, in some unfortunate circumstances, some relatives may cut themselves off from any further contact with the family, as they attempt to cope with their own issues in having a relative with an ASD diagnosis. Unfortunately, having a family member with a disability can still be perceived as stigmatizing in our society.

Challenges in Service Provision and Professional– Parent Interaction

Dealing with Service Delivery Systems

Another major challenge is the need for caregivers to navigate through a complex and ever-changing stormy sea of services and service delivery systems. Such systems vary greatly between public and private services, between educational and therapeutic services, and as children progress from the early intervention to the preschool years and into the school years. Families are expected to move easily across the requirements of different systems and to understand the laws that govern such systems and protect families' rights; however, parents can easily feel overwhelmed. Many parents have expressed the following sentiment to us: "We now feel we have reached a point where we are managing the challenges of our child's autism. However, it is no longer the autism that causes the most stress, it is the systems that we have to deal with to continue to help our child."

Dealing with Professionals and Other Service Providers

At the very least, being informed about parental rights and becoming familiar with the maze of services available may pose major problems for families. At worst, parents may have to deal with professionals who have significant decision-making power but who may not be trained in how to effectively communicate with and support families. It also is not uncommon for a mother or father to be more knowledgeable about ASD than the professionals who are arranging services for the child or who are directly responsible for the child's care. When facing these circumstances, parents may not have a great deal of confidence in those they will have to rely on. Furthermore, when competent professionals are highly stressed due to lack of support in the systems in which they work, parents who are appropriately assertive may come to be viewed as highly demanding or unreasonable. Even in those circumstances where parents are fortunate to have highly competent professionals available to them and organized, responsive systems to serve their child, we often hear these parents express concern about the many families they know who are not so fortunate. Furthermore, there is always a lingering concern that the bottom might fall out of an ideal program due to a change in staffing or funding.

Confusion Regarding Available Interventions and Models

Parents and caregivers may also be confused by the wide variety of approaches available for children with ASD and by conflicting claims regarding effectiveness of different approaches. Some professionals claim superiority of their approach over other approaches, based on what many believe to be a biased interpretation of the research literature. We and many other professionals (NRC, 2001) have questioned these claims

> The range of challenges expressed by families must be addressed in educational programming in order for families to see professional support as helpful and relevant to family life.

and consider that it is most realistic to address challenges in ASD through nonexclusive and individualized approaches (Prizant & Wetherby, 1998). We believe that there is potential for tremendous growth and positive change for children with ASD and that it is possible for many children to grow up and lead independent, happy, and fulfilling lives, but that most children will experience significant challenges for many years. As noted previously, the NRC's Committee on Educational Interventions for Children with Autism (2001), the highest impartial expert panel on autism convened to date, concluded that claims of recovery from ASD related to only specific approaches and that superiority of any one approach over other approaches was not substantiated based on a comprehensive review of the educational intervention research. We have previously written about and are in agreement with many of the NRC's conclusions regarding the significant questions that remain about efficacy of intervention (Prizant & Rubin, 1999; Prizant & Wetherby, 1998; Prizant, Wetherby, & Rydell, 2000). These important issues are explored further in Chapter 6 of this volume.

One may ask, "What harm can it cause to present extremely optimistic (even if questionable) information about the efficacy of a specific approach?" We all have observed firsthand the stress experienced by parents when they are given misinformation about the need to follow a particular approach faithfully (based on a promise of "recovery"), especially when an approach may be inconsistent with the beliefs of the family or the capability of the family to engage in the particular recommended intervention. Given that we do not put all our eggs in the basket of "recovery" from ASD as the primary goal for children and as the reference point for programmatic success, the SCERTS Model emphasizes supporting families in a comprehensive manner as an integral part of program assessment and intervention over the long term, based on family values and needs. Because each family has a unique path to follow and needs that they feel are necessary and crucial for happiness and success, the SCERTS Model asks the family, "What will make the most difference in your life and that of your child's?"

Core Challenges Requiring Support Among Professionals

Developing a Relationship with a Child

As noted previously, parents have hopes, dreams, and expectations for their child and must adapt and cope with challenges to these dreams. Successful coping and adaptation involves the ability to adjust expectations and derive joy from a child as *he or she is,* while simultaneously supporting the child's development. In a similar manner, professionals and caregivers outside of the immediate family have dreams and expectations in working with children with special needs and they need to be able to cope and adapt when such dreams are challenged. This is especially true for younger and less experienced professionals, as they most often choose a helping profession because of the strong desire to support children in challenges they face.

In many if not most cases, children with ASD present professionals and caregivers with exceptional challenges (and the potential for exceptional rewards), due to the nature of the disability. First, challenges in social communication and in developing social relationships experienced by children with ASD may create barriers to the development of positive relationships. At the very least, the development of such relationships unfolds more slowly over time than they do with most other children. Second, due to challenges in emotional regulation, children with ASD may be unpredictable and inconsistent in their behavioral responses to others. Third, due to challenges in both social communication and emotional regulation, children with ASD may develop either outwardly directed problem behaviors such as aggression and other disruptive behaviors or may shut down socially or develop self-directed behaviors such as self-injury, all of which may be extremely difficult for service providers to deal with practically as well as emotionally.

> For services to children with ASD and their families to be as effective as possible, challenges to professionals and other service providers must be addressed in a comprehensive program.

Developing and Implementing a Team Approach

As noted, the SCERTS Model works best as a team approach. Development and implementation of a team approach, however, requires mutual trust and respect among professionals and parents, time for planning and meeting, understanding of the unique contributions of professionals from different disciplines and flexibility in service provision (e.g., team teaching and collaborative consultation, rather than providing services using a pullout model). Unfortunately, barriers to a team approach often include, but are not limited to, lack of planning time, lack of administrative support, mistrust among professionals, and inflexibility into service provision due to professional "boundary" issues.

In some cases, there may be significant barriers to parent–professional collaboration as part of a team approach. For example, professionals may feel challenged when parents who feel overwhelmed express anger to professionals. This may occur when parents feel all that is not being done as it should be to help their child "get better" as quickly as possible. Misdirecting anger to others is a natural human reaction that we all have experienced and have engaged in. However, when professionals believe that they are doing the best they can and receive feedback to the contrary, there is an undeniable emotional impact. The cumulative transactional impact of these difficulties may lead professionals to question their own abilities and over time may inadvertently affect professionals' perceptions of a child as not wanting to relate to others or cooperate. It may also affect perceptions of a family or of parents as not being easy to work with, even though the parents may be doing the best they can given the circumstances. In extreme cases, some professionals may experience feelings of burnout when they feel unappreciated and may no longer have the energy or desire to work with children with ASD due to the myriad of challenges they face in their work.

These interpersonal challenges may be particularly problematic and may be amplified for professionals who feel isolated and do not have a support system available to them in the work setting. We frequently observe these types of difficulties in our professional activities, and unfortunately, they are more common than we would like to see. They are addressed as real and powerful factors in the SCERTS Model because these factors affect the ability of service providers to support children and families as effectively as possible. This can only happen through a comprehensive system and plan for transactional support for professionals as well as for family members.

Ensuring Consistency and Continuity in Educational Programming Across Settings

Research has repeatedly demonstrated the difficulties faced by students with ASD when there is limited consistency across learning environments. Thus, it is essential that services be consistent and be carefully coordinated. Such coordination is necessary between in-classroom teaching and additional support services and therapies outside of the classroom and even outside of the school environment.

Achieving this goal, however, may be extremely challenging. Too often, children receive a range of services both within and outside of school that at best are poorly coordinated and at worst are inconsistent and even fragmented. This causes confusion both for a child as well as for his or her parents. In addition, transitions from one school year to the next, and from one set of service providers to another set, make continuity and consistency that much more difficult. In fact, research has demonstrated that parents find such transitions to be among the highest times of stress due to the uncertainty inherent in such transitions and the difficulties in leaving trusted professionals and starting to work with professionals who are relative strangers.

SUMMARY

The Transactional Support domain of the SCERTS Model recognizes that we are all in it together and must form a partnership in the complex task of supporting children with ASD and their families. Thus, service providers must be able to understand the dynamics of developing individualized programs for children and families after gaining an intimate understanding of the specific challenges children and families face and the responsibility we have in supporting children and families as well as each other. The SCERTS Model builds transactional support into the very foundation of the model, as these dynamic influences on a child's development are undeniable and pervasive. When they are addressed in a comprehensive manner, everyone benefits.

Chapter 5

SCERTS Model Programmatic Priorities and Milestones

In this chapter, we specify the priorities for the Social Communication, Emotional Regulation, and Transactional Support domains of the SCERTS Model, as guided by developmental research and milestones. Challenges faced by children with ASD and their families also are discussed relative to developing menaignful goals in educational programming.

SOCIAL COMMUNICATION: PRIORITIES IN THE SCERTS MODEL

Social-communicative abilities provide an important foundation for so many aspects of a child's development that are valued and targeted in the SCERTS Model. For example, for all children, competence in social communication provides the foundation for 1) the development of positive and emotionally secure relationships with caregivers; 2) the ability to play with peers and develop friendships; 3) the requisite language and communication skills that contribute to social and academic success in school; and 4) the ability to maintain well-regulated emotional states, which contributes to the prevention and/or reduction of problem behaviors. Prioritizing abilities in social communication is especially important as the developmental challenges associated with ASD put children at greater risk for having difficulties in all these areas.

Competence in social communication is the result of a child's having countless social experiences with different partners in daily activities over time and across situations (Sameroff & Fiese, 1990). New skills are practiced as the child learns to share his or her intentions and emotions with partners in activities that are as varied as family mealtimes, playtime with brothers and sisters, and bedtime routines. A critical goal of the SCERTS Model is to profile a child's strengths and challenges in the capacities for joint attention and symbol use in everyday activities to guide educational program planning. Research on typical developmental patterns and sequences in these domains (i.e., what is learned) as well as on developmental processes that are essential for learning (i.e., how learning occurs) forms the basis for profiling abilities in joint attention and symbol use.

Capacities related to joint attention are assessed along a developmental continuum because more advanced abilities in joint attention are built on and emerge from earlier developmental achievements. For example, abilities at the Social Partner stage, such as use of communicative gaze to share attention and emotions and nonverbal expression of a range of intentions, provide a foundation for abilities at the Language Partner stage, such as using language to express a range of intentions and emotions and to respond appropriately to others' emotional expression. Abilities at the Language Partner stage, in turn, help to build the foundation for abilities at the Conversational Partner stage, including the ability to consider a communicative partner's knowledge, perspective, and emotional state to make appropriate topic selections, provide essential background information, interpret language within social contexts, and respond with empathy.

Likewise, abilities related to the capacity for symbol use are assessed along a developmental continuum. At the Social and Language Partner stages, symbolic capacities are assessed by documenting the presymbolic (e.g., gestures, vocalizations) and symbolic means (e.g., spoken language, sign language, picture systems) a child uses to communicate. As the child progresses to more sophisticated developmental stages, assessment profiles the child's capacity to use and understand grammatical structures and syntax; to demonstrate an awareness of the conventional meanings of nonverbal information (e.g., gaze, facial expressions, intonation); and to adhere to the social conventions typically used within conversational discourse to initiate interactions, exchange turns, and mark topic shifts. Symbolic capacity in play, as well as types and complexity of play, are assessed as another important aspect of symbol use.

Specific goals and a plan for supporting joint attention and symbolic capacities across partners and contexts are then formulated based on assessment results, functional needs, and family priorities. Thus, in the SCERTS Model, a developmental sequence of social-pragmatic competencies is targeted within a variety of activities and across natural environments to facilitate a child's ability to move along a developmental continuum from early stages of development such as the Social Partner and Language Partner stages to later stages such as the Conversational Partner stage.

Why Is a Developmental Framework Emphasized in the SCERTS Model?

The burgeoning literature on social, communicative, cognitive, emotional and sensory-motor development in children provides a theoretical and empirical foundation both for understanding social-communicative problems and for implementing effective and developmentally appropriate interventions. We have delineated three significant principles, drawn from the literature on social-communicative development, that we feel are crucial to understanding and enhancing social-communicative abilities of children with ASD (Prizant et al., 2000; Wetherby et al., 1997).

1. First, communication development involves continuity from preverbal to verbal communication. That is, the development of preverbal intentional communication is a necessary precursor to the development of the intentional use of language to communicate. Words are mapped onto a child's intentions, which are first expressed in preverbal communication behaviors. For children with ASD who do not speak, emphasis should be placed on developing preverbal social and communication skills, drawing from knowledge of a child's unique social-communicative profile and augmentative and alternative communicative options.

2. Second, a child's developmental profile across cognitive, linguistic, social, and emotional regulatory capacities should provide the basis for decision making for communication enhancement because the development of communicative competence is the outcome of a developmental interaction among these domains.

3. Third, all behavior should be viewed in reference to the child's relative level of functioning across developmental domains. As discussed in Chapter 4 of this volume, children with ASD usually show developmental discrepancies or discontinuities across domains; therefore, goals may need to be targeted at different levels for different domains (e.g., a child may be more advanced in symbolic language skills than joint attention skills). Many of the problem behaviors developed by children with ASD can be understood as attempts to communicate and as coping strategies in the face of significant communicative limitations if such behavior is interpreted relative to developmental discrepancies.

Information on typical development offers an organizational framework for assessment and intervention, to identify relevant and developmentally appropriate goals. However, a distinction must be made between working within a developmental model, which is the approach we advocate with the SCERTS Model, and, in contrast, teaching to a developmental checklist. Rather than merely offering a guideline for sequencing goals and objectives, developmental information can provide a frame of reference for understanding a child's behavioral competencies and for setting developmentally appropriate goals. Without careful attention to developmental issues, communication enhancement efforts can target competencies that are considerably above or below a child's capabilities. For example, a child at a one- to two-word utterance level may be taught to memorize and use long grammatical sentences well beyond his or her spontaneous language level, whereas another child may be trained to develop a large labeling vocabulary when he or she clearly is ready for higher level goals such as an emphasis on reciprocal social conversation. However, the uneven profile of abilities and disabilities in cognitive and social-communicative functioning, which in part, is definitive of ASD, should caution against the adoption of too narrow a developmental focus such as teaching children strictly according to a development checklist because differences across children provide important considerations for individualized goal setting.

Goal-Setting Framework for Social Communication

We have organized the goals for social communication in the SCERTS Model into the two areas of joint attention and symbol use and have sequenced the goals based on the social-communicative stages of Social Partner (preverbal intentional communication), Language Partner (emerging language and early language), and Conversational Partner (more advanced language) stages. The developmental patterns delineated in Chapter 2 of this volume serve not only as a reference for assessment and early identification but also as a guide for goal setting and an overall educational plan. Table 5.1 provides a summary of milestones in social communication as children progress through the Social Partner, Language Partner, and Conversational Partner stages.

Within the SCERTS framework, the capacities for joint attention and symbol use addressed along a developmental sequence. As outlined in Table 5.1, typical developmental processes involved in achieving the capacities for joint attention and symbol use are addressed in each developmental stage, in a continuum that highlights the relationship between success in early developing and preverbal social-communicative capacities and later social-communicative competence. For example, at the Social Partner stage, goals may focus on a child's ability to orient to a partner by sharing attention, showing emotion, and expressing a range of communicative intentions. In the more advanced Language and Conversational Partner stages, the ability to consider the perspective and knowledge of a communicative partner is addressed, as this ability supports communicative skills such as making appropriate topic selections, providing essential background information when discussing past or future events, and interpreting nonliteral language within social contexts (e.g., figurative expressions, humor, sarcasm). Similarly, the capacity for symbol use is addressed in a developmental sequence, beginning with a child's use of early communicative and then more conventional communicative signals (e.g., conventional gestures and gaze) at the Social Partner stage; building to a generative, rule-based linguistic system at the Language Partner stage; and culminating in an understanding of and adherence to the social conventions of conversational discourse at the Conversational Partner stage.

In the SCERTS Model, all people who interact with a child with ASD on a regular basis (e.g., parents, other caregivers, siblings, peers, educators, therapists) are viewed

Table 5.1.   SCERTS Model social communication milestones

Joint attention milestones	Symbol use milestones

Social Partner stage

Joint attention milestones	Symbol use milestones
Sharing attention	**Using learning strategies**
Shares attention by noticing and looking at people	Takes turns by repeating familiar actions and sounds after another person's turn
Shares attention by shifting gaze between people and objects	Spontaneously imitates a variety of familiar actions or sounds immediately after a model
Shares attention by looking at what another person is looking at or pointing to	Spontaneously imitates a variety of familiar actions or sounds at a later time
Sharing emotion	**Play**
Displays a variety of emotions, including happiness, sadness, anger, and fear	Uses a variety of exploratory actions on objects (e.g., banging, mouthing, dropping)
Shares negative emotion by seeking comfort	Uses a variety of familiar objects conventionally toward self in real activities (e.g., wipes with washcloth, eats with spoon, drinks with cup)
Shares positive emotion by smiling and looking	
Responds to changes in emotion expressed by others	**Understanding nonverbal cues and familiar words**
Sharing intentions	Comprehends instructions with a variety of nonverbal cues (i.e., situational, facial expression, intonation, gestural, and visual cues)
Uses early intentional behaviors (e.g., coordinates gestures and vocalizations with physical contact or gaze) to request and protest	Comprehends a small number of familiar words in a familiar context
Communicates to draw attention to self (e.g., pulls hand to request a tickle, reaches to request comfort, tugs on pant leg to get attention, waves to greet)	**Using gestures**
	Uses a variety of contact gestures (e.g., pulls another's hand to an object, gives an object, pushes away an object, shows an object)
Communicates to draw attention to objects or events of interest (e.g., shows an object to comment, claps after building a tower of blocks, points to label)	Uses a variety of conventional gestures (e.g., gives, shows, pushes away, reaches, raises arms, waves, points, claps, shakes head)
Communicates to share immediate experiences with familiar people in familiar activities and environments	Uses a variety of distal gestures (e.g., reaches, raises arms, waves, points, claps, shakes head)
Reciprocity	**Using vocalizations**
Initiates and responds to communicative bids frequently and engages in extended interactions over several turns that are reciprocal	Uses differentiated vocalizations to express distress and happiness
Persists and repairs communicative breakdowns by repeating or modifying message	Uses repertoire of vowels (e.g., "ah," "oo," "ee") and consonant–vowel combinations (e.g., "ma," "na," "ba," "da," "ga," "wa," "ya")
	Coordinating of means
	Uses a variety of communicative means for repair strategies
	Coordinates gestures and vocalizations
	Uses socially acceptable communicative means in place of unacceptable forms (e.g., aggression, tantrum, self-injury)

Language Partner stage

Joint attention milestones	Symbol use milestones
Sharing attention and emotion	**Using learning strategies**
Monitors the attentional focus of a partner	Spontaneously imitates nonverbal and verbal behavior and changes the behavior by modifying it or combining it with a different behavior
Secures attention to oneself prior to expressing intentions (i.e., nonverbal or verbal calling)	
Figures out the emotional state of another person based on nonverbal social cues	Spontaneously imitates a variety of nonverbal and verbal behavior at a later time in a different context
Sharing intentions	**Play**
Uses range of communicative functions to include more social purposes (e.g., greets, shows off, comments)	Uses a variety of objects to construct simple products (e.g., stacking a tower of blocks, putting a puzzle together)

Language Partner stage (continued)

Sharing intentions (continued)

Coordinates sharing attention, affect, and intentions to share experiences

Communicates intentions across more varied people, activities, and environments

Asks questions to seek new information about things of interest (e.g., "What's that?")

Reciprocity

Engages in extended interactions over several turns that are reciprocal

Readily initiates communication with appropriate rate of communication for the context

Shows reciprocity in speaker and listener roles (i.e., turn-taking and topic following) to share experiences

Play (continued)

Uses a variety of familiar objects conventionally directed toward self in play (e.g., feeds self with spoon without food)

Uses familiar objects conventionally directed toward others in play (e.g., feeds stuffed animal with spoon)

Combines actions with objects in play (e.g., pours, stirs, and feeds stuffed animal)

Using gestures

Uses a variety of conventional and symbolic gestures (e.g., showing, distal pointing, clapping, shaking and nodding head)

Uses sequences of gestures in coordination with gaze

Using and understanding words

Uses initial lexicon of 5–10 symbols to communicate (spoken words, signs, and/or pictures)

Uses core vocabulary of 10–50 words that are decontextualized and express early semantic relations (e.g., existence, nonexistence, recurrence, rejection)

Understands and uses vocabulary to express a variety of semantic relations (e.g., action, attribute, possession, location, agent, emotion) to predicate (i.e., describe states, qualities, and relations of objects and events)

Segments echolalic chunks to produce more conventional, creative utterances

Uses novel word combinations (or signs/pictures) to express a broad range of semantic relations (e.g., modifier + object, negation + object, agent + action + object)

Conversational Partner stage

Sharing attention and emotion

Secures attention to oneself prior to expressing intentions (i.e., nonverbal or verbal calling)

Understands nonverbal cues of shifts in attentional focus

Modifies language based on what a partner has seen or heard

Shares internal thoughts or mental plans with a partner

Understands and used advanced emotion words to describe emotional states of self and others

Figures out the emotional state of another person based on nonverbal social cues

Understands possible causal reasons behind emotions

Sharing intentions/experiences

Shares intentions for a variety of reasons (i.e., to regulate behavior, for social interaction, and for joint attention)

Shares experiences by introducing topics about past and future events, providing sufficient information for the listener

Understands that others have their own thoughts and beliefs (i.e., are mental agents)

Using learning strategies

Observes others and imitates behaviors modeled by others in a flexible manner

Internalizes adult instruction by comparing two or more perspectives simultaneously

Uses self-monitoring and metacognitive skills in solving problems

Collaborates and negotiates with a peer or group of peers in problem solving and in conversation

Play

Combines many pieces or parts to construct a representational product (e.g., builds a bridge or fort with blocks, makes a dog from playdough)

Uses planned logical sequences of actions with objects in play (e.g., prepares food and feeds stuffed animal)

Uses representational play themes that involve make-believe roles with realistic and miniature toys

Takes on a role and collaborates with a peer in dramatic play

Participates in recreational activities with peers that are rule based

(continued)

Table 5.1. *(continued)*

Joint attention milestones	Symbol use milestones

Conversational Partner stage (continued)

Sharing intentions/experiences *(continued)*

Shows awareness of another's intentions, preferences, and prior experiences by gauging the clarity of vocabulary selection and information provided without providing too much or redundant discourse

Reciprocity/relation

Modifies and responds to topic selections based on a listener's attentional focus, prior knowledge, preferences, and emotional state

Maintains topics by asking relevant questions to request information and clarification from a partner

Provides needed information based on partner's knowledge about and interest on the topic

Maintains mutually satisfying conversational exchanges by modifying language and providing transitional cues for topic shifts that are appropriate to a specific partner's perspective

Repairs communicative breakdowns and expresses feelings of success during interactions

Using and understanding generative language

Uses and understands grammatical morphemes (e.g., prepositions, articles, plurals, tense markers) and simple sentence constructions (i.e., declaratives, imperatives, negatives, and interrogatives)

Uses pronouns to correspond with speaker/listener (*I/you*) roles

Uses and understands higher level grammatical forms that express differences in meaning (e.g., subordinate clauses, conjunctions)

Understands nonverbal cues within a conversational context to interpret emotion and nonliteral meanings

Uses simple and complex sentences to organize conversational discourse in a manner that effectively conveys intent across a range of partners and settings

Using and understanding conversational rules

Recognizes and follows verbal conventions for initiating, exchanging turns, and terminating interactions

Interprets and uses language flexibly depending on the social context and the nonverbal cues of one's communicative partner (e.g., inferences, words with multiple meanings, figurative language, sarcasm)

---

as potential developmental facilitators and may benefit from guidance and support in enhancing specific competencies in joint attention and symbol use. However, a child's ability and availability for social engagement and communication, and learning in general, are greatly determined by the capacity for maintaining well-regulated emotional and arousal states. Consequently, we now turn to this second critical domain, the Emotional Regulation domain of the SCERTS Model.

EMOTIONAL REGULATION: PRIORITIES IN THE SCERTS MODEL

Due to the interdependency between abilities in social communication and emotional regulation, the SCERTS Model incorporates an integrative approach when difficulties are present in both developmental domains, as is commonly observed in ASD. The SCERTS Model directly addresses emotional regulation by targeting goals for the development of mutual and self-regulatory capacities and for recovery from extreme dysregulation. These goals are addressed by enhancing social-communicative abilities and by using specific transactional supports such as modifying interpersonal interactions, integrating learning supports, and designing activities and environments to support emotional regulation.

In determining individualized goals for a particular child, emotional regulatory capacities must be understood from a developmental perspective. That is, for children with ASD, emotional regulation may be facilitated through behavioral strategies (i.e., presymbolic sensory-motor means) and/or through higher level cognitive-linguistic means such as language strategies and metacognitive strategies (DeGangi, 2000;

Prizant & Meyer, 1993). A presymbolic child with ASD at the Social Partner stage may first develop behavioral self-regulating abilities, such as mouthing fingers or objects, averting gaze, or engaging in repetitive motor activity. As the child matures and enters the Language Partner and Conversational Partner stages, greater linguistic and cognitive abilities are developed and language and cognitive problem-solving skills become available as potential vehicles for emotional regulatory functions as well (e.g., using delayed echolalia in the form of self-talk or planning with visual supports to cope with potentially challenging situations). As noted in Chapter 3 of this volume, the emotional regulatory abilities of a child at the Social Partner stage are limited to his or her developmental capacities (e.g., a presymbolic child is not able to use language-based or other symbolic strategies). In contrast, the emotional regulatory strategies of a child with ASD at the Language Partner or the Conversational Partner stage may potentially consist of both earlier-developing behavioral strategies and higher level language and metacognitive strategies. For example, a more developmentally advanced child may engage in soothing repetitive actions such as rocking in a rocking chair, as well as reviewing a picture schedule of upcoming activities, to decrease anxiety related to uncertainty about the daily schedule. State of arousal and environmental demands often contribute to which of these specific types of strategies or combinations of strategies may be successful for an individual child in any given circumstance.

An essential aspect of the SCERTS Model is initially to assess a child's capacities to maintain well-regulated states of arousal across contexts, by documenting the primary factors supporting or interfering with emotional regulation and the specific signals that a child gives when he or she needs support. Different emotional regulatory strategies are observed and documented in different activities and with different levels of arousal, ranging from organized and well regulated to dysregulated states. Next, specific goals and a plan are developed for supporting a child in acquiring and applying mutual or self-regulatory strategies. As a plan to support emotional regulation strategies are implemented, the efficacy of the plan is documented, with adjustments made as needed.

Table 5.2 provides sample emotional regulation milestones at the Social Partner, Language Partner, and Conversational Partner stages, which form the basis for goals to be delineated in Chapter 8 of this volume as part of the SCERTS Assessment Process (SAP).

When a child is experiencing a high or low degree of arousal, partners need to read those signals and then support mutual regulation by responding in ways that promote the child's ability to focus; engage; and be in a state more conducive to relating, learning, and processing information. This is consistent with the respondent form of mutual regulation that was discussed in Chapter 3 of this volume. In the SCERTS Model, capacities for initiated mutual regulation strategies also are fostered in ways that best fit a child's developmental profile and needs. Children may be taught to request assistance or protest in socially acceptable ways through nonverbal means for children at the Social Partner stage (e.g., acquiring and using early developing gestures to request, protest, or reject) or verbal means for children at the Language Partner and Conversational Partner stages (e.g., acquiring and using specific vocabulary for expressing emotions, or to indicate refusal). These abilities often effectively preclude problem behaviors precipitated by emotional dysregulation.

In addition to mutual regulatory capacities, the SCERTS Model targets the development of self-regulatory strategies for children with ASD. Self-regulatory strategies at the Social Partner stage may include helping a child to discover and use behav-

Table 5.2. SCERTS Model emotional regulation milestones

Self-regulation milestones	Mutual regulation milestones
Social Partner stage	
Early in the Social Partner stage, emotion is primarily state dependent. Foundational milestones typically achieved between birth and 6 months include 1. Use of biologically determined mechanisms to self-soothe and self-stimulate (e.g., tactile stimulation, sucking, gaze aversion) in response to environmental stimulation, social interactions, and internal variables 2. Increasing tolerance for and ability to process a variety of sensory and social experiences 3. Development of homeostasis with regard to sleep-wake cycles, hunger/satiety, social attention, and activity level Additional milestones achieved by more advanced partners (older than 6 months developmentally) include 1. Coordination of simple motor actions and use of these actions to self-regulate through sensory-motor means 2. Engagement in responsive social interactions with caregivers 3. Development of more flexible and a broader range of strategies for self-soothing and self-stimulation (e.g., using tactile/kinesthetic, visual, and auditory means) based on interactions with caregivers 4. Development of the ability to discriminate changes in caregiver facial expressions 5. Development of the ability to anticipate familiar routines and sequences	Early in the Social Partner stage, a child is largely dependent on caregivers for assistance with regulating emotional state with regard to the environment, experiences, and emotions. Caregivers interpret and respond to a child's vocal and nonverbal cues of state, emotions, and needs. Caregivers provide a supportive context to stimulate or soothe an infant using behavioral strategies (e.g., tactile, kinesthetic, vestibular, visual, auditory stimulation) thereby promoting the child's development of differentiated emotional responses and refined emotional regulatory behavioral abilities. Caregivers' consistent responses to a child's signals promote the child's awareness of his or her ability to elicit support from others in the environment. Caregivers' responsive interactions with a child establish early understanding of social interaction and communication patterns (e.g., turn taking). Caregivers' responsiveness to child's displays of dysregulation promotes child's ability to recover with support and reengage in interaction or activity.
Language Partner stage	
In the Language Partner stage, there is a shift to intentional and symbolic communication and symbolic representation, which promotes the ability to identify and reflect on one's own emotional and arousal state changes, thereby promoting increased tolerance of changes in routine and transitions, adaptation in novel circumstances, and ability to delay gratification. Awareness of the social environment and of the ability to exert control in the social world increases. Self-control abilities emerge (e.g., the abilities to initiate actions, inhibit behaviors, and follow simple directions). Drive for mastery develops, which contributes to the development of sustained attention and persistence. Behavioral means of self-soothing and self-stimulating continue to be used. Recovery from states of dysregulation occurs more quickly and effectively, allowing for reengagement.	A child demonstrates increased initiation of requests for mutual regulation using conventional verbal and nonverbal communicative means. Caregivers respond to these readable, intentional requests. Caregivers provide sensory-motor comfort and stimulation as well as cognitive information about situations to expand on a child's regulatory abilities (e.g., the ability to use symbolic means to assist with self-regulation). Caregivers provide frequent opportunities for socialization of emotional expression through feedback and modeling. Caregivers promote the development of internal control and self-regulation by responding to a child's communicative bids using styles that are sensitive to state, emotion, and individual differences. Caregivers provide positive models of behavior related to emotional expression.

Conversational Partner stage

More complex language and cognitive development supports expanding abilities for symbolic representation and verbal control of emotions, leading to

- Increasing ability to verbally express emotional state and to resolve conflicts through communicative rather than solely through behavioral means
- The ability to think and talk about emotions and emotional memory of past and future events

Increased use of cognitive linguistic strategies assists with regulation of emotions (e.g., ability to verbally mediate experiences and use inner language and self-talk).

Emotional vocabulary expands, which further facilitates the ability to differentiate emotional experience.

Ability to reflect on the current situation with regard to previous experiences and use of emotional memory to assist with self-regulation develops and expands.

Ability to modify emotional expression during actual experiences increases.

Ability to request instrumental assistance (e.g., information, problem solving) develops and is used with greater frequency than physical comfort from caregivers.

Ability to use internalized rules, strategies, and plans to guide behavior develops and expands.

Behavioral strategies continue to be used and are employed flexibly depending on context, social norms, and communicative partners that are present.

Increasingly refined social skills in combination with cognitive and social development support executive functioning (e.g., memory, attention, goal setting, problem solving, organization sequencing).

Ability to perceive and interpret others' emotions increases.

Conscious awareness of self and capacity for self-regulation (e.g., can talk about what to do to support emotional regulation) develops.

A child at the Conversational Partner stage receives feedback from caregivers regarding the social acceptability of emotional display and regulation strategies.

Caregivers expand a child's knowledge of emotions by talking about emotional states, thus promoting greater emotional understanding and increased emotional vocabulary.

Caregivers provide instrumental assistance (e.g., information, problem solving) as requested by a child, which precludes frustration in activities.

Caregivers provide positive models of behavior and refined emotional regulation strategies.

Caregivers assist with peer negotiations, thus promoting problem solving and cooperation.

Peers exert greater influence on emotional regulation in observable ways (e.g., child responds to peers' efforts, child learns strategies from peers).

Caregivers teach problem solving, planning, and other cognitive strategies for self-regulation.

Note: In this table, the term *caregivers* refers to all transactional partners, including peers and siblings, community members, and so forth.

---

ioral means to independently maintain an organized state in which he or she is available for active learning. For instance, self-regulatory behavioral strategies for self-soothing when a child is in a heightened state of arousal may include focusing on a particular calming activity (e.g., listening to music, holding a favorite toy) or, for more advanced children, taking a break from an activity. Self-regulatory strategies may also include initiating and engaging in alerting sensory-motor activities, such as increased physical activity, when a child is in a low state of arousal and not optimally engaged in activities and interactions. At the Language Partner stage, language-based strategies may preclude negative reactions due to confusion or a lack of predictability by helping children to develop an awareness of the activity schedule, steps within activities or the duration of activities, transitions between activities, and unexpected changes in routines. Language-based strategies may therefore promote greater self-regulation abilities. Helping to develop an awareness of time concepts as well as the ability to understand language about past and future events also contributes to language-based self-regulation strategies. Metacognitive strategies for a child at the Conversational Partner stage involve helping the child to reflect on and be aware of the range of strategies that may be useful when he or she is faced with a potentially dysregulating circumstance, such as requesting assistance or a break.

Most children will experience extreme states of dysregulation, despite all attempts by partners to support emotional regulation by implementation of preventative strategies. Dysregulating experiences may include overwhelming sensory input, sudden changes in routine, inappropriate task demands related to difficulty or duration of an activity, and disorganizing social and linguistic input. Thus, a plan for recovery from dysregulation is also derived that may incorporate strategies that demand more intrusive approaches to support a child's physical and emotional well-being and that of others, especially if the child engages in behavior that is disruptive or harmful (to him- or herself or to others). Such reactive strategies to support recovery from extreme dysregulation may include removing the child from an activity to allow him or her access to a quiet space to be left alone, permitting the child to engage in a calming activity, or changing the environment such as going to a sensory-motor room or taking a walk.

To support emotional regulation, the plan also includes accommodations and modifications to environments and activities, as well as interpersonal supports, to be discussed shortly, as proactive and preventative measures to support emotional regulation (e.g., alternating sedentary activities with movement activities, reducing the level of sensory input, simplifying language). The use of transactional supports such as adjustments in interpersonal style, nonspeech communication systems, and visual supports plays an important role in these efforts. We thus now shift our attention to the Transactional Support domain of the SCERTS Model.

TRANSACTIONAL SUPPORT: PRIORITIES IN THE SCERTS MODEL

As discussed in Chapter 2 of this volume, transactional support provides the practical foundations for supporting children's development, their family, and other caregivers across contexts of living and learning. In the SCERTS Model, transactional support is provided in four areas: interpersonal support, learning support, support to families, and support among professionals and other service providers. These are summarized in Table 5.3.

Goals and Priorities in Providing Interpersonal Support

The majority of caregivers of children with ASD have had little formal training in child development. However, the most critical social-communicative and social-emotional experiences for most children occur in interactions with family members, when youngsters are developing the foundations of relationships; are learning the basic elements of social-communicative partnerships; and, eventually, are acquiring more sophisticated social-emotional and communicative abilities. Daily routines and family events provide the experiential opportunities in which children learn and practice these abilities and develop secure and trusting relationships (Prizant & Meyer, 1993). As noted, however, children with ASD are greatly challenged in social-emotional and communication development, despite the best efforts of loving and well-intentioned family members. Thus, family members are likely to experience frustration and confusion as they try their intuitive best to engage their children and support their development. In the SCERTS

Table 5.3. SCERTS Model transactional support goals

Interpersonal support

Identify specific features of communicative partners' interactive styles and language use that either support or are barriers to successful interactions (e.g., expression of emotion, language complexity and style, vocal volume, rate, physical proximity, physical contact, use of visual supports). An optimal style is one that

1. Provides enough structure to support a child's attentional focus, situational understanding, emotional regulation, and positive emotional experience
2. Fosters initiation, spontaneity, flexibility, and self-determination

Coordinate efforts across different partners in developing strategies to use more of those specific features that support more successful interaction.

Design and implement learning experiences with peers so that the child with an autism spectrum disorder (ASD) may benefit optimally from good language, social, and play models. Design motivating activities, organize supportive environments, and incorporate visual supports. Teach both typical children and children with ASD specific strategies for success in daily interactions.

Learning supports

Design and implement visual and organizational supports to

1. Expand and enhance the development of a child's expressive communication system, either as a primary modality or as an augmentative system that is one part of a child's multimodal communication system
2. Support a child's understanding of language as well as nonverbal behavior
3. Support a child's sense of organization, activity structure, and understanding of time
4. Support the development and use of behavioral, language, and metacognitive emotional regulatory strategies
5. Adapt and/or modify curriculum goals that are primarily language based to enable the child to succeed to the extent possible

Design living and learning environments to support social communication and emotional regulation (e.g., physical structure, level of auditory and visual stimulation).

Support to families (i.e., support to parents, siblings, and extended family members)

Provide families with educational support, including information, knowledge, and skills to understand the nature of ASD and to support their child's development. Support must be based on family priorities and should be offered through a variety of options such as educational activities (e.g., lectures, discussion groups), direct training of skills, observation of educational programming, and interactive guidance and modeling in natural activities.

Provide emotional support in one-to-one and group settings to

1. Enhance family members' abilities to cope with the stresses and challenges of raising a child with ASD.
2. Help parents to identify their priorities and develop appropriate expectations and realistic, achievable goals for their child's development and for family life.

Support among professionals and other service providers

Provide informal and planned opportunities for enhancing educational and therapeutic skills, through mentoring arrangements, sufficient planning time, and regular staff in-service trainings and by attending conferences.

Provide informal and planned opportunities for emotional support, whenever necessary, to cope with the challenges of working with children with ASD and to preclude burnout (e.g., retreats, support meetings, daily sharing opportunities).

Model, efforts are made to mitigate these challenges to family members by addressing causal factors related to limitations in social communication and emotional regulation directly through supportive education and sharing of resources with families.

In the SCERTS Model, there is a priority placed on supporting children to be as successful as possible in experiencing a sense of efficacy in communicating their intentions and in participating in emotionally fulfilling social engagement with a variety of partners. We believe an important key to such success is interpersonal support. A youngster's capacities in social communication and emotional regulation are directly related to the ability to experience frequent successful and joyful interactions. A history of successful interactions, in turn, provides the foundation for the development of emotionally satisfying relationships. Interwoven throughout interpersonal exchange and sharing of experiences is the communication of emotional states through the medium of verbal and nonverbal signals. Sensitive partners attune emotionally and calibrate their emotional tone to that of their partner, to do the following (Greenspan & Wieder, 1997; Prizant & Meyer, 1993; Stern, 1985):

1. Acknowledge their appreciation of the child's emotional state

2. Attempt to motivate further social and emotional engagement

3. Attempt to support the child's emotional regulation during disorganizing and emotionally arousing experiences

Interpersonal support is addressed in a variety of ways in the SCERTS Model. First, the interactive styles and language use of communicative partners are assessed for the qualities that enhance or inhibit successful interactions. Interaction style variables that warrant assessment are those that may influence a child's response to others' attempts to engage in social exchange. These include but are not limited to expression of emotion, language complexity and style, volume and rate of speech, intonation or melody of speech, physical proximity, and physical contact. For example, a well-intentioned partner may use too loud a voice and exaggerated facial expression to express delight to a hyperreactive child, or another partner may use language that is too complex, resulting in confusion or nonresponsiveness. An interactive style that is too directive and controlling (e.g., excessive physical prompting or correcting) may result in a hyporeactive child developing an even more passive and respondent style of relating or communicating. Conversely, a child with a bias toward sensory hyperreactivity may respond to a highly directive partner with frequent attempts to protest or escape. On the other end of the continuum, a partner who provides too little consistency, structure, or clarity of expectations through language or other means may not be able to support a child who needs a greater degree of external scaffolding for emotional regulation and social participation. In contrast, a supportive partner may use simplified language and slightly exaggerated intonation to support attention and language processing.

Based on an assessment of partners' interpersonal styles across contexts and a child's reaction to different styles, educational goals may include determining the features of communicative and interactive styles most supportive for a child in different settings. In the SCERTS Model, an optimal style is one that provides enough structure to support a child's attentional focus, situational understanding, emotional regulation, and positive emotional experience, but that also fosters initiation, spontaneity, flexibility, problem solving, and self-determination. With the important priorities of building a child's self-determination and communicative initiation in the SCERTS Model, a predominant behavioral pattern of passive compliance in a child is as undesirable as "difficult-to-control" behavior.

For interpersonal support to be effective, efforts must be coordinated across different partners in developing strategies to use more optimal styles of interaction, to support children's independence and development of a sense of self. Although some degree of variability across partners is natural, is to be expected, and is even desirable for some youngsters, too great a discrepancy may result in confusion for a child who is trying to learn the very rudiments of social engagement and social expectations.

Second, qualities of play interactions with other children (including siblings whenever possible) are assessed, with the goal of designing and implementing learning experiences so that the child with ASD may benefit optimally from good language, social, and play models. The goal is to develop a history of successful experiences for a child with ASD to further motivate the child to seek out other children, leading to the development of positive relationships and increased social motivation. Because children tend to be less predictable than adults, it is commonly observed that children with ASD may avoid interactions with other children. Supporting successful peer interactions involves designing motivating activities, organizing supportive environments, and teaching both typical children and children with ASD specific strategies for success.

Goals and Priorities in Providing Learning Supports: Implications of Learning Strengths and Weaknesses for Education

Due to the nature of learning differences in ASD and the complexity of learning environments, a variety of learning supports are typically needed to optimize success in school and other learning environments. We recognize that some children with more significant challenges may require substantial modifications to support active learning, such as quiet and relatively distraction-free learning environments. However, the SCERTS Model prioritizes learning in a variety of settings from the outset because we believe that any activity affords the opportunity to support social communication, emotional regulation, and adaptive skills. We believe that generalization of abilities is best accomplished when children learn skills in settings that occur naturally as part of their daily routine and that overtraining skills in contrived settings may actually limit a child's ability to apply those skills in other, more natural activities because they are learned in a situation-specific manner. Furthermore, different social settings provide more varied learning opportunities that cannot be replicated in highly repetitive one-to-one drill practice conducted primarily in restrictive settings. For example, treatment limited primarily to adult–child one-to-one interaction can not address the goal of enhancing a child's capacity to shift attention to follow the flow of interaction in a small group, to tolerate proximity to other children, and/or to anticipate one's turn in ongoing reciprocal interactions. These goals require not only well-designed, semi-structured activities but also more varied social contexts.

The SCERTS Model infuses an understanding of relative learning strengths and weaknesses in ASD by following a number of general principles in educational settings as well as everyday activities.

1. Presentation of information should be visually mediated to the extent possible. Visual supports help to maintain attention and visual information is processed and retrieved more effectively from memory.

2. It is essential to support analytic, conceptually based learning, while recognizing that the gestalt learning bias observed in ASD requires a high degree of consistency and predictability for learning to occur optimally. Gestalt processing involves learning by memorizing exact instances of experiences, including less relevant or irrelevant information, rather than learning by analyzing information and relating it to previous experiences. Analytic processing requires the ability to selectively attend to the most important information and to extract patterns, rules, and consistencies in an ongoing manner. The use of echolalia is an example of a gestalt processing style as applied to language, whereas movement to creative language reflects a shift to a more analytic approach to language acquisition.

    It is essential that efforts be made to move from purely rote memory strategies (the result of a gestalt learning bias), to more analytic-based strategies, which underlie the acquisition of flexible concepts and meanings. Introducing flexibility in all aspects of teaching, with an emphasis on conceptually based learning, rather than teaching to rote memory, fosters flexibility.

3. Related to encouraging flexibility in learning, the concept of *controlled variation,* or *flexibility within structure,* is followed in designing activities. This refers to the recognition that although predictability and consistency support learning for most children with ASD, systematic introduction of novelty, changing elements such as people, places, order of the activity, and so forth will support social and cognitive flexibility.

4. Difficulties in social understanding are the hallmark of the disability of ASD. Although strengths in some aspects of nonsocial knowledge may be quite beneficial (e.g., for visual-spatial problem solving), enhancing social knowledge and understanding must be addressed intensively in everyday experiences. This involves developing a child's social relationships with adults and peers and understanding emotions of others and self.

5. Active engagement (experiential learning) in the educational process supports attention, motivation, and sensory processing; emphasizes language concepts; and allows for reciprocity in learning through social interaction. More passive learning experiences, especially those that are mediated primarily through oral language, may result in passivity, attentional difficulties, and limited motivation.

In the SCERTS Model, educational and environmental supports are developed and implemented to enable children to be more actively engaged by supporting social communication, emotional regulation, and learning. First, it is necessary to assess the barriers to active engagement in reference to the learning style of children with ASD. For example, it is well accepted that most children with ASD are more effective at processing and retrieving visual information than auditory information (Prizant, 1983b; Wetherby et al., 1997). Therefore, visual supports may be helpful in

1. Expanding and enhancing a child's expressive communication system, either as a primary modality or as an augmentative system comprising one component of a child's multimodal communication system (e.g., pictures, gestures, signs, speech)

2. Supporting a child's understanding of language as well as others' nonverbal behavior through the use of topic boards, cue cards, and so forth

3. Supporting a child's sense of organization, activity structure, and understanding of time through the use of picture schedules and activity sequences

4. Supporting the development and use of language and metacognitive emotional regulatory strategies through the use picture sequences, break cards, personal organizers, and so forth (Groden & LeVasseur, 1995; Quill, 1998; Schuler, Wetherby, & Prizant, 1997)

When implementing the SCERTS Model, it is essential to specifically identify the types of visual and organizational supports that may be helpful, based on a child's developmental capacities and needs and relative to activities and social contexts in the child's life. Furthermore, efforts are made to modify and calibrate supports as the child develops, with the goal of greater efficiency and functionality in the use of supports over time.

In educational settings, another essential transactional support is curriculum modification. Although this is not as crucial for children in the preschool and early childhood years as it is for older children, curriculum modification also is often necessary to support a preschool child's success. For preschool children with more significant language processing limitations, curriculum goals that are primarily language based may have to be adjusted and or modified, with appropriate supports (e.g., visual supports) added to enable the child to succeed to the extent possible in the preschool curriculum.

Finally, in designing educational supports and programming, we must always be asking the questions, "What is the true purpose of this activity?" and "How will the skills being worked on make a difference in this child's life?" Activities should be designed to support the acquisition and practice of functional skills that will eventually lead to greater independence across activities and settings. If a skill being taught cannot be directly linked to the development of functional skills and the child's independence in the near or projected future, it may not be a useful skill to teach.

Goals and Priorities in Providing Support to Families

The Transactional Support domain of the SCERTS Model addresses a variety of goals and priorities in providing support to families given the challenges faced by most families. As a foundation for providing support services, the SCERTS Model draws from basic tenets definitive of family-centered practice (to be discussed in greater depth in Chapter 2 of Volume II). Support to families is operationalized in reference to two major categories: *educational support,* which involves providing families with the information, knowledge, and skills to support their child's development, and *emotional support,* or enhancing family members' abilities to cope with the inevitable stresses and challenges of raising a child with ASD. For support of either type to be most relevant for any one family, support activities must be flexible and responsive to where a particular family is in its developmental and growth process. For example, consider the differences in the following scenarios illustrating different families at different points in their journey:

- A family in which the parents are first expressing concerns about their child's development before diagnosis and are seeking information as to whether they should be concerned

- A family with a child who has been diagnosed recently, in which the parents are attempting to cope emotionally with this overwhelming news. The parents wish to understand their child's challenges better and even what ASD means and are in need of initial recommendations for approaches to support their child's development.

- A family with greater experience and knowledge, whose kindergarten-age child was diagnosed 3 years earlier and has been receiving services. The parents wish to explore additional educational options such as placement in a typical kindergarten to support their child's development.

- A family with a 10-year-old child who has been fully included in the general education classroom with support until third grade. However, a significant increase in anxiety related to the pressure of more advanced academics and more complex social expectations has resulted in an increase in behavioral difficulties; a clear need for additional supports; and, possibly, a need to reconsider educational placement.

Obviously, the educational and emotional supports for families required in these different scenarios may be dramatically distinct from one another. Furthermore, when other sources of differences among families are considered, including the severity of their child's disability, differences in family structure (e.g., single-parent versus two-parent households; number of siblings), differences in cultural and religious beliefs, lifestyle differences, and differences in socioeconomic status and educational level, it becomes readily apparent that supports must be highly individualized whether they are of an educational or emotional nature. In the SCERTS Model, it also is recognized that many stresses and challenges experienced by family members may not be attributed directly to the child's behavior or developmental needs. Great stress may be induced by systems of service delivery that parents may experience as unsupportive; disorganized; and, in general, not helpful (Domingue et al., 2000).

In reference to providing educational support, the SCERTS Model incorporates a systematic but flexible process for providing family members with information, knowledge, and skills to understand the nature of their child's disability and to support their child's development. Support that is provided must be based on family priorities, must be flexible enough to be a good fit for the needs of the family, and should be offered through a variety of options. Options may include educational support activities (e.g., informational sessions, discussion groups), direct training of skills, observations of educational programming, interactive guidance in natural activities, and collaborative problem solving through a team process.

In reference to providing emotional support, activities that may be effective with family members may occur in both one-to-one and group settings to

1. Enhance family members' abilities to cope with the stresses and challenges of raising a child with ASD

2. Support parents' efforts to deal successfully with professionals, as well as with educational and health care systems

3. Help family members to identify their own priorities and develop appropriate expectations and realistic, achievable goals for their child's development and for family life

Of course, there is no clear dichotomy between educational and emotional support, as these issues are often enmeshed when working with families. However, it may be helpful to identify activities as either educational (e.g., demonstrating and teaching educational techniques) or emotionally supportive in nature (e.g., discussing strategies to cope with emotionally challenging situations, such as resolving disagreements between parents or addressing embarrassment in public related to a child's behavior).

In the SCERTS Model, it is emphasized that to best support families' efforts, clinicians and educators must be cognizant of the whole range of possible reactions that family members may experience in raising a child with ASD (see Chapter 4 of this volume). The SCERTS Model is a developmental model for caregivers as well as for children, as it is recognized that the nature and types of emotional support will need to change as caregivers progress in their understanding of and ability to support their child. Parents and caregivers are encouraged to discuss the child's strengths and difficulties and to articulate the primary concerns and expectations regarding the child's development. When appropriate, parents and caregivers may be asked to share their sense of competence as well as limitations in fostering communicative and social-emotional development. Successful and unsuccessful strategies that family members may have employed to promote social and communicative interactions must also be explored.

Information about a child's and family's strengths and needs and family priorities, as gathered in assessment, form the basis from which specific educational goals are derived. Caregivers are supported in reference to communicative and interactive styles that are most appropriate in enhancing the child's development. Issues discussed previously such as degree of directiveness and modeling with developmentally appropriate language and communication in everyday routines are important considerations in ongoing support of caregivers. In addition to receiving assistance addressing social-communicative skills, caregivers are supported in helping the child to develop emotional regulatory capabilities. Ongoing assessment of and dialogue with caregivers about the child's reactive style to physiological and emotional factors are crucial. Strategies for the development of mutual and self-regulatory capacities within the context of the family structure and routine are also addressed.

In the SCERTS Model, it also is emphasized that clinicians and educators understand various family structures and functions and how these can be influenced by economic, ethnic, and cultural factors. For example, due to cultural and pragmatic factors, biological parents may not necessarily be the primary caregivers in some families; thus, other family members such as grandparents or older siblings may play a more active role in education. When designing educational strategies to be integrated into daily family routines, it is critical that recommendations be compatible with the family's belief systems and social-cultural characteristics (Lynch & Hanson, 2004).

Another important dimension of transactional support in the SCERTS Model is helping parents to think clearly about their priorities and develop appropriate expectations and realistic, achievable goals for their child's development. Parents are not dictated to—they are respected as having ultimate ownership of the decisions that must be made for both the child and the family. Professionals have the responsibility of keeping hope alive by emphasizing the child's strengths as well as needs, highlighting the potential for positive development and change, and helping to identify developmentally appropriate next steps. This involves helping parents to learn to recognize and celebrate even the smallest meaningful gains in social-communicative and social-emotional development. The more caregivers are attuned to positive change, the more they are likely to become invested in being actively involved in educational efforts.

Goals and Priorities in Providing Support Among Professionals

Professionals and other service providers also face considerable challenges in providing effective services to children with ASD. Therefore, in the SCERTS Model such challenges are assessed and plans are developed to systematically address the challenges. As with challenges faced by families, challenges experienced by professionals may be directly related to the child's disability (e.g., initial difficulty in engaging a child productively and supporting social communication, emotional regulation, academic learning, and so forth). Some parents of children with ASD may also be perceived as challenging due to their assertiveness in advocating for their children and their desire to stay involved with and to be on top of their child's program. In some cases, parents may disagree with educational staff about teaching philosophy and techniques, which may result in further tension. Challenges to professionals may also be more indirect, having to do with work settings, large class sizes or caseloads, inadequate equipment or supplies, limited planning time, lack of ongoing continuing educational opportunities, and so forth. Regardless of the source of these challenges, they must be addressed for services to be provided in the most effective and supportive manner for the child and family.

In the SCERTS Model, we also advocate an approach based on individualized assessment of challenges to professionals and other service providers. Depending on the results of an assessment, plans may be implemented to address the challenges in question. For example, support activities may be implemented that include informal and planned opportunities for enhancing staff members' educational and therapeutic skills.

Special meetings may also be arranged for airing grievances and providing emotional support, whenever necessary, to help staff in need cope with the challenges of working with children with ASD and their families and to prevent burnout.

SUMMARY

In summary, transactional supports addressed in the SCERTS Model are designed to enhance children's communication and social-emotional abilities in everyday social contexts that the children experience. Transactional supports may include interpersonal supports; learning supports; support to family members; and support among professionals and paraprofessionals, who play such an important role in fostering a child's development. Due to the transactional nature of development (Sameroff & Fiese, 1990), the crucial role played by all caregivers and partners is recognized, with specific efforts directed to development of mutually satisfying and effective social-emotional experiences based on an understanding of the child's and family's needs.

Chapter 6

Continuum of Current Intervention Approaches and the SCERTS Model

Discussions and debates about effective ways to educate and support the development of children with ASD have dominated the ASD literature for many years. This will no doubt continue, as professionals and parents wish to use practices that are most likely to improve children's developmental outcomes. Since the 1990s, there has been a proliferation of critical reviews on educational and treatment approaches for children with ASD published in journal articles, as well as in lengthy documents written for state agencies to guide policy regarding educational services. Given that the SCERTS Model is being offered as an additional approach to the landscape of educational options, a logical question is "How does the SCERTS compare with other educational approaches?" As will be discussed in this chapter, this is a complicated question to answer partially due to the fact that it often is difficult to define the essential, definitive elements that clearly distinguish one educational approach from other approaches. Another important question that is somewhat easier to address is "Is the SCERTS Model consistent with evidence-based practices discussed in the most contemporary literature?" We begin with this question and then delve into the more complicated issue of considering the SCERTS Model in reference to the broad landscape of available approaches for educating children with ASD.

THE CONCEPT OF EVIDENCE-BASED PRACTICE

Evidence-based practice has become an increasingly important concept in educating children with and without special needs. There is an effort within the U.S. Department of Education to promote evidence-based policy and practice nationwide, based on the mandates of the Education Sciences Reform Act of 2002 (PL 107-279). The term *evidence-based practice* refers to treatment approaches or educational practices that have been documented to be effective with scientific evidence. Methods for evaluating treatment efficacy generally emphasize evidence derived from empirical research methodology that have addressed internal and external validity and generalization of findings (APA, 2000; Lonigan, Elbert & Johnson, 1998). Lonigan et al. suggested that at least two well-conducted group-design studies with random assignment showing a treatment to be more effective than a placebo or alternate treatment are necessary to establish treatment efficacy. Because no large, randomized control-group studies with carefully controlled experimental designs involving children with ASD have been published, it is necessary to look for a convergence of other forms of evidence to make decisions about treatment efficacy for children with ASD. On the basis of a review of treatment research for children with ASD, Prizant and Wetherby (1998) made the following conclusions:

1. Research has supported the effectiveness of a range of approaches that differ in underlying philosophy and practice.

2. No evidence exists that any one approach is more effective than any other.

3. Not all children with ASD have benefited to the same degree from a specific approach, and even the most positive outcomes are in the range of 50% of children across different studies using very different approaches.

The state of the science in the autism literature underscores the importance of documenting the effectiveness of any specific treatment or educational approach for a particular child with ASD.

Jack Shonkoff (1996), a pediatrician who is widely known for his research on treatment efficacy and his expertise on public policy in early intervention, stated that the knowledge base for early childhood intervention practices comes from a variety of sources. These include *theory* (e.g., developmental theory, learning theory, family systems theory), *clinical and educational data* (i.e., documented results of practice in everyday contexts and learning environments), *knowledge of best practices* (i.e., cumulative knowledge based on clinical and educational experiences), *social values* (i.e., practices and goals based on societal and/or personal values), and *empirical data* (i.e., results of experimental research typically conducted with a minimum required level of experimental control).

Practice in the SCERTS Model is based on a convergence of evidence from multiple sources using different methodologies. First, it is rooted in theory and research on child development as well as theory and research addressing the very nature of ASD. Second, it incorporates the documentation of meaningful change through the collection of clinical and educational data, and programmatic decisions are made based on objective measurement of change in children's and partner's behavior. Third, given that it is not an exclusive model, knowledge of effective practices from approaches such as positive behavior support (PBS; Lucyshyn, Dunlap, & Albin, 2002) and augmentative and alternative communication (AAC; see Beukelman & Mirenda, 2005, for detailed descriptions of various AAC approaches) are easily infused in a program plan for a child that is based on and guided by the SCERTS Model. Fourth, the SCERTS Model is based on explicitly stated core values and guiding principles consistent with social values and practices that are respectful of families and children, including nationally published guidelines for educational practices for children with ASD (NRC, 2001), children with other developmental disabilities, and children without disabilities. Finally, practices in the SCERTS Model are supported by empirical evidence from developmental and contemporary behavioral research on children with ASD and related disabilities. It also is our hope that the SCERTS Model manual will serve as an impetus for further treatment research designed to address many of the acknowledged inadequacies of available research. In this manner, we hope to add to research that documents treatment fidelity and efficacy to add to the empirical evidence available on educational approaches for children with ASD.

HOW THE SCERTS MODEL IS CONSISTENT WITH THE NATIONAL RESEARCH COUNCIL'S RECOMMENDATIONS AND INSTRUCTIONAL PRIORITIES

There are a wide variety of claims regarding efficacy or effectiveness of educational approaches for children with ASD. Sifting through and making sense of these claims is a great challenge for professionals and families who need to make decisions about educational programming. Central to this confusing state of affairs is disagreement about some very basic issues. First, there are different opinions as to which are the appropriate measures of progress and outcome. For example, the most common measures of outcome used in the research literature are performance on tests of intelligence (IQ scores) and other standardized tests and school placement. However, the validity of these measures as the best measures of outcome has been questioned (NRC, 2001). Another basic issue of disagreement is whether children can "recover" from autism, which has been cited as one research outcome (McEachin, Smith, & Lovaas, 1993) and therefore whether recovery should be a realistic goal or whether ASD should truly be considered a life-long developmental disability for the great majority of individuals. It is important to emphasize that understanding ASD as a lifelong developmental disability for the great majority of individuals does not imply that children with ASD have limited potential for significant growth, developmental progress, and independent functioning. This position asserts that to provide support in the most effective ways, families and professionals must be cognizant of potential vulnerabilities and challenges in social communication and emotional regulation that the great majority of individuals with ASD will likely experience for much of their lives.

To attempt to provide some clarity to these complex issues, the National Research Council of the National Academy of Sciences convened an expert committee of 12 professionals who represented a variety of disciplines, and a range of philosophical orientations (e.g., applied behavior analysis [ABA], developmental orientations) to the education of students with ASD. This committee reviewed 20 years of educational and clinical research to draw conclusions and make recommendations regarding educational interventions for children with ASD from birth to 8 years of age.

Based on the review of the research, the committee (NRC, 2001) identified a number of critical features that were characteristic of effective interventions and made a number of recommendations based on these findings. We now address the recommendations of this committee in specific reference to practices in the SCERTS Model.

The National Research Council's Recommendations for Educating Children with Autism Spectrum Disorders

Entry into intervention programs as early as possible: The SCERTS Model advocates for the commencement of services at the point of early identification, with the first priorities being enhancing abilities in social communication and emotional regulation, with comprehensive family support. In fact, analytic frameworks for documenting early social and communication behavior critical for early identification have been developed by SCERTS Model collaborators (Wetherby & Prizant, 2002) and are now included in national initiatives supported by the American Academy of Pediatrics to improve early identification (Filipek, Prizant, et al., 1999, 2000; First Signs, 2001).

Active engagement in intensive instruction (at least 25 hours per week, 12 months per year): The SCERTS Model supports an intensive level of service to children and families (at least 25 hours per week, 12 months per year). Because of the emphasis on supporting children's development in everyday activities and routines, there are likely greater opportunities to provide this level of service across settings using the SCERTS Model as compared with approaches that rely on teaching sessions conducted by professionals in more restricted contexts.

Repeated, planned teaching opportunities with sufficient individualized attention daily: The NRC (2001) committee concluded that a low student–teacher ratio was one of the characteristics of effective interventions allowing for repeated, planned teaching opportunities and individualized attention. The SCERTS Model is, by its very nature, an approach that develops learning opportunities and goals based on individual differences in children, including learning strengths and needs. Social contexts for educational programming are chosen largely on the basis of which ones best support the development of capacities in social communication, emotional regulation, and functional skills. Furthermore, the use of planned activity routines provides consistent, predictable, and repeated teaching opportunities in functional activities directed toward priority goals that are important for success in natural settings.

Systematically planned developmentally appropriate activities targeting identified objectives: In the SCERTS Model, activities are chosen and/or developed based on the assessment of children's developmental capacities across a variety of domains, including social communication, emotional regulation, cognitive, sensory, and motor. Activities are planned to simultaneously address a small number of identified objectives across a variety of developmental domains, rather than artificially isolating skills to be trained one at a time through repetitive practice in learning activities.

Inclusion of a family component: As discussed in Chapter 4 of this volume, the Transactional Support domain of the SCERTS Model specifically addresses the provision of educational and emotional support for family members. Because the SCERTS Model has a family-centered philosophy, services are not imposed on families. Families are offered services and supports from a menu of possibilities, and therefore the best match may be made between a family's needs and family members' ability to gain access to and benefit from specific support services. Therefore, when a SCERTS Model plan is developed for a child and family, the support to families component of the Transactional Support domain is addressed with great specificity and tailored to each specific family (see Chapter 3 in Volume II).

Ongoing assessment of a child's progress, with adjustments in programming at least every 3 months: The SCERTS Assessment Process (SAP) consists of multiple levels of assessments, including direct observation in a number of contexts and reports from and interviews with caregivers (see Chapter 7 in this volume). Initial and ongoing assessment data can be entered into a database for monitoring short- and long-term progress and making informed programmatic decisions. This systematic process provides objective data for a child's team to make program adjustments and modifications.

Specialized instruction in settings that permit ongoing interactions with typically developing children to the extent that the interactions lead to specified educational goals: Programming in the SCERTS Model requires identification of learning opportunities across home, community, and school settings (when relevant). Progress is measured across these settings to ensure that efforts are resulting in meaningful and generalized changes in a child's life. One aspect of such programming is providing opportunities for a child with ASD to learn with typically developing children and with other children who can provide good language and social models, provided that such objectives are identified as part of the child's educational plan. This is addressed in the Interpersonal Support component of the Transactional Support domain of the model.

The National Research Council's Instructional Priorities

The NRC (2001) committee identified six instructional priorities. As with the recommendations just noted, we discuss how the SCERTS Model is consistent with these priorities.

1. Functional, spontaneous communication: The Social Communication domain of the SCERTS Model is defined by parameters of spontaneity and functionality, in contrast to focusing on training vocabulary and grammatical forms in repetitive practice outside of social contexts. The development of functional, spontaneous communication has been a focus of the work of the SCERTS Model collaborators for well over 2 decades, and the model has been built on this foundation.

2. Social instruction in various settings: The SCERTS Model recognizes that different social settings offer different learning opportunities for children with ASD. Therefore, exposure to social learning opportunities in a variety of settings is a basic tenet of practice, requiring that activities be designed to enhance generalization of social-communicative skills and understanding of different social events. When specific abilities are the focus of education programming, ongoing monitoring of progress also occurs across a minimum of three settings.

3. Teaching of play skills, focusing on play with peers and appropriate use of toys: In the SCERTS Model, the Symbol Use component of the Social Communication domain specifically addresses the development of play skills at a level developmentally appropriate for a specific child. Furthermore, social communication, by definition occurs with a variety of partners; therefore, learning and playing with peers (referred to as *LAPP* in the SCERTS Model) is seen as a necessary transactional support for enhancing social-communicative abilities and relationships.

4. Instruction leading to generalization and maintenance of cognitive goals in natural contexts: With a focus on functional activities as primary contexts for learning, the SCERTS Model prioritizes functional goals in a variety of developmental domains, including cognitive, social, and communicative, depending on priorities set for an individual child. Therefore, the SCERTS Model focuses on conceptually based understanding when the focus is on teaching cognitive skills, whether such skills involve reading, number concepts, or more general problem-solving abilities.

5. Positive approaches to address problem behaviors: In the SCERTS Model, problem behaviors are considered within the broader developmental domains of social communication and emotional regulation. They are addressed in a preventative manner by prioritizing social-communicative skills development that allows children to exert social control through socially acceptable means (e.g., by teaching acceptable ways to protest, to make choices, or to request breaks from dysregulating circumstances). Infusing emotional regulatory supports in activities across a child's day and supporting a well-regulated state also address prevention. The Emotional Regulation domain of the model also identifies specific strategies to support a child after he or she has already become dysregulated, including recovery from extreme states of dysregulation. A novel contribution of an emotional regulatory approach to problem behavior is that the SCERTS Model addresses all problem behaviors relative to a child's emotional state and physiological arousal, with the ultimate goal of helping the child develop a broad range of initiated mutual regulatory strategies and independent self-regulatory capacities.

6. Functional academic skills, when appropriate: Once again, functionality and meaningfulness of activities and skills are basic tenets of the SCERTS Model. In developing goals and activities to address these goals, service providers must be able to answer the following question when targeting skills within activities: "What difference will this activity or these skills make in this child's life?"

Other priorities: Finally, the committee (NRC, 2001) also recommended that educational approaches should address the core deficits or core challenges faced by children with ASD and that meaningful outcome measures must address the following two areas:

1. Gains in initiation of spontaneous communication in functional activities

2. Generalization of gains across activities, interactants (adults and peers), and environments

    The SCERTS Model addresses these priorities in the following ways:

1. Priority goals are established to address the core challenges of ASD, building on a child's capacity to initiate communication with a presymbolic or symbolic communication system and to regulate attention, arousal, and emotion.

2. Individualized intervention is provided based on a child's strengths and weaknesses and is guided by research in child development and developmentally appropriate practices.

3. The SCERTS Model incorporates intervention strategies derived from empirically supported practices of developmental social-pragmatic and contemporary behavioral approaches.

4. Generalization is addressed through transactional supports, and progress is measured in functional activities with a variety of partners across a variety of settings.

WHERE DOES THE SCERTS MODEL FIT IN THE CURRENT LANDSCAPE OF EDUCATIONAL APPROACHES?

We now return to the complex question of considering the SCERTS Model relative to the many approaches that currently are available. This is a difficult question to address, as different educational approaches and different programs are described, contrasted, and evaluated based on different criteria. At times, it is like trying to compare two or more different sports with different rules and playing fields, such as comparing football with baseball. In ASD, this is especially true because educational practices and priorities differ across approaches (e.g., initiated social communication versus compliance training, behavior management versus emotional regulation). Before addressing this issue more directly, we first need to consider how different approaches are described and compared in the current literature and in discussions by professionals and parents.

Similarities and Differences Among Educational Approaches for Children with Autism Spectrum Disorder

The literature on educational interventions addresses similarities and differences among educational approaches in at least three distinct ways. We use the terms *categorical, broad descriptive,* and *continuum approaches* to characterize the range of available approaches. Information describing characteristics of educational approaches and programs used in this discussion is derived, in part, from the NRC document *Educating Children with Autism* (2001), as well as from programmatic descriptions and critical reviews in published literature (e.g., Brown & Bambara, 1999; Heflin & Simpson, 1998).

Categorical Approach

A categorical approach to describing educational programs for children with ASD considers each program or approach to be a unique entity or package of elements, with the underlying assumption that there is sufficient cohesiveness and homogeneity within a particular approach as to describe it as distinct and significantly different from other approaches. An additional assumption underlying a categorical approach is that the elements or features descriptive of a particular approach do not overlap to any significant degree with other approaches. For example, the following is a partial list of approaches that have specified teaching practices and, in some cases, specific curricula that are followed: the educational approach espoused by Lovaas (1981) that is sometimes referred to as *Lovaas therapy;* the LEAP Model (Strain & Kohler, 1998); the Relationship Development Intervention (RDI) Program (Gutstein, 2000); Developmental Individual-Difference, Relationship-Based (DIR) model (Greenspan & Wieder, 1998), the Assessment of Basic Language and Learning Skills (ABLLS) curriculum (Sundberg & Partington, 1998); the Miller Method (Miller & Miller, 1989); the Picture Exchange Communication System (PECS; Frost & Bondy, 1994); and Structured Teaching of Division TEACCH (Schopler, Mesibov, & Hearsey, 1995). Clinics or schools may be developed to faithfully follow the practices of one approach, or existing public or private programs may adopt specific practices as their major approach for educating children with ASD. Hypothetically, there should be a minimum level of fidelity in curriculum content and educational practice such that a particular categorical approach is easily recognizable across different settings and practitioners.

A major shortcoming with a categorical orientation is that in practice, there may be considerable variability within the practice of an approach, as well as considerable overlap among different approaches when one analyzes the elements definitive of those approaches (NRC, 2001; Prizant & Wetherby, 1998). Furthermore, as an approach evolves over time, specific teaching practices and the curriculum that is used may change significantly. In some cases, different practitioners may implement very different versions of an approach even though the different versions are identified by the same name.

We have asserted previously (Prizant & Rubin, 1999; Prizant & Wetherby, 1998) that global arguments about comparative efficacy of different approaches remain weak and unfocused for two primary reasons. First, there is most often significant variability within the practice of a particular approach, and second, there is a general lack of consideration of overlap between different categories of approaches. As a case in point, when ABA is discussed as one distinct category as compared with other categories, significant differences within the practice of ABA may be obscured. For example, approaches that are predominated by highly directive teaching strategies, such as discrete trial training, and more natural and child-centered teaching approaches, such as contemporary ABA approaches (e.g., natural language paradigm, Koegel & Koegel, 1995) may be lumped together in a discussion of ABA approaches even though both goals and teaching practices vary greatly (Cohen, 1999; Prizant & Wetherby, 1998). In an analogous manner, important similarities between developmentally based approaches such as the DIR model (Greenspan & Wieder, 1998), the RDI Program (Gutstein, 2000), the SCERTS Model, and some contemporary ABA approaches (e.g., natural language paradigm, the Walden Preschool [McGee, 2001; McGeer, Morrier, & Daly, 1999]) may not even be considered when comparing approaches on a categorical basis. Examples of overlap among these approaches include a focus on child initiation and reciprocal turn taking and play as an important context for learning. However, despite these problems a categorical orientation still prevails in discussions of educational approaches and debates about treatment efficacy, which we believe to be unfortunate and overly simplistic.

Broad Descriptive Approach

Educational approaches also have been characterized in more general and broad terms by describing practices in reference to the primary goals or philosophical orientations of the approaches. Such characterizations address similarities across a number of approaches or programs, allowing for a higher level of categorization. Furthermore, common elements among a variety of practices are addressed when taking this tack. For example, Heflin and Simpson (1998) reviewed approaches as falling into three general categories: 1) interventions based on formation of interpersonal relationships (also referred to as *relationship-based* or *relationship-focused approaches* [e.g., Mahoney & Perales, 2005]), 2) skill-based treatment programs, and 3) physiologically oriented intervention programs. In their discussion, Heflin and Simpson acknowledged that a specific program or approach may have elements consistent with two or even three of these categories. Other commonly used characterizations consistent with a broad descriptive approach to categorizing educational programs include behavioral versus developmental, structured versus semistructured, academic versus functional, and multimodal communication versus speech based.

A benefit of a broad descriptive approach is that general similarities and differences can be identified among approaches, allowing professionals and parents to explore and select among practices more compatible with their beliefs and to make comparisons with approaches they are currently using. However, important and distinct differences between approaches may be obscured. For example, PECS (Frost & Bondy, 1994) has provided an innovative approach to AAC by introducing a way for children to express their intentions by exchanging symbols. PECS and the SCERTS Model both use visual supports extensively; however, PECS follows a more prescriptive teaching protocol based primarily on the ABA skill-based learning literature and to a lesser extent on the child language development literature, whereas SCERTS is greatly influenced by research on early language development, tends to be less prescriptive and more individualized, and is greatly influenced by the activity-based learning literature.

Continuum Approach

Prizant and Wetherby (1998) noted that approaches to enhance communication and social-emotional abilities for children with ASD can be described in at least two ways: First, different categorical approaches may be considered along a continuum using descriptive terms based on the philosophical orientation and research literature from which the educational practices were derived. The continuum includes traditional behavioral practices at one end and social-pragmatic approaches on the other end, with middle-ground approaches or hybrid approaches occupying the middle (see Warren, 1993). In decribing this continuum, Prizant and Wetherby (1998) addressed the evolution of current educational approaches from a historical perspective. Second, a number of more specific continua may be identified that are more closely related to actual implementation and practice within an approach, thus allowing for a more precise description of specific elements of programs. This introduces the notion of considering each of the many dimensions of educational programming along a continuum as a way to characterize educational programs and as an alternative to categorical debates and broad descriptive approaches.

In our effort to break down walls created by the predominance of categorical descriptions in the ASD literature, we noted that multiple dimensions of educational approaches may be identified and that each may be viewed along a continuum of practice

(Prizant & Wetherby, 1998; Prizant, Wetherby, & Rydell, 2000). These dimensions are discussed in the next section. We saw the need to describe programs along multi-dimensional continua, as many contemporary educational programs increasingly integrate elements of different categorical approaches, which results in greater flexibility in and individualization of programming for children. For an individual child, appropriateness of a program may vary depending upon factors such as the child's social-communicative abilities, emotional regulatory capacities, and developmental capacities in other areas; history of success with a particular approach; and parental preferences and priorities.

Consideration of programs along multidimensional continua has a number of advantages over categorical and broad descriptive characterizations:

1. Similarities as well as differences among different categorical approaches can be analyzed in a finer grained manner.

2. In specific reference to an individual student, elements that vary along each continuum may be systematically manipulated to best suit the needs and learning style of that student.

3. Teaching practices may be drawn from a variety of approaches as they are determined to best meet the needs of an individual student.

4. Movement toward greater independence for a student may be conceived as changes along various continua (e.g., greater flexibility in teaching; use of a less directive interactive style in teaching; an increase in child-centered activities, with increased choice making).

5. Future research may address specific elements and combinations of elements that may be most effective with students who demonstrate different developmental capacities and learning profiles, rather than focusing on comparing different approaches at a more global categorical level.

Dimensions of Educational Practices

As just noted, a continuum approach requires scrutiny of educational practice along a variety of dimensions. Table 6.1 presents these dimensions as organized in four major categories: teaching practices, learning contexts, child characteristics, and programmatic goals. We now discuss these dimensions with examples relative to different categorical approaches. It will be evident that these dimensions are not mutually exclusive.

Teaching Practices

Theoretical and Research Underpinnings

A broad continuum that has framed discussions about different approaches is whether an approach draws from developmental research and practice or from behavioral research and practice or both. All treatment and educational approaches have the potential to draw from the extensive literature on the development of children with and without disabilities and the literature on developmentally appropriate practice in educational settings. On one end of the continuum, however, approaches may not draw from child development research and may teach children primarily in a one-to-one adult–child teaching format, with a focus on increasing or decreasing skills based on a prescriptive program or on professionals' prior decisions about what a child needs to learn and how teaching is to occur. On the other end of the continuum, developmental research is used to provide a foundation for making decisions about goals and teaching strategies to be used to achieve those goals, as well as for making decisions about appropriate contexts for learning. Approaches for working with children with ASD vary greatly in this dimension.

Table 6.1. Dimensions of educational programming for children with ASD

Teaching practices
Theoretical and research underpinnings
Degree of prescription versus flexibility in teaching
Use of directive versus facilitative interactional and teaching styles
Approaches to problem behavior
Measurement of progress, including type and intensity of data collection
Involvement and role of parents
Use of visual supports and visually mediated activities

Learning contexts
Naturalness of teaching activities or contexts
Skill- or activity-based learning opportunities
Social complexity (e.g., one to one, small group, large group)
Role of typical or more developmentally advanced peers

Child characteristics
Individual differences in learning
Consideration of the child's emotional regulatory profile
Age and developmental range covered

Programmatic goals
Educational and treatment priorities in goal setting (i.e., domains of development)
Augmentative and alternative communication (AAC) goals and strategies
Spontaneous, initiated communication
Goals based on developmental as well as functional criteria

Traditional ABA approaches draw primarily from operant learning theory and behavioral research and practice, whereas contemporary ABA approaches integrate practices from developmentally based early childhood practice while still relying on a learning theory framework for accounting for and documenting behavioral change in children. However, contemporary ABA practices (e.g., as exemplified by the works of Koegel and Koegel, McGee, Strain, and Schreibman) may not be guided by frameworks based on the extensive research in child development to the same extent as developmentally based approaches such as the DIR Model and the SCERTS Model (Prizant & Rubin, 1999). Nevertheless, information about developmental sequences and developmental support based on child development research has had a significant influence on contemporary ABA practices. For example, primary contexts of intervention now include play-based interaction with peers and natural activities and routines, with a focus on initiated communication and age-appropriate play.

Approaches that draw most heavily from child development research and practice use developmental frameworks and developmental processes as the core foundation for determining goals, measuring progress, and selecting developmentally appropriate teaching practices. For example, the SCERTS Model is driven largely by developmental research in language and communication development, social development, development of social-emotional capacities such as emotional regulation, and development of sensory processing capacities. As noted, priority goals in the SCERTS Model are identified in the areas of social communication, emotional regulation, and transactional support. The SCERTS Model has a strong developmental focus; however, a child's functional needs and family priorities are factors that are considered along with goals guided by research on child development. Furthermore, teaching strategies based on effective learning processes derived from developmental research are infused into educational opportunities for children with ASD.

Other major bodies of research and literature relevant to underlying theoretical and research foundations are family systems theory and family-centered intervention. The SCERTS Model is heavily influenced by family systems theory and is consistent with family-centered intervention practices (e.g., Mahoney & Perales, 2005) as well as research on PBS as reported in the contemporary ABA literature (Fox et al., 2000). Greenspan and Wieder's (1998) DIR model is based on Greenspan's (1992) model of emotional development, with priority goals identified in social-emotional capacities and related abilities. The DIR model does not draw directly from research or literature on ABA practices.

Degree of Prescription versus Flexibility in Teaching

Some approaches are prescriptive, in that teaching practices and goal sequences are clearly specified with recommendations to follow them faithfully. This may include how teaching materials are to be presented, how the teaching environment is to be structured or arranged, which types of child responses are considered acceptable or correct, and how adults should respond to acceptable as well as unacceptable responses. In prescriptive approaches, children's behavior may also be defined as *on task* or *off task.* Such terms are used in specific reference to how a child's behavior relates to a specified activity or to the teacher's agenda, regardless of its relevance to events in the situation or a child's focus of attention or intention. For example, if a child comments on the noise of a truck outside the window or requests a toy on a shelf within sight, the child may simply be redirected back to the task at hand, despite the potential for using the child's interests and spontaneous communication as teachable moments.

In contrast, other approaches may not follow a predetermined agenda or prescription for teaching. On this end of the continuum, there are greater possibilities for flexibly creating learning opportunities and for spontaneously capitalizing on teachable moments based on a child's focus of attention and interest and how activities and events evolve. In the examples mentioned in the previous paragraph, the child may be brought to the window to observe the truck, with a short conversation about what it is doing, or the toys may be brought down from the shelf to encourage further spontaneous communication. For this dimension, middle-ground approaches may have some degree of structure with specified goals that are predetermined. However, the child's partner is better able to depart from a prearranged agenda either for short periods or for longer periods, depending on the potential for creating and capitalizing on new and more effective learning opportunities regardless of the original agenda. In general, this approach is characteristic of the SCERTS Model.

Use of Directive versus Facilitative Interactional and Teaching Styles

A facilitative style, which currently is advocated by developmental and some contemporary behavioral literature, is characterized by

- Following a child's attentional focus

- Offering choices and alternatives within activities

- Responding to and acknowledging children's intent

- Modeling a variety of communicative functions, including commenting on a child's activities

- Expanding and elaborating on the topic of a child's verbal and nonverbal communication

An extreme facilitative style is known as *following the child's lead,* in which minimal direction is provided on the part of the communicative partner. When primarily a facilitative style is used, an underlying assumption is that a child's spontaneous and self-directed behavior is sufficiently organized and goal directed such that the partner can create productive learning opportunities with appropriate responses and guidance but with minimal intrusion or redirection.

On the other end of the continuum is a directive style of interaction and teaching. As the name implies, this style is characterized by greater imposition by the partner on the child to communicate, respond, and behave in a particular manner. Directive styles are characterized by

- Frequent attempts to bring the child's attention to events or activities chosen by the partner

- A large proportion of questions designed to elicit specific answers or directions designed to have the child respond or perform in a particular manner

- Frequent use of more intrusive prompting strategies (physical or verbal) to support the child to respond correctly

- Evaluative comments indicating whether the child's responses are appropriate or correct

The ultimate goal of this style of teaching is for the child to comply with the partner's directives to achieve goals designated by the partner.

The middle ground on this continuum would be selective use of directive or facilitative elements depending on the nature of the activity, a child's ability relative to demands of activity, and the child's emotional regulatory status. For example, in teaching a child to tie his or her shoes, a more directive approach may initially be necessary as acquisition of this skill may initially require hand-over-hand direction due to the visual-motor and motor planning requirements. However, in fostering social-communicative abilities for this same child, a less directive approach would be warranted due to the very different nature of learning to participate in social-communicative interactions.

The SCERTS Model has a strong bias toward more facilitative styles of fostering social communication and emotional regulation. (The concept of a *facilitative style* was first introduced in the child language development literature and does not refer to the method known as *facilitated communication* [Biklen, 1990], an AAC approach used for individuals with ASD and other severe communication disabilities.) The justification is that research has demonstrated that the benefits of a more facilitative style include the following

1. Providing a child with a sense of social control and communicative power, which has been found to result in increased initiations and more elaborate communicative attempts (Mirenda & Donnellan, 1986; Peck, 1985)

2. Following the child's attentional focus and motivation, which reduces problems of noncompliance and may result in increased learning due to motivation and affective involvement

3. Providing elaborated information and feedback appropriate to the child's level and attentional focus, which supports the child's communicative and language development through modeling of vocabulary and more varied language forms and functions. For example, Mirenda and Donnellan (1986) found that compared with a directive style, the use of a facilitative style resulted in higher rates of student-initiated interactions, question asking, and conversational initiation in students with ASD. Rydell and Mirenda (1991) found that higher frequencies of generative utterances,

initiations, and increased comprehension followed adult-facilitative utterances. Facilitative strategies have also been found to increase communicative initiation and social-affective signaling of children with ASD with limited or no language abilities (Dawson & Adams, 1984; Peck, 1985; Tiegerman & Primavera, 1984).

Appropriateness of style along the continuum of facilitativeness to directiveness is a child-specific issue and can only be determined by observing the effect of partner style on interactions. Relative to a child's typical abilities, a good stylistic match should result in

1. Increased self-regulation of attention (i.e., ability to maintain a mutual focus of attention with minimal prompting)

2. Active involvement in selecting and participating in activities

3. Frequent verbal and nonverbal communicative initiations

4. More elaborate communicative initiations

5. Positive affective involvement with the partner

A style may be thought to be more facilitative when these characteristics can be observed in children's behavior. For example, for a highly active and distractible child, a style that promotes a mutual attentional focus and more active involvement, even though it may have some directive qualities (e.g., physical prompting, limit setting), must be viewed as facilitative for that child. This same style, however, may have detrimental effects for a child with a lower activity level and greater attentional regulation. As Marfo (1990) noted, the function of adult directiveness in supporting interactions is of overriding concern, not the presence or absence of features thought to be directive. In the SCERTS Model, we advocate incorporating facilitative features in play and teaching interactions and gradually modifying style along the facilitativeness–directiveness continuum until an optimal match is found.

Approaches to Problem Behavior

Another important dimension of programming is how educational staff and others respond to circumstances in which a child is emotionally dysregulated or demonstrates behavior that is considered to be problematic. This continuum is presented in greater detail in Table 6.2. On one end of the continuum are approaches referred to as *behavior management approaches* that attempt to stop a child from engaging in problem behavior in reaction to when it occurs. These behavior reduction strategies may range from using extinction (e.g., ignoring problem behaviors when they occur) to using aversive procedures or punishment, which are less preferred and considered unacceptable in most contemporary programs. In reaction to more traditional behavior management approaches, a strong movement referred to as *positive behavior support (PBS)* emerged in the 1990s. PBS approaches focus on developing preventative and nonaversive, positive reactive strategies and address factors related to patterns of behavior that are considered problematic, such as limited social-communicative skills. The SCERTS Model builds on PBS practices by including more of a developmental focus, with the long-term preventative goal of developing a child's emotional regulatory capacities, along with reactive strategies to address problem behaviors related to emotional dysregulation.

PBS and the SCERTS Model have in common a focus on positive approaches; manipulation of environmental variables, including factors that cause dysregulation and problem behaviors; and a strong focus on functional social communication. Clearly, the SCERTS Model has been influenced by PBS practices and research. However, there also

Table 6.2. A comparison of approaches addressing problem behavior

Traditional behavior management[a]	Positive behavior support[a]	Emotional regulation approach in the SCERTS Model
Is grounded in traditional behavioral orientation (e.g., change external problem behavior by manipulating consequences). No consideration of functions of behavior or developmental variables	Is grounded in contemporary behavioral orientation (e.g., change external problem behavior by manipulating consequences and antecedents and considering other variables such as setting events and functions of behavior)	Is grounded in a transactional and developmental orientation. Problem behavior is viewed in terms of a child's attempts to cope or adapt to environmental or physiological stressors relative to the child's developmental capacities and emotional history with a person or activity.
Views the person as the problem	Views the system, setting, or skill deficiency as the problem	Views mismatches among interpersonal, environmental, or activity demands and the child's abilities/skills and emotional regulatory capacities as the problem
Focuses on manipulation of external variables—not on the child's perspective. This is an "outside of the child" approach.	Focuses on manipulation of external variables and functions of behavior using positive approaches to teach replacement skills. This is not from child's perspective and is an "outside of the child" approach.	Considers child's intentions, emotional arousal, previous emotional history and experience, and relationship history. This is an "inside out" approach.
Emphasizes reducing or eliminating behavior. Primarily a reactive approach	Identifies and teaches replacement skills and builds relationships. Reactive and proactive strategies are used.	Enhances social communication, relationships, and emotional regulatory capacities proactively from a developmental perspective. Reactive strategies include effective means to support a child's emotional regulation (mutual regulatory strategies) at the time of dysregulation.
Relies frequently on negative consequences	Relies primarily on positive approaches	Relies on positive, relationship-based approaches focused on a child's socioemotional responses
Has "quick fix" expectations	Has a goal of sustained results achieved over time (with a focus on reduction of identified problem behavior)	Has a life-span goal of developing foundation of emotional regulatory capacities and related developmental capacities that prevent development of problem behaviors
Is designed by "experts" in reaction to problem behavior	Is developed by a collaborative team in reaction to problem behavior. However, proactive strategies also may be developed to preclude problem behavior from developing in the future.	Is developed by a team proactively as an inherent part of overall developmental plan, not initiated solely as a reaction to the appearance of problem behavior.

[a]*Source:* U.S. Department of Education, Office of Special Education and Rehabilitative Services, Office of Special Education Programs, n.d.

are some significant distinctions. One distinction is that the SCERTS Model uses a developmental, emotional regulatory framework rather than a behavior analytic framework to analyze and develop approaches to address problem behavior. Due to the interdependence of emotional state and physiological arousal state, there must be careful monitoring and interpretation of behavioral indicators of physiological and emotional arousal, as well as knowledge of a child's mutual and self-regulatory capacities.

In the SCERTS Model, problem behavior is analyzed relative to contextual and historical factors to determine the possible underlying intentions or communicative functions. Other factors such as a child's health status, arousal bias (hyper- or hypo-arousal), and emotional regulatory abilities and environmental stressors also are taken into consideration. Based on scrutiny of these factors, a preventative plan is put into place, which may include some or all of the following strategies: significant modifications to a child's schedule and/or daily activities and experiences; modifications to interpersonal and learning supports; implementation of sensory processing and emotional regulatory supports; and, when appropriate, biological and/or nutritional interventions to address factors shown to be related to problem behaviors (e.g., gastrointestinal problems, food allergies). A plan to support a youngster's emotional regulation at the time that he or she is engaging in problem behavior also is developed. Finally, in the SCERTS Model, it is recognized that whether a behavior is or is not considered problematic in the first place may vary greatly based on individual differences in families, cultural groups, and even the gender of the parent. Thus, educators and clinicians must work closely with families and set priorities related to patterns of problem behavior, should they arise.

Measurement of Progress, Including Type and Intensity of Data Collection

Measuring progress and accountability of services provided are now considered essential obligations for all service providers. Different approaches, however, may address measurement of progress in different ways.

Qualitative versus Quantitative Approaches

On one end of the continuum, progress may be measured informally and subjectively using qualitative means. For example, professionals may keep descriptive notes based on observations of students or may ask parents their impressions of their child's progress. Descriptions may be very general or may be more specific depending on requirements of different agencies, skills of the professional, areas being monitored, and the profession involved. Such approaches may lack specificity and objectivity in monitoring progress; however, they may tap into the social validity of progress that is measured (i.e., how changes in a child's behavior increase functional abilities and affect partners across a variety of settings). On the other end of the continuum, professionals may use intensive ongoing data collection and analysis of a child's behavioral reactions and responses, in most, if not all teaching interactions. This may include frequency counts of objectively defined behaviors, which yield quantitative data to document increases and decreases in targeted behavioral responses, with a plan for multiple observations by different staff to ensure reliability of observations. Strengths of intensive data collection include the careful documentation of progress toward target goals. However, possible shortcomings of ongoing intensive data collection include

1. The risk that some data collection approaches interfere with educators' ability to be closely observant, highly responsive, and spontaneous with children in reciprocal teaching interactions

2. The possibility that frequency counts of behavior may address presence or absence of specific targeted behavioral responses but may not capture more meaningful developmental change (i.e., socially valid change) for a child

Measuring Generalization and Carryover to Natural Environments

Another continuum related to measurement of progress is whether the emphasis is on measuring change in specific training contexts or whether there is equal if not greater concern for measuring progress across a variety of more naturally occurring activities, contexts, and partners. It has been argued (NRC, 2001; Prizant & Wetherby, 1998) that traditional static measures of developmental progress, such as changes in IQ scores or in scores on standardized tests or a sole reliance on frequency counts of behaviors, may not address the dynamic nature of social-communicative and emotional development and core challenges faced by children with ASD.

One factor complicating the issue of measurement of progress is that approaches with different underlying philosophies each measure progress in a manner consistent with the philosophy underlying the approach. For example, many behaviorally oriented approaches use frequency counts of the correctness of objectively defined responses as primary evidence of skill development and, ultimately, "mastery" of skills. Developmentally oriented educators may focus more on qualitative patterns of behavior indicative of developmental shifts rather than focusing primarily on frequency counts of correct or incorrect responses. Middle-ground approaches that address both skill acquisition and changes in underlying developmental capacities may use frequency counts of objectively defined behaviors and frameworks and procedures to monitor developmental shifts.

In the SCERTS Assessment Process (SAP) of the SCERTS Model, such a middle-ground approach is used. In the SAP, less intrusive data collection procedures are used, including observations of a child across different contexts and partners, as well as different events and activities. We also use socially valid measures of a child's abilities and of progress such as interviews with and questionnaires (SCERTS Assessment Process–Report [SAP-R]) completed by caregivers.

Involvement and Role of Parents

Most educational approaches value participation of parents because parent involvement is an important factor related to children's progress. The nature of such participation, however, may vary greatly. On one end of the continuum, educators or consultants responsible for a child's program may recruit parents to provide additional learning experiences as prescribed. In essence, parents are asked to become teachers or to hire additional personnel to carry out similar teaching programs in educational settings. On the other end of the continuum, parent involvement and direct participation is predicated largely on priorities set by parents relative to their goals for their child across different activities and settings, as well as their ability and desire to be actively involved.

In the SCERTS Model, family priorities and family members' abilities to be actively involved are important factors in developing an individualized program for a child, including setting goals that are functional, developmentally appropriate, and valued by family members. Furthermore, family members' participation in their child's program is calibrated to their ability to support the child's development relative to different activities and contexts. This is not a static issue, as family members may either become increasingly involved or less involved in activities addressing goals designated by the child's team depending on factors affecting the family. However, because of the activity-based focus of the SCERTS Model, there is an emphasis on involvement in supporting skills in the context of everyday activities and routines, rather than in separate teaching sessions. In our experience, this enables family members to take a more active role in their child's program as using everyday routines and activities creates opportunities that tend to be in harmony with the culture and lifestyle of the family.

Use of Visual Supports and Visually Mediated Activities

It is now widely accepted that the use of visual supports and visually mediated activities are effective practices for the great majority of children with ASD (Mirenda & Erickson, 2000; Wetherby et al., 1997). Visual supports may be used in a variety of ways: as primary expressive communication systems (e.g., low-tech communication boards, overlays on high-tech communication devices), as aids to understanding language and expectations communicated by others, or as organizational supports such as picture schedules. Nevertheless, approaches vary greatly as to extent to which visual supports are considered an essential part of the approach. For example, approaches that rely heavily on visual supports include Structured Teaching of Division TEACCH (Schopler et al., 1995), the SCERTS Model, and PECS (Frost & Bondy, 1994). In contrast, other approaches such as the natural language paradigm (Koegel & Koegel, 1995), Lovaas therapy (Lovaas, 1981), and Applied Verbal Behavior and the ABLLS Curriculum (Sundberg & Partington, 1998) may minimize the use of visual supports or may treat them only as secondary alternatives for expressive communication when speech does not develop.

Learning Contexts

Naturalness of Teaching Activities or Contexts

We define *naturalness* in reference to whether an activity or event designed for learning already occurs or can be scheduled to occur as a regular routine in a child's life experiences across a number of different partners, contexts, or environments. The quality of that event should be sufficiently similar to other events to enable the child to perceive the similarities and therefore generalize skills and understanding of the events across different occurrences. Less natural or more contrived activities or contexts are those that are much less likely to occur in a child's daily experiences or those that, even if they can be set up to occur, still bear little resemblance to more general activities of daily living. The setting(s) for natural activities must also support a child's emotional regulation and ability to learn optimally; therefore, some children may benefit from a larger proportion of one-to-one and small-group learning opportunities, *as long as those activities and the skills being focused on relate directly to other events and activities occurring concurrently in the children's lives.* The ultimate goal in the SCERTS Model is for a child to be able to learn and practice emerging skills in naturalistic interactions across people, settings, and circumstances. We believe that true learning must involve a child's understanding and following of natural cues, conventions, and rules of interactions with partners across a variety of contexts.

In addition, in teaching children skills necessary to participate successfully, there is an overriding concern for providing only the minimal support necessary (i.e., strategic support) so that children have opportunities to problem solve and develop and apply skills as independently as possible. Extensive use of transactional learning supports delineated as part of a child's educational plan allows for this to occur.

Skill- or Activity-Based Learning Opportunities

Closely related to the issue of naturalness of the learning context is whether activities are designed to focus primarily on teaching skills or helping children to develop a sense of the meaning and purpose of activities or both. On one end of the continuum, children may be taught skills in isolation in a manner that is not linked to or embedded within a logical sequence of events that relates to a predictable outcome of the activity or event. On the other end of the continuum, children may be exposed to activities or events with the hope that they will learn based primarily on exposure to or observation of those events. In such situations, too little attention may be given to the need for direct instruction to support the children in learning the skills that are required for successful participation.

The middle ground, which is characteristic of the SCERTS Model, is to primarily use activities and events for learning in contrast to teaching skills in an isolated manner outside of the context of events or activities, but to provide direct instruction on an as-needed basis within the context of those activities or events. We believe that a primary reliance on repetitive practice of skills isolated from activities in which the skills are used may actually inhibit understanding and generalization of those skills to larger events and activities in a child's life. Such approaches that use a "train skills to mastery, and then generalize skills to other contexts" approach may actually contribute to situation-specific learning and interfere with functional use of skills.

In the SCERTS Model, considerable attention also is given to providing children with multiple opportunities to practice skills (e.g., motor, communicative, cognitive). Teaching and learning, however, occur in activities and events that relate as closely as possible to more general life experiences in meaningful activities that already occur or that can be planned to occur outside of the specific teaching contents.

Social Complexity

To be as independent as possible and to enjoy life to its fullest, a child must be able to engage in interpersonal interactions with a variety of partners in different social contexts. In general, children with ASD have greater difficulty in larger, more complex social groupings, largely due to the differing social-communicative and emotional regulatory requirements of participating in groups with more people, more stimulation, and more complex social rules. Educational approaches vary greatly as to how children are exposed to groupings of different social complexity. On one end of the continuum are approaches in which children are taught primarily in a one-to-one (adult–child) learning context, especially in the first few years of educational programming but in some cases for many years. An often-stated belief underlying this kind of approach is that children with ASD are not able to learn in more complex settings until they acquire particular "readiness" skills such as eye contact, attentional skills, compliance with directions, and imitation skills. It is important to note that there is no evidence to support such a claim (Strain, McGee, & Kohler, 2001). On the other end of the continuum, children may be educated primarily in group settings, such as a typical preschool classroom or kindergarten, in small- or large-group activities, with few or no one-to-one learning opportunities.

In the SCERTS Model, decisions regarding social groupings in educational settings are highly individualized depending on a child's social-communicative and emotional regulatory capacities and challenges posed by available educational settings. However, given that settings of different social complexity offer different types of social learning opportunities, most children with ASD benefit from a program involving one-to-one and small-group instruction, as well as larger group activities. For example, it obviously is not possible for a child to learn to play and learn with peers or even learn to tolerate being in the proximity of other children when a program uses primarily a one-to-one adult–child teaching format. However, placement in primarily large groups may not provide opportunities for a youngster to learn to attend to the salient social-communicative cues and to participate successfully in small-group nonverbal and verbal interaction. In the SCERTS Model, it is recognized that it is desirable for children to learn in social groupings of differing complexity and that for each child the proportion of time spent in different size groups must be tailored to the goals that are set relative to different groupings and a youngster's ability to benefit from such learning opportunities. In addition, the design and use of appropriate transactional learning supports, such as visual supports, often play a major role in supporting children in group settings. The bottom line is that decisions regarding the proportion of time spent in one-to-one, small-group, and large-group learning activities must be made on an individual basis, and the need for changes in how services are provided must be monitored by a child's team as the child develops.

Role of Typical or More Developmentally Advanced Peers

For most educational approaches, a shared goal is to support children's success in activities with other children as well as to support the development of social relationships. Different approaches, however, place different priorities on activities with more developmentally advanced or typical peers. On one end of the continuum, in some approaches, it is believed that a child must acquire certain readiness skills (e.g., compliance to requests, imitation) before they can benefit from being with other children, similar to the readiness criterion that may be applied before children are placed in group settings. On the other end of the continuum, opportunities for learning with peers are considered essential from the earliest stages of educational programming because initial goals may include the development of communication and play skills with other children. In the SCERTS Model, we specifically target activities that involve learning and playing with peers (LAPP) as a high priority, given the focus on social communication and play in everyday activities, as long as activities are designed to optimize a child's emotional regulation and active participation. The long-term goals for children with regard to learning and playing with peers are to develop a sense of social membership and develop friendships and long-term relationships.

Child Characteristics

Individual Differences in Learning

The degree to which individual differences across children are recognized and addressed is another dimension where different approaches may vary greatly. Although most children with ASD experience challenges in social communication, emotional regulation, and learning, significant individual differences across children clearly may be observed. On one end of the continuum, most if not all children may be exposed to the same teaching curriculum with the same sequence of goals and teaching strategies regardless of individual differences. On the other end of the continuum, approaches may be highly individualized depending on a child's profile of strengths and needs. In the SCERTS Model, goals are derived individually based on the results of the in-depth and individually designed SCERTS Assessment Process (SAP). The selection of goals and contexts for learning occurs as part of a systematic process guided by the developmental frameworks of the SCERTS Model in social communication and emotional regulation, as well as a child's functional needs and family priorities.

Consideration of the Child's Emotional Regulatory Profile

One area of challenge that has been documented for many years in the literature on ASD (NRC, 2001; Ornitz & Ritvo, 1968) as well as by adults with ASD (Grandin, 1995; Shore, 2001; Williams, 1992) is emotional regulation. As discussed in Chapter 3 in this volume, challenges in emotional regulation are closely related to learning style differences and difficulties in social communication and social understanding, as well as to sensory sensitivities and sensory processing difficulties. However, approaches vary greatly as to the degree to which these challenges are directly addressed. As noted above, a behavior management approach has dominated practice in ASD for many years, in which problem behaviors are identified and procedures are introduced to reduce and/or eliminate them.

In the SCERTS Model, problem behaviors are always considered in reference to a child's emotional regulatory abilities and factors that precipitate dysregulation, as emotional regulation is the primary dimension of focus, in contrast to a focus on specific problem behaviors alone. Multiple factors related to emotional regulation and dysregulation are specifically identified and addressed (e.g., social, cognitive, and sensory processing difficulties are considered in specific reference to emotional regulation and arousal modulation). A child's difficulties are assessed systematically and the development of specific mutual and self-regulatory strategies are targeted along with the implementation of a range of transactional supports, to support the child's ability to deal with daily challenges to maintaining well-regulated states.

Age and Developmental Range Covered by an Approach

Another important consideration that varies among approaches is the chronological age and developmental age range for which a particular approach is designed. For example, PECS is most relevant for children from an early intentional communication stage to single-word and early multiword stages of communication. Comprehensive programs have been designed for inclusive education for preschool children, such as the LEAP Model (Strain & Kohler, 1998) and the Walden Preschool approach. The SCERTS Model, in its current form, is applicable for children from the earliest developmental stages to conversational stages, including the age range from birth to 10–12 years of age. However, feedback from families and practitioners is that the model also is applicable for older people with ASD, due to the focus on the life-span issues of social communication, emotional regulation, and transactional supports.

Programmatic Goals

Educational and Treatment Priorities in Goal Setting

Different educational approaches may vary greatly as to the educational priorities (i.e., domains of development) focused on in a child's overall program. Children with ASD often have multiple developmental needs, ranging from the acquisition of functional skills for self-help; to the development of social-communicative and emotional regulatory capacities; to cognitive skills, motor skills, and academic learning needs. Most approaches address a broad range of developmental needs; however, the focus of a particular program may be skewed toward particular areas of need. For example, approaches such as the SCERTS Model and the DIR model (Greenspan & Wieder, 1998) place a great deal of emphasis on social and emotional development, and the SCERTS Model has a particular focus on addressing social communication with great specificity. Social communication also is a focus of the natural language paradigm (Koegel & Koegel, 1995), and peer interaction is a focus of the LEAP Model (Strain & Kohler, 1998) and the Walden Preschool.

Another related factor is whether the needs addressed are closely related to the core challenges experienced by children with ASD as reported in research on ASD. On one end of the continuum, approaches may be based largely on teaching rote cognitive and language skills, with an emphasis on teaching a repertoire of correct responses in prescriptive teaching programs. On the other end of the continuum are approaches focused on enhancing abilities to directly address the core challenges in ASD. The SCERTS Model is consistent with this latter focus, with priorities based on enhancing capacities in social communication and emotional regulation.

Augmentative and Alternative Communication Goals and Strategies

AAC goals and strategies include the implementation of nonspeech communication modalities used either instead of or in addition to speech as a means of communication. Although there are clear individual variations among children, a child with ASD typically demonstrates a strong preference for nontransient visual information due to learning style differences, as discussed in Chapter 4 in this volume. *Nontransient* refers to information that remains static or fixed in place over time, such as objects, visual-spatial patterns, pictures, and written words (Wetherby et al., 1997). Different approaches place different degrees of emphasis on identifying AAC goals and strategies and the types of AAC strategies used.

In general, approaches that place greater emphasis on social communication tend to value a wide range of AAC strategies as part of efforts to support communication development (Mirenda & Erickson, 2000). However, other approaches may not advocate the use of AAC (e.g., Walden Preschool) or support only a limited range of AAC options (e.g., Applied Verbal Behavior only uses sign language), despite the fact that research has demonstrated that use of different forms of AAC do not preclude and likely support speech and language development (Mirenda & Erickson, 2000; NRC, 2001). Some approaches may begin with AAC options for nonspeaking children but may quickly abandon AAC when any speech is acquired. The SCERTS Model has a bias toward the use of a multimodal approach (i.e., pictures, objects, written words, signs, speech). This approach must be appropriately designed for an individual child to support the development of a broad foundation of communication abilities with movement into language and conversational stages, to support communicative flexibility and adaptability across contexts and partners.

Spontaneous, Initiated Communication

For more than 2 decades, SCERTS Model collaborators have advocated for working on spontaneous, initiated communication as a priority for children with ASD (Prizant, 1982; Prizant & Wetherby, 1993; Wetherby et al., 1997). Research has demonstrated the importance of focusing on initiated, spontaneous communication because a child's ability to initiate communication early in development has been found to be highly predictive of more positive social-communicative outcomes (Koegel et al., 1999). Furthermore, as discussed previously, the NRC guidelines highlighted "functional spontaneous communication" (2001, p. 6) as among the highest priorities in educational programming. Finally, clinical experience suggests that initiation leads to greater participation and increased self-determination in everyday activities and precludes the development of problem behaviors due to increased competence in communicating needs more independently.

Different approaches vary greatly to the extent to which initiated communication is emphasized as a goal. For example, more traditional ABA approaches (e.g., Lovaas, 1981) place children primarily in a respondent role, especially when discrete trial training is the instructional method of choice. Contemporary ABA approaches such as the natural language paradigm (Koegel & Koegel, 1995) emphasize the importance of communicative initiation. As noted previously, the SCERTS Model values initiated spontaneous communication across partners and contexts as a high priority goal in any child's program from the outset of the program.

Goals Based on Developmental as Well as Functional Criteria

Approaches vary as to the basis on which goals are established. Some approaches use functional criteria. That is, goals are based on skills that are viewed as necessary to address a child's everyday needs; however, the specific goals that are set for a child may not be chosen specific to the child's developmental capacities. For example, focusing on speech training for a presymbolic child or on teaching children at early stages of single-word or early multiword communication to say whole sentences would be developmentally inappropriate, although such a goal may be selected with the good intentions of teaching functional skills. Other approaches that may be developmentally based may be inconsistent in selecting goals that specifically address functional skills in daily routines and functional needs across settings, as teaching may occur to address goals on a developmentally sequenced checklist.

In the SCERTS Model, the approach used is functional as well as developmentally grounded because goals are developed based on parental priorities and actual communicative needs in everyday living routines and environments so that there is a clear and natural incentive for a child to communicate. Stated differently, the perspective of the child and family is adopted so that goals are relevant to family members' daily experiences. The SCERTS Model also is grounded in a child's developmental abilities so that educational efforts do not under- or overshoot the child's capacity for learning. A child's "zone of proximal development" (Vygotsky, 1978) is determined across all domains of learning so that learning may be optimized because what is being learned is within the developmental reach of the child.

SUMMARY

It is now recognized that many complex factors must be considered in developing appropriate educational programs for children with ASD. As noted, this is especially true for determining goals and teaching strategies to enhance social-communicative abilities, a clear priority for all individuals with ASD. Given that there is no evidence that any one categorical approach is more effective than other approaches (Dawson & Osterling, 1997; NRC, 2001; Prizant & Wetherby, 1998), we have argued that comparing different approaches from a categorical orientation provides little insight and offers less potential for individualized programming, now considered essential for best meeting the educational needs of individuals with ASD (NRC, 2001). There is evidence, however, that there needs to be a focus on initiated communication; on enhancing social-communicative abilities in social activities in a variety of contexts that are as natural as possible; and on fully understanding and integrating knowledge about the relationships of social-communicative abilities, problem behavior, and emotional regulation (NRC, 2001; Prizant et al., 2000; Wetherby & Prizant, 1999)—all of which are of the highest priority in the SCERTS Model.

As an alternative to categorical comparisons, we also have argued that it is potentially more fruitful to examine and scrutinize practices relative to a variety of dimensions, including teaching practices, learning contexts, child characteristics, and programmatic goals. The SCERTS Model is characteristic of this multidimensional approach and therefore allows for individualization of programming along all dimensions. Furthermore, because the SCERTS Model is not exclusionary of other approaches, parents and practitioners can continue to use methods or strategies that are associated with other approaches as long as goals reflect clear priorities in the areas of social communication, emotional regulation, and transactional supports.

Chapter 7

The SCERTS Assessment Process
Overview and Implementation

We begin this chapter with a definition of terms about assessment to clarify the purpose and scope of the SCERTS Assessment Process (SAP). We then describe how the SAP is different from traditional assessment approaches, delineate the parts of the SAP, and describe in some detail the steps for administering the SAP.

DEFINITION OF TERMS ABOUT ASSESSMENT

From a broad perspective, assessment is the measurement of a child's knowledge, abilities, and achievement (Meisels, 1996). There is not a clear boundary between assessment and intervention (or educational programming); rather, assessment should be viewed as part of the educational programming process. The purpose of assessment for young children is twofold: 1) to identify or rule out the existence of a developmental problem and 2) to understand the nature of the developmental problem to guide educational programming decisions.

The regulations governing the implementation of the Individuals with Disabilities Education Act (IDEA) Amendments of 1997 (PL 105-17) distinguish between the terms *evaluation* and *assessment* (Early Intervention Programs, 2004, § 300.322[2][b]). *Evaluation* refers to the process used to determine a child's initial and continuing eligibility for services and includes screening, developmental evaluation, and diagnostic evaluation. Screening may be the first step in evaluation and includes the process of referral and identification of children who are at high risk of having developmental delays or disabilities and thus need to have an evaluation. Developmental evaluation is the process of confirming the presence or absence or a delay or disability and determining eligibility for services. Diagnostic evaluation is a more in-depth process of examining the nature of or classification of the developmental delay or disability. *Assessment* refers to the ongoing procedures used to document a child's unique strengths and needs as well as the family's concerns, priorities, and resources regarding the child's development, to plan intervention or educational programming services (Crais, 1995). Assessment should provide information about a child's abilities or specific skills across domains as well as guidelines for educational programming. Assessment would usually be done after the evaluation when it has been determined that a child needs an IEP or an IFSP. *The SAP is designed to meet the purpose of assessment for intervention or educational planning. The SAP would only be implemented with a child who is suspected of having ASD or another developmental disability affecting social communication and emotional regulation and who therefore needs an IEP or an IFSP.*

The tools and strategies used for evaluation may be very different from those used for assessment because of their distinct purposes. Evaluation typically is conducted during a brief period, typically using one or more testing sessions and using standardized, norm-referenced evaluation instruments. Norm-referenced instruments use measurements that rank or compare a child's performance with that of a group. Both the testing and the scoring procedures are standardized and present normative scores that describe the average performance of groups of children. In contrast, assessment procedures are ongoing and usually entail multiple strategies and sources of information using criterion-referenced or curriculum-based instruments.

The SAP is a criterion-referenced, curriculum-based tool designed for assessment. Criterion-referenced instruments measure a child's level of performance, degree of mastery on specific tasks, or expected developmental skills within a domain. Often developmental progressions are used as guidelines for standards of the domains assessed. For example, developmental progressions in language or imaginative play may be used as the standards to document a child's behavior as part of the assessment process. Criterion-referenced measures are more appropriate than norm-referenced measures for educational planning because they provide specific information about what a child can do on each task, as well as the developmental skills that are present, emerging, or absent. Curriculum-based assessments are criterion-referenced tools that measure a child's performance on skills or objectives that are part of a curriculum.

The SAP is a curriculum-based assessment, which is a criterion-referenced tool that is linked to the SCERTS Model curriculum (described in Volume II), and many of the items in the SAP are based on developmental progressions documented in research on the development of children with and without disabilities. For example, one objective for Social Communication at the Social Partner stage is that a child *spontaneously imitates familiar actions or sounds immediately after a model,* with the criterion being *The child accurately imitates or closely approximates a familiar action or sound spontaneously (i.e., without direction to do so) immediately after a partner models the behavior. The child imitates at least two different behaviors. A familiar action or sound is one that the child will readily display spontaneously (e.g., clapping, imitating animal sounds).* The child's behavior is measured against this standard for the child to receive credit for this ability.

Curriculum-based refers to the fact that the focus of what is being assessed is directly tied to a curriculum or sequence of goals and objectives that is developmentally based and that will be used to guide the process of program planning for a child. In the example just given, if the child is not demonstrating this ability of spontaneous imitation, it may be an appropriate objective to target in educational programming as part of the curriculum sequence. The SAP is not a norm-referenced tool. That is, it is not based on comparing a child's observable behavior with that of a sample group of children selected from a large population of children. Therefore, it is not designed for *evaluation,* which is intended to provide developmental age equivalents, standard scores, or percentile rankings based on normative data. *The SAP is not intended to serve the purpose of determining, based on quantitative data, whether a child has a disability. It is designed for profiling relative strengths, needs, and priorities to inform program development and goal setting and to monitor progress.*

THE SCERTS ASSESSMENT PROCESS VERSUS TRADITIONAL ASSESSMENT APPROACHES

Serious concerns have been raised about the use of traditional, norm-referenced testing practices for young children with special needs. Neisworth and Bagnato stated

It is long overdue for our interdisciplinary fields to *abandon decontextualized testing practices* and to champion the use of measurement techniques that capture authentic portraits of the naturally occurring competencies of young exceptional children in everyday settings and routines—the natural developmental ecology for children. (2004, p. 198)

More specific to communication and social-emotional development, approaches to the assessment of communication and related abilities traditionally have focused on the structure or form of language (e.g., producing and understanding words and sentences) and are based on having children respond to requests in adult-directed tasks, most often outside the context of everyday functional activities. Likewise, assessments of a child's emotional regulatory abilities often are restricted to caregiver questionnaires and behavior sampling directly related to sensory processing difficulties, rather than to the child's ability to employ regulatory skills and maintain engagement in the context of meaningful daily activities. As discussed in Chapters 2 and 3 of this volume, the communication and emotional regulatory difficulties associated with ASD and related disabilities are most apparent in the areas of social use of speech, language, and nonverbal communication across communicative partners and activities and the ability to maintain a well-regulated state to support availability for learning and engaging socially. Because most formal assessment instruments focus primarily on language form outside the context of everyday activities, they often provide little insight into a child's unique profile of strengths and needs in the critical areas of social communication and emotional regulation across settings and partners. Therefore, those instruments also are of limited use in determining meaningful goals and teaching strategies.

Research and theory on how children acquire language and social-communicative abilities suggest that the following features are critical to the assessment of communication and emotional regulation in children with significant social-communicative problems:

1. Social communication and emotional regulation should be assessed within interactive, meaningful contexts and everyday activities in which a child has opportunities to initiate communication and social interaction and in which the child may experience challenges to emotional regulation.

2. Caregivers, teachers, and other familiar partners should be integrally involved in assessments 1) as active participants in assessment activities, 2) as informants about a child's abilities, and 3) as collaborators in programmatic decision making.

3. Assessment should not only identify relative developmental weaknesses but should also provide information about relative strengths in social communication, emotional regulation, and related areas of development.

4. Assessment should be viewed as a dynamic process in which a child's capacity for developing social-communicative and emotional regulatory capacities is understood across partners and settings and over time.

Wetherby and Prizant (1992) identified several major limitations of the most frequently used communication assessment instruments. We briefly consider each limitation and note how the SCERTS Model addresses each assessment challenge:

1. Most assessment approaches do not allow for the family to collaborate in decision making about the assessment process or to participate to the extent desired by family members and thus are not family centered. In the SCERTS Model, assessment information is gathered across a variety of social contexts (home, community, and school), including activities with family members. Furthermore, parents are asked to provide information on questionnaires or through interviews (i.e.,

SCERTS Assessment Process–Report, or SAP-R), and to make judgments about the accuracy of assessment results so that professionals know whether they are obtaining an accurate picture of the child.

2. Most assessment approaches are primarily adult directed, placing the child being assessed in a respondent role and thus limiting observations of spontaneous, initiated communication. In the SCERTS Model, there is an emphasis on gathering information about social communication, emotional regulation, and related abilities as a child spontaneously participates in communicative interactions as part of everyday activities with a variety of partners. We also use a variety of assessment contexts and activities that vary in structure, social complexity, and sensory-motor demands, depending on the information being gathered.

3. Most formal instruments emphasize language milestones and forms of communication (e.g., number of different sounds, words, word combinations), rather than social communication in everyday interactions and the social-communicative and symbolic foundations of language and communicative competence. In the SCERTS Model, assessment focuses on the functional use of language and nonverbal communication, social-emotional abilities such as specific aspects of social interaction and emotional regulation, and play. In this way, an individual child's relative strengths and weaknesses, as well as coping strategies may be identified. Thus, in the SCERTS Model, we address the critical need to move toward more authentic assessment of children with ASD by ensuring ecological validity of assessment practices and by using dynamic assessment to explore aspects of contexts that support or impede a child's acquisition of communicative competence and emotional regulatory abilities.

Assessment of a child's developing capacities is most relevant when it pinpoints specific educational goals and teaching strategies, that is, when it provides specific directions for education and treatment. Limitations in intentional communication, language comprehension, emotional regulation, and associated developmental discontinuities and problem behaviors make it very difficult to rely on standardized and other formal instruments for many children with ASD. We cannot, therefore, take for granted that children with ASD understand the social expectations and have the social knowledge and the regulatory capacities necessary for the successful use of formal, adult-directed tools. Likewise, the utility of formal testing for the purposes of educational planning has significant limitations, particularly at more advanced developmental stages. Visual, linguistic, and contextual cues are, in fact, rarely static (i.e., fixed in place), as presented within a formal language or developmental testing battery. Rather, successful processing of social, linguistic, visual, and situational cues requires the ability to *rapidly register and integrate* multiple pieces of information (e.g., verbal, visual) within spontaneous and quickly paced interactions. Thus, difficulties in processing multimodal, transient information often are overlooked on formal testing and are best captured within observations of relatively natural social exchanges in everyday activities. In the SCERTS Model, a variety of assessment techniques are used to capture the most accurate and representative picture of a child's abilities across a variety of settings and social partners. This yields a profile of a child's strengths and needs, which is critical in determining how social communication, emotional regulation, and related abilities may be enhanced.

RANGE OF ASSESSMENT APPROACHES IN THE SCERTS MODEL

Assessment is an ongoing process rather than an end in itself; therefore, different assessment approaches are used in the SCERTS Model, including interviews and questionnaires, naturalistic observational assessment, behavior sampling, and semistructured assessment. Assessment approaches vary in the degree of structure and intrusion that is imposed on the assessment context and the child. Figure 7.1 presents a continuum of assessment options from less intrusive to more intrusive.

The variability in children's behavior, particularly as observed in children with ASD across contexts and partners, necessitates the use of multiple assessment strategies implemented in different contexts and over time. Furthermore, if significant variability in social communication and emotional regulation is documented as it relates to different contexts and communicative partners, such variability may then be investigated further because factors that may affect social communication and emotional regulation are greatly influenced by characteristics of the social context and partners. In other words, it is important to identify the factors in different situations that contribute to a child's behavioral variability. The range of possible assessment strategies includes the following.

1. *Interviewing significant others and/or having familiar people complete assessment questionnaires* is an important initial method for gathering information about a child's social communication, emotional regulation, and related abilities. This approach is considered the least intrusive because information is gathered without any direct observation or interaction with a child. People who know a child well and spend time with the child in different settings and who may be familiar with the child's development over time are essential resources and can potentially provide a wealth of information about a child's abilities. The SCERTS Model uses information reported by family members or teachers who can serve in this capacity through questionnaires referred to as the SAP-R, or through an interview process guided by the SAP-Report (SAP-R) Form. In this initial stage of information gathering, interviews and questionnaires also allow professionals:

    a. To begin to develop a trusting relationship with parents and other caregivers

    b. To ask parents and other caregivers about their perception of the child's strengths and needs

    c. To determine the priorities of parents and/or other primary caregivers for intervention services

    d. To respond to any general questions the parents may have that may not be directly related to their child's assessment or future services

2. *Observation of daily activities that occur in natural environments* is the next least intrusive approach. In this approach, important information is gathered about a child's spontaneous communication and emotional regulatory capacities in relatively

Figure 7.1. Approaches to assessment.

comfortable and familiar situations. Such observations may be made across school, home, and community settings. Naturalistic observation also provides information about motivating activities and transactional support (interpersonal and learning support) that have already been implemented, and has the potential to capture the most accurate picture of child's functional abilities in daily activities. In the SCERTS Model, we refer to this part of the assessment process as the SCERTS Assessment Process–Observation (SAP-O).

3. *Behavior sampling and elicited responses* may also be used, when appropriate, to address more specific questions about a child's social-communicative and emotional regulatory abilities. Behavior sampling involves the use of activities that are set up specifically to gather a sample of a child's social-communicative and emotional regulatory response to specific challenges posed to the child. For behavior sampling, there is no right or wrong response. The information gathered is used to develop a profile of the child's abilities. For example, at the Social Partner stage, a snack activity may be used in which a child must make choices, request actions, or protest undesired choices. In elicited responses, more specific abilities may be targeted. For example, at the Language Partner stage, a child may be asked a number of *wh*-questions during a play activity, and his or her responses to different questions may be documented to determine the number and complexity of *wh*-questions the child is able to respond to, thus providing direct information for determining goals. At the Conversational Partner stage, a conversational sample could be gathered by initiating a range of developmentally appropriate topics and gathering information related to the child's understanding of social conventions for exchanging turns and/or his or her awareness of the listener's need for background information related to past events. Behavior sampling for emotional regulatory abilities may look similar across the partner stages and may include creating opportunities to observe a child in situations that may put the child at risk for dysregulation such as making transitions away from a preferred activity, participating in a new environment, and/or engaging in a dynamic environment (e.g., caregivers leaving an ongoing activity). Specific information may be gathered about social communication and emotional regulation with both behavior sampling and elicited responses; however, responses are not typically related to normative data. Rather, the child's behavior is compared with established criteria that are either individualized (i.e., clinician-designed probe) or part of a curricular-based assessment tool, such as the SAP. In the SCERTS Model, behavior sampling may also be used as part of the SAP-O.

4. *Standardized testing is the most intrusive and restrictive form of assessment* because there are constraints on both the assessor, in reference to how test items are presented or administered, and on the child, because responses are determined to be correct or incorrect based on predetermined criteria. Furthermore, a child's performance is compared with that of other children, yielding a numeric score, developmental age, and/or percentile ranking. Although some standardized testing serves the purposes of determining developmental levels and eligibility for services, it is not used as part of the SAP, which is designed as an assessment for intervention planning, a purpose for which most standardized tests were not designed. In summary, in the SAP, assessment approaches are developed on an individual basis from the options just discussed, except for standardized testing, and the approaches used are individualized and depend on the child and the specific questions asked.

Since, by nature, social-communicative disabilities not only affect the child but also his or her partners, the challenges are not isolated to child variables alone. Thus, the SAP is not limited to the assessment of child variables only; it is extended across situations and people, including the transactional support that may or may not be available for supporting social communication and emotional regulation. Assessment of these factors is critical, as the SCERTS Model places high priority on supporting children's capacities across contexts and partners.

ASSESSMENT PRACTICES FOR SUPPORTING FAMILIES USED IN THE SCERTS MODEL

We now highlight assessment principles and practices employed during the SAP that are critical in supporting families.

1. *The SAP is designed to yield useful information directly linked to educational programming, which is compatible and consistent with the needs expressed by the family.* When parents play an active role and are satisfied with the assessment process and the information they receive, positive and trusting parent–professional relationships are supported. However, major mistrust and tension can develop between parents and professionals when families receive information that they feel is not helpful or is only marginally relevant, especially when they must expend considerable emotional energy and, in some cases, fiscal resources in pursuing assessments to answer questions they may have. Far too often, parents feel they do not receive honest and frank answers to their questions, even when they are clear about their primary reasons for seeking an assessment. In the SAP, all efforts are made to support parents in making assessment a meaningful and positive experience that addresses their primary questions.

2. *The SAP always involves direct observation of a child in natural activities and settings and should use multiple sources of information.* In the SCERTS Model, direct observation across activities and settings is incorporated as part of the SAP. Checklists and questionnaires completed by individuals familiar with the child in a variety of settings are also used. Videotapes provided by parents may also provide an opportunity to observe a child in natural activities or different settings. The results of using multiple sources of information are a more accurate picture of a child and a clear and concrete message to parents that assessment practices are committed to developing a comprehensive understanding of a child's strengths and needs.

3. *In the SAP, parents and family members are recognized, respected, and supported as experts about their child.* The SAP acknowledges the expertise of family members as they are asked to share their observations of the child's strengths or assets, as well as their primary concerns and priorities. They are also asked to validate whether the SAP captures an accurate picture of the child. Parents are requested to specify the information they wish to acquire from the SAP and the major concerns of the family. When parents are actively engaged in the SAP, not only are they educated about the process itself, but also there is more of an opportunity to build a consensus about a child's developmental strengths and needs based on a shared set of observations.

4. *Following the SAP, immediate feedback is given to parents and directly addresses the strengths and needs of the child.* As part of the SAP, primary concerns identified by the family are addressed directly, and ample time is provided for questions and discussion. The manner in which professionals provide assessment feedback has a profound effect on parents' perceptions of their child, of themselves as parents, and of the professionals involved in the assessment. Stated simply, the behavior of professionals directly contributes to parents' perceptions of professionals as being helpful or as an additional source of stress, and the SAP attempts to support positive relationships from the onset of the process.

5. To the extent possible, information shared throughout and subsequent to the SAP is presented with a minimal amount of technical language or professional jargon, and when jargon must be used, terms are fully explained to caregivers. ASD is an extremely complex spectrum of disabilities, for professionals as well as family members. This complexity is exacerbated when families receive information that is difficult to decipher and use, whether it is received verbally or in written form. In general, to the extent possible, professionals must provide feedback and respond to questions at a level appropriate to family members' understanding. As it may be difficult for professionals to completely avoid technical jargon, parents should be offered detailed explanations and, as noted, ample time to ask questions. In the SAP, efforts are made to clearly explain any jargon that may be unavoidable and to discuss a child's profile in a manner that can be understood and validated by parents.

Special Considerations Regarding the Role of Brothers and Sisters in Assessment

In the SAP, brothers and sisters are recognized as a unique source of information and as important partners. Therefore, to the extent possible, they should be actively included in assessment. Of course, the specific types of involvement depend on the age and developmental abilities of the brother or sister, the nature of assessment activities (e.g., SAP-R questionnaires versus observation of activities), and the location of assessment activities (e.g., home versus school or center based).

Depending on these factors, brothers and sisters may be involved in assessment in a variety of ways and play multiple assessment roles similar to caregivers. First, parents may be encouraged to ask brothers and sisters to provide information when filling out the SAP-R. Siblings may have unique opportunities, experiences, and observations of their brother or sister that parents do not have. This strategy is consistent with the use of multiple informants in assessment, a SCERTS Model assessment strategy used as part of the SAP.

Second, brothers and sisters may be direct participants in assessment by engaging in play interactions either during a clinic- or home-based observational assessment or during other observations of natural routines (included as part of the SAP-O). In such circumstances, it is helpful to observe everyday routines such as snack or mealtime and provide siblings with choices of play activities to encourage interactions to be as natural as possible. For clinic- or school-based assessments involving a brother or sister, caregivers can be encouraged to bring favorite toys or activities used by the children in play interactions at home so that relatively familiar routines may be observed. Alternatively, introduction of new toys or activities provides an opportunity to observe interactive patterns and whether and how the sibling may assume a teaching or supportive role. The types of communicative adjustments and successful strategies that brothers and sisters demonstrate to foster successful communication and to support emotional regulation may be an important source of information in planning educational efforts. On the other hand, if there are significant interactive difficulties, these may also be observed and addressed directly in working with siblings and caregivers, especially when caregivers identify such concerns as a priority goal in educational programming.

Third, brothers and sisters may also fulfill the role as interpreter of subtle, unconventional, or unintelligible language and communicative behavior or signals of dysregulation. This role is most relevant for a child with ASD who has limited conventional means to communicate, as may be observed for a child at the Social Partner stage or even at an early Language Partner stage. In our experience, it is striking how often parents report that brothers and sisters are better interpreters of the communication of their child with ASD than are adults. Therefore, siblings should be considered potential valuable resources in explaining what a child is attempting to communicate and in reading signals of dysregulation. Educators may encourage brothers and sisters to interpret communicative signals or signs of dysregulation during play interactions by asking the sibling what the brother or sister means or is attempting to communicate or how they know their brother or sister is becoming upset.

Fourth, brothers and sisters may also play the role of validators of observations, that is, providing information as to whether the child's behavior as observed is typical of what the sibling usually sees. Finally, older siblings who have a more clear awareness and understanding of the child's disability may be asked to discuss situations in which the child has the greatest difficulty and strategies that are most successful in helping the child to communicate, stay well-regulated emotionally, and participate successfully in social interaction.

A few notes of caution are in order when brothers and sisters are involved in the assessment process as just described. First, they should be given an explanation as to why the assessment is occurring. Usually, a simple explanation for young children will suffice, such as, "We would like to see how you play with blocks with Justin so that we can get an idea of how Justin plays and communicates. Is that okay?" Second, siblings should always be voluntary participants in assessment activities and should be given the option to decline. Praise should be given to siblings for their participation; however, a sibling's discomfort or refusal should be accepted and respected, with no negative consequences. In addition, siblings should be commended for specific aspects of their interpersonal behavior that supports the child's social communication and emotional regulation. For example, siblings may be praised for use of specific adjustments such as simplifying linguistic input, modeling, and encouraging communicative initiation and play by following their brother's or sister's interests.

Seven Ways to Be Family-Centered in Assessment Practices

In addition to the principles discussed previously, the following are seven specific ways to be family-centered in assessment practices that we recommend and/or use in implementing the SAP:

1. Make a personal contact (telephone or visit) before the date of the first formal meeting to discuss the SAP.

2. In early stages of implementing the SAP, always ask families, "What is the information you hope to get from this assessment?" and be sure to address those questions when giving live feedback and in the assessment report.

3. Invite family members to be actively involved in the assessment by observing the child in activities with family members in familiar settings or by bringing familiar activities in the office, clinic, or school where assessment is to take place.

4. Ask parents to rate how typical the child's behavior was during the SAP-O, and note any variations from reports of typical behavior in the assessment report. In the SAP, we document this information in the Family Perception and Priorities section of the SAP Summary Form (SAP Sum).

5. Provide ample opportunity for feedback and discussion during and following the SAP (SAP Sum).

6. Integrate parents' observations or comments about their child's behavior and development directly in the body of the report, to validate their collaborative role in the assessment process and to acknowledge their expertise about their child.

7. Provide parents with the opportunity to 1) provide feedback about the report, 2) edit the report for inaccuracies or omitted information, and 3) approve the accuracy of the final report before it is signed and distributed.

OVERVIEW OF THE SCERTS ASSESSMENT PROCESS

To provide for the type of educational approach advocated in the SCERTS Model, assessment is designed to focus on a child's current capacity for social communication and emotional regulation in a variety of natural environments and to document current transactional supports that are effective for the child and/or his or her partners. The primary function of the SAP is to provide information that can be directly translated into goals for enhancing social-communicative and emotional regulatory abilities and that can be used in the documentation of educational efforts. In fact, we see assessment and educational programming as dynamically interwoven: assessment guides educational programming intervention, and progress toward educational goals continues to refine and expand assessment questions. Assessment must be a multistage process.

The SAP is an ongoing assessment process. It is completed initially as the starting point of assessment to gather sufficient information on social communication, emotional regulation, and transactional support in a relatively brief period. The function of the initial assessment is to accurately document a child's developmental profile of strengths and needs and the family's priorities, from which initial educational goals and strategies are derived. Furthermore, additional assessment questions may be raised that require further consideration. Because the SCERTS Model is a curriculum-based assessment, a child's changing profile of strengths and needs is documented on an ongoing basis to track meaningful change in social communication, emotional regulation, and transactional support. Ongoing assessment serves a variety of purposes, including the following:

1. Documentation of progress, which allows for adjustments in goals and strategies

2. Identification of developmental areas that are particularly challenging and that require a more in-depth consideration of goals and strategies

3. Documentation of new questions that arise as a child progresses, including a plan to address those questions

A child's progress on Social Communication and Emotional Regulation objectives is tracked on daily logs, summarized on weekly logs, and updated quarterly with the SAP-R and SAP-O. This ongoing monitoring of progress informs the team as to whether changes in programming are needed.

Thus, the SAP is an ongoing assessment process

1. To establish a child's profile of developmental strengths and needs

2. To determine meaningful, purposeful, and motivating goals based on a child's profile and functional needs

3. To select the most appropriate learning contexts and teaching strategies

4. To determine the necessary transactional support (i.e., interpersonal support, learning support, support to families, support to professionals)

5. To monitor progress over time

Furthermore, the SAP does not focus primarily on limitations or deficits; it also identifies specific developmental strengths and motivations, emerging abilities, and other critical factors that contribute to the enhancement of social communication, emotional regulation, and related abilities.

The SAP is guided by core questions about social communication (i.e., joint attention and symbol use), emotional regulation (i.e., mutual and self-regulation), and transactional support (e.g., interpersonal and learning support), which are continually redefined on the basis of a child's overall developmental level, functional needs, and preliminary assessment outcomes. These core assessment questions pertain not only to the Social Communication, Emotional Regulation, and Transactional Support domains of the SCERTS Model but also to the interrelationship among these domains so that areas of greatest needs as well as strengths are identified in a comprehensive manner.

SCERTS Assessment Process Domains, Components, Goals, Objectives, and Stages

The SAP addresses three domains—Social Communication, Emotional Regulation, and Transactional Support. Each domain is divided into two core curricular components. Joint Attention and Symbol Use are the core components of the Social Communication domain; Mutual Regulation and Self-Regulation are the core components of the Emotional Regulation domain; and Interpersonal Support and Learning Support are the core curricular components of the Transactional Support domain. The Transactional Support domain has two additional components at the program level, support to families and support among professionals, which are addressed in greater detail in Chapter 4 of this volume and Chapter 3 of Volume II. Goals in each component are addressed with reference to three stages of social communication development—the Social Partner, Language Partner, and Conversational Partner stages. The goals for each core component in the three SAP domains at each language stage are presented in Tables 7.1–7.3. In the SAP, each goal is subdivided into objectives with specific criteria.

In addition to profiling abilities in social communication, emotional regulation, and transactional support, a child's scores on selected SAP objectives are combined to measure progress on eight Social-Emotional Growth Indicators. These indicators reflect common priorities and concerns expressed by parents and professionals about children with ASD in everyday discussions. Collectively, these indicators are a composite of a child's growth in social and emotional development, which influences the child's engagement with the environment and people and capacity to learn. The eight Social-Emotional Growth Indicators measured on the SAP are as follows:

1. *Happiness:* the capacity to experience and express positive emotion from everyday activities

2. *Sense of Self:* the capacity to take pride in one's special qualities and achievements

3. *Sense of Other:* the capacity to understand the perspective of others

4. *Active Learning and Organization:* the capacity to be engaged actively and organized in learning activities

5. *Flexibility and Resilience:* the ability to flow with changes and stick with new challenges

6. *Cooperation and Appropriateness of Behavior:* the capacity to cooperate and regulate behavior in social interaction

7. *Independence:* the ability to use one's own resources to be successful

8. *Social Membership and Friendships:* the capacity to be part of a social group and develop a network of friends

Table 7.1. Social Partner stage: Overview of the domains, components, and goals in the SCERTS Assessment Process (SAP)

SOCIAL COMMUNICATION	EMOTIONAL REGULATION	TRANSACTIONAL SUPPORT
Joint Attention	**Mutual Regulation**	**Interpersonal Support**
JA1 Engages in reciprocal interaction	MR1 Expresses range of emotions	IS1 Partner is responsive to child
JA2 Shares attention	MR2 Responds to assistance offered by partners	IS2 Partner fosters initiation
JA3 Shares emotion	MR3 Requests partners' assistance to regulate state	IS3 Partner respects child's independence
JA4 Shares intentions to regulate the behavior of others	MR4 Recovers from extreme dysregulation with support from partners	IS4 Partner sets stage for engagement
JA5 Shares intentions for social interaction		IS5 Partner provides developmental support
JA6 Shares intentions for joint attention	**Self-Regulation**	IS6 Partner adjusts language input
JA7 Persists and repairs communication breakdowns	SR1 Demonstrates availability for learning and interacting	IS7 Partner models appropriate behaviors
	SR2 Uses behavioral strategies to regulate arousal level during familiar activities	**Learning Support**
Symbol Use	SR3 Regulates emotion in new and changing situations	LS1 Partner structures activity for active participation
SU1 Learns by imitation of familiar actions and sounds	SR4 Recovers from extreme dysregulation by self	LS2 Partner uses augmentative communication support to foster development
SU2 Understands nonverbal cues in familiar activities		LS3 Partner uses visual and organizational support
SU3 Uses familiar objects conventionally in play		LS4 Partner modifies goals, activities, and learning environment
SU4 Uses gestures and nonverbal means to share intentions		
SU5 Uses vocalizations to share intentions		
SU6 Understands a few familiar words		

Table 7.2. Language Partner stage: Overview of the domains, components, and goals in the SCERTS Assessment Process (SAP)

SOCIAL COMMUNICATION

Joint Attention

JA1 Engages in reciprocal interaction

JA2 Shares attention

JA3 Shares emotion

JA4 Shares intentions to regulate the behavior of others

JA5 Shares intentions for social interaction

JA6 Shares intentions for joint attention

JA7 Persists and repairs communication breakdowns

JA8 Shares experiences in reciprocal interaction

Symbol Use

SU1 Learns by observation and imitation of familiar and unfamiliar actions and words

SU2 Understands nonverbal cues in familiar and unfamiliar activities

SU3 Uses familiar objects conventionally in play

SU4 Uses gestures and nonverbal means to share intentions

SU5 Uses words and word combinations to express meanings

SU6 Understands a variety of words and word combinations without contextual cues

EMOTIONAL REGULATION

Mutual Regulation

MR1 Expresses range of emotions

MR2 Responds to assistance offered by partners

MR3 Requests partners' assistance to regulate state

MR4 Recovers from extreme dysregulation with support from partners

Self-Regulation

SR1 Demonstrates availability for learning and interacting

SR2 Uses behavioral strategies to regulate arousal level during familiar activities

SR3 Uses language strategies to regulate arousal level during familiar activities

SR4 Regulates emotion during new and changing situations

SR5 Recovers from extreme dysregulation by self

TRANSACTIONAL SUPPORT

Interpersonal Support

IS1 Partner is responsive to child

IS2 Partner fosters initiation

IS3 Partner respects child's independence

IS4 Partner sets stage for engagement

IS5 Partner provides developmental support

IS6 Partner adjusts language input

IS7 Partner models appropriate behaviors

Learning Support

LS1 Partner structures activity for active participation

LS2 Partner uses augmentative communication support to foster development

LS3 Partner uses visual and organizational support

LS4 Partner modifies goals, activities, and learning environment

Table 7.3. Conversational Partner stage: Overview of the domains, components, and goals in the SCERTS Assessment Process (SAP)

SOCIAL COMMUNICATION

Joint Attention

JA1 Shares attention

JA2 Shares emotion

JA3 Shares intentions for a variety of purposes

JA4 Shares experiences in reciprocal interaction

JA5 Persists and repairs communication breakdowns

Symbol Use

SU1 Learns by imitation, observation, instruction, and collaboration

SU2 Understands nonverbal cues and nonliteral meanings in reciprocal interactions

SU3 Participates conventionally in dramatic play and recreation

SU4 Uses appropriate gestures and nonverbal behavior for the context

SU5 Understands and uses generative language to express meanings

SU6 Follows rules of conversation

EMOTIONAL REGULATION

Mutual Regulation

MR1 Expresses range of emotions

MR2 Responds to assistance offered by partners

MR3 Responds to feedback and guidance regarding behavior

MR4 Requests partners' assistance to regulate state

MR5 Recovers from extreme dysregulation with support from partners

Self-Regulation

SR1 Demonstrates availability for learning and interacting

SR2 Uses behavioral strategies to regulate arousal level during familiar activities

SR3 Uses language strategies to regulate arousal level during familiar activities

SR4 Uses metacognitive strategies to regulate arousal level during familiar activities

SR5 Regulates emotion during new and changing situations

SR6 Recovers from extreme dysregulation by self

TRANSACTIONAL SUPPORT

Interpersonal Support

IS1 Partner is responsive to child

IS2 Partner fosters initiation

IS3 Partner respects child's independence

IS4 Partner sets stage for engagement

IS5 Partner provides developmental support

IS6 Partner adjusts language input

IS7 Partner models appropriate behaviors

Learning Support

LS1 Partner structures activity for active participation

LS2 Partner uses augmentative communication support to foster development

LS3 Partner uses visual and organizational support

LS4 Partner modifies goals, activities, and learning environment

IMPLEMENTING THE SCERTS ASSESSMENT PROCESS

In the SAP, information is gathered from multiple sources using the SAP-R for information reported by parents, teachers, and/or other familiar caregivers and the SAP-O for information based on naturalistic observation and, if needed, using behavior sampling. Following are detailed descriptions of the steps involved in implementing the SAP.

Step 1: Determine the Child's Communication Stage

The first step in implementing the SAP is to determine the child's communication stage as a first step because the SAP-R and SAP-O each have three different forms, one for each of the three major stages of communication development, Social Partner, Language Partner, and Conversational Partner, which are described in detail in Chapter 2 of this volume.

Determining a child's communication stage for the SAP is based on answers to questions about the child's expressive communication that appear on the Worksheet for Determining Communication Stage. This worksheet lists each set of questions as a series of separate yes/no questions. Information from family members and educational staff who interact with the child on a regular basis should be used to answer these questions. This information may be gathered by reviewing the child's records or by interviewing caregivers by telephone or in person. The questions should be answered in the order listed. If any question is answered *no,* the appropriate communication stage forms can be determined and subsequent questions do not need to be answered. For example, if Question 1a is answered *no,* then the Social Partner stage forms should be used and no further questions need to be considered. If a question is answered *yes,* then proceed to the next question. For the first set of questions, a *yes* answer is required for all four questions (i.e., 1a, 1b, 1c, and 1d) to proceed to the second set of questions. If the answer is *no* to any of these questions, this would indicate that the child is not yet solidly using words and that the Social Partner stage forms should be used for the SAP. If the answer to all four of these questions is *yes,* this would indicate that the child is using words and that the second set of questions needs to be answered to decide whether to use the Language Partner or Conversational Partner forms.

A similar process should be followed in answering the second set of questions. If any question is answered *no,* the appropriate communication stage can be determined and subsequent questions do not need to be answered. For example, if the answer to Question 2a is *no,* then the Language Partner stage forms should be used and no further questions need to be considered. If a question is answered *yes,* then proceed to the next question. If the answer is *no* to any of the questions in the second set (i.e., 2a, 2b, 2c, 2d, and 2e), this would indicate that the child is not yet solidly using a variety of words and phrases and that the Language Partner stage forms should be used for the SAP. If the answer to all five of these questions is *yes,* this indicates that the child is using a variety of words and phrases and that the Conversational Partner stage forms should be used. For example, consider the following:

> Joey is 30 months old and communicates primarily with contact gestures (e.g., giving objects; simple motor actions such as pulling another's hand), guttural vocalizations, the protoword "ma" for "more," and has tantrums to protest or refuse. The SAP forms for the Social Partner stage should be used for Joey.

> Mary is 4 years old and communicates with immediate echolalia and about 10 different spontaneous words or phrases. The SAP forms for the Language Partner stage should be used for Mary.

John is 7 years old, uses well over 100 words, and regularly combines words creatively in phrases. However, John has very limited ability to engage in conversation, especially with peers. The SAP forms for the Conversational Partner stage should be used for John.

If there is any doubt about a child's communication stage, it is better to err on the side of underestimating and use the earlier communication stage to ensure that information is gathered about critical foundation skills.

The domains of Social Communication and Emotional Regulation are organized developmentally, when appropriate, so that foundation skills build from stage to stage. Although some overlap is included across the stages to check that children have acquired the foundation skills from earlier stages, new skills are added at each stage. The domain of Transactional Support has much overlap across stages, and developmental expectations are reflected in the criteria.

Special Considerations for Children Who Use Echolalia

As noted in Chapter 2 of this volume, the majority of children with ASD who do learn to talk go through a period of using echolalia, the imitation of speech of others, either immediately (i.e., immediate echolalia) or at some time later (i.e., delayed echolalia; Prizant et al., 1997). An echolalic utterance may be equivalent to a single word or a label for a situation or event. Current understanding of echolalia indicates that it may serve a variety of communicative and cognitive functions (Prizant & Rydell, 1993) and often represents a productive language learning strategy for many children with ASD, not unlike imitation for typically developing children. The way children who use echolalia learn to talk is by imitating phrases associated with situations or emotional states, then learning meanings by using phrases and seeing how they work. Over time, many children learn to use these gestalt forms purposefully in communicative interactions and eventually are able to break down the echolalic chunks into smaller meaningful units as part of the process of making the transition to a rule-governed, generative language system. Pronoun reversals (e.g., using "you" to refer to oneself) are a by-product of echolalia because a child repeats the pronoun heard, thus reversing the pronouns used in reference to self and other. For example, a child may use the echolalic utterance "Do you want a piece of candy?" as a way to request candy, although it sounds as if the child is offering it.

In the SCERTS Model, echolalia is one means that a child may use to express intentions and is considered in relation to the repertoire of other means (i.e., gestures, gaze, facial expression, creative speech) that the child uses for social communication. The SAP provides for the documentation of a child's use of echolalia as one aspect of social communication, and movement from echolalia to functional, creative language is targeted and tracked as an important achievement in symbol use. Efforts should be made to determine the size and flexibility of the gestalt forms used by a child with ASD and to help the child acquire creative language by following the developmental progression of language and social-communicative abilities delineated in the stages of the SCERTS Model.

In determining the expressive communication stage for the SAP with a child who uses echolalia, special consideration needs to be given to decisions about how many words and phrases the child has in his or her communicative repertoire. Three major questions should be asked in considering level of language production for echolalia. First, do the echolalic words have referential meaning? That is, are they used to refer to specific objects or events in a relevant manner and only those objects or events? Children who use words or phrases communicatively but not referentially typically cycle through their repertoire of utterances, guessing the object name in an attempt to request an object, until they produce the correct label and the partner provides the desired object.

A second question to be explored in considering a child's language level is how many different words and word combinations are used referentially. For a child with ASD who is producing echolalic utterances, the number of different utterances used referentially may be a better measure of language level than utterance length or complexity. If a child spontaneously produces fewer than 20 different utterances, it is likely that his or her overall language level is at a first-word level rather than at a level of first word combinations, placing the child at the Language Partner stage. A third question for a child who uses word combinations is whether the child uses the individual words alone and in other word combinations or whether an utterance is equivalent to a single word for that child. It is likely that children who do not combine words creatively are functioning at a first-word level of language development rather than at a level of first word combinations, even though they produce multiword units or "gestalt forms" (Prizant & Rydell, 1993) that appear to be indicative of the higher level of word combinations. Although this seems paradoxical, it is important to determine a child's generative language capabilities and not be misled by the surface form of rotely learned utterances or gestalt forms that may give a misleading picture of language competence. Children at the Conversational Partner stage must be using a large number of words and creating generative phrases and thus are likely moving beyond echolalia.

Step 2: Gather Information with the SAP-R Form

The next step in the SAP is to gather information from families and teachers or other caregivers using the SAP-R Form. This can be used as a questionnaire that is filled out by the family independently, or it can be used as a guide during a live interview. We recommend that the SAP-R Form be completed before the SAP-O, if possible, to assist in the planning for the observation. The SAP-R Forms for each of the three communication stages appear in Appendix A of this volume. This section describes the procedures for completing the SAP-R as Step 2 in the SAP. It would be helpful to bookmark the SAP-R Forms in Appendix A to refer to them when reading through this chapter.

Select the SAP-R Form that corresponds with the child's communication stage. The SAP-R Form gathers information about factors contributing to developmental capacities in social communication and emotional regulation and dysregulation and variables related to transactional support. The SAP-R Form also includes a needs assessment for the family to identify 1) the most significant family needs relative to the family's priorities and stresses; 2) the most significant strengths and needs that family members observe in the child; 3) the opportunities to see the child at his "best" and "worst," to determine the best times and places to observe the range of the child's abilities; 4) the child's typical social partners (e.g., immediate family, close friends and relatives, acquaintances, other caregivers, partners in the community), who are sometimes collectively referred to as the child's circle of friends or social network; and 5) the typical contexts of the child's life (e.g., home, child care, playground, school, dance class).

As noted above, the SAP-R Form is designed to be used in one of two ways. It can be used as a questionnaire that is completed by a parent, a teacher, or another adult who has daily or regular interactions with the child. Alternately, it can be used as a guide in an interview that can be completed face-to-face or by telephone. We strongly recommend a face-to-face interview for parents of children who are newly diagnosed and for parents with limited English or reading proficiency or limited education levels. We also recommend that the SAP-R Form be completed as an interview the very first time that it is used with a family to make sure that parents are comfortable with the terminology. We feel that interviewing families to gather information for the SAP-R will help educate families about the SCERTS Model and will set the stage for successful collaboration with families. After the initial interview, the SAP-R can be sent home as a questionnaire for quarterly or annual updates. (Each SAP-R Form is 4 pages long and can be photocopied double sided onto 11″ × 17″ paper and folded, for ease of use and storage.)

Step 3: Identify Assessment Team Members and Plan the SAP-O

The next step in the SAP is to use the SAP Map for Planning the SAP-Observation to identify the assessment team members and their roles and responsibilities and to determine where the observations will take place and who will plan the observation schedule. In addition, team members should consider if any referrals for outside assessments are warranted based on presenting concerns. The SAP is designed to be a team assessment, ideally including family members and professionals from pertinent disciplines (e.g., speech-language pathology, occupational therapy, psychology, early intervention, early childhood special education, general education, applied behavior analysis). First, we describe the variables that need to be considered in planning the SAP-O and then we describe how to plan the SAP-O using the SAP Map.

The SAP-O is designed to gather *representative* information about a child's range of abilities and needs within natural environments, including typical behavior, optimal functioning, and factors and circumstances that are most challenging. Special attention needs to go into planning the observations that will yield this information. So that the SAP-O will gather a representative portrayal of a child and the child's learning environments, we have identified six observational variables that influence the child's behavior and have established guidelines for addressing each of these variables in the observations.

Natural Contexts

Natural contexts include familiar settings that a child spends time in during regularly scheduled activities and routines. Three primary natural contexts should be considered as observational contexts for the SAP-O: the *home* (i.e., where the child sleeps/resides), the child's *learning center or school* (i.e., where the child learns on a frequent basis), and the *community* (i.e., places the family goes on a regular basis).

Threshold for Representative Observation

All children should be observed in either the home or at a learning center or school. It is recommended that all children be observed in at least two contexts. If this is not possible, information about the child's behavior in other contexts can be gathered from the SAP-R Form and/or from videotapes of the child in other natural contexts. If information gathered from parent or teacher report is inconsistent with information gathered from observation, this would indicate that an observation in one or more additional contexts would be needed.

Length of Observation

The representativeness of an observation may be affected by the length of the observation because children's behavior can be variable across a period of time. For the SAP-O, every effort should be made to observe the child for sufficient time to ensure that the information is representative.

Threshold for Representative Observation

Social Partner and Language Partner stages—total observation time that is at least 2 hours in duration

Conversational Partner stage—total observation time that is at least 3–4 hours in duration

We strongly recommend that all children be observed on at least two different days (i.e., at least 1 hour on each day). These are minimum guidelines, and more time or more observations may be needed for children whose behavior is more variable.

Partners

Children's behavior varies according to the familiarity of the partner and the age of the partner relative to the child's age. A familiar partner is one whom the child knows well and interacts with on a regular basis. A child of the same age would be another child who is close to the child's age (i.e., within 6 months for toddlers; within 1 year for preschool children, within 1 or 2 years for elementary-age children) and may be a peer or sibling.

Threshold for Representative Observation

All children should be observed with familiar partners.

Children at the Language and Conversation Partner stages should be observed with both familiar and unfamiliar partners.

Children who are in school or child care settings should be observed with both adults and children.

Group Size

Children's behavior varies according to the adult–child ratio and the number of children in groups. A child can be observed during activities in three possible group sizes—one to one (one adult to one child), small group, and large group—if these group sizes are part of the child's natural routines and activities. What defines the specific sizes of small and large groups depends on the age and stage of the child and the range of opportunities for varying group sizes in the child's natural routines. We offer the following examples as a general guideline: For a toddler at the Social Partner stage, a small group may be two to four other children and a large group may be more than four other children. For a school-age child at the Conversational Partner stage, a small group may be two to eight other children and a large group may be more than eight other children.

Threshold for Representative Observation

Children at the Social, Language, and Conversational Partner stages should be observed in at least two group sizes.

Children not yet in school, child care, or playgroup settings may be observed in only a one-to-one setting if this is most typical of daily routines.

Activity Variables

Children's behavior can vary depending on the nature of the activity. Variables that are likely to influence children's behavior include whether the activity is 1) unstructured versus structured; 2) a must-do caregiving or work activity versus a fun, play activity; 3) adult directed versus child directed, 4) motor based versus sedentary; 5) familiar versus unfamiliar; 6) preferred versus nonpreferred; 7) easy versus difficult; 8) language based versus non–language based or visually supported; 9) social versus solitary; and 10) in a busy, noisy, and cluttered setting versus in a calm, quiet, and soothing setting.

Threshold for Representative Observation

Each child should be observed in at least four activities that vary along at least four variables that are most important for that child. It is critical that a child be observed while he or she is well regulated and, if possible, in varying levels of dysregulation (i.e., mild and extreme, if the child is reported to display extreme dysregulation). For younger children, activities are likely shorter; therefore, the observation should include more activities to meet the minimum criterion for length of observation (discussed previously).

Transitions

Children's behavior can vary as children are faced with transitions. A transition is the point when one activity ends and another begins (e.g., transition from circle time to playground time; transition from eating breakfast to getting ready to leave the house) or when there is a change in the situation during an activity (e.g., Mom leaves the room; a new child joins the group).

Threshold for Representative Observation

All children should be observed during at least three transitions. A transition is defined as when a child is involved in a significant change or disengagement from the initial physical location or from the ongoing focus of attention, including a change of activity, setting, or social partner. A change within an ongoing activity (e.g., introducing new tasks within table work or during circle activities) when other factors remain constant, such as setting or partner, does not qualify as a transition.

Process for Completing the SAP Map

A team meeting should be held to make decisions that are delineated on the SAP Map for Planning the SAP-Observation. If all team members are not available, it is important that the key team members who will be conducting the observation participate in this meeting. It must be decided who will serve as the team leader and complete the SAP Map. The SAP-R should be reviewed to use information about the child's strengths and needs and the family's priorities in planning the observation. Next, the SAP Map should be used to designate the location, date, and time of the observation and the assessment team members who will observe the child and complete the SAP-Observation (SAP-O) Form. The six variables just delineated need to be considered to ensure a representative sample.

The SAP Map provides boxes to fill in for each of the six variables and keys that specify the threshold for representative observations for each language stage.

1. Enter the child's name and the date. Use additional pages if more than two observations are completed, and number each page.

2. Enter the observation numbers: 1 for the first observation number and 2 or higher for subsequent observations.

3. For *Location,* record the specific natural context of the observation (e.g., preschool classroom, home, community playground).

4. For *Date and time,* specify the date and the estimated beginning and ending time of the observation. Calculate the length of the observation, and enter this in the *Length* area.

5. List the team members who will observe the child and who will complete the SAP-O.

6. For *Partners and group size,* list the specific names, titles, or relationships of the partners and the numbers of partners. Include all of the partners and group sizes that will occur during the observation.

7. For *Activities,* describe the different activities that will occur during the observation and list the number of the activity variables that best characterize each activity, using the key for activity variables from 1a to 10b. More than one activity variable can be listed for each activity.

8. For *Transitions,* describe the nature of the change in activity, setting, location, and/or partner for each transition.

For example, for 5-year-old Samantha, circle time is an activity identified as problematic by her teacher and therefore needed to be observed. *Circle time* would be written under *Activities,* and 1a, 3a, 4b, and 6b would be listed under *Variables* because this activity is structured; adult directed; sedentary; and, for this child, nonpreferred. For *Transitions,* the transitions that are anticipated would be described across activities (e.g., *circle time to dramatic play center*) and/or contexts (e.g., *classroom to cafeteria*).

The areas for each observation are completed, and additional pages are used as needed. Make sure to plan at least 2 hours of total observation time for children at the Social Partner and Language Partner stages and at least 3–4 hours of total observation time for children at the Conversational Partner stage, if possible, with this time spread over at least 2 different days.

Step 4: Complete the SAP-O Form

The next step is to observe the child and document information from the observation using the SAP-O Form. The SAP-O Forms for each of the three communication stages are presented in Appendix A in this volume, and the criteria defining each objective for each stage are presented in Chapter 8 of this volume. This section describes the procedures for completing the SAP-O as Step 4 in the SAP. It would be helpful to bookmark the SAP-O Forms and criteria so that you may to refer to them when reading the rest of this chapter. (Chapters 5–7 of Volume II contain filled-in versions of some of the SAP-O Forms and other SAP forms.)

1. Select the SAP-O Form that corresponds with the child's stage of expressive communication (i.e., Social Partner, Language Partner, or Conversational Partner). On the cover page of the SAP-O, enter the child's name, date of birth, pertinent background information (e.g., notable information from a medical or developmental history, allergies), and the team members who will be observing the child. Each SAP-O Form has space to record up to four quarters of SAP-O data for a child; however, if the child has progressed to the next communication stage, that stage's corresponding SAP-O Form would instead need to be used.

2. Enter the date of the first observation for the initial assessment in the box for *Qtr 1 (Quarter 1) start date* in the box labeled *Date of observation.* When the observations are completed, enter the total length of the observations in the box labeled *Length of total observation.*

3. During each observation check off the variables that occur on the cover page of the SAP-O Form to document the representativeness of each observation and the set of observations collectively. That is, on the cover page of the SAP-O Form, check the appropriate box for group size, the familiarity and ages of the partners, and the natural contexts; circle all of the activity variables that apply to each activity; and write a brief description of the transitions as encountered by the child as you are observing the child. You will need to refer back to the cover page periodically during an observation to circle new variables as they occur.

Pages 2–7 of the SAP-O Form are organized into the three domains, two addressing the child's strengths and needs (i.e., Social Communication and Emotional Regulation) and one addressing the partners and environment (i.e., Transactional Support). Given that the SAP is designed to be a team assessment, it is highly desirable to include two or more team members in documenting the child's behaviors during observations. For example, different team members may each document behaviors in each of the three domains, or one team member may document behaviors in the two domains addressing the child's skills (i.e., Social Communication and Emotional Regulation) and another team member may document behaviors addressing transactional support used by partners in the learning environment.

Documenting Observed Behaviors

During the observation, to track the occurrence of behaviors, an assessor may want to put plus (+) signs to the right of behaviors as they are observed. Each domain area has specific skills delineated into behaviors that correspond with goals, which are delineated into objectives. The assessor needs to determine if the child meets the operational criteria provided for each behavior. The objectives for each goal are listed in developmental progression or complexity, if applicable, so that once the child meets all of the objectives under one goal, then that child has achieved that goal. Generally, lower numbered objectives are developmentally easier than (i.e., appear earlier in development) and often are foundational abilities for higher numbered objectives. Because children with ASD may learn different skills at different rates, it is possible that a child may have a higher score for a more advanced objective than for a lower objective under the same goal. For example, for the Social Partner stage, children usually respond to bids for interaction (JA1.1) before they initiate bids for interaction (JA1.2); however, it is possible for a child with ASD to achieve a higher score on JA1.2 than on JA1.1.

It is important to note that there is no ceiling on the SAP-O due to the differential rate of learning just noted. Therefore, all of the objectives for all of the goals should be assessed. In some cases, however, behaviors are ordered developmentally so that a 0 score on a lower objective implies a 0 score on a higher objective for that goal. For example, for the Social Partner stage, if a child does not meet the criteria for JA2.1, *Looks toward people,* then that child would also not meet the criteria for JA2.2, *Shifts gaze between people and objects.* For the Language and Conversational Partner stages, if the child receives lower ratings (e.g., primarily 0 or 1) on the first objective for the majority of the goals, then the team should consider backing up to the previous stage's forms (i.e., change to the Social and Language Partner stage forms, respectively).

Linked Objectives

On the SAP-O Form, three symbols are used to link objectives within or across the Social Communication and Emotional Regulation domains. The symbol = is used when two objectives are identical or nearly identical and are important objectives that fall under more than one component. For example, for the Social Partner stage, JA1.2, *Initiates bids for interaction,* is the same as SR1.4 at that stage. The symbol ≈ is used when two objectives are nearly identical or are so similar they are addressing a common skill or behavior or one objective is addressing a subset of the other objective. We cross-reference objectives to more than one component to indicate the importance of the objective within the component and domain. Referring to the example above, a child's ability to initiate bids for interaction is critical for the developing capacity in both joint attention and self-regulation. There are many objectives that overlap across components and/or domains that reflect the interdependence of the components of Social Communication and Emotional Regulation.

The third symbol used is ↔ which indicates that two objectives should be linked when targeting these objectives in intervention. For example, for the Social Partner stage, Joint Attention objectives for the goal *Shares intentions to regulate behavior* should be linked with Symbol Use objectives for the goal *Uses gestures and nonverbal means to share intentions.* In other words, one objective should be formed that states the communicative intention to be targeted (e.g., JA4.3, *Requests help or other action*) and the means used to express this intention (e.g., SU4.4, *Uses conventional contact gestures*). The Expression of Intentions and Emotions Worksheet, which appears with the Social Partner stage SAP-O Form in Appendix A in this volume, was developed to help users document the relationship of intentions and communicative means during the observation by checking the means a child uses to express specific intentions. This information will help in decision making about which means to target with which intentions.

At the end of the observation, each behavior should be rated using a scoring system (0, 1, or 2 points) with the definitions shown in Figure 7.2. The numerical scores are recorded on the SAP-O Form in the boxes to the left of the numbered objectives.

If the child does not display the skill during the observation, information gathered from the SAP-R should be used to supplement the observation and refine the scoring of 0, 1, or 2. In addition, the assessor should use behavior sampling techniques, described later in Step 5, in an effort to gather information about behaviors that did not occur at all or that rarely occurred during the observation. This step may be skipped if all behaviors are observed. If many behaviors are not observed, then more time should be devoted to behavior sampling or consideration should be given to using the SAP-O Form from the previous stage. The child's behavior displayed during behavior sampling would be scored the same as during the observation. Thus, the score of 0, 1, or 2 should be entered in the box to the left of each objective, based on the combined information from the observation, SAP-R, and behavior sampling. It may be necessary

---

2—Child is using this skill independently and criterion is met consistently.
- Child meets criterion **independently** (i.e., without assistance).
- Child meets criterion **regularly** (e.g., skill is displayed at least two times in an observation for low-frequency behaviors, skill is displayed often for high-frequency behaviors, skill is displayed in at least two of three opportunities observed).

For the Social Partner stage
- Child meets criterion in at least two different activities (e.g., caregiving routines, play) or contexts (e.g., school, home).
- Child meets criterion with at least two different partners.

For the Language Partner stage
- Child meets criterion in at least two different activities (e.g., caregiving routines, play) or contexts (e.g., school, home).
- Child meets criterion with at least three different partners.

For the Conversational Partner stage
- Child meets criterion in at least two different activities (e.g., caregiving routines, play) and two different contexts (e.g., school, home).
- Child meets criterion with at least three different partners, at least one of whom must be a peer.

1—Child is practicing this skill and criterion is met inconsistently.
- Child meets criterion in one activity (e.g., caregiving routines, play).
- Child meets criterion with assistance.
- Child meets criterion occasionally or inconsistently.

0—Child is learning this skill and criterion is not met without partner support.
- Child does not meet criterion when given the opportunity.
- Child does not meet the criterion based on reported information (e.g., from SAP-R, from parent or teacher report).
- Child would not be expected to meet criterion based on other performance.

Figure 7.2. Definitions in the scoring system for the SCERTS Assessment Process–Observation (SAP-O).

to gather additional information from parent or teacher report on the use of certain behaviors across contexts or partners that were not observed or that could not be sampled.

Tabulation of Scores on the SAP-O Cover Page

A child's scores of 0, 1, or 2 on the SAP objectives should be determined based on the combined performance during the observation, behavior sampling, and information provided on the SAP-R. Based on the point scale for each objective, two sets of scores should be summarized on the cover page of the SAP-O Form. First, a sum of the scores for each of the components of the three SCERTS domains (i.e., Joint Attention, Symbol Use, Mutual Regulation, Self-Regulation, Interpersonal Support, and Learning Support) should be entered in the appropriate Qtr (Quarter) column in the box in the lower left corner of the page that is labeled *SCERTS Profile Summary.* This box shows the total possible score for each component so that the child's relative score can be judged. Second, in the lower right-hand corner of the cover page, a sum of the scores for each of the eight Social-Emotional Growth Indicators should be entered in the Qtr 1 column. This box shows that the total possible score for each indicator is 10 so that the child's progress can be judged. The Social-Emotional Growth Indicators and the objectives that contribute to each indicator are described next.

Social-Emotional Growth Indicators in the SCERTS Model

On the SAP-O Forms, specific objectives are delineated under each goal area for Social Communication, Emotional Regulation, and Transactional Support. This comprehensive and highly specific breakdown provides a detailed profile of a child and partners' current abilities, informs decision making for the next logical goals to consider in program planning, and provides a framework for documenting short- and long-term progress. We also recognize, however, that professionals and parents often discuss and are concerned about more general qualities of a child's behavior, as reflected in everyday discussions about the child's strengths and needs. Such general qualities valued by parents and professionals are apparent in statements such as "I want him to have friends and feel a like a member of his class," "We want her to be happy," and "We wish that he could be more independent and flexible in daily activities."

To address these concerns, we derived a list of Social-Emotional Growth Indicators by considering the more generic aspects of a child's development valued by parents and professionals. This process involved analyzing the SCERTS curriculum-based assessment goals and objectives across the domains of Social Communication and Emotional Regulation for key indicators of these important qualities that are meaningful to parents and professionals. The generic Social-Emotional Growth Indicators we identified include 1) Happiness, 2) Sense of Self, 3) Sense of Other, 4) Active Learning and Organization, 5) Flexibility and Resilience, 6) Cooperation and Appropriateness of Behavior, 7) Independence, and 8) Social Membership and Friendships. We have found that these qualities can be operationally defined by clusters of objectives measured in the SAP. This provides another level of analysis in which progress in such Social-Emotional Growth Indicators can be measured as part of the SAP, with changes in social-emotional growth documented over time. We believe that by documenting these indicators, we enhance the meaningfulness of what we document with the SAP, which more closely addresses the social validity of changes that can be observed in a child's behavior. We now briefly define and discuss the rationale for selecting each of these Social-Emotional Growth Indicators.

1. *Happiness:* Happiness involves a child's experience and expression of positive emotion and the ability to derive joy from social experiences and learning opportuni-

ties, which fuels many aspects of the child's development and social relationships. Furthermore, a child who has the ability to experience and express happiness draws others to him- or herself, creating further opportunities for learning and social participation. We define *Happiness* as the capacity to experience, express, and derive positive emotion from everyday activities and engagement with partners, and we document the extent to which this is characteristic of a child's emotional experience.

2. *Sense of Self:* A child who develops a sense of self is able see him- or herself as distinct from others and demonstrates greater confidence in formulating and achieving personal goals. We define *Sense of Self* as the capacity to see oneself relative to one's special personal qualities (as compared with others), personal history, and relationships with others and to take pride in one's achievements. Parents and professionals value this quality as it underlies the development of self-esteem, self-determination, and the desire to master challenges in everyday activities.

3. *Sense of Other:* A child who is able to develop a sense of other people as distinct human beings with their own goals, opinions, and feelings is more capable of becoming a more sensitive and empathetic social partner and friend. A child who is able to take another person's feelings and thoughts into account (perspective-taking) also becomes more desirable as a partner from the perspective of others. We define *Sense of Other* as the capacity to understand and appreciate another's feelings and thoughts and to adjust one's behavior accordingly based on such understanding. This capacity underlies such qualities as thoughtfulness, empathy, and kindness, qualities that are so valued by parents and professionals.

4. *Active Learning and Organization:* A child who is an active learner is inquisitive and curious, views others as a source of information and learning, and is a hypothesis tester and a problem solver. When we add the quality of organization, a child's experience in learning in social and nonsocial settings becomes an exercise that naturally leads to efficiency and effectiveness in dealing with cognitive and social challenges in everyday activities. We define *Active Learning and Organization* as the ability to initiate efforts to engage others for learning, to seek information, to problem-solve, to relate new experiences to previous experiences, and to remain organized and engaged in activities in a manner that contributes to learning. These qualities also involve the ability to engage in goal-directed behavior, maintain attention, and remain emotionally well regulated and focused in planning and carrying out activities across settings. These qualities are valued by parents and professionals, as a child who is an active learner and is organized becomes more of a true partner in learning, rather than a passive respondent partner, which places considerably less of a burden on adult partners to be primarily responsible for a child's learning.

5. *Flexibility and Resilience:* One of the great challenges observed in children with ASD is discussed in the *Diagnostic and Statistical Manual of Mental Disorders, Fourth Edition, Text Revision,* as an "inflexible adherence to specific, nonfunctional routines or rituals" (APA, 2000, p. 75) and was discussed by Kanner (1943) in his seminal article on autism as "an insistence on preservation of sameness." Such inflexibility may occur for many reasons; for example, it may be representative of the cognitive or learning style observed in ASD, or it may be an emotional regulatory

strategy used in the face of confusion and stress. In contrast, flexibility, or the ability to go with the flow and to tolerate sudden and unpredictable changes as well as new and changing aspects of experiences, is a marker of important cognitive and emotional regulatory progress. For parents and educators, an increase in flexibility quite simply makes daily life easier for the child with ASD and all partners. Resilience also requires flexibility, and it is defined as the capacity to persist and stick to it in mastering new skills and achieving goals and to recover quickly and stay on track when challenged cognitively, socially, and/or emotionally. With *Flexibility and Resilience,* a child is better able to cope, adapt, and even thrive when faced with challenges faced in everyday life.

6. *Cooperation and Appropriateness of Behavior:* By cooperation, we are not referring to passive compliance. We are referring to a child's choice to actively participate, which often entails accepting and following another's agenda, rather than primarily following one's own agenda. Difficulty with this aspect of cooperation can be the source of frequent conflict and stress for some children with ASD. *Cooperation* entails the capacity to engage with adult and child partners in play, communication, and social interaction in a manner that conforms to accepted social conventions of behavior relative to a child's chronological age and societal expectations specific to different social contexts. The extent to which a child's behavior conforms to social conventions is directly related to the degree to which such behavior is considered appropriate or inappropriate by others. Due to the fact that learning in social contexts and social understanding provides the foundation for socially conventional behavior, the very nature of the disability of ASD poses great challenges for a child to behave appropriately in social contexts. Clearly, *Appropriateness of Behavior* is one area highly valued by parents and professionals, for as a child is more able to engage in activities with greater cooperation and behavioral appropriateness, the child becomes a more desirable social partner and is more likely to look and act in a manner more similar to children without special needs.

7. *Independence:* We define *Independence* as the extent to which one is able to engage in daily routines with success and meet challenges of daily activities using one's own resources, rather than depending on support from others. This requires a greater understanding of daily routines, as well as the ability to use skills to participate with minimal or no assistance. It also requires the ability to make judgments about such crucial issues as safety. A child who is more independent typically has greater capacities in self-determination and has more options for participating in a greater variety of activities across a variety of partners and settings. Therefore, there is less of a burden on parents and professionals to make decisions for a child and less of a need to provide constant supervision and support.

8. *Social Membership and Friendships:* The quality of social membership and development of friendships is a challenge for children with ASD, due to the primarily social nature of the disability. However, these qualities are highly valued by parents and professionals. We define *Social Membership and Friendships* as the capacity to view oneself as a participant and identify with a social group with two or more other members and to engage in behavior that illustrates identification with the group. Such identification may include the development of friendships, which is the capacity to have a special relationship with a peer or a small number of peers

at a level of intimacy that is qualitatively different from relationships with a broader network of people. In addition to the emotional satisfaction of feeling connected to others, this quality also enhances learning in a group context and motivates a child to be like others and to communicate and engage socially with other children.

Each of these Social-Emotional Growth Indicators is measured in the SAP by distinct clusters of five objectives within the domains of Social Communication and Emotional Regulation. Table 7.4 provides a summary listing of the five objectives for each Social-Emotional Growth Indicator for each SAP stage.

Step 5: Conduct Behavior Sampling

Although observations of natural contexts provide critical information about a child's spontaneous behavior, it may be rather time consuming to wait for some behaviors to occur naturally, especially low-frequency behaviors that may only occur in specific types of circumstances. Therefore, some of a child's abilities or potential may not be demonstrated even during an extended observation period. In these circumstances, behavior sampling may be used to supplement information gathered from observation. The purpose of behavior sampling is to collect a representative sample of behavior typ-

Table 7.4. Computing Social-Emotional Growth Indicators from Social Communication and Emotional Regulation objectives of the SAP-O

Social-Emotional Growth Indicators	Social Partner stage objectives	Language Partner stage objectives	Conversational Partner stage objectives
1. Happiness	JA3.2, JA5.4 MR1.1, MR2.4 SR1.7	JA3.1, JA5.2 MR1.2, MR2.5 SR1.8	JA2.1, JA3.2, JA5.6 MR1.5 SR1.6
2. Sense of Self	JA4.4, JA7.1 MR2.6, MR3.3 SR4.1	JA4.4, JA7.1 MR3.4, MR3.7 SR5.1	JA1.2, JA5.6 SU1.4, SU5.2 MR1.3
3. Sense of Other	JA1.3, JA5.4 SU2.7 MR2.4, MR2.5	JA3.4, JA5.4 SU2.4 MR2.4, MR2.7	JA1.4, JA4.3, JA4.5, JA4.7, JA5.6
4. Active Learning and Organization	SU1.3, SU1.4, SU3.4, SU4.7 SR2.1	SU1.4, SU3.4 MR2.7, MR3.3 SR4.1	JA5.3 SU1.3, SU3.4 SR3.5, SR4.2
5. Flexibility and Resilience	JA7.3 MR4.3 SR3.1, SR4.3, SR4.4	JA7.2 SR2.3, SR4.1, SR5.4, SR5.5	JA5.4 MR3.5 SR5.5, SR5.6, SR6.4,
6. Cooperation and Appropriateness of Behavior	JA1.1 SU2.7, SU4.5 MR2.1 SR4.2	JA5.7 SU2.3, SU4.1, SU5.6 SR1.5	SU3.6, SU6.1, SU6.4 MR3.5 SR1.4
7. Independence	JA4.4 SU2.6 MR2.6 SR3.3, SR4.1	JA4.4 MR2.6, MR3.5 SR5.1, SR5.3	JA3.1 SU1.4 SR6.1, SR6.2, SR6.3
8. Social Membership and Friendships	JA1.4, JA2.1, JA5.1 MR2.3 SR1.4	JA1.1, JA2.3, JA5.4, JA8.3 MR2.3	JA4.7, JA4.8 SU3.7 MR2.3, MR3.4

ical of a child's range of functioning in a relatively short period using naturalistic procedures. Structured communicative situations may be staged to entice a child to interact and to use a variety of communicative functions. Opportunities can also be set up for the use of toys or objects instrumentally and symbolically to assess a child's level of symbol use. In sampling spontaneous behavior, we have found that it is critical for the child to have the opportunity to initiate behavior; therefore, the partner should use a facilitative style and not overly direct the child to behave in a certain manner.

After completing the SAP-O, the team should review the information that has been recorded based on the observation as well as information gathered from the SAP-R. The team should identify any objectives that have not been scored or that the team feels underestimate the child's abilities. Behavior sampling procedures should be planned to set up opportunities that are very likely to elicit those particular behavioral patterns. Opportunities can be conceptualized as brief activities that can vary in the degree of structure that is offered by the partner and the learning supports. For example, if a child was observed in a classroom that is highly structured and teacher directed, it would be important to see how the child responds in a situation with less structure and more opportunities for initiation.

For children at the Social and Language Partner stages who do not readily initiate interaction, one technique that is valuable to elicit increased instances of intentional communication is the use of *communicative temptations,* which have been described by Wetherby and colleagues (Wetherby & Prizant, 1989, 1993, 2002; Wetherby & Prutting, 1984). Communicative temptations involve opportunities designed to tempt or entice specific attempts at communication. The idea is to create a situation that is highly enticing to the child, while requiring some active signaling by the child that is directed to the partner. Once the child anticipates that the communicative partner will act in a predictable way (e.g., by opening a container, by rolling a ball back, by blowing more bubbles), the situation makes sense to the child. One example is activating a wind-up toy, letting it deactivate, and then waiting and looking expectantly at the child. This provides opportunities for the child to request assistance at getting the toy to activate, to protest about the ceasing of action, or to draw attention to the spectacle of the wind-up toy. Another example is giving the child a block to put away in a box; repeating this several times so that the child expects a block; and then giving a different object, such as a toy animal or a book. The novel object may tempt the child to communicate about the unexpected object or to protest over the change in objects.

Because temptations may be presented nonverbally, they circumvent the problem of a child's limited comprehension of language. In other words, they illustrate to the child that the partner wants and expects the child to communicate. It is important to present a communicative temptation and then wait and look expectantly at the child to encourage the child to initiate communication. Following are examples of communicative temptations for some of the communicative intentions measured on the SAP (see Table 7.5).

Although each temptation should be designed with at least one particular communicative intention in mind, we have found in our research using communicative temptations that any one temptation may potentially elicit a variety of communicative intentions (Wetherby & Prizant, 1993; Wetherby & Rodriguez, 1992). It is informative to compare how a child initiates communication with the structure provided during communicative temptations with the way in which he or she does this in less structured

Table 7.5. Examples of communicative temptations to elicit a variety of communicative intentions

Communicative intention	Communicative temptation
Requests desired food or objects	Place desired object on shelf out of the child's reach. Offer the child choices.
Protests/refuses undesired food or objects	Offer the child undesired objects. Place the child's hands in a cold, wet, or sticky substance.
Requests help	Place desired object in a container that the child cannot open.
Protests undesired actions	Remove or block access to desired object. Offer undesired activity. End a preferred activity abruptly or unexpectedly.
Requests social game	Present a social game such as "I'm gonna get you" by waving your hands in front of the child and tickling the child, and then hold out before repeating this.
Takes turns	Set up a turn-taking interaction that is predictable and has spaces for the child to take a turn; wait and look expectantly when it is the child's turn.
Greets	Wave and say "hi" when entering room; knock on a table and bring a stuffed animal from under the table to greet the child, then have the stuffed animal say bye-bye when leaving; repeat this between other temptations.
Comments on objects	Put some interesting objects in an opaque container and encourage the child to pull one out at a time. Give the child several of the same object to put in a container and then give the child something different.
Comments on actions	Present objects that create interesting spectacles, such as balloons, bubbles, and wind-up toys. Suddenly spill some substance or do something unexpected in front of the child.

play interactions to understand how transactional supports help the child communicate better. Communicative repair opportunities can be built into the communicative temptations once the child is displaying a consistent signal by having a partner hold out and not respond to the child's signal.

Structured situations can also be designed to probe a child's comprehension of different types of messages. To supplement observation in natural environments, it may be necessary to systematically present instructions with varying levels of complexity to determine what the child actually comprehends. For example, an instruction can first be given using only verbal input. If the child does not follow the instruction, nonverbal cues can systematically be added to determine which ones aid understanding. Structured situations can also be designed to probe a child's level of play through systematic presentation of sets of materials and offering of different levels of support (e.g., verbal instructions, nonverbal modeling, physical prompting).

For a child at the Conversational Partner stage, more sophisticated situations can be presented to entice the child to not only use language in conversation but use the array of higher level skills measures on the SAP. Table 7.6 shows examples of structured situations for children at advanced language stages.

Behavior sampling may also be used to assess emotional regulatory skills not observed in more natural routines and activities. The purpose is to obtain an observational sample of a child's reactions to varying degrees of potentially dysregulating circumstances. Some emotional regulation skills may be observed using some of the behavior sampling strategies for social communication, whereas for other emotional regulation

Table 7.6.   Examples of structured situations for the Conversational Partner stage

Structured situation	Description
Referential communication task, or barrier game	Have the child sit face to face with a partner, but have a barrier block the child's and partner's view of each other. Give the child and the partner identical materials that need to be constructed in a particular way (e.g., drawing a picture; making a clay figure; building a scene with magnetic pieces). Have the child and partner take turns instructing each other how to construct the product. Then have the partners remove the barrier and show each other the products to see if they are the same.
Scavenger hunt	Create a list or map of the child's favorite items that are hidden around the room to create an opportunity for the child to use questions or advanced relational meanings to locate the items.
Procedural narrative	Have the child describe to a partner how to make something (e.g., peanut butter and jelly sandwich) or carry out a familiar activity (e.g., brushing teeth, taking a bath).
Personal event narrative	Have the child tell a story about a personal experience when he or she was very excited, scared, or sad.
Story grammar narrative	Have the child retell a familiar story that has a plot (e.g., *Finding Nemo, Spiderman*), or use a picture book with no words to elicit a story.
Peer tutoring	Ask the child to teach a peer how to complete a task that the child is competent with but that the peer does not know how to do; ask a peer to teach the child a task.
Video monitoring	Videotape the child in a communicative situation and then have the child watch the videotape and reflect on the success of the situation, the emotion expressed, or other aspects to probe the child's understanding and ability to reflect on the situation.

skills, special circumstances may need to be designed. Thus, behavior sampling for emotional regulation can be accomplished within the communicative temptations but can also be done as a separate step or through unique circumstances. For example, as previously noted in the list of temptations, favorite, familiar activities or desired objects and edibles may be presented and access to them may be limited to assess how a child copes with the inherent challenges to remain well regulated. Unique circumstances may be created by manipulating sensory input along a variety of dimensions that are likely to put a child at risk for dysregulation. For example, music may be played too loudly, a partner may use highly exaggerated emotional expression, the child may be touched too frequently, and so forth to assess a child's strategies to remain well regulated. Finally, familiar and fixed routines may be sabotaged to assess a child's reactions.

Because some of these behavior sampling strategies may cause mild to more extreme distress, their use should be time limited for the purpose of sampling behavior related to emotional regulation, which will have the long-term benefit for the child of selecting appropriate goals and strategies to address emotional regulation. When such behavior sampling approaches are used that may result in varying degrees of dysregulation, their purpose should be explained and permission should be obtained from the parents. Under all circumstances, partners should be prepared to support recovery from dysregulation and document the effectiveness of strategies to support recovery, which provides critical information for educational programming. In our experience, parents intuitively know the importance of observing their child under more difficult and challenging circumstances. Observing a child only in a well-regulated state limits the information that may be gathered for educational programming. In many instances, parents can be asked to suggest and even demonstrate strategies to tap into a child's emotional regulatory reactions and strategies.

The use of behavior sampling should be viewed as a dynamic process in assessment in that decisions about what to do next are based on what a child is currently able to do. Therefore, behavior sampling approaches need to be flexible and to unfold in reaction to the child's responses. For example, in setting up a communicative temptation to have a child at the Social Partner or Language Partner stage request help, one can present a container with a desired object in it to the child. If the child mouths and shakes the container but does not initiate a communicative signal to request, then verbally offer help and follow by offering an open-hand gesture. If the child does not respond to these supports, then hold your hand right over the lid to see if the child will push your hand to the lid to request help. Likewise, in setting up a communicative temptation for a child at the Conversational Partner stage to provide information about past events, one might have the child tell a story about a personal experience when he or she was very excited, scared, or sad (as discussed previously). If the child does not respond to this temptation, however, then it might be helpful to request a photograph album from home so that the child has access to visual supports for a specific event, as this may elicit more elaborate descriptions. Thus, the behavior sample offers a systematic opportunity to explore the levels of support that the child needs for optimal social communication and emotional regulation.

Step 6: Compile and Integrate Information with the SAP Summary Form

Following completion of the SAP-R and the SAP-O, the results of the SAP should be summarized on the SAP Summary Form (SAP Sum) to compile and integrate information. The SAP Sum provides a format to summarize two key sources of information: 1) the child's strengths and needs identified on the SAP-O, which incorporates information from the SAP-R, and 2) family perception of the SAP-O results and priorities for goal setting.

Key Information Source 1: Summarize Strengths and Needs

A child's profile of strengths and needs in the Social Communication, Emotional Regulation, and Transactional Support domains should be charted on pages 1 and 2 of the SAP Sum by filling in the boxes to the left of each goal, starting from left and moving to the right. Each box corresponds with 1 possible point. For example, for the first goal under Joint Attention at the Social Partner stage, there are four objectives, which total 8 possible points (because each objective is awarded 0–2 points) and correspond with the eight boxes. If a child earned 2 for the first objective, 1 for the second and third objectives, and 0 for the fourth objective, then the first four boxes beside JA1 on the SAP Sum should be shaded in $(2 + 1 + 1 + 0 = 4)$, which would indicate that the child has earned half of the points for this goal. Filling in the scores for each of the goals in the SCERTS Profile provides a graphic portrayal of the strengths and needs of the child and his or her partners. Goals for which fewer than half of the boxes are filled in are relative needs, and goals for which more than half of the boxes are filled in are relative strengths.

Similarly, a child's profile of strengths and needs in the eight Social-Emotional Growth Indicators should be charted on page 2 of the SAP Sum. Each Social-Emotional Growth Indicator is based on five objectives (see Figure 7.4) and a total possible score of 10 (again because each objective is awarded 0–2 points). Indicators with fewer than five boxes shaded in show relative needs and indicators with more than five boxes shaded in indicate relative strengths.

Key Information Source 2: Family Perception of SAP-O Results and Priorities

Before identifying the specific goals and objectives for a child's educational program, family members should be asked during a team meeting to share their perceptions of the SAP-O to validate that the assessment findings are representative of the child's behavior. In other words, is the child's profile of strengths and needs accurately captured on the SAP Sum? At this point, family members are asked to suggest any additional information that is needed to develop their child's educational plan. Documenting the family's perception of the validity of information gathered in the SAP-O is a critical step in building consensus with the family about the child's strengths and needs.

In addition, the family should be given the opportunity to reflect on and express their priorities for their child by answering the questions listed on page 2 of the SAP Sum regarding where they want to focus their energies and what skills they hope their child will achieve in the next 3 months. This information should be used to prioritize weekly objectives targeted for the next quarter. The family's perceptions and priorities should be summarized on page 2 of the SAP Sum.

Step 7: Prioritize Goals and Objectives

Based on the information compiled and integrated from the SAP-O and SAP-R and from the profiles documented on the SAP Sum, the assessment team members should work together to prioritize weekly objectives that 1) are the most *functional* (i.e., the skill will make a difference in a child's life), 2) directly *address family priorities* (i.e., the skill is valued by families), and 3) match the *developmental areas of need* revealed on the SCERTS Profile (i.e., the skill is developmentally appropriate based on the child's profile of strengths and needs). As noted previously, some objectives marked with the symbol = on the SAP-O Form are identical across component areas. Objectives marked with the symbol ↔ on the SAP-O Form need to be linked to form one objective.

A child's developmental level on the SAP Sum is not the sole factor for selecting weekly objectives. Equal consideration should be given to those objectives that would be the most functional and those that most closely match the family's priorities. Although this process occasionally results in selection of objectives that might appear out of sequence in reference to the structure of goals and objectives in the SAP, this flexibility and individualization is actually considered critical for successful implementation of a SCERTS Model program. (See Chapter 1 in Volume II for more detail on guiding principles and practice guidelines for prioritizing objectives.)

It is recommended that at least four and no more than eight objectives across the Social Communication and/or Emotional Regulation domains and four to eight objectives in the Transactional Support domain be targeted to work on weekly. As a child or partner achieves an objective, new objectives should be introduced. The objectives should be listed on page 3 of the SAP Sum. There should be at least one Transactional Support objective that is likely to support behaviors targeted for each Social Communication and Emotional Regulation objective. However, there may not be a one-to-one correspondence with the Social Communication and Emotional Regulation objectives and the Transactional Support objectives, as more than one Social Communication and Emotional Regulation objective may be supported by one Transactional Support objective.

Step 8: Recommend Further Assessment

The SAP Sum includes an area on page 4 to enter information about further assessment. This box is designed to enter information from outside assessments that have been completed and/or to make recommendations for further assessments that need to be completed. Such assessments may be conducted by outside agencies or professionals who are not on the SCERTS assessment team. Alternately, they may be conducted by one member of the SCERTS assessment team independent of the team or in collaboration with professionals who are not on the SCERTS team. Examples of outside assessments include a hearing evaluation conducted by an audiologist, a sensory integration or motor skill assessment conducted by an occupational therapist, an oral-motor evaluation conducted by a speech-language pathologist, or a functional assessment of behavior problems conducted by a behavior specialist or an interdisciplinary team.

Step 9: Design a SCERTS Educational Program

Step 9 of the SAP involves identifying a number of key meaningful activities and purposeful activities (i.e., MA & PA), defining the levels of support within these activities (i.e., the roles and responsibilities of educational team members), identifying familiar partners who will play a critical role in service provision, and targeting multiple objectives within these activities. This process is described in detail in Chapter 1 of Volume II. Two SAP Activity Planning Forms should be used for each child to plan activities for the morning and afternoon schedule, respectively. This is critical to ensure that the SCERTS intervention program is intensive and approximates at least 25 hours per week of active engagement in productive learning activities. On the SAP Sum, in the box labeled SCERTS Activity Planning, the boxes for *Morning schedule* and *Afternoon schedule* should be checked to document that these have been completed. More than two SAP Activity Planning Forms can be completed by an education team, if desired, as this may be helpful for planning a child's program in community setting, in therapeutic contexts, and for contexts that include more activities than would fit in the space alloted on these forms.

Next, the SAP assessment team should discuss and formulate a SCERTS Family Support Plan and a SCERTS Support Plan for Professionals and Service Providers to provide both educational support and emotional support. These are the two important programmatic components of the Transactional Support domain which are not directly measured or targeted in the SAP curricular goals and objectives. The process for documenting these support plans is described in detail in Chapter 3 of Volume II, and these plans are viewed as critical pieces of a comprehensive service delivery plan, rather than as elements of a plan that are considered optional. These should be documented on page 4 of the SAP Sum.

Step 10: Perform Ongoing Tracking

Once the four to eight weekly objectives in Social Communication and Emotional Regulation and in Transactional Support are identified and being targeted, the child's performance should be monitored daily using a SAP Daily Tracking Log. Two versions of the SAP Daily Tracking Log are provided. The first version has one activity box for each objective, and the second version has two activity boxes per objective. The second version would be used for chronologically or developmentally younger children whose daily activities are relatively brief. The process for targeting multiple objectives in multiple activities is described in detail in Chapter 1 of Volume II. Although it is not feasible to record data on every objective in every activity, it is critical to track a child's progress to inform decision making about the effectiveness of program implementation. We recommend that behavior be tracked on every objective at least once per week and ideally once per day in one or two activities. Because multiple objectives are targeted in multiple activities, one or two objectives should be identified to track behaviors on the SAP Daily Tracking Log in any one activity. Over the course of the week, each objective should be tracked in the array of activities in which it is targeted.

The child's name, communication stage, and date should be entered on the top of each Daily Tracking Log. The child's Social Communication and Emotional Regulation objectives and the partner's Transactional Support objectives should be entered in the left column. In the space labeled *Activity,* the activity should be described by characterizing the group size, partner, context, and activity variables. In the space labeled *Notes,* the behavior of the child or partner can be documented quantitatively (e.g., use + for each initiation or correct response) or qualitatively (e.g., describe the child's or partner's best behavior during that activity).

The information documented on the SAP Daily Tracking Logs should be used to complete the SAP Weekly Tracking Log. The scoring (0–2 points) as defined previously and used on the SAP-O for each language stage should also be used on the Weekly Tracking Log. The child's name and communication stage should be entered on the top and the start date of each week should be entered in the boxes across the top numbered 1–12. The child's Social Communication and Emotional Regulation objectives and the partner's Transactional Support objectives should be entered down the side in the left column. A score of 0, 1, or 2, should be assigned for each objective, based on the information documented for each objective.

As noted previously, it is critical to track a child's progress from week to week to inform decision making about the effectiveness of program implementation. We recommend that if a score of 0 is entered 3–4 weeks in a row for an objective, then some aspect of the program should be changed, which may involve targeting a lower level objective or modifying some aspect of the activity or transactional support.

The SAP-O Form can be updated each quarter by using a different color pen or pencil when recording information. Objectives that had scores of 0 or 1 should be updated. Information can be derived from the weekly tracking logs, new observations, sampling behavior, and the SAP-R to update the SAP-O Form. It is recommended that a new SAP Sum should be completed each quarter because either the targeted objectives have been achieved and therefore new objectives are needed or the lack of progress necessitates a change in the objectives targeted. It is critical to a child's success to monitor progress and then to modify the educational program based on the tracking information. The SAP provides a mechanism for ongoing monitoring of progress and program modification every 3 months.

Chapter 8

The SCERTS Assessment Process
Using the SAP-O
Forms and Criteria

As described in Chapter 7 of this volume, the SAP addresses three domains—Social Communication, Emotional Regulation, and Transactional Support. Each domain is divided into two core components: Joint Attention and Symbol Use are the core components of the Social Communication domain; Mutual Regulation and Self-Regulation are the core components of the Emotional Regulation domain; Interpersonal Support and Learning Support are the core components of the Transactional Support domain. Goals in each domain are organized into three communication stages—the Social Partner, Language Partner, and Conversational Partner stages, and the goals in each domain are subdivided into objectives with specific criteria. This chapter discusses the SAP-O Forms and presents the criteria for the SAP-O. The SAP-O Forms appear in Appendix A of this volume, and it may be useful to bookmark the forms to refer to them while reading this chapter.

Some of the child objectives for different goals or components are related, and we use three symbols to indicate these relationships. On the forms and criteria for the SAP-O, the symbol = is used when two objectives are identical and fall under more than one component. The symbol ≈ is used when two objectives are nearly identical or are so similar they are addressing a common skill or behavior or one objective is addressing a subset of the other objective. In these cases, one or the other objective should be targeted at one time because targeting both at the same time may be duplicative or unnecessary. The other objective should be considered subsequently if it is not fully achieved once the first objective is achieved. The symbol ↔ is used to indicate that two goals or sets of objectives should be linked when targeting objectives under these goals in intervention. In other words, one objective from each set of objectives should be incorporated into a more comprehensive objective, if appropriate for the individual child. The steps for implementing the SAP are described in detail in Chapter 7 of this volume.

In addition to yielding a profile of social communication, emotional regulation, and transactional support, a child's scores on selected SAP objectives are combined to measure progress on eight Social-Emotional Growth Indicators. These indicators reflect common priorities and concerns expressed by parents and professionals about children with ASD in everyday discussions. Collectively, these indicators are a composite of a child's growth in social and emotional development, which affect a child's engagement with the environment and people and capacity to learn. These indicators are discussed in greater detail in Chapter 7 of this volume.

SAP-O FORMS FOR THE SOCIAL PARTNER STAGE

The Social Partner stage encompasses two major transitions that enable a child to be an active social partner: the transition to communicating with purpose or intent and the transition to the acquisition and use of conventional gestures and vocalizations.

We have developed the Expression of Intentions and Emotions Worksheet, an optional worksheet, to assist in gathering data for the SAP-O at the Social Partner stage. This worksheet appears in Appendix A of this volume after the Social Partner stage SAP-O Form. Communicative intentions, measured in objectives JA4.1 through JA6.2, and expression of emotions, measured in objectives MR1.1 through MR1.4, are listed down the side. Presymbolic and symbolic communicative means, measured in objectives SU4.1 through SU5.4, are listed across the top. This grid can depict patterns in the means used for each intention and emotions, which can be helpful in making decisions about targeting and linking these objectives.

SAP-O CRITERIA FOR THE SOCIAL PARTNER STAGE

Following are the criteria for each objective at the Social Partner stage. The criteria define the behavior to be measured for each objective. Some criteria specify a minimum number of times that the child is required to display the behavior to achieve the objective. For criteria that do not specify a minimum number, the child should display the behavior regularly or appropriately for the context. *For all objectives at the Social Partner stage, a rating of 2 requires observations of behaviors with at least two different partners in at least two different contexts unless otherwise noted.*

SOCIAL COMMUNICATION

JOINT ATTENTION

1

Engages in reciprocal interaction

JA1.1   Responds to bids for interaction (= MR2.3)
Criterion: The child responds to a familiar person's bid for interaction. The bid and/or response may be nonverbal or verbal. The child's response must be immediate (i.e., displayed within 5 seconds following the other person's bid) and contingent (i.e., maintains the focus of attention or topic). The child's response does not need to demonstrate comprehension of a verbal bid.

JA1.2   Initiates bids for interaction (= SR1.4)
Criterion: The child initiates a bid for interaction through nonverbal or vocal means. The behavior must be *directed* to another person by proximity (moving toward or away from another person), physical contact (touching another person with a gesture or an action), or gaze. The behavior must be *initiated* by the child, meaning that it is not a response to another person's behavior.

JA1.3   Engages in brief reciprocal interaction (= SR1.5)
Criterion: The child initiates and responds to bids for interaction with a familiar person for at least two consecutive exchanges.*

JA1.4   Engages in extended reciprocal interaction (= SR1.6)
Criterion: The child initiates and responds to bids for interaction with another person for at least four consecutive exchanges between the child and partner.*

*An *exchange* consists of a turn from the child and a turn from the partner. At least one of the exchanges must be initiated by the child.

2
Shares attention

JA2.1   Looks toward people
Criterion: The child directs gaze spontaneously (without prompting) toward another person's face. Looking toward people may occur without a communicative signal or may support communication.

JA2.2   Shifts gaze between people and objects
Criterion: The child shifts or alternates gaze spontaneously (without prompting) between a person and an object and back at least three times. The gaze must be directed to another person's face. Gaze shifts may occur without a gesture or vocalization or may support communication. The shift must be smooth and immediate (i.e., the entire sequence should occur within 2 seconds). The gaze shift must be three point or four point. A *three-point gaze shift* may be either a person–object–person gaze shift (i.e., when the child is looking at a person, shifts gaze to an object, and then immediately shifts back to the person) or an object–person–object gaze shift (i.e., the child is looking at an object, shifts gaze to a person, and then immediately shifts back to the object). A *four-point gaze shift* is an object–Person A–Person B–object gaze shift (i.e., the child is looking at an object, shifts gaze to Person A, then immediately shifts gaze to Person B, and then immediately shifts back to the object).

JA2.3   Follows contact point (= SU2.4)
Criterion: The child follows the reference of another person's contact point (e.g., touching an object or a picture with an extended index finger) by directing gaze where the person is pointing at least two times. The instruction can be accompanied by calling the child's name and saying, "Look," or saying, "Give me that," or "Get that," but no other gestural, situational, or verbal cues (e.g., labeling the object) should be used.

JA2.4   Follows distal point (= SU2.5)
Criterion: The child follows the reference of another person's point at a distance (e.g., pointing to an object or picture at least 3–5 feet away) by turning the head and directing gaze or getting an object where the person is pointing at least two times. The reference should be to the side or behind the child so that the child needs to turn his or her head at least 45°. The instruction can be accompanied by calling the child's name and saying, "Look," or saying, "Give me that," or "Get that," but no other gestural, situational, or verbal cues (e.g., labeling the object) should be used.

3
Shares emotion

**JA3.1   Shares negative emotion using facial expressions or vocalizations
              (≈ MR3.1)**
Criterion: The child displays *negative emotion* (i.e., a clear vocal or facial expression of distress or frustration, which may be accompanied by a gesture or change in body posture) and shares it with another person by looking at, approaching (e.g., crawling over to), gesturing toward (e.g., raising arms to be picked up), or touching that person (e.g., pulling on pant leg).

**JA3.2   Shares positive emotion using facial expressions or vocalizations
              (≈ MR3.2)**
Criterion: The child displays *positive emotion* (i.e., a clear facial expression of pleasure or excitement, which may or may not be accompanied by a vocalization, e.g., laughing, squealing) and shares it by directing gaze toward another person's face, immediately before, during, or after displaying the emotion.

JA3.3   Responds to changes in partners' expression of emotion (= MR2.4, SU2.7)

Criterion: The child responds to changes in partners' expression of emotion by changing his or her behavior (e.g., pausing, focusing on a partner's face, dropping a toy, moving toward or away).

JA3.4   Attunes to changes in partners' expression of emotion (= MR2.5)

Criterion: The child attunes to changes in partners' expression of emotion by mirroring the emotional tone (e.g., smiles and laughs in response to a partner's positive affect; frowns and stops moving in response to a negative expression).

4
Shares intentions to regulate the behavior of others (↔ JA7.2, JA7.3, SU4–SU5)

For the objectives within this goal, the signals must be *directed* to another person by proximity (moving toward or away from another person), physical contact (touching another person with a gesture or an action), or gaze.

JA4.1   Requests desired food or objects (≈ MR2.6)

Criterion: The child directs nonverbal or vocal signals (e.g., reaches toward an object, bangs and looks toward an object out of reach) to get another person to give a desired food item or object.

JA4.2   Protests/refuses undesired food or objects (≈ MR3.4)

Criterion: The child directs nonverbal or vocal signals (e.g., pushes away) to get another person to remove an undesired food item or object.

JA4.3   Requests help or other actions (≈ MR3.3)

Criterion: The child directs nonverbal or vocal signals to get another person to provide help or assistance in carrying out an action that the child cannot do (e.g., opening containers, activating toys) or other actions (e.g., taps chair to request partner to sit down).

JA4.4   Protests undesired actions or activities (≈ MR3.4)

Criterion: The child directs nonverbal or vocal signals (e.g., pushes away, cries paired with gaze) to get another person to cease an undesirable action or get out of an undesirable activity.

5
Shares intentions for social interaction (↔ JA7.2, JA7.3, SU4–SU5)

For the objectives within this goal, the signals must be *directed* to another person by proximity (moving toward or away from another person), physical contact (touching another person with a gesture or an action), or gaze.

JA5.1   Requests comfort (≈ MR3.1)

Criterion: The child directs nonverbal or vocal signals to seek another's attention for comfort from distress, frustration, or fear/wariness.

JA5.2   Requests social game

Criterion: The child directs nonverbal or vocal signals to direct another person to begin or to continue carrying out a game-like social interaction.

JA5.3   Takes turns

Criterion: The child directs nonverbal or vocal signals as a turn filler to keep a cooperative social exchange going at least two times. This involves waiting for the partner to take a turn.

JA5.4   Greets

Criterion: The child directs nonverbal or vocal signals to indicate notice of a person or object entering or leaving the immediate situation or to mark the initiation or termination of an interaction (e.g., waves).

JA5.5   Calls

Criterion: The child directs nonverbal or vocal signals to gain the attention of another person, followed by an additional communicative signal (e.g., touching arm followed by a reach to request, vocalizing followed by a point to comment).

JA5.6   Shows off

Criterion: The child directs nonverbal or vocal signals to attract another's attention to a display of oneself or an action for social sharing (e.g., making a funny face, playing an instrument, going down a slide).

6

Shares intentions for joint attention (↔ JA7.2, JA7.3, SU4–SU5)

For the objectives within this goal, the signals must be *directed* to another person by proximity (moving object toward another person), physical contact (touching another person with a gesture or an action), or gaze. The signals are not part of a highly practiced and repetitive routine.

JA6.1   Comments on object

Criterion: The child directs nonverbal or vocal signals to get another person to notice or look at an object or entity (e.g., points to picture in a book, shows a toy brought out of a bag).

JA6.2   Comments on action or event

Criterion: The child directs nonverbal or vocal signals to get another person to notice or look at an action, a spectacle, or an event (e.g., reaching toward and looking at partner when bubbles pop or a tower of blocks falls over; pulling a partner to a preferred television program to point out a special character).

7

Persists and repairs communication breakdowns

JA7.1   Uses appropriate rate of communication for context

Criterion: The child directs nonverbal or vocal signals at an appropriate rate for the context (e.g., at least once per minute during one-to-one interaction, once every 3 minutes during a small-group interaction, once every 5–10 minutes during a large-group interaction). Lower rates would be expected with unfamiliar partners than with familiar partners and with adults than with peers.

JA7.2   Repeats communication to repair breakdowns (↔ JA4–JA6)

Criterion: When there is a *communication breakdown* (i.e., the child is not understood and/or does not achieve a desired goal), the child repeats all or part of the same communicative signal to repair or fix the breakdown.

JA7.3   Modifies communication to repair breakdowns (↔ JA4–JA6)

Criterion: When there is a breakdown in communication, the child modifies the communicative signal to repair the breakdown in one of the following ways: 1) shifts to a different communicative means (i.e., different gesture, different sound, or different combination of gesture and sound), 2) changes a quality of the signal (e.g., clear increase in loudness, syllable added to the vocalization), or 3) repeats the same act but directs it to a different person.

SYMBOL USE

1
Learns by imitation of familiar actions and sounds

A *familiar action or sound* is one that the child will readily display spontaneously (e.g., clapping, imitating animal sound).

SU1.1   Takes turns by repeating own actions or sounds
Criterion: The child takes turns by repeating his or her own actions or sounds (e.g., child rolls a ball, partner rolls the ball back, then child rolls it again) using at least two different behaviors (i.e., two different actions, two different sounds, or one action and one sound) during the course of an activity. The partner needs to take a turn in between the child's actions or sounds, but the child's turn does not need to be the same behavior as the partner's turn.

SU1.2   Imitates familiar actions or sounds when elicited immediately after a model
Criterion: The child accurately imitates or closely approximates a familiar action or sound immediately after a partner directs the child (e.g., "Do this," "Say this") using at least two different behaviors.

SU1.3   Spontaneously imitates familiar actions or sounds immediately after a model
Criterion: The child accurately imitates or closely approximates a familiar action or sound spontaneously (i.e., without direction to do so) immediately after a partner models the behavior. The child imitates at least two different behaviors.

SU1.4   Spontaneously imitates familiar actions or sounds at a later time
Criterion: The child accurately imitates or closely approximates a familiar action or sound spontaneously (i.e., without direction to do so) at a later time after a partner has modeled the behavior. The child imitates at least two different behaviors. A later time is at least three turns or at least a minute after the model but can be within the same activity or at a much later time.

2
Understands nonverbal cues in familiar activities

SU2.1   Anticipates another person's actions in familiar routines (= SR3.1)
Criterion: The child anticipates another person's actions in at least two different familiar routines by hesitating before, shifting body orientation, or requesting the expected behavior (e.g., during a familiar tickle game, adult tickles child and then stops and child does any of the following: 1) waits and positions body to be tickled again; 2) pulls adult's hand to request more tickling; 3) shifts gaze between adult's approaching hands and adult's face; or 4) displays giggling and smiling during a pause in the tickle routine, which reflects the anticipation).

SU2.2   Follows situational cues in familiar activities
Criterion: The child follows a simple instruction in a familiar activity with at least two different situational cues (e.g., partner says, "Wash hands," when standing in front of the sink and child holds hands out under faucet; partner says, "Clean up," when activity is done and holds out a bag for the toys and child puts toys in the bag).

SU2.3   Follows gestural cues other than a point
Criterion: The child follows a simple instruction with at least two different gestural cues other than a point (e.g., partner says, "Come here," with open arms extended to-

ward child; partner says, "Give it to me," with palm-up open hand extended near an object).

SU2.4   Follows a contact point (= JA2.3)

Criterion: The child follows the reference of another person's contact point (e.g., touching an object or a picture with an extended index finger) by directing gaze where the person is pointing at least two times. The instruction can be accompanied by calling the child's name and saying, "Look," or saying, "Give me that," or "Get that," but no other gestural, situational, or verbal cues (e.g., labeling the object) should be used.

SU2.5   Follows a distal point (= JA2.4)

Criterion: The child follows the reference of another person's point at a distance (e.g., pointing to an object or picture at least 3–5 feet away) by turning the head and directing gaze or getting an object where the person is pointing at least two times. The reference should be to the side or behind the child so that the child needs to turn his or her head at least 45°. The instruction can be accompanied by calling the child's name and saying, "Look," or saying, "Give me that," or "Get that," but no other gestural, situational, or verbal cues (e.g., labeling the object) should be used.

SU2.6   Responds to visual cues (photographs or pictures)

Criterion: The child follows a simple instruction with at least two different visual cues (e.g., partner says, "Get the ball," and shows a picture of a ball; partner says, "Let's play Ring Around the Rosy," and shows a photograph of the child playing this game and the child goes to the circle and holds out hands ready to play). The instruction should be given with no gestural or situational cues.

SU2.7   Responds to facial expression and intonation cues (≈ JA3.3)

Criterion: The child responds to a simple instruction with at least two different facial expressions or intonation cues (e.g., partner says, "I'm gonna get you," with a happy face and rising intonation, and child laughs, runs away, and then stops in anticipation of being tickled; partner says, "No, no, no, don't touch," with an angry face and stern intonation, and child puts object down and backs away). The instruction is given with no gestural or situational cues.

3

Uses familiar objects conventionally in play

SU3.1   Uses exploratory actions on objects (↔ SR2.1)

Criterion: The child uses at least five different exploratory actions (actions that examine physical properties) on objects (e.g., grasps, rolls, squeezes, drops, bangs, rubs, twirls, mouths, shakes).

SU3.2   Uses familiar objects in constructive play

Criterion: The child uses at least three objects in combination to construct at least two different products (e.g., stacks a tower of blocks or rings, puts puzzle pieces together, puts cars together to make a train, strings beads). Taking blocks off a stack, banging objects together, or putting objects in a container do not count as a combinatorial action.

SU3.3   Uses familiar objects conventionally toward self

Criterion: The child uses familiar objects conventionally (i.e., for the conventional or functional use) toward self (e.g., drinks with a bottle or cup, eats or stirs with a spoon, pours with a cup or pitcher, puts hat on, puts shoes on, washes face with cloth, combs or brushes hair, brushes teeth, puts telephone to ear). The object needs to be used in the *proper orientation* (e.g., holding the handle of the spoon; demonstrating brushing motion with toothbrush, but not biting toothbrush). The child can receive credit for imitation of an action using the same object modeled by another person only if the child demonstrates the action a second time.

SU3.4   Uses familiar objects conventionally toward other
Criterion: The child uses familiar objects conventionally toward another person or an inanimate object (e.g., hugs or kisses stuffed animal, feeds stuffed animal with utensil, puts blanket on doll, rolls ball or car to another person). The object needs to be used in the proper orientation. The child receives credit for an imitation of an action using the same object modeled by another person only if the child demonstrates the action a second time during the course of the activity.

4

Uses gestures and nonverbal means to share intentions (↔ JA4–JA6, MR1, MR3.3, MR3.4)

SU4.1   Uses proximity
Criterion: The child uses proximity (i.e., moves or positions self near another person) as a communicative signal (i.e., expecting a specific response from the partner).

SU4.2   Uses facial expressions
Criterion: The child directs facial expressions (e.g., smile, frown) to others to indicate pleasure and distress.

SU4.3   Uses simple motor actions
Criterion: The child uses at least three different simple motor actions (i.e., actions or movements that are not conventional or symbolic gestures) as a communicative signal (e.g., taking another person's hand and putting it on an object to request help, pulling on another person's pant leg to call, leading a person to the door to request *out,* moving body back and forth to signal *go*).

SU4.4   Uses conventional contact gestures
☐ *give*   ☐ *push away*   ☐ *show*   ☐ *reach/touch*   ☐ *point/touch*

Criterion: The child uses at least three different contact gestures (i.e., the child's hand touches another person, an object, or a picture) that are conventional (i.e., having shared meaning that is widely recognized).

SU4.5   Uses conventional distal gestures
☐ *wave*   ☐ *distal reach*   ☐ *distal point*   ☐ *clap*   ☐ *head shake*   ☐ *head nod*

Criterion: The child uses at least three different distal gestures (i.e., the child's hand does not touch another person, an object, or a picture) that are conventional (i.e., having shared meaning that is widely recognized). A reach or clap must be accompanied by a gaze shift prior to, during, or immediately following the reach or clap.

SU4.6   Uses reenactment or symbolic distal gestures
Criterion: The child uses at least three different reenactment or symbolic gestures that are also distal gestures. A *reenactment gesture* is a re-presentation or replication of an action from an event that is used at a later time (e.g., making a flying motion with the hand to request continuation of a tickle game, using an action that replicates the tickling movement). A *symbolic gesture* is a pantomime action that is referential or like a word (e.g., turning the hand back and forth to indicate *open,* making a flying motion with the hand when the thumb and pinky are extended out to indicate *airplane*).

SU4.7   Uses sequence of gestures or nonverbal means

Criterion: The child uses a sequence of two or more gestures or nonverbal means as a communicative signal (e.g., pulls a person by the hand to the closet, then points to an object out of reach; taps to get a person's attention, then shows the person an object).

SU4.8   Coordinates gestures and gaze

Criterion: The child uses gaze in coordination with at least three different gestures. The gaze may be looking at people's faces and/or gaze shifts.

**5
Uses vocalizations
to share intentions
(↔ JA4–JA6, MR1,
MR3.3, MR3.4)**

SU5.1   Uses differentiated vocalizations (↔ MR1)

Criterion: The child uses at least two different vocalizations. A vocalization *must include a vowel sound* and may also include a consonant that precedes or follows the vowel. For example, a whine produced with the mouth closed approximating the /m/ sound would not contain a vowel and thus would not be counted. Nonspeech sounds such as laughs, cries, sighs, lip smacks, trills, and raspberries should not be included. Vocalizations can be produced either spontaneously or imitatively but must be used as a communicative signal (i.e., directed to others to accomplish a goal).

SU5.2   Uses a variety of consonant + vowel combinations

Criterion: The child uses at least five different consonant + vowel combinations as communicative signals. The consonants of particular interest are the ones that emerge earliest. Following is a list of the 10 consonants that are most likely to be used by children in the early stages of communication development (Wetherby & Prizant, 1993a):

Early consonant sounds

/m/ as in "mamamama," "Mama," or "moo"

/n/ as in "nununu" or "no no"

/b/ or /p/ as in "babababa," "bibo," "poo," or "bye-bye"

/d/ or /t/ as in "dodododo," "titi," or "Daddy"

/g/ or /k/ as in "googoo," "cookie," or "gone gone"

/w/ as in "woowoo," "weewee," or "wagon"

/l/ as in "lalala," "balloon," or "little"

/y/ as in "yayaya," "yum yum," or "you"

/s/ as in "sasasa," "sock," or "kiss"

/sh/ as in "shashasha," "hush," or "shoe"

The communicative signal need not include a recognizable word. The consonant may precede or follow the vowel.

SU5.3   Uses words bound to routines

Criterion: The child uses at least three different words that are bound to a routine as communicative signals. A **word bound to a routine,** also called a *protoword* or an *early word-like form,* may be spoken or signed or may be a picture that is used as a word or lexical form and is defined as 1) a consistent sound pattern or sign that approximates a conventional word and 2) a form that is used to refer to a specific object, action, or attribute and that is used only in a highly specific context (e.g., "uh oh" when dropping things, "muh" to request more, "baba" for bottle).

SU5.4 **Coordinates vocalizations with gaze and gestures**
Criterion: The child uses gaze in coordination with vocalizations. The gaze may be looking at people's faces and/or gaze shifts.

6
Understands a few familiar words

SU6.1 **Responds to own name**
Criterion: The child responds to his or her name at least two times by turning toward or looking at the person immediately (within 2 seconds) after the child's name is called.

SU6.2 **Responds to a few words in familiar social games**
Criterion: The child responds to at least three different words in familiar social games (e.g., child points to correct body parts when caregiver asks, "Where's your nose?" and "Where's your tummy?" in a bathtub routine of finding these body parts; child is the first to fall down when partner says "and we all . . . fall . . . down" in Ring Around the Rosy). The instruction should be given with no gestural cues.

SU6.3 **Responds to a few familiar person, body part, or object names**
Criterion: The child follows a simple instruction with at least two different person or object names by touching, showing, or making a clear change in direction of eye gaze to identify correctly the person, body part, or object (e.g., partner says, "Where's Mommy?" and child reaches toward his mom; partner says, "Where's your feet?" and child touches his feet; partner says, "Get your cup," with several choices of objects, and child picks up cup). The instruction should be given with no gestural or situational cues.

SU6.4 **Responds to a few frequently used phrases in familiar routines**
Criterion: The child responds correctly to two simple instructions (at least two different phrases) (e.g., at the end of the school day, teacher says, "Time to go home—put your coat on," and child goes across the room and gets her coat; after dinner; parent tells child, "Time for a bath," and the child runs upstairs to the bathroom; caregiver says, "Let's go for a ride," and child goes to the door and sits down to have her shoes put on). The instruction should be given with no gestural cues.

EMOTIONAL REGULATION

MUTUAL REGULATION

1
Expresses range of emotions
(↔ SU4–SU5)

MR1.1 **Expresses happiness**
Criterion: The child expresses happiness with facial expression or vocalization (e.g., smiling, laughing) in appropriate situations.

MR1.2 **Expresses sadness**
Criterion: The child expresses sadness with facial expression or vocalization (e.g., frowning, pouting, crying) in appropriate situations.

MR1.3 **Expresses anger**
Criterion: The child expresses anger with facial expression or vocalization (e.g., whining, fussing, crying) in appropriate situations.

MR1.4 **Expresses fear**
Criterion: The child expresses fear or wariness with facial expression or vocalization (e.g., widened eyes with tense lower eyelids) in appropriate situations.

**2
Responds
to assistance
offered by partners**

MR2.1   Soothes when comforted by partners
Criterion: The child soothes or calms down quickly (i.e., within 30 seconds) when partners offers comfort verbally or nonverbally, with the exception of periods of time when the child is experiencing extreme dysregulation, fear, or violations of expectations.

MR2.2   Engages when alerted by partners
Criterion: The child becomes actively engaged when partners introduce alerting and organizing stimulation through social routines and motor play.

MR2.3   Responds to bids for interaction (= JA1.1)
Criterion: The child responds to a familiar person's bid for interaction. The bid and response may be nonverbal or verbal. The child's response must be immediate (i.e., displayed within 5 seconds following the other person's bid) and contingent (i.e., maintains the focus of attention or topic). The child's response does not need to demonstrate comprehension of a verbal bid.

MR2.4   Responds to changes in partners' expression of emotion (= JA3.3)
Criterion: The child responds to changes in partners' expression of emotion by changing his or her behavior (e.g., pausing, focusing on a partner's face, dropping a toy, moving toward or away).

MR2.5   Attunes to changes in partners' expression of emotion (= JA3.4)
Criterion: The child attunes to changes in partners' expression of emotion by mirroring the emotional tone (e.g., smiles and laughs in response to a partner's positive affect; frowns and stops moving in response to a negative expression).

MR2.6   Makes choices when offered by partners (≈ JA4.1)
Criterion: The child directs nonverbal or vocal signals to make a choice when offered by the partner at least two times.

**3
Requests partners'
assistance to
regulate state**

MR3.1   Shares negative emotion to seek comfort (≈ JA3.1; ↔ JA5.1)
Criterion: The child displays *negative emotion* (i.e., a clear vocal or facial expression of distress or frustration, which may be accompanied by a change in body posture or gesture) and shares it with another person by looking at, approaching (e.g., crawling over to), gesturing toward (e.g., raising arms to be picked up), or touching that person (e.g., pulling on pant leg) to seek comfort.

MR3.2   Shares positive emotion to seek interaction (≈ JA3.2)
Criterion: The child displays *positive emotion* (i.e., a clear facial expression of pleasure or excitement, which may or may not be accompanied by a vocalization, e.g., laughing, squealing) and shares it by looking at, approaching (e.g., crawling over to), gesturing toward (e.g., raising arms to be picked up, showing an object), or touching that person (e.g., pulling on pant leg, tapping arm) to seek interaction.

MR3.3   Requests help when frustrated (≈ JA4.3; ↔ SU4–SU5)
Criterion: The child directs nonverbal or vocal signals when distressed to get another person to give help or carry out an action that challenges or exceeds the child's skill level.

MR3.4   Protests when distressed (≈ JA4.2, JA4.4; ↔ SU4–SU5)
Criterion: The child directs nonverbal or vocal signals (e.g., pushing away, vocalizations, crying paired with gaze) to get another person to remove an undesired food item or object or to cease an undesired action or to get out of an undesired activity at least two times.

4
Recovers from extreme dysregulation with support from partners

Extreme dysregulation is a state in which a child is not available for engagement or learning and may experience intense emotions. By definition, a state of extreme dysregulation must preclude the child's ability to engage with people and activities in a productive manner. Extreme dysregulation typically is not brief or episodic, and it may be continuous or cyclical within a period of time. Behavioral evidence of extreme dysregulation may include 1) expression of intense and seemingly inconsolable distress; 2) complete loss of attention to the activity or to other people; 3) intense, disruptive vocalizations (e.g., crying, screaming, moaning) and/or nonverbal behavior (flailing, self- or other-directed hitting, slapping, biting); 4) frenetic motor activity; 5) extreme shutdown and disengagement for an extended period; and so forth. Extreme dysregulation may be associated with arousal levels that are very high (i.e., extreme distress or excitement) or very low (i.e., extremely passive, disengaged state), either of which precludes engagement.

MR4.1   Responds to partners' efforts to assist with recovery by moving away from activity
Criterion: The child responds to partners' attempts to assist with recovery and to change the child's attentional focus by moving away from activities that are overstimulating or undesired after reaching an extreme state of dysregulation.

MR4.2   Responds to partners' use of behavioral strategies
Criterion: The child responds to partners' use of behavioral strategies (i.e., simple motor actions or sensory-motor strategies) that are implemented to help the child to recover from an extreme state of dysregulation.

MR4.3   Responds to partners' attempts to reengage in interaction or activity
Criterion: The child responds to partners' attempts to reengage in interaction or activity after recovery (i.e., return to a well-regulated state) from extreme dysregulation.

MR4.4   Decreases amount of time to recover from extreme dysregualtion due to support from partners
Criterion: The amount of time the child takes to *recover* (i.e., return to an available state for learning and engaging) from extreme dysregulation decreases over time when the child is supported by partners.*

MR4.5   Decreases intensity of dysregulated state due to support from partners
Criterion: The intensity of emotional response and the changes in the child's state of arousal or energy level during episodes of dysregulation decrease over time with support from partners.*

You may need to rely on information gathered from interviews with others who observe the child over time to establish child-specific criteria for objectives MR4.4 and MR4.5 at the Social Partner stage.

SELF-REGULATION

1
Demonstrates availability for learning and interacting

SR1.1   Notices people and things in the environment
Criterion: The child takes notice of people in his environment by looking at or by visually tracking and approaching them. The child also takes notice of objects (e.g., toys, household items) in the environment by looking at them, reaching for them, and/or actively exploring them through physical manipulation.

SR1.2   Shows interest in a variety of sensory and social experiences

Criterion: The child shows interest in a variety of sensory experiences (e.g., looking, touching, tasting, smelling, moving) and social experiences by actively exploring familiar environments during solitary play and social interactions.

SR1.3   Seeks and tolerates a variety of sensory experiences

Criterion: The child seeks and tolerates at least five different sensory experiences (e.g., looking, listening, rubbing, mouthing, smelling, climbing, jumping, rocking).

SR1.4   Initiates bids for interaction (= JA1.2)

Criterion: The child initiates a bid for interaction through nonverbal or vocal means. The behavior must be *directed* to another person by proximity (moving toward or away from another person), physical contact (touching another person with a gesture or an action), or gaze. The behavior must be *initiated* by the child, meaning that it is not a response to another person's behavior.

SR1.5   Engages in brief reciprocal interaction (= JA1.3)

Criterion: The child initiates and responds to bids for interaction with a familiar person for at least two consecutive exchanges.*

SR1.6   Engages in extended reciprocal interaction (= JA1.4)

Criterion: The child initiates and responds to bids for interaction with another person for at least four consecutive exchanges between the child and partner.*

*An **exchange** consists of a turn from the child and a turn from the partner. At least one of the exchanges must be initiated by the child.*

SR1.7   Responds to sensory and social experiences with differentiated emotions

Criterion: The child responds to different sensory and social experiences with differentiated emotions (e.g., shows happiness and excitement in fun activities, distress in stressful or unpleasant activities, and fear or wariness in unfamiliar or scary activities).

2
Uses behavioral strategies to regulate arousal level during familiar activities

Behavioral strategies are simple motor actions or sensory-motor strategies that the child engages in that regulate arousal level, evident by the child's level of attention, alertness, activity level, affect, and engagement.

SR2.1   Uses behavioral strategies to regulate arousal level during solitary activities (↔ SU3.1)

Criterion: The child uses behavioral strategies in solitary activities to increase arousal level (when underaroused) and decrease arousal level (when overaroused). Examples of behavioral strategies that may be used in solitary activities include sucking a thumb or pacifier, rocking, rubbing a soft blanket, hiding under a big pile of blankets, making repetitive vocalizations, flapping hands, grinding teeth, walking on toes, jumping, swinging, spinning, eating, or listening to music. *Overarousal* may be due to excessive sensory stimulation, too much excitement, or stressful events. *Underarousal* may be due to fatigue, boredom, or lack of organizing stimulation and may result in lack of attention or nonresponsiveness.

SR2.2   Uses behavioral strategies to regulate arousal level during social interactions

Criterion: The child uses behavioral strategies (i.e., simple motor actions or sensory-motor strategies) to increase and decrease arousal level during social interactions. Examples of behavioral strategies that may be used during social interaction include sucking a thumb or pacifier, rocking, rubbing a soft blanket, averting gaze away from people, moving away to be alone, jumping, flapping hands, mouthing, chewing, toe walking, approaching another person to play a social game, rocking, or spinning.

SR2.3   Uses behavioral strategies modeled by partners to regulate arousal level
Criterion: The child uses behavioral strategies (i.e., simple motor actions or sensory-motor strategies) that are imitated either immediately or at a later time from behaviors modeled by partners to regulate arousal level (e.g., squeezing hands, jumping).

SR2.4   Uses behavioral strategies to engage productively in an extended activity
Criterion: The child is able to engage productively for an extended activity (i.e., at least 10–15 minutes) and uses behavioral strategies (i.e., simple motor actions or sensory-motor strategies) as needed to regulate arousal level (e.g., mouths or bites a chewy toy or piece of food or gum, squeezes object or stress ball, bounces leg, rocks in chair, plays with fidget toy).

**3
Regulates emotion during new and changing situations**

SR3.1   Anticipates another person's actions in familiar routines (= SU2.1)
Criterion: The child anticipates another person's actions in at least two different familiar routines by hesitating before the other person's actions, shifting body orientation, or requesting the expected behavior (e.g., during a familiar tickle game, adult tickles child and then stops, and child does any of the following: 1) waits and positions body to be tickled again; 2) pulls adult's hand to request more tickling; 3) shifts gaze between adult's approaching hands and adult's face; or 4) displays giggling and smiling during a pause in the tickle routine, which reflects the anticipation).

SR3.2   Participates in new and changing situations
Criterion: The child is willing to participate in new and changing situations. Participation must include some degree of active involvement and engagement, not simply tolerance without involvement or passive attention. *New situations* are activities or features of activities that are unfamiliar to the child (e.g., an activity that the child has not participated in; a new person joining a familiar activity). *Changing situations* are ones that have variation in key features (e.g., sensory stimulation, activity level, activity sequence, task difficulty) or that have unexpected features (e.g., unpredictable events such as changes in place or sequence of common routines, activities terminated prematurely).

SR3.3   Uses behavioral strategies to regulate arousal level in new and changing situations
Criterion: The child uses behavioral strategies to regulate arousal level and intensity of emotional response in new (i.e., unfamiliar) and changing (i.e., having unexpected features) situations.

SR3.4   Uses behavioral strategies to regulate arousal level during transitions
Criterion: The child uses behavioral strategies to regulate arousal level and intensity of emotional response during transitions between activities.

**4
Recovers
from extreme
dysregulation
by self**

Extreme dysregulation is a state in which a child is not available for engagement or learning, and may experience intense emotions. By definition, a state of extreme dysregulation must preclude the child's ability to engage with people and activities in a productive manner. Extreme dysregulation typically is not brief or episodic, and it may be continuous or cyclical within a period of time. Behavioral evidence of extreme dysregulation may include 1) expression of intense and seemingly inconsolable distress; 2) complete loss of attention to the activity or to other people; 3) intense, disruptive vocalizations (e.g., crying, screaming, moaning) and/or nonverbal behavior (flailing, self- or other-directed hitting, slapping, biting); 4) frenetic motor activity; 5) extreme shutdown and disengagement for an extended period; and so forth. Extreme dysregulation may be associated with arousal levels that are very high (i.e., extreme distress or excitement) or very low (i.e., extremely passive, disengaged state), either of which precludes engagement.

SR4.1 Removes self from overstimulating or undesired activity
Criterion: The child moves away from activities that are overstimulating or undesired after reaching an extreme state of dysregulation.

SR4.2 Uses behavioral strategies to recover from extreme dysregulation
Criterion: The child uses behavioral strategies (i.e., simple motor actions or sensory-motor strategies) to *recover* (i.e., return to an optimal level of arousal) from an extreme state of dysregulation.

SR4.3 Reengages in interaction or activity after recovery from extreme dysregulation
Criterion: The child is able to reengage or bring him- or herself back to an interaction or activity after *recovery* (i.e., return to an optimal level of arousal) from extreme dysregulation.

SR4.4 Decreases amount of time to recover from extreme dysregulation
Criterion: The amount of time the child takes to *recover* (i.e., return to an optimal level of arousal) from extreme dysregulation decreases over time.*

SR4.5 Decreases intensity of dysregulated state
Criterion: The intensity of emotional response and the changes in the child's state of arousal or energy level during episodes of extreme dysregulation decrease over time.*

You may need to rely on baseline information gathered from interviews with others who observe the child over time to determine child-specific criteria for objectives SR4.4 and SR4.5 at the Social Partner stage.

TRANSACTIONAL SUPPORT

**INTER-
PERSONAL
SUPPORT**

**1
Partner is
responsive to child**

IS1.1 Follows child's focus of attention
Criterion: The partner follows the child's focus of attention by looking at and/or talking about what the child is attending to most of the time.

IS1.2   Attunes to child's emotion and pace

Criterion: The partner attunes to the child's emotion and pace by mirroring the emotional tone of the child's behavior and adjusting nonverbal behavior and vocalizations to the child's behavior (e.g., partner smiles and laughs in response to child's positive emotion, partner looks sad in response to child's distressed expression).

IS1.3   Responds appropriately to child's signals to foster a sense of communicative competence

Criterion: The partner responds to the child's intentional communicative signals (i.e., nonverbal or vocal signals directed to partner) for behavioral regulation, social interaction, or joint attention by responding appropriately to the child's intended goal. For example, if the child is requesting an object, the partner gives the child that object. If the child is protesting or refusing an object, the partner removes that object. If the child is seeking comfort, comfort is provided, and if the child is drawing attention to an event, the partner focuses attention on the event.

IS1.4   Recognizes and supports child's behavioral strategies to regulate arousal level

Criterion: The partner recognizes the child's use of behavioral strategies to regulate arousal level and supports these strategies. For example, if the child is trying to jump or move as an alerting and energizing strategy, the partner modifies the interaction to support or incorporate this strategy; if the child persistently seeks pressure as a means of organization by pressing into partners, the partner provides pressure through hugs; and so forth.

IS1.5   Recognizes signs of dysregulation and offers support

Criterion: The partner recognizes the child's signs of dysregulation. For example, the partner provides support when behavioral signs indicate that the child is not available for learning or engaging due to an arousal state that is too high, including distress or extreme excitement, or too low, including disinterest or fatigue. The partner provides appropriate assistance contingent on the child's arousal state in an effort to help the child regulate arousal.

IS1.6   Imitates child

Criterion: The partner imitates the child's verbal and/or nonverbal behavior and gives the turn back to the child when doing so is appropriate to the context. For example, when the child acts on objects or vocalizes, the partner imitates or approximates these behaviors and pauses, waiting for a further response from the child.

IS1.7   Offers breaks from interaction or activity as needed

Criterion: The partner schedules, offers, or allows for breaks from interaction or activities when the child's behavior suggests that a break is needed (e.g., as demonstrated by a change in arousal state, focus of attention, activity level, or emotional state) or when the child has been engaged in one activity for a long time. Breaks may involve a temporary pause from or cessation of an ongoing activity, with no specific demands being made for the child to attend or participate during the break. Breaks may also involve redirection to motivating and organizing activities.

IS1.8   **Facilitates reengagement in interactions and activities following breaks**
Criterion: The partner facilitates reengagement in interactions and activities following break times when the child is demonstrating appropriate arousal level and emotional state to participate fully in ongoing activities.

2 **Partner** **fosters initiation**	IS2.1 **Offers choices nonverbally or verbally** Criterion: The partner offers choices to the child nonverbally or verbally. Choices may include what to eat, what to wear, what activity to participate in, what objects to use in an activity, and so forth.

IS2.2   **Waits for and encourages initiations**
Criterion: The partner waits for the child to initiate using nonverbal or vocal signals and looks expectantly at the child to encourage initiation. For example, in activities in which opportunities for initiation are provided (e.g., choice making, playing a fun social game with clear turns) or needs are created for the child to communicate (e.g., desired objects are visible but put out of reach), the child is allowed sufficient time to direct a communicative signal to the partner with proximity (moving toward or away from another person), physical contact (touching another person with a gesture or an action), or gaze. The partner does not intervene unless it becomes clear that the child is not going to initiate and that the child needs additional support. Initiations are encouraged regardless of whether they are nonverbal or vocal.

IS2.3   **Provides a balance of initiated and respondent turns**
Criterion: The partner does not ask too many questions or give too many commands (either of which limits a child to primarily a respondent mode) and provides a balance of taking turns in relation to the child's initiations and responses.

IS2.4   **Allows child to initiate and terminate activities**
Criterion: The partner shares control with the child over when to initiate and terminate activities when appropriate. For example, the child may indicate that he is done with an activity nonverbally (e.g., walking away when finished, pushing away materials) or verbally (saying or signing "done"). If the child is engaged in a must-do activity (e.g., dressing, washing) or if the activity is very close to successful completion, the partner verbally acknowledges the child's communicative bid to end the activity (and may indicate steps to completion), even if it is not possible for the activity to be terminated immediately.

3 **Partner** **respects child's** **independence**	IS3.1 **Allows child to take breaks to move about as needed** Criterion: The partner allows the child to take breaks from activities when appropriate for the context to move about as needed (e.g., after participating for some time, particularly in activities that require sitting and focusing attention).

IS3.2   **Provides time for child to solve problems or complete activities at own pace**
Criterion: The partner gives the child adequate time to actively solve problems and to finish activities at the child's pace in most activities. For example, the partner refrains from rushing the child or providing premature prompting as long as the child is progressing in an activity and does not need additional support.

IS3.3　Interprets problem behavior as communicative and/or regulatory

Criterion: The partner recognizes, interprets, and responds to problem behavior as serving a communicative purpose. For example, if the child pushes or hits to protest, the partner acknowledges the child's intent and may model a more socially acceptable means for the child (if appropriate). Likewise, if the child is vocalizing loudly in an effort to block out disorganizing environmental sounds, the partner recognizes this and encourages the use of other regulatory strategies.

IS3.4　Honors protests, rejections, or refusals when appropriate

Criterion: The partner honors the child's signals to protest, reject, or refuse an object or activity when appropriate for the context. For example, in situations in which the child clearly does not wish to accept offered items or engage in activities, the partner does not continue to demand that the child do so under appropriate circumstances (e.g., during nonessential activities, when other choices of foods or toys are available).

4

Partner sets stage for engagement

IS4.1　Gets down on child's level when communicating

Criterion: The partner positions him- or herself and gets down on the child's level to encourage face-to-face interaction or physical proximity when communicating with the child.

IS4.2　Secures child's attention before communicating

Criterion: The partner secures the child's attention nonverbally or verbally before communicating with the child. For example, the partner calls the child's name or touches the child before directing communicative signals to the child.

IS4.3　Uses appropriate proximity and nonverbal behavior to encourage interaction

Criterion: The partner uses appropriate proximity (closeness and orientation to the child) and enticing nonverbal behavior (facial expression, gesture, intonation) to invite and encourage interaction. For example, rather than attempting to engage the child from a distance (e.g., calling to child from across the room), the partner comes close to the child and uses clear gestures, objects, and animated facial expression to engage the child. Similarly, when looking at picture books, the partner may use a face-to-face orientation to promote gaze shifting and sharing of attention.

IS4.4　Uses appropriate words and intonation to support optimal arousal level and engagement

Criterion: The partner uses appropriate words and intonation to support the child's optimal arousal level and engagement. For example, the partner either uses exaggerated, more intense vocalizations or verbalizations for an alerting effect or quieter, less intense vocalizations or verbalizations for a calming effect, as appropriate.

5

Partner provides developmental support

IS5.1　Encourages imitation

Criterion: The partner encourages the child to imitate behavior spontaneously by following the child's attentional focus, waiting, taking turns, and modeling behaviors for the child to imitate. Behaviors modeled may include vocalization, word approximations, or nonverbal action.

IS5.2   Encourages interaction with peers

Criterion: The partner encourages the child to interact with peers by drawing peers to the child, helping the child to respond to bids from peers, helping the child initiate bids for interaction directed to peers, and mediating successful interactions with peers. The partner may use verbal and/or nonverbal means to encourage interaction.

IS5.3   Attempts to repair breakdowns verbally or nonverbally

Criterion: The partner attempts to repair *communication breakdowns* (i.e., situations in which the partner does not understand the child's signal or the child does not understand the partner's message) either verbally or nonverbally by clarifying the meaning of the signal. For example, the partner may repeat the verbal or nonverbal signal or may modify the signal by adding words or gestures.

IS5.4   Provides guidance and feedback as needed for success in activities

Criterion: The partner provides support, guidance, and feedback as needed in activities so that the child maintains an optimal arousal level and experiences success. For example, the partner provides social praise or uses appropriate guided participation strategies (i.e., additional cues or prompts), without excessively prompting or directing the child.

IS5.5   Expands on child's play and nonverbal communication

Criterion: The partner expands on the child's play and nonverbal communication by adding to the child's behavior and following the child's attentional focus and topic of communication or play. For example, when the child rolls a car to the partner, the partner puts a pretend figure in the car and rolls it back to the child; the child gives a jar of chips to request open and the partner opens the jar and says "more chips" or "open jar."

**6
Partner adjusts
language input**

IS6.1   Uses nonverbal cues to support understanding

Criterion: When talking to the child, the partner uses clear and appropriate nonverbal cues (gestures, facial expressions, intonation) to support the child's understanding of the message. Words are not used in isolation as the only means to communicate.

IS6.2   Adjusts complexity of language input to child's developmental level

Criterion: When talking to the child, the partner adjusts the complexity of the language so that it is appropriate for the child's developmental level. For example, if the child does not yet understand words, the partner uses mostly single words or simple phrases when talking to the child. If the child does understand some words, the partner uses mostly two- and three-word phrases when talking to the child or consistently simplifies longer utterances (e.g., partner follows up the request, "Time to sit down and eat dinner," with "Sit down" and "Time for dinner").

IS6.3   Adjusts quality of language input to child's arousal level

Criterion: When talking to the child, the partner adjusts the quality of the language, which may include the content, complexity, or intonation, to support the child's arousal level. For example, the partner uses a soothing vocal tone, less exaggerated intonation, and simplified language when the child is highly aroused or more exaggerated vocal tone and volume when the child is underaroused.

7
Partner models appropriate behaviors

IS7.1   Models appropriate nonverbal communication and emotional expressions

Criterion: The partner provides clear and appropriate models of nonverbal communication (e.g., gestures) and emotional expressions (e.g., smiling and laughing to indicate pleasure).

IS7.2   Models a range of communicative functions

Criterion: The partner models a range of communicative functions verbally and nonverbally, for the following:

a. *behavioral regulation:* For example, the partner models pointing or holding out an open palm paired with saying "more ball" to request, the partner models a giving gesture paired with saying "help" to request actions, the partner models a pushing-away gesture while stating "all done" to protest or refuse an object, or the partner models reaching paired with saying an object label to request a desired object.

b. *social interaction:* For example, the partner models waving to greet on arrival and departure, the partner models making a reaching gesture to request comfort, the partner initiates a social game through nonverbal reenactments (e.g., hides own face to initiate a game of Peekaboo, starts the motions of a fingerplay song) and/or verbal means (e.g., saying "Peekaboo" or "The itsy-bitsy spider . . . "), or the partner models clapping to seek another's praise following completion of routines and activities.

c. *joint attention:* For example, the partner models a nonverbal comment by showing objects or pointing to interesting events and pairs these comments with a developmentally appropriate verbal model (e.g., saying "a ball," "big ball," or "ball roll").

IS7.3   Models appropriate play

Criterion: The partner models appropriate play for the child's developmental level and provides a variety of experiences with sensorimotor, symbolic, and constructive play. For example, with a duplicate set of play materials, the partner models single-scheme imaginative play, such as feeding a doll for the child making the transition to the early stages of symbolic play. Opportunities for sensorimotor exploration and constructive play (e.g., playing with blocks and puzzles) are provided on regular basis.

IS7.4   Models appropriate behavior when child uses inappropriate behavior

Criterion: In situations in which the child displays inappropriate behavior but is regulated enough to benefit from models, the partner models appropriate behavior. For example, the partner models making a pushing-away gesture and saying "no" if the child screams to reject a food item that is offered or models the use of a picture symbol, word, and/or sign for "all done" if the child is forcefully attempting to escape from an activity. Likewise, for a child who is chewing on his clothing and biting others in an effort to regulate arousal, appropriate mouthing and biting activities are modeled and provided (e.g., provision of a cup or toys).

IS7.5   Models "child-perspective" language

Criterion: The partner models language from the perspective of the child and considers the child's intentions and developmental level. For example, if the child is reaching for a toy car that is out of reach, the partner provides a model that matches the child's intention and developmental level, such as "car" or "car down." If the child produces an angry vocalization directed to the partner, the partner models saying "mad," "Billy's mad," or "I am mad."

<table>
<tr><td>

LEARNING SUPPORT

1

Partner structures activity for active participation

</td></tr>
</table>

LS1.1   Defines clear beginning and ending to activity
Criterion: The partner structures the activity so that the beginning and ending are clearly defined for the child. Natural or planned rituals are used. For example, a swinging activity begins with saying, "Ready, set, go," and ends with saying and signing "stop," or the beginning of an activity is marked with taking out toys and the end of the activity is marked with the words and sign for "all done."

LS1.2   Creates turn-taking opportunities and leaves spaces for child to fill in
Criterion: The partner structures the activity by creating turn-taking opportunities and leaving spaces for the child to fill in a turn. The child's turn may be nonverbal or verbal. For example, when initiating an activity, the partner models "Ready, set . . . " and allows the child to vocalize "go"; the partner rocks with child to music and pauses for the child to indicate verbally or nonverbally to continue; or spaces are left for the child to fill in during book routines that provide frequent repetition and carrier phrases (e.g., as found in the *Brown Bear, Brown Bear* books).

LS1.3   Provides predictable sequence to activity
Criterion: The partner provides a predictable sequence to the activity by the nature of the activity itself, through repetition so that the steps become familiar or through the use of other support to make the activity predictable to the child. For example, the partner practices a constructive play activity requiring a fixed sequence of steps to completion (e.g., nesting cups, combining ingredients to create a product), or the partner refers to a picture sequence to indicate progress in an activity and steps to completion. This strategy is also used during caregiving routines.

LS1.4   Offers repeated learning opportunities
Criterion: The partner consistently and predictably repeats aspects of activities across contexts throughout the child's day (e.g., choice-making opportunities at snack, circle time, and lunch) or repeats similar activities over time (e.g., pretend play with a feeding set one day and a grooming set another day) to provide predictable learning opportunities for the child. Predictable repetition is in contrast to introducing too many novel activities within a time frame.

LS1.5   Offers varied learning opportunities
Criterion: Within the context of repetition and expectation, the partner varies an aspect of the activity, which provides novelty for the child to learn from. For example, once the child is familiar with a play activity (e.g., blowing bubbles), the partner may vary this routine by pausing just prior to blowing to provide an opportunity for the child to request continuation. Similarly, once the child is familiar with a snack routine, the partner may vary the activity by providing a cup while withholding the juice or milk to encourage an opportunity for a request. The partner may vary a predictable activity to elicit commenting (e.g., removing objects from a "surprise" box to entice child to hold up and show an object and comment about the object; the objects removed should be sufficiently novel or ever changing to draw the child's attention and interest).

**2
Partner uses augmentative communication support to foster development**

LS2.1 Uses augmentative communication support to enhance child's communication and expressive language

Criterion: The partner makes available and encourages the child to use an augmentative communication support (i.e., nonspeech communication, e.g., gestures, signs, objects, pictures, photographs, picture symbols) to enhance the child's ability to communicate using one or a variety of nonspeech modalities.

LS2.2 Uses augmentative communication support to enhance child's understanding of language and behavior

Criterion: The partner uses and refers to an augmentative communication support (i.e., nonspeech communication, e.g., gestures, signs, objects, photographs, picture symbols) to enhance the child's ability to understand language and behavior. For example, during greeting routines, a partner may show a picture of a familiar family member (e.g., Mom, Dad, a sibling) just prior to his or her arrival home to provide the child with a greater understanding of this social event.

LS2.3 Uses augmentative communication support to enhance child's expression and understanding of emotion

Criterion: The partner makes available and encourages the child to use an augmentative communication support (i.e., nonspeech communication, e.g., gestures, signs, objects, photographs, picture symbols) to enhance his or her ability to express emotions and understand the emotions of others.

LS2.4 Uses augmentative communication support to enhance child's emotional regulation

Criterion: The partner makes available and encourages the child to use an augmentative communication support (i.e., nonspeech communication, e.g., gestures, signs, objects, photographs, picture symbols) to enhance the child's ability to regulate his or her arousal level, by providing a way to express mutual regulation, such as requesting an organizing activity, a break from an activity, or assistance during an activity, through nonspeech means.

**3
Partner uses visual and organizational support**

Visual support is a way of presenting information using visual aids, including individual or sequences of objects, photographs, logos, picture symbols, to enhance the child's active participation and understanding. *Organizational support* is a way of organizing materials or physical space or marking time concepts to enhance the child's organization.

LS3.1 Uses support to define steps within a task

Criterion: The partner uses visual and organizational support to define the goals or steps within a task or activity. For example, the partner refers to a within-activity picture sequence to define steps (e.g., in a scavenger hunt game, the partner may provide a visual map of all of the items that the child is seeking, such as Thomas the Tank Engine figurines or Sesame Street characters). Sophistication of the visual support is commensurate with the child's developmental level.

LS3.2 Uses support to define steps and time for completion of activities

Criterion: The partner uses visual and organizational support to define the steps and the time for completion of activities. For example, a visual timer may provide visual depiction of the time remaining, or a countdown strip with pull-off Velcro numbers may indicate the steps remaining in an activity.

LS3.3   Uses visual support to enhance smooth transitions between activities
Criterion: The partner uses visual support so that transitions from one activity to another are smooth and the child maintains a well-regulated state. For example, the partner uses a now–next visual sequence or refers to a picture schedule to indicate what is coming next. Likewise, the partner may use a visual timer to emphasize that a transition is about to occur.

LS3.4   Uses support to organize segments of time across the day
Criterion: The partner uses visual and organizational support to organize segments of time across the day. For example, the partner refers to a picture or object schedule to review upcoming activities as well as completed activities over a longer time than single transitions.

LS3.5   Uses visual support to enhance attention in group activities
Criterion: The partner uses visual support to enhance the child's attention to the activity and to peers in group activities. For example, the partner uses photographs or picture symbols to cue the child to direct attention to the activity, by using copies of visuals used by the activity leader in circle time, or by exchanging pictures with peers as part of the activity.

LS3.6   Uses visual support to foster active involvement in group activities
Criterion: The partner uses visual support to foster the child's initiation and active participation in group activities. For example, the partner uses visual support to offer choices within activities, including choices of songs, materials, play partners, and so forth.

**4
Partner modifies goals, activities, and learning environment**

LS4.1   Adjusts social complexity to support organization and interaction
Criterion: The partner provides a smaller group setting or one-to-one support or increases as needed to support the child's organization and success in interaction. The partner appropriately judges when to provide more or less social complexity.

LS4.2   Adjusts task difficulty for child success
Criterion: The partner adjusts the task difficulty as needed to foster the child's success and to help the child maintain an optimal level of arousal. For example, the partner reduces the number of steps or simplifies steps in an activity when the child is becoming agitated.

LS4.3   Modifies sensory properties of learning environment
Criterion: The partner modifies the sensory properties of the learning environment as needed to help the child maintain an optimal level of arousal. For example, the partner adjusts lighting and controls for noise level and visual distraction.

LS4.4   Arranges learning environment to enhance attention
Criterion: The partner modifies the arrangement of the learning environment as needed to help the child focus attention. For example, the partner may use chairs organized in a semicircle or small rugs to mark where children sit for small-group activities or may use physical barriers to demarcate boundaries of centers or near doorways.

LS4.5   Arranges learning environment to promote child initiation
Criterion: The partner modifies the arrangement of the learning environment as needed to help the child initiate interactions. For example, the partner organizes ma-

terials out of reach or sight to promote initiation of requests throughout daily routines rather than providing all materials in specified activities.

LS4.6 Designs and modifies activities to be developmentally appropriate

Criterion: The partner designs activities that are developmentally appropriate for the child's level. For example, activities are designed with appropriate expectations for communication, attention, and active participation for the child, taking into account language, motor, and attentional requirements.

LS4.7 Infuses motivating materials and topics in activities

Criterion: The partner infuses materials and topics that are interesting and motivating to the child in activities. For example, materials and topics are chosen based on the child's preferences and learning strengths (e.g., favorite characters from stories, gross motor play). The partner recognizes that the child's intrinsic motivation to communicate is fostered in these contexts in contrast to activities that are selected by the adult and imposed on the child regardless of the child's interest.

LS4.8 Provides activities to promote initiation and extended interaction

Criterion: The partner provides activities in which the child has the opportunity to initiate communication and participate in extended interactions. For example, the partner captures the child's interest in toys or activities that require another's assistance (e.g., bubbles, wind-up toys, paint bottles with tight lids); the partner places a few of the child's preferred or desired objects out of reach (e.g., placing motivating toys or objects on a high shelf or in a sealed but see-through container that will require assistance to open); or the partner adds repeated turns or new steps to the activity to maintain and extend interaction.

LS4.9 Alternates between movement and sedentary activities as needed

Criterion: The partner alternates between activities in which the child has the opportunity to engage in organizing movement activities with those in which the child is expected to be sedentary or still. The frequency and types of movement activities are selected with respect to the child's arousal bias.

LS4.10 "Ups the ante" or increases expectations appropriately

Criterion: The partner "ups the ante" or increases expectations for active participation, communication, and/or problem solving when the child is being successful and is at a more optimal level of arousal. This may occur through "sabotage," or holding out for more sophisticated communication or problem solving, with modeling or prompting as needed.

SAP-O FORMS FOR THE LANGUAGE PARTNER STAGE	The Language Partner stage encompasses two transitions to symbolic communication: the transition to first words, which is usually slow and gradual, and the transition to word combinations, which usually occurs when children go through a burst in vocabulary growth.

We have developed several optional worksheets to assist in gathering data for the SAP-O at the Language Partner stage. These worksheets appear in Appendix A of this volume after the Language Partner SAP-O Form. The Expression of Intentions and Emotions Worksheet for the Language Partner stage is similar to that for the Social Partner stage, with slight differences in the categories included that correspond with objectives in the SAP-O for this stage. Communicative intentions measured in objectives JA4.1 through JA6.3 and expression of emotions measured in objectives JA3.1, JA3.2, MR1.1, and MR1.2 are listed down the side. Presymbolic and symbolic communicative means, which are measured in objectives SU4.1 through SU5.6, are listed across the top. This grid can depict patterns in the means used for each intention and emotion, which can be helpful in making decisions about targeting and linking these objectives.

Two additional worksheets have been developed to assist in recording the word meanings used by children at the Language Partner stage. The Word Meanings Worksheet lists the categories of early relational words, names, and advanced relational words measured in objectives SU5.3, SU5.4, SU5.5, SU6.3, and SU6.4. The Relational Meanings in Word Combinations Worksheet lists the categories of relational meanings in word combinations measured in objectives SU5.6 and SU6.5. The number of boxes to be checked when the word meanings are observed corresponds with the minimum number required to achieve each objective for word use and understanding, respectively.

SAP-O CRITERIA FOR THE LANGUAGE PARTNER STAGE

Following are the criteria for each objective at the Language Partner stage. The criteria define the behavior to be measured for each objective. Some criteria specify a minimum number of times that the child is required to display the behavior to achieve the objective. For criteria that do not specify a minimum number, the child should display the behavior regularly or appropriately for the context. *For all objectives at the Language Partner stage, a rating of 2 requires observations of behaviors with at least three different partners in at least two different contexts unless otherwise noted.*

SOCIAL COMMUNICATION

JOINT ATTENTION

1 Engages in reciprocal interaction

JA1.1 Initiates bids for interaction (= SR1.1)
Criterion: The child initiates a bid for interaction through nonverbal or verbal means. The behavior must be *directed* to another person by proximity (moving toward or away from another person), physical contact (touching another person with a gesture or an action), gaze, or verbalizations paired with gaze. The behavior must be *initiated* by the child, meaning that it is not a response to another person's behavior.

JA1.2 Engages in brief reciprocal interaction (= SR1.2)
Criterion: The child initiates and responds to bids for interaction for at least two consecutive exchanges. An *exchange* consists of a turn from the child and a turn from the partner. At least one of the exchanges must be initiated by the child.

JA1.3 Engages in extended reciprocal interaction (= SR1.3)
Criterion: The child initiates and responds to bids for interaction for at least four consecutive exchanges between the child and partner. An *exchange* consists of a turn from the child and a turn from the partner. At least one of the exchanges must be initiated by the child, and the child's turns need to be related to the partner's turns in topic or focus.

2
Shares attention

JA2.1   Shifts gaze between people and objects
Criterion: The child shifts or alternates gaze spontaneously (without prompting) between a person and an object and back at least three times. The gaze must be directed to another person's face. Gaze shifts may occur without a gesture or word or may support communication. The shift must be smooth and immediate (i.e., the entire sequence should occur within 2 seconds). The gaze shift must be three point or four point. A *three-point gaze shift* may be either a person–object–person gaze shift (i.e., the child is looking at a person, shifts gaze to an object, and then immediately shifts back to the person) or an object–person–object gaze shift (i.e., the child is looking at an object, shifts gaze to a person, and then immediately shifts back to the object). A *four-point gaze shift* is an object–Person A–Person B–object gaze shift (i.e., when the child is looking at an object, shifts gaze to Person A, then immediately shifts gaze to Person B, and then immediately shifts back to the object).

JA2.2   Follows contact and distal point (= SU2.2)
Criterion: The child follows the reference of another person's 1) contact point (e.g., touching an object or a picture with an extended index finger) by directing gaze where the person is pointing at least two times *and* 2) distal point (e.g., pointing to an object or picture at least 3–5 feet away) by turning the head and directing gaze or getting an object where the person is pointing at least two times. The reference should be to the side or behind the child so that the child needs to turn his or her head at least 45°. The instruction can be accompanied by calling the child's name and saying, "Look" or saying, "Give me that," or "Get that," but no other gestural, situational, or verbal cues (e.g., labeling the object) should be used.

JA2.3   Monitors attentional focus of a social partner
Criterion: The child spontaneously follows the reference of another person's attentional focus during an ongoing activity. Evidence includes the child following the reference of another person's gesture, looking at what someone else is paying attention to, or communicating about what someone else is doing.

JA2.4   Secures attention to oneself prior to expressing intentions (≈ JA5.5)
Criterion: The child secures the attention of a social partner by calling nonverbally (e.g., tapping on shoulder or arm) or verbally (e.g., saying partner's name, signing partner's name, holding up a picture) prior to expressing communicative intentions (e.g., requesting, commenting)

3
Shares emotion

JA3.1   Shares negative and positive emotion (= MR1.1; ≈ MR3.1, MR3.2)
Criterion: The child displays 1) *negative emotion* (i.e., a clear vocal, verbal or facial expression of distress or frustration, which may be accompanied by a gesture or change in body posture) *and* 2) positive emotion (i.e., a clear facial expression of pleasure or excitement, which may or may not be accompanied by a vocalization, e.g., laughing, squealing, words). The child must share emotions with others by directing gaze toward another person's face, immediately before, during, or after displaying the emotion.

**JA3.2   Understands and uses symbols to express a range of emotions
           (≈ MR1.2, SR3.5)**
Criterion: The child understands and uses symbols (i.e., words, signs, or pictures) to express at least one positive emotion (e.g., *happy, fun, silly*) *and* at least one negative emotion (e.g., *mad, angry, sad*).

JA3.3   Attunes to changes in partners' expression of emotion ($\approx$ SU2.4, $=$ MR2.5)

Criterion: The child attunes to changes in the expression of emotion of at least three partners by mirroring the emotional tone (e.g., smiles and laughs in response to partner's positive emotion; frowns and stops moving in response to a negative expression).

JA3.4   Describes the emotional state of another person ($\leftrightarrow$ SU5.6)

Criterion: The child notices and describes the emotional state of another person by commenting about it (e.g., "Mommy sad," "Daddy mad").

4

Shares intentions to regulate the behavior of others ($\leftrightarrow$ JA7.2, JA8.2, SU4–SU5, MR3.7)

For the objectives within this goal, the signals must be *directed* to another person by proximity (moving toward or away from another person), physical contact (touching another person with a gesture or an action), or gaze.

JA4.1   Requests desired food or objects ($\approx$ MR2.6)

Criterion: The child directs nonverbal (e.g., unconventional or conventional gestures, vocalizations) or verbal (e.g., words, signs) signals to get another person to give a desired food item or object.

JA4.2   Protests/refuses undesired food or objects ($\approx$ MR3.4)

Criterion: The child directs nonverbal or verbal signals (e.g., pushing away, saying "no") to get another person to remove an undesired food item or object.

JA4.3   Requests help or other actions ($\approx$ MR3.3)

Criterion: The child directs nonverbal or verbal signals to get another person to provide help or assistance in carrying out an action that the child cannot do (e.g., opening containers, activating toys) or other actions (e.g., taps chair and says "sit" to request partner to sit down).

JA4.4   Protests undesired actions or activities ($\approx$ MR3.4)

Criterion: The child directs nonverbal or verbal signals (e.g., pushing away, saying "no," giving stop sign picture) to get another person to cease an undesirable action or get out of an undesirable activity.

5

Shares intentions for social interaction ($\leftrightarrow$ JA7.2, JA8.2, SU4–SU5)

For the objectives within this goal, the signals must be *directed* to another person by proximity (moving toward or away from another person), physical contact (touching another person with a gesture or an action), use of verbalizations (e.g., partner name), or gaze.

JA5.1   Requests comfort ($\approx$ MR3.1)

Criterion: The child directs nonverbal or verbal signals to seek comfort from distress, frustration, or fear/wariness.

JA5.2   Requests social game

Criterion: The child directs nonverbal or verbal signals to direct another person to begin or to continue carrying out a game-like social interaction (e.g., says "down" or gestures toward ground to direct others to fall down during Ring Around the Rosy).

JA5.3   Takes turns

Criterion: The child directs nonverbal or verbal signals as a turn filler to keep a cooperative social exchange going at least two times. This involves waiting for the partner to take a turn.

JA5.4 Greets

Criterion: The child directs nonverbal or verbal signals to indicate notice of a person entering or leaving the immediate situation or to mark the initiation or termination of an interaction (e.g., waves and says "hi" or "bye-bye").

JA5.5 Calls (≈ JA2.4)

Criterion: The child directs nonverbal or verbal signals to gain the attention of another person, followed by an additional communicative signal (e.g., touching arm followed by a reach to request, calling someone's name followed by a point to comment).

JA5.6 Shows off

Criterion: The child directs nonverbal or verbal signals (e.g., clapping, sharing emotion) to attract another's attention to a display of oneself or an action for social sharing (e.g., making a funny face, playing an instrument, reciting a nursery rhyme).

JA5.7 Requests permission

Criterion: The child directs nonverbal or verbal (i.e., word, sign, or picture) signals to seek another's consent to carry out an action (e.g., child says, "Open door?" to get permission to open the door and go outside; child says, "Eat cookie," or exchanges a picture to get permission to eat a cookie).

6
Shares intentions for joint attention (↔ JA7.2, JA8.2, SU4–SU5)

For the objectives within this goal, the signals must be **directed** to another person by proximity (moving object toward another person), physical contact (touching another person with a gesture or an action), or gaze. The signals are not part of a highly practiced and repetitive routine.

JA6.1 Comments on object

Criterion: The child directs nonverbal or verbal signals to get another person to notice or look at an object or entity (e.g., points to picture in a book, shows a toy brought out of a bag).

JA6.2 Comments on action or event

Criterion: The child directs nonverbal or verbal signals to get another person to notice or look at an action, a spectacle, or an event (e.g., looking at a partner and saying "pop" when bubbles pop or "uh oh" when a tower of blocks falls over; pulling a partner to a preferred television program to point out a special character).

JA6.3 Requests information about things of interest

Criterion: The child directs nonverbal or verbal signals to get another person to provide requested information about object or an event (e.g., showing an unfamiliar object paired with a quizzical look; pointing to a picture and saying, "What that?"; showing a horse figure and saying, "Doggie?").

7
Persists and repairs communication breakdowns

JA7.1 Uses appropriate rate of communication for context

Criterion: The child directs nonverbal or verbal signals to a variety of partners at an appropriate rate for the context (e.g., at least once per minute during one-to-one interaction, once every 3 minutes during a small-group interaction, and once every 5–10 minutes during a large-group interaction). Lower rates would be expected with unfamiliar partners, with peers, in highly adult directed contexts, and when activities provide fewer opportunities.

JA7.2   Repeats and modifies communication to repair (↔ JA4–JA6)
Criterion: When there is a *communication breakdown* (i.e., the child is not understood and/or the child does not achieve a desired goal), the child repeats all or part of the same communicative signal to repair or fix the breakdown, or modifies the communicative signal to repair when not understood. Modifying a signal occurs when the child 1) shifts to a different communicative means (i.e., different gesture, different sound, or different combination of gesture and sound), 2) changes a quality of the signal (e.g., clear increase in loudness, syllable added to the vocalization), or 3) repeats the same act but directs it to a different person.

JA7.3   Recognizes breakdowns in communication
Criterion: The child recognizes when there is a breakdown in communication during ongoing interactions in activities by clarifying his or her intention when the partner does not respond appropriately (e.g., saying "want *apple*" after being given a banana following a request) or by clearly indicating that the message is not heard or understood (e.g., saying, "What?" or "Huh?").

8
Shares experiences in reciprocal interaction

JA8.1   Coordinates attention, emotion, and intentions to share experiences
Criterion: The child coordinates the sharing of attention, emotion, and nonverbal or verbal signals to share experiences. This should include sharing some experiences about events remote in time or place (e.g., child comments about new dog to a partner at school; child comments at home about a fun school event).

JA8.2   Shows reciprocity in speaker and listener roles to share experiences (↔ JA4–JA6)
Criterion: The child provides and requests needed information in both the speaker and listener roles to share experiences. The child is able to focus on a topic about sharing experiences for at least four consecutive exchanges between the child and partner. An *exchange* consists of a turn from the child and a turn from the partner.

JA8.3   Initiates interaction and shares experiences with a friend
Criterion: The child initiates interaction and shares experiences with a friend who is a peer similar in age and/or status; that is, the peer is not a tutor or in a teaching role.

SYMBOL USE

1
Learns by observation and imitation of familiar and unfamiliar actions and words

SU1.1   Spontaneously imitates familiar actions or words immediately after a model
Criterion: The child accurately imitates or closely approximates a familiar action or word spontaneously (i.e., without direction to do so) immediately after a partner models the behavior. The child imitates at least two different behaviors. A familiar action or word is one that the child readily displays spontaneously.

SU1.2   Spontaneously imitates unfamiliar actions or words immediately after a model
Criterion: The child accurately imitates or closely approximates an unfamiliar action or word spontaneously (i.e., without direction to do so) immediately after a partner models the behavior. The child imitates at least two different behaviors. An unfamiliar action or word is one that the child does not readily display spontaneously.

SU1.3   Spontaneously imitates actions or words and adds a different behavior

Criterion: The child accurately imitates or closely approximates an action or word spontaneously (i.e., without direction to do so) after a partner has modeled the behavior, and the child adds a different behavior (e.g., imitating clapping hands and adding reaching hands into air). The child engages in at least two different sequences of similar behaviors.

SU1.4   Spontaneously imitates a variety of behaviors later in a different context

Criterion: The child observes a stream of behaviors and accurately imitates or closely approximates a variety of actions or words spontaneously (i.e., without direction to do so) at a later time after a partner has modeled the behavior and in a different context than the behavior was modeled. The child imitates at least five different behaviors. A later time is at least three turns or at least 1 minute after the model or a much later time. A different context is either a different activity or a similar activity with a different partner.

2

Understands nonverbal cues in familiar and unfamiliar activities

SU2.1   Follows situational and gestural cues in familiar and unfamiliar activities (= SR4.2)

Criterion: The child follows a simple instruction in familiar and unfamiliar activities with at least two different situational cues (e.g., partner says, "Wash hands," when standing in front of the sink, and child holds hands out under faucet; partner says, "Clean up," when activity is done and holds out a bag for the toys, and child puts toys in the bag) *and* at least two different gestural cues other than a point (e.g., partner says, "Come here," with open arms extended toward child; partner says, "Give it to me," with palm-up open hand extended near an object).

SU2.2   Follows contact and distal point (= JA2.2)

Criterion: The child follows the reference of another person's contact point (i.e., touching an object or a picture with an extended index finger) by directing gaze where the person is pointing at least two times *and* distal point (i.e., pointing to an object or picture at least 3–5 feet away) by turning the head and directing gaze or getting an object where the person is pointing at least two times. The references should be to the side or behind the child so that the child needs to turn his or her head at least 45°. The instruction can be accompanied by calling the child's name and saying, "Look," or saying, "Give me that," or "Get that," but no other gestural, situational, or verbal cues (e.g., labeling the object) should be used.

SU2.3   Follows instructions with visual cues (photographs or pictures)

Criterion: The child follows a simple instruction with at least two different visual cues (e.g., partner says, "Get the ball," and shows a picture of a ball; partner says, "Let's play Ring Around the Rosy," and shows a photograph of child playing this game, and child goes to the circle and holds out hands ready to play). The instruction should be given with no gestural or situational cues.

SU2.4   Responds to facial expression and intonation cues (≈ JA3.3)

Criterion: The child responds to simple instructions with at least two different facial expressions or intonation cues (e.g., partner says, "I'm gonna get you," with a happy face and rising intonation, and child laughs, runs away, and then stops in anticipation of being tickled; partner says, "No, no, no, don't touch," with an angry face and stern intonation, and child puts object down and backs away). The instruction is given with no gestural or situational cues.

3

Uses familiar objects conventionally in play

SU3.1 Uses a variety of objects in constructive play
Criterion: The child uses at least four similar objects in combination to construct at least three different products (e.g., stacks a tower of blocks or rings, puts puzzle pieces together, puts cars together to make a train, strings beads). Taking blocks off a stack, banging objects together, or putting objects in a container do not count as a combinatorial action.

SU3.2 Uses a variety of familiar objects conventionally toward self
Criterion: The child uses at least five different familiar objects conventionally (i.e., for the conventional or functional use) toward self (e.g., drinks with a bottle or cup, eats or stirs with a spoon, pours with a cup or pitcher, puts hat on, puts shoes on, washes face with cloth, combs or brushes hair, brushes teeth, puts telephone to ear). The object needs to be used in the *proper orientation* (e.g., holding the handle of the spoon; demonstrating brushing motion with toothbrush, but not biting toothbrush). The child can receive credit for imitation of an action using the same object modeled by another person only if the child demonstrates the action a second time without an immediate model.

SU3.3 Uses a variety of familiar objects conventionally toward other
Criterion: The child uses at least five different familiar objects conventionally toward another person or an inanimate object (e.g., hugs or kisses stuffed animal, feeds stuffed animal with utensil, puts blanket on doll, brushes partner's hair, rolls ball or car to another person). The object needs to be used in the proper orientation. The child receives credit for an imitation of an action using the same object modeled by another person only if the child demonstrates the action a second time during the course of the activity without an immediate model.

SU3.4 Combines a variety of actions with objects in play
Criterion: The child combines a variety of actions with familiar objects conventionally toward self or other (e.g., pours into bowl, stirs, and scoops with spoon to feed stuffed animal; kisses stuffed animal, then puts blanket on animal to go to bed; drives toy car, then parks it). The object needs to be used in the proper orientation. The child receives credit for an imitation of an action using the same object modeled by another person only if the child demonstrates the action a second time during the course of the activity or combines the action with a different action without an immediate model.

4

Uses gestures and nonverbal means to share intentions (↔ JA4–JA6, MR3.3, MR3.4)

SU4.1 Uses a variety of conventional and symbolic gestures
Criterion: The child uses at least five different conventional or symbolic gestures. A conventional gesture is a gesture that has shared meaning that is widely recognized. A symbolic gesture is a pantomime action that is referential or like a word (e.g., turning the hand back and forth to indicate *open*, shrugging the shoulders with the arms extended and palms up to indicate *I dunno*, making a flying motion with the hand when the thumb and pinky are extended out to indicate *airplane*). During the Language Part-

ner stage, the child should be using the following gestures, if these were not already acquired during the Social Partner stage: a) show, b) wave, c) distal reach/point, d) clap, e) head shake, f) head nod, and g) other symbolic gestures.

SU4.2 Uses a sequence of gestures or nonverbal means in coordination with gaze

Criterion: The child uses a sequence of two or more gestures or nonverbal means as a communicative signal (e.g., pulls a person by the hand to the closet, then points to an object out of reach; taps to get a person's attention, then shows the person an object) in coordination with gaze (i.e., either looking at people's faces and/or gaze shifts).

5 **Uses words and word combinations to express meanings** (↔ JA4–JA6, MR3.3, MR3.4)	**SU5.1 Coordinates sounds/words with gaze and gestures** Criterion: The child uses gaze in coordination with sounds and/or words. The gaze may be looking at people's faces and/or gaze shifts.

SU5.1 Coordinates sounds/words with gaze and gestures

Criterion: The child uses gaze in coordination with sounds and/or words. The gaze may be looking at people's faces and/or gaze shifts.

SU5.2 Uses at least 5–10 words or echolalic phrases as symbols

Criterion: The child uses at least 5–10 different words or echolalic chunks as symbols. A *word* may be spoken or signed or may be a picture and is defined as 1) a consistent sound pattern or sign that approximates a conventional word *and* 2) a form that is used to refer to a specific object, action, or attribute and that is used to refer to only that word meaning (e.g., "uh oh" when dropping things, "muh" to request more, "baba" to ask for a bottle).

SU5.3 Uses early relational words

Criterion: The child spontaneously expresses all of the following early relational meanings with at least one spoken word, sign, or picture in each category:

a. *existence:* notes the existence of something or directs attention to it (e.g., *this, that, her, what's that?*)

b. *nonexistence/disappearance:* notes that something is not there when expected or that something was there and has disappeared (e.g., *no, gone, all gone, bye-bye*)

c. *recurrence:* requests an object to replace an absent object or notes that an object appears after having been gone (e.g., *more, again, another*)

d. *rejection:* refuses something that is offered (e.g., *no, bye-bye, stop*)

SU5.4 Uses a variety of names for objects, body parts, and agents

Criterion: The child spontaneously expresses all of the following names with speech, signs, or pictures:

a. *objects:* at least 10 different words naming an entity or thing that is the recipient of an action (e.g., *milk, juice, water, cookie, cup, bottle, ball, car, hat, shoe*)

b. *body parts:* at least 3 different words naming a part of the body (e.g., *eye, nose, hand, tummy*)

c. *agents:* at least 3 different words naming a person or animal that can be the source of an action (e.g., *Mommy, Daddy, baby, doggie, kitty*)

SU5.5 Uses a variety of advanced relational words

Criterion: The child spontaneously expresses all of the following advanced relational meanings:

a. *personal-social:* at least two different words to acknowledge someone (e.g., *hi, bye-bye, please, thank you*)

b. *action:* at least five different words to describe general or specific actions that may or may not involve objects (e.g., *do, want, give, look, see, push, drink, throw, kiss, eat, walk, sleep, laugh*)

c. *modifier:* at least five different words to describe states, qualities, and relationships of things, including

- *attribute* (describes characteristics of or differences between things, e.g., *hot, big, stinky, dirty*)

- *possession* (notes that an agent possesses something, e.g., *mine, Mommy*)

- *location* (notes direction or spatial relationship of two objects, e.g., *up, on, off, in, out, under*)

- *denial* (denies the existence of something, e.g., *no, not*)

d. *wh- word:* at least two different *wh-* words to pose questions about the name or location of things (e.g., *what, where*)

SU5.6   Uses a variety of relational meanings in word combinations (↔ JA3.4)
Criterion: The child spontaneously uses at least 20 different word combinations with at least five different utterances in each of the following three major categories:

a. *modifier + object*

- *recurrence + object (more cookie, 'nuther jump)*

- *attribute + object (big shoe, dirty diaper, one baby, nice kitty)*

- *possessor + possession (Mommy shoe, Daddy hair, my cup)*

- *demonstrative + object (this cup, that ball)*

- *location + object (on table, in box)*

b. *negation + object*

- *nonexistence (no juice, water gone)*

- *disappearance (bubbles bye-bye, milk gone)*

- *rejection (no night-night)*

- *denial (no baby, not shoe)*

c. *agent + action + object*

- *action + object (eat cookie, throw ball, drink juice, lookit that, get me, put table, shirt off)*

- *agent + action (Mommy go bye-bye, baby sleep, Daddy throw, doggie sit)*

- *agent + object (Daddy cookie, Mommy bottle, doggie ball, dolly chair)*

- *agent + action + object (Daddy throw ball, Daddy push car, Mommy kiss baby, Mommy get bottle)*

6
Understands
a variety of
words and word
combinations
without
contextual cues

SU6.1   Responds to own name
Criterion: The child responds to his or her name at least two times by turning toward or looking at the person immediately (within 2 seconds) after the child's name is called.

SU6.2   Responds to a variety of familiar words and phrases (= SR1.6)
Criterion: The child responds correctly to at least five different simple instructions with familiar words or phrases in familiar activities or environments (e.g., at the end of the school day, teacher says, "Time to go home—put your coat on," and child goes across the room, gets his coat; after dinner; parent tells child, "Time for a bath," and child runs upstairs to the bathroom; partner says, "Let's go for a ride," and child goes to the door and sits down to have his shoes put on). The instruction should be given with no gestural cues.

SU6.3   Understands a variety of names without contextual cues
Criterion: The child follows a simple instruction with at least 10 different object names, at least 3 different body parts, and at least 3 different person names. The child's response may include touching, showing, or looking (i.e., child must make a clear change in direction of eye gaze) to identify correctly the object, body part, or person (e.g., partner says, "Where's Mommy?" and child turns and looks at his mom; partner says, "Where are your feet?" and child touches his feet; partner says, "Get your cup," with several choices of objects, and child picks up cup). The instruction should be given with no gestural or situational cues.

SU6.4   Understands a variety of relational words without contextual cues
Criterion: The child follows at least three different instructions with each of the following relational meanings (for a total of nine different instructions):

a.   *action* (e.g., partner says, "Give me," "Throw," or "Push ball")

b.   *modifier*

   •   *attribute* (e.g., partner says, "Give me big/little cup")

   •   *possession* (e.g., partner says, "Where's Mommy's/baby's hair?")

   •   *location* (e.g., partner says, "Put ball in/on box")

   •   *denial* (e.g., partner says, "Is this a ball?" while holding up a cup)

c.   *wh- word* (e.g., partner says, "What is this?" while holding up a picture of a ball; partner says, "Where is the ball?" when the ball is on a high shelf)

The instructions should be given with no gestural or situational cues.

SU6.5   Understands a variety of relational meanings in word combinations
**   without contextual cues**
Criterion: The child follows at least 5 different instructions with word combinations expressing each of the following three categories of relational meanings (for a total of 15 different instructions):

a.   *modifier + object* (e.g., partner says, "Jump again," "Give me big shoe," "Give me Mommy's shoe/Daddy's hat/child's shirt," "Put the ball on table/in box")

b.   *negation + object* (e.g., partner says "no blankie," and child puts blanket away; partner says "not shoe" while holding a shirt and shoe, and child takes the shirt)

c. *agent* + *action* + *object*

- *action* + *object* (e.g., partner says, "Throw ball," with several objects out; partner says, "Drink juice," when several choices of food and drink are out; partner says "Put closet," while handing a ball to the child; partner says, "Turn on light," before entering a room; partner says, "Take shirt off," when child is fully dressed)

- *agent* + *action* (e.g., partner says, "Johnny go bye-bye," and child gets jacket to go outside; partner says, "Baby sleep," and child positions doll to sleep; partner says, "Doggie ride," and child gives a stuffed dog a ride in a wagon)

- *agent* + *object* (e.g., partner says "Mommy bottle," and child feeds bottle to Mommy; partner says "Doggie ball," and child throws the ball to the dog, partner says "dolly chair," and child puts the doll in a chair)

- *agent* + *action* + *object* (e.g., partner says, "Johnny throw ball," with several choices of objects out; partner says, "Johnny kiss Mommy/doggie"; partner says, "Doggie push car," with several animal figures and vehicles out)

The instructions should be given with no gestural or situational cues.

EMOTIONAL REGULATION

MUTUAL REGULATION

1 Expresses range of emotions (↔ SU4–SU5)

MR1.1   Shares negative and positive emotion (= JA3.1)

Criterion: The child displays *negative emotion* (i.e., a clear vocal, verbal or facial expression of sadness, anger, or frustration, which may be accompanied by a gesture or change in body posture) and 2) *positive emotion* (i.e., a clear facial expression of pleasure or excitement, which may or may not be accompanied by a vocalization, e.g., laughing, squealing, words). The child must share emotions with others by directing gaze toward another person's face, immediately before, during, or after displaying the emotion.

MR1.2   Understands and uses symbols to express a range of emotions (≈ JA3.2; = SR3.5)

Criterion: The child understands and uses symbols (i.e., words, signs, or pictures) to express at least one positive emotion (e.g., *happy, fun, silly*) *and* at least one negative emotion (e.g., *sad, angry, frustrated*).

MR1.3   Changes emotional expression in familiar activities based on partners' feedback

Criterion: The child changes emotional expression based on verbal or nonverbal feedback from partners in familiar activities (e.g., child changes from having a fearful expression to smiling when partner says, "It's okay, it won't hurt you," when a wind-up toy approaches child).

**2
Responds
to assistance
offered by partners**

MR2.1 Soothes when comforted by partners
Criterion: The child soothes or calms down quickly (i.e., within 30 seconds) when partners offer comfort verbally or nonverbally, with the exception of periods of time when the child is experiencing extreme dysregulation, fear, or violations of expectations.

MR2.2 Engages when alerted by partners
Criterion: The child becomes actively engaged when partners introduce alerting and organizing stimulation through social routines and motor play.

MR2.3 Responds to bids for interaction
Criterion: The child responds to another person's bid for interaction. The bid and response may be nonverbal or verbal. The child's response must be immediate (i.e., displayed within 5 seconds following the other person's bid) and contingent (i.e., maintains the focus of attention or topic). The child's response does not need to demonstrate comprehension of a verbal bid.

MR2.4 Responds to changes in partners' expression of emotion
Criterion: The child responds to changes in partners' expression of emotion by changing his or her behavior (e.g., pausing, dropping a toy, moving toward or away).

MR2.5 Attunes to changes in partners' expression of emotion (= JA3.3)
Criterion: The child attunes to changes in the expression of emotion of at least three partners by mirroring the emotional tone (e.g., smiles and laughs in response to partner's positive emotion; frowns and stops moving in response to a negative expression).

MR2.6 Makes choices when offered by partners (≈ JA4.1)
Criterion: The child directs nonverbal or verbal signals to make a choice when offered by the partner at least two times.

MR2.7 Changes regulatory strategies based on partners' feedback in familiar activities
Criterion: The child changes regulatory strategies (i.e., behavioral or language strategies) based on feedback provided by partners in familiar activities. For example, a child who crashes into his parent to seek pressure to decrease arousal level modifies this strategy when he is redirected to a hugging game, or a child who is vocalizing loudly in anger responds to a picture card for *mad* that is presented to her by touching the card or by saying "mad."

**3
Requests partners'
assistance to
regulate state**

MR3.1 Shares negative emotion to seek comfort (≈ JA3.1; ↔ JA5.1)
Criterion: The child displays *negative emotion* (i.e., a clear vocal or facial expression of distress or frustration, which may be accompanied by a change in body posture or gesture) and shares it with another person by looking at, approaching (e.g., crawling over to), gesturing toward (e.g., raising arms to be picked up), or touching that person (e.g., pulling on pant leg) to seek comfort.

MR3.2 Shares positive emotion to seek interaction (≈ JA3.1)
Criterion: The child displays *positive emotion* (i.e., a clear facial expression of pleasure or excitement, which may or may not be accompanied by a vocalization, e.g., laughing, squealing) or word and shares it by looking at, approaching (e.g., crawling over to), gesturing toward (e.g., raising arms to be picked up, showing an object), or touching that person (e.g., pulling on pant leg, tapping arm) to seek interaction.

MR3.3   Requests help when frustrated (≈ JA4.3; ↔ SU4–SU5)
Criterion: The child directs nonverbal or verbal signals to a partner to get another person to help when a task exceeds the child's skill level.

MR3.4   Protests when distressed (≈ JA4.2, JA4.4; ↔ SU4–SU5)
Criterion: The child directs nonverbal or verbal signals (e.g., pushing away, saying "no" paired with gaze) to get another person to remove an undesired food item or object or to cease an undesired action or to get out of an undesired activity at least two times.

MR3.5   Uses language strategies to request a break
Criterion: The child uses verbal language (i.e., speech, signs, or pictures) to request a break from an activity that is too difficult, overwhelming, boring, long, or undesired (e.g., child says, "Need break," or "Stop, please," or exchanges stop sign icon).

MR3.6   Uses language strategies to request regulating activity or input
Criterion: The child uses verbal language (i.e., speech, signs, or pictures) to request an activity or sensory input that will have a regulating effect on the child's state of arousal (e.g., child says, "Play computer," when the computer would be a calming activity or says, "Go outside," when child needs to be aroused and get a break from sedentary activities).

MR3.7   Uses language strategies to exert social control (↔ JA4)
Criterion: The child uses verbal language (i.e., speech, signs, or pictures) to initiate social control in appropriate situations. For example, the child uses agent + action word combinations to direct others actions in environment (e.g., "Mommy go bye-bye," "Baby sleep," Daddy throw," "Do it").

4
Recovers from extreme dysregulation with support from partners

Extreme dysregulation is a state when a child is not available for engagement or learning, and may experience intense emotions. By definition, a state of extreme dysregulation must preclude the child's ability to engage with people and activities in a productive manner. Extreme dysregulation typically is not brief or episodic, and it may be continuous or cyclical within a period of time. Behavioral evidence of extreme dysregulation may include 1) expression of intense and seemingly inconsolable distress; 2) complete loss of attention to the activity or to other persons; 3) intense, disruptive vocalizations (e.g., crying, screaming, moaning) and/or nonverbal behavior (flailing, self- or other-directed hitting, slapping, biting); 4) frenetic motor activity; 5) extreme shutdown and disengagement for an extended period; and so forth. Extreme dysregulation may be associated with arousal levels that are very high (i.e., extreme distress or excitement) or very low (i.e., extremely passive, disengaged state), either of which precludes engagement.

MR4.1   Responds to partners' efforts to assist with recovery by moving away from activity
Criterion: The child responds to partners' attempts to assist with recovery and to change the child's attentional focus by moving away from activities that are overstimulating or undesired after reaching an extreme state of dysregulation.

MR4.2   Responds to partners' use of behavioral strategies
Criterion: The child responds to partners' use of behavioral strategies (i.e., simple motor actions or sensory-motor strategies) that are implemented to help the child to recover from an extreme state of dysregulation.

MR4.3   Responds to partners' use of language strategies
Criterion: The child responds to partners' use of language strategies (e.g., soothing voice, recitation of familiar nursery rhyme, counting to 10 slowly) that are implemented to help the child recover from an extreme state of dysregulation.

MR4.4   Responds to partners' attempts to reengage in interaction or activity
Criterion: The child responds to partners' attempts to reengage in interaction or activity after recovery (i.e., return to available state) from extreme dysregulation.

MR4.5   Decreases amount of time to recover from extreme dysregulation due to support from partners
Criterion: The amount of time the child takes to *recover* (i.e., return to an available state for learning and engaging) from extreme dysregulation decreases over time when the child is supported by partners.*

MR4.6   Decreases intensity of dysregulated state due to support from partners
Criterion: The intensity of emotional response and the changes in the child's state of arousal or energy level during episodes of dysregulation decrease over time with support from partners.*

   *You may need to rely on baseline information gathered from interviews with others who observe the child over time to determine child-specific criteria for objectives MR4.5 and MR4.6 at the Language Partner stage.

SELF-REGULATION

1 Demonstrates availability for learning and interacting

SR1.1   Initiates bids for interaction (= JA1.1)
Criterion: The child initiates a bid for interaction through nonverbal or verbal means. The behavior must be *directed* to another person by proximity (moving toward or away from another person), physical contact (touching another person with a gesture or an action), gaze, or verbalizations paired with gaze. The behavior must be *initiated* by the child, meaning that it is not a response to another person's behavior.

SR1.2   Engages in brief reciprocal interaction (= JA1.2)
Criterion: The child initiates and responds to bids for interaction for at least two consecutive exchanges. An *exchange* consists of a turn from the child and a turn from the partner. At least one of the exchanges must be initiated by the child.

SR1.3   Engages in extended reciprocal interaction (= JA1.3)
Criterion: The child initiates and responds to bids for interaction for at least four consecutive exchanges between the child and partner. An *exchange* consists of a turn from the child and a turn from the partner. At least one of the exchanges must be initiated by the child, and the child's turns need to be related to the partner's turns in topic or focus.

SR1.4   Responds to sensory and social experiences with differentiated emotions
Criterion: The child responds to different sensory and social experiences with differentiated emotions (e.g., shows happiness and excitement in fun activities, distress in stressful or unpleasant activities, and fear or wariness in unfamiliar or scary activities).

SR1.5   Demonstrates ability to inhibit actions and behaviors
Criterion: The child demonstrates the ability to inhibit actions or behaviors in situations in which the child knows the behaviors are inappropriate. This is done without prompting from the partner. For example, the child reaches to grab a toy that another child has and then withdraws her hand and waits her turn.

SR1.6   Responds to a variety of familiar words and phrases (= SU6.2)
Criterion: The child responds correctly to at least five different simple instructions with familiar words or phrases in familiar activities or environments (e.g., at the end of the school day, teacher says, "Time to go home—put your coat on," and child goes across the room, gets his coat; after dinner; parent tells child, "Time for a bath," and child runs upstairs to the bathroom; partner says, "Let's go for a ride," and child goes to the door and sits down to have his shoes put on). The instruction should be given with no gestural cues.

SR1.7   Persists during tasks with reasonable demands
Criterion: The child persists in trying to complete tasks when the demands are reasonable. Reasonable demands are considered relative to the developmental appropriateness of the task and whether the child is at an optimal level of arousal. The child does not need to successfully complete tasks but needs to demonstrate the effort to complete tasks.

SR1.8   Demonstrates emotional expression appropriate to context
Criterion: The child expresses a range of emotions (i.e., positive, neutral, and negative) that are appropriate given the social and sensory variables present in the environment. For example, the child laughs and smiles appropriately when engaged in a fun social game (e.g., London Bridge) with the class.

**2
Uses behavioral strategies to regulate arousal level during familiar activities**

Behavioral strategies are simple motor actions or sensory-motor strategies that the child engages in that regulate arousal level, evident by the child's level of attention, alertness, activity level, emotion, and engagement.

SR2.1   Uses behavioral strategies to regulate arousal level during solitary and social activities
Criterion: The child uses behavioral strategies to increase arousal level (when underaroused) and decrease arousal level (when overaroused) in solitary activities and during social interactions. Examples of behavioral strategies that may be used in solitary activities include sucking a thumb, rocking, rubbing a soft blanket, hiding in a tight corner, making repetitive vocalizations, flapping hands, grinding teeth, walking on toes, jumping, swinging, spinning, eating, or listening to music. Examples of behavioral strategies that may be used during social interaction include sucking a thumb, holding a comfort object, averting gaze, moving away to be alone, jumping, flapping hands, mouthing, chewing, toe walking, approaching another person to play a social game, rocking, or spinning. *Overarousal* may be due to excessive sensory stimulation, too much excitement, or stressful events. *Underarousal* may be due to fatigue, boredom, or lack of organizing stimulation and may result in lack of attention or nonresponsiveness.

SR2.2   Uses behavioral strategies modeled by partners to regulate arousal level

Criterion: The child uses behavioral strategies (i.e., simple motor actions or sensory-motor strategies) that are imitated either immediately or at a later time from behaviors modeled by partners to regulate arousal level (e.g., squeezing hands, jumping).

SR2.3   Uses behavioral strategies to engage productively in an extended activity

Criterion: The child is able to engage productively for an extended activity (i.e., at least 10–15 minutes) and uses behavioral strategies (i.e., simple motor actions or sensory-motor strategies) as needed to regulate arousal level (e.g., mouths or bites a chewy toy or piece of food or gum, squeezes object or stress ball, bounces leg, rocks in chair, plays with fidget toy).

**3
Uses language
strategies to
regulate arousal
level during
familiar activities**

Language strategies are words or other symbols (i.e., signs, pictures) that the child uses that regulate arousal level, evident by the child's level of attention, alertness, activity level, emotion, and engagement. Language strategies may include creative utterances or delayed echolalia.

SR3.1   Uses language strategies to regulate arousal level during solitary activities

Criterion: The child uses language strategies to increase arousal level (when underaroused) and decrease arousal level (when overaroused) in solitary activities. Examples of language strategies that may be used in solitary activities include the child's repeating, "I'm okay," after falling down; the child's saying "mad" during solitary play; or the child's stating "Don't worry," when afraid, all of which correctly identify the child's emotional state but are not directed to others. *Overarousal* may be due to excessive sensory stimulation, too much excitement, or stressful events. *Underarousal* may be due to fatigue, boredom, or lack of organizing stimulation and may result in lack of attention or nonresponsiveness.

SR3.2   Uses language strategies to regulate arousal level during social interactions

Criterion: The child uses language strategies to increase arousal level (when underaroused) and decrease arousal level (when overaroused) during social interactions. Examples of language strategies that may be used in social interactions include the child's identifying his or her emotional state or using delayed echolalia to help promote organization and attention.

SR3.3   Uses language strategies modeled by partners to regulate arousal level

Criterion: The child uses language strategies (i.e., words or other symbols, e.g., signs, pictures) that are imitated either immediately or at a later time (i.e., delayed echolalia) from language modeled by partners to regulate arousal level (e.g., child uses language to cope with stressful events, such as "Fire alarm all done"; "Mommy happy"; or "First finish work, then time for snack").

SR3.4   Uses language strategies to engage productively in an extended activity

Criterion: The child is able to engage productively for an extended activity (i.e., at least 10–15 minutes) and uses language strategies (i.e., words or other symbols, e.g., signs, pictures) to regulate arousal level. For example, the child may identify his emotions or repeat instructions (e.g., "Bead on"; "Build tower"; "Three more, then all done") to help maintain focus of attention.

SR3.5   Uses symbols to express a range of emotions ($\approx$ JA3.2; = MR1.2)
Criterion: The child uses symbols (i.e., words, signs, or pictures) to express at least one positive emotion (e.g., *happy, fun, silly*) *and* at least one negative emotion (e.g., *sad, angry, frustrated*).

4
Regulates emotion during new and changing situations

SR4.1   Participates in new and changing situations
Criterion: The child is able to participate in new and changing situations. Participation must include some degree of active involvement and engagement, not simply tolerance without involvement or passive attention. *New situations* are activities or features of activities that are unfamiliar to the child (e.g., an activity that the child has not participated in; a new person joining a familiar activity). *Changing situations* are ones that have variation in key features (e.g., sensory stimulation, activity level, activity sequence, task difficulty) or that have unexpected features (e.g., unpredictable events such as changes in place or sequence of common routines, activities terminated prematurely).

SR4.2   Follows situational and gestural cues in unfamiliar activities
(= SU2.1)
Criterion: The child follows a simple instruction in familiar and unfamiliar activities with at least two different situational cues (e.g., partner says, "Wash hands," when standing in front of the sink, and child holds hands out under faucet; partner says, "Clean up," when activity is done and holds out a bag for the toys, and child puts toys in the bag) *and* with at least two different gestural cues other than a point (e.g., partner says, "Come here," with open arms extended toward child; partner says, "Give it to me," with palm-up open hand extended near an object).

SR4.3   Uses behavioral strategies to regulate arousal level in new and
changing situations
Criterion: The child uses behavioral strategies to regulate arousal level and intensity of emotional response in new (i.e., unfamiliar) and changing (i.e., unexpected features) situations. Such strategies may include conventional sensory-motor actions such as the child tapping his toes or chewing gum. These strategies may also be idiosyncratic actions as long as they help the child to attain or maintain a more regulated state (e.g., walking on toes, flapping, rocking).

SR4.4   Uses language strategies to regulate arousal level in new and
changing situations
Criterion: The child uses language strategies (e.g., delayed echolalia, emotion words, language pertaining to the activity) to regulate arousal level and intensity of emotional response in new (i.e., unfamiliar) and changing (i.e., unexpected features) situations.

SR4.5   Uses behavioral strategies to regulate arousal level during transitions
Criterion: The child uses behavioral strategies to regulate arousal level and intensity of emotional response during transitions between activities. For example, the child holds a ball to squeeze while walking from the classroom to the cafeteria.

SR4.6   Uses language strategies to regulate arousal level during transitions
Criterion: The child uses language strategies to regulate arousal level and intensity of emotional response during transitions between activities. For instance, the child sings a familiar song during transition; repeats a partner's model "First playdough, then slide"; or uses symbols to label emotions.

**5
Recovers
from extreme
dysregulation
by self**

Extreme dysregulation is a state when a child is not available for engagement or learning, and may experience intense emotions. By definition, a state of extreme dysregulation must preclude the child's ability to engage with people and activities in a productive manner. Extreme dysregulation typically is not brief or episodic, and it may be continuous or cyclical within a period of time. Behavioral evidence of extreme dysregulation may include 1) expression of intense and seemingly inconsolable distress; 2) complete loss of attention to the activity or to other people; 3) intense, disruptive vocalizations (e.g., crying, screaming, moaning) and/or nonverbal behavior (flailing, self- or other-directed hitting, slapping, biting); 4) frenetic motor activity; 5) extreme shutdown and disengagement for an extended period; and so forth. Extreme dysregulation may be associated with arousal levels that are very high (i.e., extreme distress or excitement) or very low (i.e., extremely passive, disengaged state), either of which precludes engagement.

SR5.1   Removes self from overstimulating or undesired activity
Criterion: The child moves away from activities that are overstimulating or undesired after reaching an extreme state of dysregulation.

SR5.2   Uses behavioral strategies to recover from extreme dysregulation
Criterion: The child uses behavioral strategies (i.e., simple motor actions or sensory-motor strategies) to recover from an extreme state of dysregulation.

SR5.3   Uses language strategies to recover from extreme dysregulation
Criterion: The child uses language strategies (i.e., words or other symbols, e.g., signs, pictures) to recover from an extreme state of dysregulation.

SR5.4   Reengages in interaction or activity after recovery from extreme dysregulation
Criterion: The child is able to independently reengage or bring him- or herself back to an interaction or activity after recovery (i.e., return to optimal level of arousal) from extreme dysregulation.

SR5.5   Decreases amount of time to recover from extreme dysregulation
Criterion: The amount of time the child takes to *recover* (i.e., return to an optimal level of arousal) from extreme dysregulation decreases over time.*

SR5.6   Decreases intensity of dysregulated state
Criterion: The intensity of emotional response and the changes in the child's state of arousal or energy level during episodes of extreme dysregulation decrease over time.*

You may need to rely on baseline information gathered from interviews with others who observe the child over time to determine child-specific criteria for objectives SR5.5 and SR5.6 at the Language Partner stage.

TRANSACTIONAL SUPPORT

INTER-PERSONAL SUPPORT

1

Partner is responsive to child

IS1.1   Follows child's focus of attention

Criterion: The partner follows the child's focus of attention by looking at and/or talking about what the child is attending to most of the time.

IS1.2   Attunes to child's emotion and pace

Criterion: The partner attunes to the child's emotion and pace by mirroring the emotional tone of the child's behavior and adjusting nonverbal behavior and vocalizations to the child's behavior (e.g., partner smiles and laughs in response to child's positive emotion, partner looks sad in response to child's distressed expression).

IS1.3   Responds appropriately to child's signals to foster a sense of communicative competence

Criterion: The partner responds to the child's nonverbal or verbal signals directed to the partner for behavioral regulation, social interaction, or joint attention by responding appropriately to the child's intended goal. For example, if the child is requesting an object, the partner gives the child that object. If the child is protesting or refusing an object, the partner removes that object. If the child is seeking comfort, comfort is provided, and if the child is drawing attention to an event, the partner focuses attention on the event.

IS1.4   Recognizes and supports child's behavioral and language strategies to regulate arousal level

Criterion: The partner recognizes the child's use of behavioral and language strategies to regulate arousal level and supports these strategies. For example, if the child is trying to jump or move as an alerting and energizing strategy, the partner modifies the interaction to support or incorporate this strategy; if the child persistently seeks pressure as a means of organization by pressing into partners, the partner provides pressure through hugs; and so forth. If the child is continually talking about a loud noise in the environment, the partner attempts to provide identifying information about the noise.

IS1.5   Recognizes signs of dysregulation and offers support

Criterion: The partner recognizes the child's signs of dysregulation. For example, the partner provides support when behavioral signs indicate that the child is not available for learning or engaging due to an arousal state that is too high, including distress or extreme excitement, or too low, including disinterest or fatigue. The partner provides appropriate assistance contingent on the child's arousal state in an effort to help the child regulate arousal. Assistance may be in the form of behavioral or language strategies.

IS1.6   Imitates child

Criterion: The partner imitates the child's verbal and/or nonverbal behavior and gives the turn back to the child when doing so is appropriate to the context. For example, if the child acts on objects or talks, the partner imitates or approximates these behaviors and pauses, waiting for a further response from the child.

IS1.7   Offers breaks from interaction or activity as needed
Criterion: The partner schedules, offers, or allows for breaks from interaction or activities when the child's behavior suggests that a break is needed (e.g., as demonstrated by a change in arousal state, focus of attention, activity level, or emotional state) or when the child has been engaged in one activity for a long time. Breaks may involve a temporary pause from or cessation of an ongoing activity, with no specific demands being made for the child to attend or participate during the break. Breaks may also involve redirection to motivating and organizing activities.

IS1.8   Facilitates reengagement in interactions and activities following breaks
Criterion: The partner facilitates reengagement in interactions and activities following break times when the child is demonstrating appropriate arousal level and emotional state to participate fully in ongoing activities.

2
Partner
fosters initiation

IS2.1   Offers choices nonverbally or verbally
Criterion: The partner offers choices to the child nonverbally or verbally, dependent on arousal state. For example, if a child is in a very high state of arousal, a choice is offered nonverbally; however, when the child is in a well-regulated state, choices are offered verbally. Choices may include what to eat, what to wear, what activity to participate in, what objects to use in an activity, and so forth.

IS2.2   Waits for and encourages initiations
Criterion: The partner waits for the child to initiate using nonverbal or verbal signals and looks expectantly at the child to encourage initiation. For example, in activities in which opportunities for initiation are provided (e.g., choice making, playing a fun social game with clear turns) or needs are created for the child to communicate (e.g., desired objects are visible, but put out of reach), the child is allowed sufficient time to direct a communicative signal to the partner with proximity (moving toward or away from another person), physical contact (touching another person with a gesture or an action), or gaze. The partner does not intervene unless it becomes clear that the child is not going to initiate and that the child needs additional support. Initiations are encouraged regardless of whether they are nonverbal or verbal; however, there should be an increasing bias to facilitate the use of symbolic strategies or the child's most sophisticated means in initiation.

IS2.3   Provides a balance of initiated and respondent turns
Criterion: The partner does not ask too many questions or give too many commands (either of which limits a child to primarily a respondent mode) and provides a balance of taking turns in relation to the child's initiations and responses.

IS2.4   Allows child to initiate and terminate activities
Criterion: The partner shares control with the child over when to initiate and terminate activities when appropriate. For example, the child may indicate that he is done with an activity nonverbally (e.g., walking away when finished, pushing away materials) or verbally (e.g., saying or signing "done"). If the child is engaged in a must-do activity (e.g., dressing, washing) or if the activity is very close to successful completion, the partner verbally acknowledges the child's communicative bid to end the activity (and may indicate steps to completion), even if it is not possible for the activity to be ter-

minated immediately. Initiations and terminations are encouraged regardless of whether they are nonverbal or verbal; however, there should be an increasing bias to facilitate the use of symbolic strategies or the child's most sophisticated means to be used in initiations and terminations.

3
Partner respects child's independence

IS3.1   Allows child to take breaks to move about as needed
Criterion: The partner allows the child to take breaks from activities when appropriate for the context to move about as needed (e.g., after participating for some time, particularly in activities that require sitting and focusing attention).

IS3.2   Provides time for child to solve problems or complete activities at own pace
Criterion: The partner gives the child adequate time to actively solve problems and to finish activities at the child's pace in most activities. For example, the partner refrains from rushing the child or providing premature prompting as long as the child is progressing in an activity and does not need additional support.

IS3.3   Interprets problem behavior as communicative and/or regulatory
Criterion: The partner recognizes, interprets, and responds to problem behavior as serving a communicative purpose. For example, if the child pushes or hits to protest, the partner acknowledges the child's intent and may model a more socially acceptable means for the child (if appropriate). Likewise, if a child is talking loudly in an effort to block out disorganizing environmental sounds, the partner recognizes this and encourages the use of other regulatory strategies.

IS3.4   Honors protests, rejections, or refusals when appropriate
Criterion: The partner honors the child's signals to protest, reject, or refuse an object or activity when appropriate for the context. For example, in situations in which the child clearly does not wish to accept offered items or engage in activities, the partner does not continue to demand that the child do so under appropriate circumstances (e.g., during nonessential activities, when other choices of foods or toys are available).

4
Partner sets stage for engagement

IS4.1   Gets down on child's level when communicating
Criterion: The partner positions him- or herself and gets down on the child's level to encourage face-to-face interaction or physical proximity when communicating with the child.

IS4.2   Secures child's attention before communicating
Criterion: The partner secures the child's attention nonverbally or verbally before communicating with the child. For example, the partner calls the child's name or touches the child before directing communicative signals to the child.

IS4.3   Uses appropriate proximity and nonverbal behavior to encourage interaction
Criterion: The partner uses appropriate proximity (closeness and orientation to the child) and enticing nonverbal behavior (facial expression, gesture, intonation) to invite and encourage interaction. For example, rather than attempting to engage the child from a distance (e.g., calling to child from across the room), the partner comes close to the child and uses clear gestures, objects, and animated facial expression to engage the

child. Similarly, when looking at picture books, the partner may use a face-to-face orientation to promote gaze shifting and sharing of attention.

IS4.4 Uses appropriate words and intonation to support optimal arousal level and engagement

Criterion: The partner uses appropriate words and intonation to support the child's optimal arousal level and engagement. For example, the partner either uses exaggerated, more intense vocalizations or verbalizations for an alerting effect or quieter, less intense vocalizations or verbalizations for a calming effect, as appropriate.

5
Partner provides developmental support

IS5.1 Encourages imitation

Criterion: The partner encourages the child to imitate behavior spontaneously by following the child's attentional focus, waiting, taking turns, and modeling behaviors for the child to imitate. Behaviors modeled may include vocalization, word approximations, or nonverbal action.

IS5.2 Encourages interaction with peers

Criterion: The partner encourages the child to interact with peers by drawing peers to the child, helping the child to respond to bids from peers, helping the child initiate bids for interaction directed to peers, and mediating successful interactions with peers. The partner may use verbal and/or nonverbal means to encourage interaction.

IS5.3 Attempts to repair breakdowns verbally or nonverbally

Criterion: The partner attempts to repair *communication breakdowns* (i.e., situations in which the partner does not understand the child's signal or the child does not understand the partner's message) either verbally or nonverbally by clarifying the meaning of the signal. For example, the partner may repeat the verbal or nonverbal signal or may modify the signal by adding words or gestures.

IS5.4 Provides guidance and feedback as needed for success in activities

Criterion: The partner provides support, guidance, and feedback as needed in activities so that the child maintains optimal arousal and experiences success. For example, the partner provides social praise or uses appropriate guided participation strategies (i.e., additional cues or prompts), without excessively prompting or directing the child.

IS5.5 Provides guidance on expressing emotions and understanding the cause of emotions

Criterion: The partner provides support, guidance, and feedback as needed in activities so that the child expresses appropriate emotions and understands the cause of his or her emotions. For example, the teacher says, "You don't like it when Samantha hits you. That hurts and makes you mad. Tell her, 'Stop it.'"

6
Partner adjusts language input

IS6.1 Uses nonverbal cues to support understanding

Criterion: When talking to the child, the partner uses clear and appropriate nonverbal cues (gestures, facial expressions, intonation) to support the child's understanding of the message. Words are not used in isolation as the only means to communicate.

IS6.2 Adjusts complexity of language input to child's developmental level

Criterion: When talking to the child, the partner adjusts the complexity of the language so that it is appropriate for the child's developmental level. For example, if the child does understand some words, the partner uses mostly two- and three-word phrases when talking to the child or consistently simplifies longer utterances (e.g., partner follows up the request, "Time to sit down and eat dinner," with "Time for dinner" and "Sit down").

IS6.3   Adjusts quality of language input to child's arousal level

Criterion: When talking to the child, the partner adjusts the quality of the language, which may include the content, complexity, or intonation, to support the child's arousal level. For example, the partner uses a soothing vocal tone, less exaggerated intonation, and simplified language when the child is highly aroused or more exaggerated vocal tone and volume when child is underaroused.

7
Partner models appropriate behaviors

IS7.1   Models appropriate nonverbal communication and emotional expressions

Criterion: The partner provides clear and appropriate models of nonverbal communication (e.g., gestures) and emotional expressions (e.g., smiling and laughing to indicate pleasure).

IS7.2   Models a range of communicative functions

Criterion: The partner models a range of communicative functions verbally and nonverbally, for the following:

a. *behavioral regulation:* For example, the partner models pointing or holding out an open palm paired with saying "more ball" to request, the partner models a giving gesture paired with saying "help" to request actions, the partner models a pushing-away gesture while stating "all done" to protest or refuse an object, or the partner models reaching paired with an object label to request a desired object.

b. *social interaction:* For example, the partner models waving with "Hi, Tommy," or "Bye, Tommy," to greet on arrival or departure; the partner models making a reaching gesture while saying, "Want hug," to request comfort; the partner initiates a social game through nonverbal and verbal reenactments (e.g., hides own face to initiate a game of Peekaboo, starts the motions of a fingerplay song) and/or verbal means (e.g., saying "Peekaboo" or "I'm gonna get you"); or the partner models clapping to seek another's praise following completion of routines and activities.

c. *joint attention:* For example, the partner models a nonverbal comment by showing objects or pointing to interesting events and pairs these comments with a developmentally appropriate verbal model (e.g., saying "a ball," "big ball," or "ball roll").

IS7.3   Models appropriate constructive and symbolic play

Criterion: The partner models appropriate play for the child's developmental level and provides a variety of experiences with sensorimotor, symbolic, and constructive play. For example, with a duplicate set of play materials, the partner models single-scheme imaginative play, such as feeding a doll for a child making the transition to the early stages of symbolic play. Opportunities for sensorimotor exploration and constructive play (e.g., playing with blocks and puzzles) are provided on regular basis.

IS7.4   Models appropriate behavior when child uses inappropriate behavior

Criterion: In situations in which the child displays inappropriate behavior but is regulated enough to benefit from models, the partner models appropriate behavior. For example, the partner models making a pushing-away gesture and saying "no carrot" if the child screams to reject a food item that is offered, or models the use of a picture symbol, word, and/or sign for "all done" if the child is forcefully attempting to escape from an activity. Likewise, for a child who is chewing on her clothing and biting others in an effort to regulate arousal, appropriate mouthing and biting activities are modeled and provided (e.g., provision of a cup or toys).

IS7.5 Models "child-perspective" language

Criterion: The partner models language from the perspective of the child and considers the child's intentions and developmental level. For example, if the child is reaching for a toy car that is out of reach, the partner provides a model that matches the child's intention and developmental level, such as "car" or "car down." If the child produces an angry vocalization directed to the partner, the partner models saying "mad," "Billy's mad," or "I am mad."

LEARNING SUPPORT

1 Partner structures activity for active participation

LS1.1 Defines clear beginning and ending to activity

Criterion: The partner structures the activity so that the beginning and ending are clearly defined for the child. Natural or planned rituals are used. For example, a swinging activity begins with saying, "Ready, set, go," and ends with saying and signing "stop," or the beginning of an activity is marked with taking out toys and the end of the activity is marked with the words and sign for "all done."

LS1.2 Creates turn-taking opportunities and leaves spaces for child to fill in

Criterion: The partner structures the activity by creating turn-taking opportunities and leaving spaces for the child to fill in a turn. The child's turn may be nonverbal or verbal. For example, when initiating an activity, the partner models "Ready, set . . . " and allows the child to say "go"; the partner rocks with child to music and pauses for the child to indicate verbally or nonverbally to continue; or spaces are left for the child to fill in during book routines that provide frequent repetition and carrier phrases (e.g., as found in the *Brown Bear, Brown Bear* books).

LS1.3 Provides predictable sequence to activity

Criterion: The partner provides a predictable sequence to the activity by the nature of the activity itself, through repetition so that the steps become familiar or the use of other support to make it predictable to the child. For example, the partner practices a constructive play activity requiring a fixed sequence of steps to completion (e.g., nesting cups, combining ingredients to create a product), or the partner refers to a picture sequence to indicate progress in an activity and steps to completion. This strategy is also used during caregiving routines.

LS1.4 Offers repeated learning opportunities

Criterion: The partner consistently and predictably repeats aspects of activities across contexts throughout the child's day (e.g., choice-making opportunities at snack, circle time, and lunch) or repeats similar activities over time (e.g., pretend play with a feeding set one day and a grooming set another day) to provide predictable learning opportunities for the child. Predictable repetition is in contrast to introducing too many novel activities within a time frame.

LS1.5   Offers varied learning opportunities

Criterion: Within the context of repetition and familiar routines, the partner varies an aspect of the activity, which provides novelty for the child to learn from. For example, once the child is familiar with a play activity (e.g., blowing bubbles), the partner may vary this routine by pausing just prior to blowing to provide an opportunity for the child to request continuation. Similarly, once the child is familiar with a snack routine, the partner may vary the activity by providing a cup while withholding the juice or milk to encourage an opportunity for a request. The partner may vary a predictable activity to elicit commenting (e.g., removing objects from a "surprise" box to entice child to hold up and show an object and comment about the object by ensuring that the objects removed are sufficiently novel or ever changing).

2

Partner uses augmentative communication support to foster development

LS2.1   Uses augmentative communication support to enhance child's communication and expressive language

Criterion: The partner makes available and encourages the child to use an augmentative communication support (i.e., nonspeech communication, e.g., gestures, signs, objects, pictures, photographs, picture symbols) to enhance the child's ability to communicate using one or a variety of nonspeech modalities.

LS2.2   Uses augmentative communication support to enhance child's understanding of language and behavior

Criterion: The partner uses and refers to an augmentative communication support (i.e., nonspeech communication, e.g., gestures, signs, objects, photographs, picture symbols) to enhance the child's ability to understand language and behavior. For example, a partner may show a picture symbol sequence during a snack routine of the agent + action combination "Andrew eat" while the child is eating or may show a picture of a familiar family member (e.g., Mom, Dad, or a sibling) just prior to his or her arrival home to provide the child with a greater understanding of this social event.

LS2.3   Uses augmentative communication support to enhance child's expression and understanding of emotion

Criterion: The partner makes available and encourages the child to use an augmentative communication support (i.e., nonspeech communication, e.g., gestures, signs, picture symbols) to enhance his or her ability to express emotions and understand the emotions of others through use of word combinations.

LS2.4   Uses augmentative communication support to enhance child's emotional regulation

Criterion: The partner makes available and encourages the child to use an augmentative communication support (i.e., nonspeech communication, e.g., gestures, signs, objects, photographs, picture symbols) to enhance the child's ability to regulate his or her arousal level, by providing a way to express mutual regulation, such as requesting an organizing activity, a break from an activity, or assistance during an activity, through nonspeech means.

3

Partner uses visual and organizational support

Visual support is a way of presenting information using visual aids, including individual or sequences of objects, photographs, logos, picture symbols, to enhance the child's active participation and understanding. *Organizational support* is a way of organizing materials or physical space or marking time concepts to enhance the child's organization.

LS3.1   Uses support to define steps within a task
Criterion: The partner uses visual and organizational support to define the goals or steps within a task or activity. For example, the partner refers to a within-activity picture sequence to define steps (e.g., in a scavenger hunt, partner may provide a visual map of all of the items that the child is seeking; in an art activity, partner may provide a visual listing of three steps, including picture symbols for 1) cut paper, 2) glue paper, and 3) color paper). Sophistication of the visual support is commensurate with the child's developmental level.

LS3.2   Uses support to define steps and time for completion of activities
Criterion: The partner uses visual and organizational support to define the steps and the time for completion of activities. For example, a visual timer may provide visual depiction of the time remaining, or a countdown strip with pull-off Velcro numbers may indicate the steps remaining in an activity.

LS3.3   Uses visual support to enhance smooth transitions between activities
Criterion: The partner uses visual support so that transitions from one activity to another are smooth and the child maintains an optimal level of arousal. For example, the partner uses a now–next visual sequence or refers to a picture schedule to indicate what is coming next. Likewise, the partner may use a visual timer to emphasize that a transition is about to occur.

LS3.4   Uses support to organize segments of time across the day
Criterion: The partner uses visual and organizational support to organize segments of time across the day. For example, the partner refers to a picture schedule to review upcoming activities as well as completed activities over a longer time than single transitions.

LS3.5   Uses visual support to enhance attention in group activities
Criterion: The partner uses visual support to enhance the child's attention to the activity and to peers in group activities. For example, the partner uses photographs or picture symbols to cue the child to direct attention to the activity, by using copies of visual support used by the activity leader in circle time or by exchanging pictures with peers as part of the activity.

LS3.6   Uses visual support to foster active involvement in group activities
Criterion: The partner uses visual support to foster the child's initiation and active participation in group activities. For example, the partner uses visual support (e.g., a spinner with children's pictures on segments of the spinner, a turn card) to offer choices within activities, including choices of songs, materials, and play partners, and/or to signal turns in activities.

**4
Partner modifies
goals, activities,
and learning
environment**

LS4.1   Adjusts social complexity to support organization and interaction
Criterion: The partner provides a smaller group setting or one-to-one support as needed to support the child's organization and success in interaction. The partner appropriately judges when to provide more or less social complexity.

LS4.2   Adjusts task difficulty for child success
Criterion: The partner adjusts the task difficulty as needed to foster the child's success and to help the child maintain an optimal level of arousal. For example, the partner reduces the number of steps or simplifies steps in an activity when the child is becoming agitated.

LS4.3   Modifies sensory properties of learning environment

Criterion: The partner modifies the sensory properties of the learning environment as needed to help the child maintain an optimal level of arousal. For example, the partner adjusts lighting and controls for noise level and visual distraction.

LS4.4   Arranges learning environment to enhance attention

Criterion: The partner modifies the arrangement of the learning environment as needed to help the child focus attention. For example, the partner may use chairs organized in a semicircle or small rugs to mark where children sit for small-group activities or may use physical barriers to demarcate boundaries of centers or near doorways.

LS4.5   Arranges learning environment to promote child initiation

Criterion: The partner modifies the arrangement of the learning environment as needed to help the child initiate interactions. For example, the partner organizes materials out of reach or sight to promote initiation of requests throughout daily routines rather than providing all materials in specified activities.

LS4.6   Designs and modifies activities to be developmentally appropriate

Criterion: The partner designs activities that are developmentally appropriate for the child's level (e.g., activities are designed with appropriate expectations for communication, attention, and active participation for the child) or modifies the developmental difficulty of activities (e.g., activities are simplified if the child becomes frustrated or has difficulty with the task), taking into account language, motor, and attentional requirements.

LS4.7.   Infuses motivating materials and topics in activities

Criterion: The partner infuses materials and topics that are interesting and motivating to the child in activities. For example, materials and topics are chosen based on the child's preferences and learning strengths (e.g., favorite characters from stories, gross motor play). The partner recognizes that the child's intrinsic motivation to communicate is fostered in these contexts in contrast to activities that are selected by the adult and imposed on the child regardless of the child's interest.

LS4.8   Provides activities to promote initiation and extended interaction

Criterion: The partner provides activities in which the child has the opportunity to initiate communication and participate in extended interactions. For example, the partner captures the child's interest in toys or activities that require another's assistance (e.g., bubbles, wind-up toys, paint bottles with tight lids); the partner places a few of the child's preferred or desired objects out of reach (e.g., placing motivating toys or objects on a high shelf or in a sealed but see-through container that will require assistance to open); or the partner adds repeated turns or new steps to the activity to maintain and extend interaction.

LS4.9   Alternates between movement and sedentary activities as needed

Criterion: The partner alternates between activities in which the child has the opportunity to engage in organizing movement activities with those in which the child is expected to be sedentary or still. The frequency and types of movement activities are selected with respect to the child's arousal bias.

LS4.10   "Ups the ante" or increases expectations appropriately

Criterion: The partner "ups the ante" or increases expectations for active participation, communication, and/or problem solving when the child is being successful and is at a more optimal level of arousal. This may occur through "sabotage," or holding out for more sophisticated communication or problem solving, with modeling or prompting as needed.

SAP-O FORMS FOR THE CONVERSATIONAL PARTNER STAGE

The Conversational Partner stage encompasses two major transitions: the transition to sentence grammar and the transition to conversational discourse.

We have developed several optional worksheets to assist in gathering data for the SAP-O at the Conversational Partner stage. These worksheets appear after the Conversational Partner SAP-O Form in Appendix A of this volume. The Intentions, Presupposition, and Conversational Rules Worksheet can be used to record communicative intentions measured in objectives JA3.1 through JA3.3 and MR4.3 through MR4.5; presupposition measured in objectives JA1.4, JA1.5, JA4.5, and JA4.6; and conversational rules measured in objectives JA4.1 through JA4.4, JA4.6, JA5.2 through JA5.6, SU4.1 through SU4.4, and SU6.1 through SU6.4. The Expression and Understanding of Emotions Worksheet can be used to record early and advanced emotion words measured in objectives JA2.1 through JA2.7, SU2.2, MR1.1 through MR1.5, and SR3.1 through SR3.3. These worksheets include columns to record these behaviors in two different contexts and with three different partners.

Two additional worksheets have been developed to assist in recording the understandings and use of generative language in the Conversational Partner stage. The Language Elements Worksheet lists the categories of advanced relational meanings, reference to things, and verb phrases measured in objectives SU5.1 through SU5.3. The Sentence Constructions Worksheet lists the categories of sentence constructions measured in objective SU5.4. The number of boxes to be checked when the word meanings are observed corresponds with the minimum number required to achieve each objective.

SAP-O CRITERIA FOR THE CONVERSATIONAL PARTNER STAGE

Following are the criteria for each objective at the Conversational Partner stage. The criteria define the behavior to be measured for each objective. Some criteria specify a minimum number of times that the child is required to display the behavior to achieve the objective. For criteria that do not specify a minimum number, the child should display the behavior regularly or appropriately for the context. *For all objectives at the Conversational Partner stage, a rating of 2 requires observations of behaviors with at least three different partners in at least two different contexts unless otherwise noted.*

SOCIAL COMMUNICATION

JOINT ATTENTION

1
Shares attention

JA1.1   **Monitors attentional focus of a social partner (= SR1.2)**
Criterion: The child spontaneously follows the reference of another person's attentional focus during an ongoing activity. Evidence includes the child's following the reference of another person's gesture, looking at what someone else is paying attention to, or communicating about what someone else is doing or talking about.

JA1.2   **Secures attention to oneself prior to expressing intentions**
Criterion: The child secures the attention of a social partner by calling nonverbally (e.g., tapping on shoulder, gesturing toward, securing gaze) or verbally (e.g., saying

partner's name, signing partner's name, holding up a picture) prior to expressing communicative intentions (e.g., requesting, commenting)

JA1.3 Understands nonverbal cues of shifts in attentional focus
Criterion: The child demonstrates appropriate adjustment in attentional focus in response to a partner's change in body orientation and eye gaze. The child needs to demonstrate an awareness of the partner's disengagement and shift to a new focus of attention. Evidence includes the child's shifting his or her gaze to what the partner has shifted to, responding to a partner's change in body orientation, or commenting about a partner's shift in orientation or gaze.

JA1.4 Modifies language based on what partners have seen or heard
Criterion: The child demonstrates an awareness that someone needs to perceive (e.g., see, hear) a specific event to know that it has happened and therefore adds background information for those who did not perceive the event (e.g., were not present when an event occurred). The child needs to provide at least two pieces of clarifying information about who or what happened to a partner who did not witness the event so that the partner can understand the referent and gist of the event. For example, the child comes home from school and states, "Ms. Peters read a book called *The Enormous Turnip.*"

JA1.5 Shares internal thoughts or mental plans with partners
Criterion: The child demonstrates *metacognitive skills* (i.e., the ability to reflect on and talk about thoughts and plans) by sharing internal thoughts or mental plans with partners. For example, in talking about how she will make a house out of blocks, the child verbalizes the steps to a partner prior to beginning, such as indicating where the door will go, which part will be the kitchen, and so forth.

2
Shares emotion

JA2.1 Understands and uses early emotion words (= MR1.1, SR3.1)
Criterion: The child uses verbal language (i.e., speech, signs, or pictures) that emerge early in language development to express at least two positive emotions (e.g., *happy, fun, silly, good*) *and* at least two negative emotions (e.g., *mad, angry, sad, sick, tired*).

JA2.2 Describes others' emotional states with early emotion words
Criterion: The child notices and describes the emotional state of another person by commenting about it with at least two positive (e.g., "Mommy feels good," "John is having fun") and two negative (e.g., "My brother feels sad," "Daddy is mad") early emotion words.

JA2.3 Understands and uses advanced emotion words (= MR1.2, SR3.2)
Criterion: The child uses advanced words to express at least two positive emotions (e.g., *content, hopeful, excited, proud, delighted, interested*) *and* at least two negative emotions (e.g., *frustrated, scared, worried, bored, stressed, terrified, embarrassed, guilty, jealous*).

JA2.4 Describes others' emotional states with advanced emotion words
Criterion: The child notices and describes the emotional state of another person by commenting about it with at least two positive and two negative advanced emotional words (e.g., saying "Sara is frustrated," when observing that a classmate is dissatisfied with an outcome of a negotiation).

JA2.5 Understands and uses graded emotions (= MR1.3, SR3.3)
Criterion: The child demonstrates the ability to understand and express emotions with regard to their relative intensity. For example, the child says that he likes to watch a

preferred television program but loves playing video games (his most favorite thing to do), or the child says that he is bothered by the activity level in the lunchroom at school but is terrified of the fire alarm going off.

JA2.6 Understands nonverbal cues of emotional expression (= SU2.2)

Criterion: The child demonstrates appropriate responses to a partner's change in emotional expression with 1) gestures, 2) facial expressions, and/or 3) intonation (prosody). For example, the child takes a step backward when his partner gives a stern look and raises a hand in an effort to stop the child's actions.

JA2.7 Describes plausible causal factors for emotions of self and others

Criterion: The child provides causal factors for 1) positive emotions (e.g., child indicates that a friend was excited because she received a gift she had wanted for her birthday), and 2) negative emotions (e.g., child indicates that teacher was frustrated when two students asked him questions at the same time).

3 **Shares intentions for a variety of purposes** (↔ JA5.2, SU4–SU5)	**JA3.1 Shares intentions to regulate the behavior of others (= MR4.3)** Criterion: The child directs verbal language (i.e., speech, signs, or pictures) for all of the following reasons: a) requests objects and activities to get another person to give a desired object or carry out an action, such as turning on the computer; b) requests help to get another person to provide help or assistance in carrying out an action that the child cannot do independently; c) requests a break from an ongoing activity; and d) protests/refuses to get another person to remove an undesired object or cease an undesirable action or activity.

JA3.2 Shares intentions for social interaction (= MR4.4)

Criterion: The child directs verbal language (i.e., speech, signs, or pictures) for all of the following reasons: a) greets to indicate notice of a person entering or leaving the immediate situation or to mark the initiation or termination of an interaction (e.g., waves and says "hi" or "bye" plus person's name); b) calls to gain the attention of another person; c) requests comfort to seek comfort from distress, frustration, or fear; d) regulates interaction to keep turn taking going; e) requests permission to seek another's consent to carry out an action; f) praises partner to indicate regard for the partner's success or accomplishment; g) expresses empathy about a positive or negative experience of the partner; and h) shares secrets to confide in another person.

JA3.3 Shares intentions for joint attention (= MR4.5)

Criterion: The child directs verbal language (i.e., speech, signs, or pictures) for all of the following reasons: a) comments to get another person to notice events that are immediate, past, *and* imagined; b) provides requested information about events that are immediate and past in response to *what, what doing, who, where,* and *yes/no* questions; c) requests information about immediate, past, and future events; d) expresses feelings and opinions; and e) anticipates and plans outcomes.

4 **Shares experiences in reciprocal interaction**	**JA4.1 Shows reciprocity in speaker and listener roles to share experiences** **(= SR1.3)** Criterion: The child participates in both the speaker and listener roles to share experiences. The child is able to focus on a topic for at least four consecutive exchanges be-

tween the child and partner. An *exchange* consists of a turn from the child and a turn from the partner.

JA4.2   Initiates a variety of conversational topics
Criterion: The child initiates at least four different conversational topics that span different categories (e.g., *school,* such as classwork, recess, or meals; *after school,* such as sports, movies, or video games; *family,* such as vacations, pets, or siblings; *school subjects,* such as astronomy or science).

JA4.3   Initiates and maintains conversations that relate to partners' interests
Criterion: The child initiates and maintains conversations about topics of interest to a partner. For example, the child asks a peer about her favorite movie and maintains the discussion despite the fact that he has not seen the movie. Conversations must last for at least four consecutive exchanges.

JA4.4   Maintains interaction by requesting or providing relevant information
Criterion: The child maintains interaction with a balance of providing and requesting information that is relevant to the topic. The child is able to provide on-topic comments that demonstrate interest, excitement, and/or empathy (e.g., a partner says, "I saw the *Spy Kids 3-D* movie," and the child responds, "Cool! That's a fun movie!"). The child not only provides comments, but also asks questions (e.g., partner says, "I have a dog at home," and child says, "What's its name?" rather than saying "Oh, that's nice").

JA4.5   Provides needed information based on partners' knowledge of topic
Criterion: The child provides more information to a less familiar partner and less information to a more familiar partner. The child gauges the clarity of vocabulary selection and information provided without providing too much or redundant information.

JA4.6   Gauges length and content of conversational turn based on partners
Criterion: The child considers a specific partner's previous experiences and knowledge base to provide more detailed background information (e.g., who was there, what happened, where it happened). The child monitors the amount of information to provide based on the information already provided to that partner and/or that partner's interest.

JA4.7   Prefers to be engaged with partners
Criterion: The child chooses to be engaged with partners more often than being alone during unstructured periods of time. The child spends more than half of each hour engaged in activities with adults or peers.

JA4.8   Has friendships with partners who share interests
Criterion: The child spends more time with (hangs out with) at least two different peers who have common interests in nonacademic activities (e.g., video games, book series, art) or nonschool settings (e.g., martial arts class, skate park, mall).

**5
Persists and repairs
communication
breakdowns**

JA5.1   Uses appropriate rate of communication for context
Criterion: The child directs words to a variety of partners at an appropriate rate for the context (e.g., at least once per minute during one-to-one interaction, once every 3 minutes during a small-group interaction, once every 5–10 minutes during a large-group interaction). Lower rates would be expected with unfamiliar partners, with peers, in highly adult-directed contexts, and when activities provide fewer opportunities.

JA5.2   Repeats and modifies communication to repair breakdowns (↔ JA3)
Criterion: When there is a *communication breakdown* (i.e., the child is not understood and/or does not achieve a desired goal), the child repeats all or part of the same communicative signal to repair or fix the breakdown or modifies the communicative signal to repair when not understood. Modifying a signal occurs when the child 1) shifts to a different communicative means (i.e., different gesture, different word, or different combination of gesture and word), 2) changes a quality of the signal (e.g., clear increase in loudness, gesture added to a word, different word added), or 3) repeats the same act but directs it to a different person.

JA5.3   Recognizes breakdowns in communication and requests clarification
Criterion: The child recognizes when there is a breakdown in communication during ongoing interactions in activities and requests clarification. The child recognizes breakdowns by clarifying his or her intention when the partner does not respond appropriately (e.g., saying, "I want an *apple*," after being given a banana following a request) or by clearly indicating that the message is not heard or understood (e.g., saying, "What did you say?" or "Which one did you mean?").

JA5.4   Modifies language and behavior based on partners' change in agenda
Criterion: The child modifies the quantity or quality of his language and behavior when partners change the agenda (e.g., topic of conversation, shortens the activity, desires to continue the activity). For example, the child makes a brief comment to end a conversation when it becomes apparent that his partner wishes to switch topics.

JA5.5   Modifies language and behavior based on partners' emotional reaction
Criterion: The child modifies the quantity or quality of his language and behavior when partners express an emotional reaction (e.g., keen interest in the conversation, boredom with the topic, anger with something child has done). For example, the child provides additional details about a recent field trip when his partner expresses excitement and interest.

JA5.6   Expresses feelings of success and confidence during interactions
Criterion: The child expresses emotions during reciprocal interactions that indicate feelings of success (e.g., "I did it!" "Look how good I did"; "I'm really good at _____"; "Wow, I finished my work") and confidence (e.g., "I think I can do that").

SYMBOL USE

**1
Learns by
imitation,
observation,
instruction,
and collaboration**

**SU1.1   Spontaneously imitates a variety of behaviors later in a different
context**
Criterion: The child accurately imitates a sequence of behaviors spontaneously (i.e., without direction to do so) and/or closely approximates a variety of actions or words spontaneously at a later time after a partner has modeled the behavior and in a different context than the behavior was first modeled. The child imitates at least five different behaviors (verbal or nonverbal). A later time is at least three turns or at least a minute after the model or a much later time. A different context is either a different activity or a similar activity with a different partner.

SU1.2 Uses behaviors modeled by partners to guide social behavior (= MR3.3)

Criterion: The child displays behaviors that he or she has observed partners using. The child uses these modeled behaviors to guide how he or she is acting in social contexts. For example, the child observes a peer in class raise her hand to get the teacher's attention, and the child then stays in his seat and raises his hand while waiting for the teacher to call on him.

SU1.3 Uses internalized rules modeled by adult instruction to guide behavior (= SR4.1)

Criterion: The child acts in accordance with rules modeled by adult instruction consistent with cultural norms. For example, the child raises hand to ask permission; the child thanks partner when given object; or the child says "Excuse me" or I'm sorry" when bumping into someone.

SU1.4 Uses self-monitoring and self-talk to guide behavior (= SR4.3)

Criterion: The child uses language as a tool for emotional regulation; to prepare for changes in routine; to organize behavior; and/or to discuss potentially problematic, emotionally dysregulating situations. For example, the child observes that another child is teasing and says, "I'll just ignore her and walk away," as he does so.

SU1.5 Collaborates and negotiates with peers in problem solving (= MR3.4)

Criterion: The child uses language as a tool to collaborate with peers and negotiate when faced with a problem to solve. For example, in a group puzzle activity, the child asks a peer to trade a puzzle piece with him so that each can complete a section of a puzzle, or the child negotiates roles with a peer in a pretend restaurant activity (e.g., decides with peer who will play waiter and customer, collaborates with peer in designing rules for a game).

2 Understands nonverbal cues and nonliteral meanings in reciprocal interactions

SU2.1 Understands nonverbal cues of turn taking and topic change

Criterion: The child recognizes cues and responds appropriately to cues that signal the end of a partner's turn and/or a partner's disengagement with the interaction (e.g., pausing, looking at or away from partner, using rising or falling intonation).

SU2.2 Understands nonverbal cues of emotional expression (= JA2.6)

Criterion: The child demonstrates appropriate response to a partner's change in emotional expression with 1) gestures, 2) facial expressions, and 3) intonation (prosody). For example, the child takes a step backward when his partner gives a stern look and raises his hand in an effort to stop the child's actions.

SU2.3 Understands nonverbal cues and nonliteral meanings of humor and figures of speech

Criterion: The child responds in a manner that demonstrates understanding of a partner's change in 1) facial expression and 2) intonation (prosody) to express humor, understand idioms, identify target words (that might have multiple interpretations), and identify important contextual cues (e.g., environment, speaker's perspective) to help clarify the meaning of figures of speech.

SU2.4 **Understands nonverbal cues and nonliteral meanings of teasing, sarcasm, and deception**
Criterion: The child responds to 1) contextual cues, 2) gestural cues, 3) facial expressions, and 4) intonation (prosody) to recognize instances in which words are used in a teasing, sarcastic, or deceptive manner.

3
Participates conventionally in dramatic play and recreation

SU3.1 **Uses logical sequences of actions in play about familiar events**
Criterion: The child combines at least four actions in a logical sequence involving events that the child experiences regularly (e.g., preparing, serving, and eating food; getting a stuffed animal ready for bed; putting figures in a bus and driving them to school).

SU3.2 **Uses miniature or abstract objects as props**
Criterion: The child uses miniature objects (e.g., small toy figures and vehicles) or substitute props (e.g., a stick used as a sword, a block used as a telephone) in pretend play.

SU3.3 **Uses logical sequences of actions in play about less familiar events**
Criterion: The child combines at least four actions in a logical sequence involving events that the child has experienced occasionally (e.g., going to a birthday party, going to the doctor's office, having hair shampooed and cut).

SU3.4 **Takes on a role and engages in dramatic play**
Criterion: The child takes on a role by narrating with a different voice quality or acting out the role nonverbally while engaging in dramatic play (e.g., child pretends to be a hairdresser and "shampoos" and "cuts" a doll's hair; child pretends to be Peter Pan and acts as if he were flying).

SU3.5 **Plays in a common activity with other children**
Criterion: The child participates in a common play activity along with other children and focuses on the same play goal. For example, the child helps to builds a structure with blocks, plays tag, or takes turn pulling and riding in a wagon.

SU3.6 **Takes on a role and cooperates with peers in dramatic play**
Criterion: The child takes on a role by narrating or acting out the role nonverbally while engaging in dramatic play in cooperation with a peer. For example, one child pretends to be the doctor and another child pretends to be the patient, and they act out a scene together; or one child pretends to be Peter Pan and another child pretends to be Captain Hook, and they act out a scene together.

SU3.7 **Participates in rule-based group recreation**
Criterion: The child collaborates with peers and participates in a recreational activity that is rule based. For example, the child participates in game of kickball and follows the basic rules of waiting for a turn, kicking the ball, running to the bases, and running home and, when in the field, trying to the catch the ball and tag a runner from the other team.

4
Uses appropriate gestures and nonverbal behavior for the context
(↔ JA3, MR1)

SU4.1 **Uses appropriate facial expressions for the context and partner**
Criterion: The child uses appropriate facial expression (not too restricted or exaggerated) based on the partner and the context.

SU4.2 **Uses appropriate gestures for the context and partner**
Criterion: The child uses appropriate gestures to call attention (e.g., tapping on another's shoulder), to clarify meaning (e.g., pointing or raising hands), and to share emo-

tions. The gestures need to be appropriate based on the partner and context and should respect a partner's personal space and privacy.

SU4.3   Uses appropriate body posture and proximity for the context and partner

Criterion: The child uses appropriate body posture (e.g., orients to the front when class, faces partner in conversation) and proximity (positions self at an appropriate distance) based on the partner and context and should respect a partner's personal space and privacy.

SU4.4   Uses appropriate vocal volume and intonation for the context and partner

Criterion: The child adjusts the volume (loudness) and intonation (e.g., pitch, vocal quality, rate, stress, fluency) of his or her voice depending on who he or she is talking to and the nature of the context (e.g., loud voice on the playground, quiet voice in the classroom).

5 **Understands** **and uses** **generative** **language to** **express meanings** **(↔ JA3, MR1)**	**SU5.1 Understands and uses a variety of advanced relational words** Criterion: The child spontaneously uses at least five examples of each of the following advanced relational meanings:

a.   *wh- words* (e.g., *what, where, who, when, why*)

b.   *temporal relations* (e.g., *now, later, before after, in a minute*)

c.   *physical relations* (e.g., colors, shapes, *hard/soft, big/little, tall/short*)

d.   *numerical relations* (e.g., numbers to indicate how many, *few, some, many, more/less*)

e.   *location terms* (e.g., *in, on, under, next to, behind, in back of, in front of, above, below, left, right*)

f.   *kinship terms* (e.g., *mother, father, sister, brother, grandmother*)

g.   *causal terms* (e.g., *but, so, because, if, or*)

SU5.2   Understands and uses reference to things

Criterion: The child understands and uses appropriately word forms (spoken, signed, pictures, or written) to reference things in all of the following categories:

a.   at least five *subject pronouns* (e.g., *I/you, he/she, it, we/they*)

b.   at least five *other pronouns* (e.g., *me/you, him/her, your/my, some, any, none, this/that*)

c.   both *determiners* (i.e., *the, a*)

d.   at least five *plurals* (e.g., *cats, cookies, cows, sheep*)

SU5.3   Understands and uses a variety of verb phrases

Criterion: The child understands and uses at least five different appropriate forms of the following types of verb phrases:

a.   *main verbs* (e.g., *open, run, to be, think*)

b.   *tense markers* (e.g., *is walking, barks, dropped, will, should*)

c. *helping verbs* (e.g., *has, have, had, do, does, did, am, is, are, was, were, been*)

d. *modals* (e.g., *wanna, gonna, may, might, can, could*)

e. *negation* (e.g., *no, not, won't, can't, wasn't*)

SU5.4 Understands and uses a variety of sentence constructions
Criterion: The child understands and uses at least five different appropriate forms of the following sentence constructions:

a. *declarative* (e.g., *I need a break. The boy is riding a bike.*)

b. *imperative* (e.g., *Go outside now. Pick up your toys.*)

c. *negative* (e.g., *I don't know. I can't do that.*)

d. *interrogative* (e.g., *Can you help me? Who is in the house?*)

e. *embedding* (e.g., *The bird is in the cage. I wanna go outside. I think I should go first. The man selling the balloons gave one to me.*)

f. *conjoining* (e.g., *There is a little boy and he is running home. The boy is crying because he fell down. When I am done with my work, I get to go outside.*)

SU5.5 Understands and uses connected sentences in oral and written discourse
Criterion: The child understands and uses a sequence of at least four connected sentences that relate to each other in ongoing discourse (maintaining topic and linking reference to person, place, and thing). The child is able do this in both oral and written discourse.

**6
Follows rules
of conversation**

SU6.1 Follows conventions for initiating conversation and taking turns
Criterion: The child initiates topics and follows conventions for taking turns by following the topic when it is his turn, taking turn of an appropriate length (not dominating the exchange), and waiting for a turn without interruptions.

SU6.2 Follows conventions for shifting topics in conversation
Criterion: The child follows verbal conventions when shifting topics by making it clear how one topic relates to the next (e.g., "That makes me think of . . . ") or informing the partner that they are changing topics (e.g., "Let's talk about something else").

SU6.3 Follows conventions for ending conversation
Criterion: The child knows when a dialogue is finished and provides an appropriate concluding statement and salutation (e.g., "I've got to go now," "It was good to see you").

SU6.4 Follows conventions of politeness and register
Criterion: The child demonstrates appropriate topic selection, use of vocabulary, and vocal register (intonation) based on partner status (e.g., teacher/parent versus a peer), familiarity (e.g., unfamiliar partner versus familiar partner), and relationship with a specific partner (e.g., casual versus formal).

EMOTIONAL REGULATION

MUTUAL REGULATION

1
Expresses range of emotions
(↔ SU4–SU5)

MR1.1   Understands and uses early emotion words (= JA2.1, SR3.1)
Criterion: The child uses verbal language (i.e., speech, signs, or pictures) that emerges early in language development to express at least two positive emotions (e.g., *happy, fun, silly, good*) and at least two negative emotions (e.g., *mad, angry, sad, sick, tired*).

MR1.2   Understands and uses advanced emotion words (= JA2.3, SR3.2)
Criterion: The child uses advanced words to express at least two positive emotions (e.g., *content, hopeful, excited, proud, delighted, interested*) and at least two negative emotions (e.g., *frustrated, scared, worried, bored, stressed, terrified, embarrassed, guilty, jealous*).

MR1.3   Understands and uses graded emotions (= JA2.5, SR3.3)
Criterion: The child demonstrates the ability to understand and express emotions with regard to their relative intensity. For example, the child says that he likes to watch a preferred television program but loves playing video games (his most favorite thing to do), or the child says he is bothered by the activity level in the lunchroom at school but is terrified of the fire alarm going off.

MR1.4   Changes emotional expression in familiar activities based on partners' feedback
Criterion: The child changes emotional expression based on verbal or nonverbal feedback from partners (e.g., child stops laughing when partner gives nonverbal feedback that laughter is inappropriate in the current context).

MR1.5   Uses nonverbal cues of emotional expression
Criterion: The child demonstrates the ability to express emotions with appropriate nonverbal behavior, including 1) gestures, 2) facial expressions, and 3) intonation (prosody).

2
Responds to assistance offered by partners

MR2.1   Soothes when comforted by partners
Criterion: The child soothes or calms down quickly (i.e., within 30 seconds) when a partner offers comfort verbally or nonverbally, with the exception of periods of time when the child is experiencing extreme dysregulation, fear, or violations of expectations.

MR2.2   Engages when alerted by partners
Criterion: The child becomes actively engaged when partners introduce alerting and organizing stimulation. For example, when a partner uses energetic verbal and nonverbal means to interact, the child becomes engaged.

MR2.3   Responds to bids for interaction
Criterion: The child responds to another person's bid for interaction. The bid and response may be nonverbal or verbal. The child's response must be immediate (i.e., displayed within 3 seconds following the other person's bid) and contingent (i.e., maintains the focus of attention or topic). The child's response does not need to demonstrate comprehension of a verbal bid.

MR2.4   Responds to changes in partners' expression of emotion
Criterion: The child responds to changes in partners' expression emotion by changing his or her behavior (e.g., pausing, moving quickly, moving toward or away). For example, the child persists in an activity when he sees his partner nodding and smiling.

MR2.5   Attunes to changes in partners' expression of emotion
Criterion: The child attunes to changes in the expression of emotion of at least three partners, including peers, by mirroring the emotional tone (e.g., smiles and laughs in response to caregiver's positive emotion, frowns and stops moving in response to partner's negative expression).

MR2.6   Responds to information or strategies offered by partners
Criterion: The child responds to information or strategies that have been taught, practiced, and/or discussed by adults and peers. The child uses this information to regulate arousal level, which is evident by the child's level of attention, alertness, activity level, emotion, and engagement. For example, the child may tell a classmate to stop teasing him or stop bothering him or may ask to do another activity at another table, based on suggestions from the teacher, or the child may demonstrate a decrease in arousal when the teacher provides him with information related to the structure of an unanticipated assembly.

**3
Responds
to feedback
and guidance
regarding behavior**

MR3.1   Responds to feedback regarding the appropriateness of emotional display
Criterion: The child modifies her emotional expression based on feedback from partners. The child responds differentially to feedback that is given with respect to the appropriateness of display in the particular social context. For example, the child begins to vocalize in an angry manner, but then says, "I'm mad, I want to take a turn on the swing," after her teacher says, "Tell me what's wrong."

MR3.2   Responds to feedback regarding the appropriateness of regulatory strategies
Criterion: The child modifies regulatory strategies based on feedback from partners. The child responds differentially to feedback that is given with respect to appropriateness of the strategy given the social context. For example, the child attempts to crash into a partner but then says, "I need a hug," after the partner prevents her from crashing and asks her, "What do you need?"

MR3.3   Uses behaviors modeled by partners to guide behavior (= SU1.2)
Criterion: The child displays behaviors that he or she has observed partners using. The child uses these modeled behaviors to guide how he or she is acting in social contexts. For example, the child observes a peer in class raise her hand to get the teacher's attention, and the child then stays in his seat and raises his hand while waiting for the teacher to call on him.

MR3.4   Collaborates and negotiates with peers in problem solving (= SU1.5)
Criterion: The child uses language as a tool to collaborate with peers and negotiate when faced with a problem to solve. For example, in a group puzzle activity, the child asks a peer to trade a puzzle piece with him so that each can complete a section of a puzzle, or the child negotiates roles with a peer in a pretend restaurant activity (e.g.,

decides with peer who will play waiter and customer, collaborates with peers in designing rules for a game).

MR3.5   Accepts ideas from partners during negotiation to reach compromise
Criterion: The child acknowledges and agrees to ideas that are suggested by a partner during a negotiation to reach a compromise. For example, before going out to recess, the child says to his classmate, "I want to play basketball outside," but his friend says, "It's my turn to choose, and I want to play Four Square." The child then responds, "Okay, Four Square first, and then we can play basketball after."

**4
Requests
partners'
assistance to
regulate state**

MR4.1   Shares negative emotion to seek comfort
Criterion: The child displays *negative emotion* (i.e., a clear vocal, verbal, or facial expression of distress or frustration, which may be accompanied by a change in body posture or gesture) or language and shares it with another person by looking at, approaching (e.g., walking toward), gesturing toward (e.g., waving over), or touching that person (e.g., tapping arm) to seek comfort.

MR4.2   Shares positive emotion to seek interaction
Criterion: The child displays *positive emotion* (i.e., a clear facial expression of pleasure or excitement, which may or may not be accompanied by a vocalization, e.g., laughing, squealing, or language) and shares it by looking at, approaching (e.g., walking toward), gesturing toward (e.g., waving over), or touching that person (e.g., tapping arm) to seek interaction.

MR4.3   Shares intentions to regulate the behavior of others (= JA3.1)
Criterion: The child directs verbal language (i.e., speech, signs, or pictures) for all of the following reasons: a) requests objects and activities to get another person to give a desired object or carry out an action, such as turning on the computer; b) requests help to get another person to provide help or assistance in carrying out an action that the child cannot do independently; c) requests a break from an ongoing activity; and d) protests to get another person to remove an undesired food object or cease an undesirable action or activity.

MR4.4   Shares intentions for social interaction (= JA3.2)
Criterion: The child directs verbal language (i.e., speech, signs, or pictures) for all of the following reasons: a) greets to indicate notice of a person entering or leaving the immediate situation or to mark the initiation or termination of an interaction (e.g., waves and says "hi" or "bye" plus person's name); b) calls to gain the attention of another person; c) requests comfort to seek comfort from distress, frustration, or fear; d) regulates interaction to keep turn taking going; e) requests permission to seek another's consent to carry out an action; f) praises partners to indicate regard for the partner's success or accomplishment; g) expresses empathy about a positive or negative experience of the partner; and h) shares secrets to confide in another person.

MR4.5   Shares intentions for joint attention (= JA3.3)
Criterion: The child directs verbal language (i.e., speech, signs, or pictures) for all of the following reasons: a) comments to get another person to notice events that are immediate, past, *and* imagined; b) provides requested information about events that are immediate and past in response to *what, what doing, who, where,* and *yes/no* questions; c) requests information about immediate, past, and future events; d) expresses feelings and opinions; and e) anticipates and plans outcomes.

MR4.6   Requests assistance to resolve conflict and problem-solve situations
Criterion: The child is able to ask for assistance in situations to resolve conflict or to problem-solve. For example, the child observes that another child is teasing and seeks the teacher's help in figuring out how to get that child to stop, or the child anticipates that he will miss his bus and asks his mother what he should do.

**5

Recovers from extreme dysregulation with support from partners**

Extreme dysregulation is a state in which a child is not available for engagement or learning and may experience intense emotions. By definition, a state of extreme dysregulation must preclude the child's ability to engage with people and activities in a productive manner. Extreme dysregulation typically is not brief or episodic, and it may be continuous or cyclical within a period of time. Behavioral evidence of extreme dysregulation may include 1) expression of intense and seemingly inconsolable distress; 2) complete loss of attention to the activity or to other people; 3) intense, disruptive vocalizations (e.g., crying, screaming, moaning) and/or nonverbal behavior (flailing, self- or other-directed hitting, slapping, biting); 4) frenetic motor activity; 5) extreme shutdown and disengagement for an extended period; and so forth. Extreme dysregulation may be associated with arousal levels that are very high (i.e., extreme distress or excitement) or very low (i.e., extremely passive, disengaged state), either of which precludes engagement.

MR5.1   Responds to partners' efforts to assist with recovery by moving away from activity
Criterion: The child responds to partners' attempts to assist with recovery and to change the child's attentional focus by moving away from activities that are overstimulating or undesired after reaching an extreme state of dysregulation.

MR5.2   Responds to partners' use of behavioral strategies
Criterion: The child responds to partners' use of behavioral strategies (e.g., simple motor actions or sensory-motor strategies such as accepting a hug, breathing deeply, or squeezing a ball) that are implemented to help the child to recover from an extreme state of dysregulation.

MR5.3   Responds to partners' use of language strategies
Criterion: The child responds to partners' use of language strategies (e.g., soothing voice, providing information, counting to 10 slowly) that are implemented to help the child recover from an extreme state of dysregulation.

MR5.4   Responds to partners' attempts to reengage in interaction or activity
Criterion: The child responds to partners' attempts to reengage him or her in an interaction or activity after recovery (i.e., return to a well-regulated state) from extreme dysregulation.

MR5.5   Decreases amount of time to recover from extreme dysregulation due to support from partners
Criterion: The amount of time the child takes to recover from extreme dysregulation (i.e., return to an well-regulated state) decreases over time when the child is supported by partners.*

MR5.6   Decreases intensity of dysregulated state due to support from
         partners

Criterion: The intensity of emotional response and the changes in the child's state of arousal or energy level during episodes of extreme dysregulation decrease over time with support from partners.*

You may need to rely on baseline information gathered from interviews with others who observe the child over time to determine child-specific criteria for objectives MR5.5 and MR5.6 at the Conversational Partner stage.

SELF-REGULATION

1 Demonstrates availability for learning and interacting

SR1.1   Responds to sensory and social experiences with differentiated
         emotions

Criterion: The child responds to different sensory and social experiences with differentiated emotions (e.g., shows happiness and excitement in fun activities, distress in stressful or unpleasant activities, and fear or wariness in unfamiliar or anxiety-arousing activities).

SR1.2   Monitors attentional focus of a social partner (= JA1.1)

Criterion: The child spontaneously follows the reference of another person's attentional focus during an ongoing activity. Evidence includes the child's following the reference of another person's gesture, looking at what someone else is paying attention to, or communicating about what someone else is doing or talking about.

SR1.3   Shows reciprocity in speaker and listener roles to share experiences
         (= JA4.1)

Criterion: The child participates in both the speaker and listener roles to share experiences. The child is able to focus on a topic for at least four consecutive exchanges between the child and partner. An *exchange* consists of a turn from the child and a turn from the partner.

SR1.4   Demonstrates ability to inhibit actions and behaviors

Criterion: The child demonstrates the ability to inhibit actions or behaviors in situations in which the child knows the behaviors are inappropriate. This is done without prompting from the partner. For example, the child waits until he is called on to answer teacher's question, rather than calling out, or the child begins an inappropriate behavior such as throwing an object or striking out and then stops.

SR1.5   Persists during tasks with reasonable demands

Criterion: The child persists in trying to complete tasks when the demands are reasonable. Reasonable demands are considered relative to the developmental appropriateness of the task and whether the child is in a well-regulated state. The child does not need to successfully complete tasks but needs to demonstrate the effort to complete tasks. For example, the child may struggle with completing a math worksheet or is having difficulty waiting in line but makes an effort to succeed in these tasks rather than giving up.

SR1.6   Demonstrates emotional expression appropriate to context
Criterion: The child expresses a range of emotions (i.e., positive, neutral, and negative) that are appropriate given the social and sensory variables present in the environment. Range of emotions expressed is expanded from those seen in previous stages to include those that are contingent on social understanding (e.g., pride, guilt, embarrassment). For example, the child stands tall and smiles broadly at the teacher or gives a "high five" after completing a challenging activity.

**2
Uses behavioral strategies to regulate level of arousal during familiar activities**

Behavioral strategies are simple motor actions or sensory-motor strategies that the child engages in that regulate arousal level, evident by the child's level of attention, alertness, activity level, emotion, and engagement.

SR2.1   Uses behavioral strategies to regulate arousal level during solitary and social activities
Criterion: The child uses behavioral strategies that are flexible depending on context, social norms, and communicative partners present, to increase arousal level (when underaroused) and decrease arousal level (when overaroused) in solitary activities and during social interactions. Examples of behavioral strategies that may be used in solitary activities include chewing gum, rocking, squeezing hands together, standing on toes, flapping hands, grinding teeth, jumping, spinning, eating, or listening to music. Examples of behavioral strategies that may be used during social interaction include holding a comfort object, averting gaze, squeezing hands tightly, jumping, hugging, eating, chewing, toe walking, or approaching another person to play a social game. *Overarousal* may be due to excessive sensory stimulation, too much excitement, or stressful events. *Underarousal* may be due to fatigue, boredom, or lack of organizing stimulation and may result in lack of attention or nonresponsiveness.

SR2.2   Uses behavioral strategies modeled by partners to regulate arousal level
Criterion: The child uses behavioral strategies (i.e., simple motor actions or sensory-motor strategies) that are imitated either immediately or at a later time from behaviors modeled by partners to regulate arousal level (e.g., squeezing hands, jumping, stomping feet, taking a deep breath).

SR2.3   Uses behavioral strategies to engage productively in an extended activity
Criterion: The child is able to engage productively for an extended activity (i.e., at least 10–15 minutes) and uses behavioral strategies (i.e., simple motor actions or sensory-motor strategies) as needed to regulate arousal level (e.g., chews gum, squeezes object or stress ball, bounces leg, rocks in chair, plays with fidget toy).

**3
Uses language strategies to regulate arousal level during familiar activities**

Language strategies are words or other symbols (i.e., signs, pictures) that the child uses to regulate arousal level, as is evident by the child's level of attention, alertness, activity level, emotion, and engagement. Language strategies may include creative utterances or delayed echolalia.

SR3.1   Understands and uses early emotion words (= JA2.1, MR1.1)
Criterion: The child uses verbal language (i.e., speech, signs, or pictures) that emerges early in language development to express at least two positive emotions (e.g., *happy, fun, silly, good) and* at least two negative emotions (e.g., *mad, angry, sad, sick, tired*).

SR3.2   Understands and uses advanced emotion words (= JA2.3, MR1.2)
Criterion: The child uses advanced words to express at least two positive emotions (e.g., *content, hopeful, excited, proud, delighted, interested) and* at least two negative emotions (e.g., *frustrated, scared, worried, bored, stressed, terrified, embarrassed, guilty, jealous*).

SR3.3   Understands and uses graded emotions (= JA2.5, MR1.3)
Criterion: The child demonstrates the ability to understand and express emotions with regard to their relative intensity. For example, the child says that he likes to watch a preferred television program but loves playing video games (his most favorite thing to do), or the child says that he is bothered by the activity level in the lunchroom at school but is terrified of the fire alarm going off.

SR3.4   Uses language strategies to regulate arousal level during solitary and social activities
Criterion: The child uses language strategies to increase arousal level (when underaroused) and decrease arousal level (when overaroused) in solitary and social activities. Examples of language strategies that may be used in solitary activities include the child's repeating, "I'm okay, it doesn't hurt," after falling down; and the child's stating, "Don't worry," when afraid, which correctly identify the child's emotional state but are not directed to others. Examples of language strategies that may be used in social interactions include the child's identifying his or her emotional state or commenting on his or her internal state or activity such as by saying "I need to stay awake," or "I'm trying hard," to help promote organization and attention. Although the language is used in a social context, it does not appear to be an attempt to elicit support from others, which would be mutual regulation. *Overarousal* may be due to excessive sensory stimulation, too much excitement, or stressful events. *Underarousal* may be due to fatigue, boredom, or lack of organizing stimulation and may result in lack of attention or nonresponsiveness.

SR3.5   Uses language strategies modeled by partners to regulate arousal level
Criterion: The child uses language strategies (i.e., words or other symbols, e.g., signs pictures) that are imitated either immediately or at a later time (i.e., delayed echolalia) from language modeled by partners to regulate arousal level (e.g., "Recess is finished," "Mommy is happy," "After work I will have snack").

SR3.6   Uses language strategies to engage productively in an extended activity
Criterion: The child is able to engage productively for an extended activity (i.e., at least 10–15 minutes) and uses language strategies (i.e., words or other symbols, e.g., signs, pictures) to regulate arousal level and attention. For example, the child may identify his emotions or repeat instructions (e.g., "Put bead on top," "Three more then all done," "First scoop and spread peanut butter on bread, then scoop and spread jelly") to help maintain focus of attention.

**4
Uses metacognitive strategies to regulate arousal level during familiar activities**

SR4.1   Uses internalized rules modeled by adult instruction to guide behavior (= SU1.3)
Criterion: The child acts in accordance with rules modeled by adult instruction consistent with cultural norms. For example, the child raises a hand to ask permission; the child thanks a partner when given an object; or the child says, "Excuse me," or "I'm sorry," when bumping into someone.

SR4.2   Uses metacognitive strategies to plan and complete activities
Criterion: *Metacognitive strategies* involve the abilities to reflect on and talk about cognitive processes that support organization and that regulate attention and arousal level to guide behavior. The child is able to use or refer to metacognitive strategies as supports to help him focus his attention and fulfill task expectations. For example, the child might make a list to help remember homework assignments or might create a schedule to help organize and sequence the steps of a task.

SR4.3   Uses self-monitoring and self-talk to guide behavior (= SU1.4)
Criterion: The child uses language as a tool for emotional regulation; to prepare for changes in routine; to organize behavior; and/or to discuss potentially problematic, emotionally dysregulating situations. For example, the child observes that another child is teasing and says, "I'll just ignore her and walk away," as he does so.

SR4.4   Uses emotional memory to assist with emotional regulation
Criterion: The child is able to reflect on previous emotional experience related to specific events or people and applies strategies to help regulate emotion when faced with the same or similar circumstances. For example, the child hears an announcement about an impending fire drill and gets the noise-reducing headphones that he learned to use after a previous negative experience with fire drills, or the child avoids another child at school who has teased him in the past.

SR4.5   Identifies and reflects on strategies to support regulation
Criterion: The child demonstrates and reflects on effective self-regulatory capacities. For example, when the child is asked what she can do when feeling stressed and when alone, she states that she can listen to calming music, jump on the trampoline, or look at a favorite book.

**5
Regulates emotion during new and changing situations**

SR5.1   Uses behavioral strategies to regulate arousal level in new and changing situations
Criterion: The child uses behavioral strategies to regulate arousal level and intensity of emotional response in new (i.e., unfamiliar) and changing (i.e., unexpected features) of familiar situations. Such strategies may include conventional sensory-motor actions such as the child tapping his toes or chewing gum. These strategies may also be idiosyncratic actions as long as they help the child to attain or maintain a more regulated state (e.g., walking on toes, flapping, rocking). *New situations* are activities or features of activities that are unfamiliar to the child (e.g., an activity that the child has not participated in; a new person joining a familiar activity). *Changing situations* are ones that have variation in key features (e.g., sensory stimulation, activity level, activity sequence, task difficulty) or that have unexpected features (e.g., unpredictable events, such as changes in place or sequence of common routines; activities terminated prematurely).

SR5.2 Uses language strategies to regulate arousal level in new and changing situations

Criterion: The child uses language strategies (e.g., creative language pertaining to the situation or delayed echolalia) to regulate arousal level and intensity of emotional response in new (i.e., unfamiliar) and changing (i.e., unexpected features) situations. For example, the child may say repeatedly, "I'm excited to see the hippopotamus at the zoo," in an effort to maintain his focus and direct his nervous energy as he enters the zoo for the first time.

SR5.3 Uses metacognitive strategies to regulate arousal level in new and changing situations

Criterion: The child uses metacognitive strategies (e.g., the ability reflect on and talk about strategies for self-regulation) to regulate arousal level and intensity of emotional response in new (i.e., unfamiliar) and changing (i.e., unexpected features) situations. For example, at the start of a movie the child says to himself, "If the movie becomes too scary, I can go get a drink at the concession stand," and then does so when the sound of the movie becomes too loud for him.

SR5.4 Uses behavioral strategies to regulate arousal level during transitions

Criterion: The child uses behavioral strategies to regulate arousal level and intensity of emotional response during transitions between activities. For example, the child may use conventional sensory-motor actions such as squeezing his hands together or breathing deeply or may use idiosyncratic actions (e.g., jumping, bending fingers) to help him attain or maintain a regulated state when making transitions between activities.

SR5.5 Uses language strategies to regulate arousal level during transitions

Criterion: The child uses language strategies to regulate arousal level and intensity of emotional response during transitions between activities. For instance, the child sings a familiar song during transition; repeats a partner's model of saying, "First I have science class, then I go outside for recess"; or says, "We have to wait, soon we can go," while waiting away from other children to be dismissed from the classroom to go to the school bus.

SR5.6 Uses metacognitive strategies to regulate arousal level during transitions

Criterion: The child uses metacognitive strategies to regulate arousal level and intensity of emotional response during transitions between activities. For example, the child may develop an idea to count the number of paintings on the wall in the school hallway during transitions from the classroom to the cafeteria, which supports a well-regulated state; informs his teacher of the plan; and carries it out. Likewise, a child may understand that uncertainty during transitions is a source of discomfort for her; therefore, she may decide to ask her partners for key pieces of information pertaining to the transition (e.g., where? when? how long?), with the intention of repeating this information to herself during the actual transition. The child then does so.

**6
Recovers
from extreme
dysregulation
by self**

Extreme dysregulation is a state in which a child is not available for engagement or learning and may experience intense emotions. By definition, a state of extreme dysregulation must preclude the child's ability to engage with people and activities in a productive manner. Extreme dysregulation typically is not brief or episodic, and it may be continuous or cyclical within a period. Behavioral evidence of extreme dysregulation may include 1) expression of intense and seemingly inconsolable distress; 2) complete loss of attention to the activity or to other people; 3) intense, disruptive vocalizations (e.g., crying, screaming, moaning) and/or nonverbal behavior (flailing, self- or other-directed hitting, slapping, biting); 4) frenetic motor activity; 5) extreme shutdown and disengagement for an extended period; and so forth. Extreme dysregulation may be associated with arousal levels that are very high (i.e., extreme distress or excitement) or very low (i.e., extremely passive, disengaged state), either of which precludes engagement.

SR6.1   Removes self from overstimulating or undesired activity
Criterion: The child moves away from activities that are overstimulating or undesired after reaching an extreme state of dysregulation.

SR6.2   Uses behavioral strategies to recover from extreme dysregulation
Criterion: The child uses behavioral strategies (e.g., simple motor actions, sensory-motor strategies) to recover from an extreme state of dysregulation.

SR6.3   Uses language strategies to recover from extreme dysregulation
Criterion: The child uses language strategies (i.e., words or other symbols, e.g., signs, pictures) to recover from an extreme state of dysregulation.

SR6.4   Reengages in interaction or activity after recovery from extreme dysregulation
Criterion: The child is able to independently reengage or bring him- or herself back to an interaction or activity after recovery from extreme dysregulation (i.e., return to a well-regulated state).

SR6.5   Decreases amount of time to recover from extreme dysregulation
Criterion: The amount of time the child takes to *recover* (i.e., return to a well-regulated state) from extreme dysregulation decreases over time.*

SR6.6   Decreases intensity of dysregulated state
Criterion: The intensity of emotional response and the changes in the child's state of arousal or energy level during episodes of extreme dysregulation decrease over time.*

   You may need to rely on baseline information gathered from interviews with others who observe the child over time to determine child-specific criteria for objectives SR6.5 and SR6.6 at the Conversational Partner stage.

TRANSACTIONAL SUPPORT

INTER-PERSONAL SUPPORT

1
Partner is responsive to child

IS1.1   Follows child's focus of attention
Criterion: The partner follows the child's focus of attention 1) by looking at and/or talking about what the child is attending to or 2) by acknowledging the child's focus before redirecting the child back to the activity at hand. Examples include the following: 1) the child is looking out the window while playing at home and his mother joins him by looking and pointing to the cars driving by; the child is playing with blocks during free play, and his teacher notices and comments on his play: "That looks like a castle";

and 2) a teacher observes the child initiating a conversation about a special area of interest (e.g., Harry Potter) during a math lesson and follows the child's attentional focus by validating the topic but redirects the child to the social activity by saying, "I can see you like that movie. We can talk about Harry Potter after math during lunchtime."

IS1.2 Attunes to child's emotion and pace

Criterion: The partner recognizes the child's emotional expression and adjusts his or her interpersonal style accordingly. For example, the partner smiles and responds with enthusiasm when the child expresses joy with an accomplishment, looks concerned and provides reassurance when the child appears frustrated, or slows the pace of the interaction when the child looks confused and is lagging behind his classmates.

IS1.3 Responds appropriately to child's signals to foster a sense of communicative competence

Criterion: The partner responds to the child's nonverbal or verbal signals directed to the partner. If the child's signal is socially inappropriate or unconventional, the partner acknowledges the child's communicative bids and then responds contingently by modeling a more appropriate means. For example, if the child says with excitement, "It's raining cats and dogs," when it begins to snow, the partner responds, "Yes, it is snowing heavily."

IS1.4 Recognizes and supports child's behavioral, language, and metacognitive strategies to regulate arousal level

Criterion: The partner recognizes and supports the child's use of 1) behavioral, 2) language, and 3) metacognitive strategies to regulate arousal level. For example, if the child is trying to jump or move as an alerting and energizing strategy, the partner modifies the interaction to support or incorporate this strategy; if the child persistently seeks pressure by pressing into partners as a means of organization, the partner provides pressure through hugs; and so forth. If the child is continually talking about a loud noise in the environment, the partner attempts to provide identifying information about the noise. If the child asks about what he needs to do to cope with anxiety around the first week of school, the partner discusses strategies the child can use to be well regulated.

IS1.5 Recognizes signs of dysregulation and offers support

Criterion: The partner recognizes the child's signs of dysregulation. For example, the partner provides support when behavioral signs indicate that the child is not available for learning or engaging due to an arousal state that is too high, including distress or extreme excitement, or too low, including disinterest or fatigue. The partner provides appropriate assistance contingent on the child's arousal state in an effort to help the child regulate arousal. The partner provides assistance by 1) modeling appropriate behavioral, language, or metacognitive strategies; 2) giving instruction as to how to self-talk through dysregulated states; and/or 3) collaborating with the child on determining an appropriate means for regulation.

IS1.6 Provides information or assistance to regulate state

Criterion: The partner helps the child maintain a regulated state or prevents dysregulation, rather than only dealing with dysregulation when it occurs. For example, 1) a partner may recognize a potentially distressful upcoming event and may model self-talk and self-monitoring (e.g., "When the fire alarm goes off, I can plug my ears so the noise is not too loud"), and 2) a partner may validate the child's opinion in an interaction while modeling collaboration with peers (e.g., "Friends can compromise when they have different ideas. Each friend can share his or her ideas and be willing to change them so that everyone is happy").

IS1.7 Offers breaks from interaction or activity as needed

Criterion: The partner schedules, offers, or allows for breaks from interaction or activities when the child's behavior suggests that a break is needed (e.g., as demonstrated by a change in arousal state, focus of attention, activity level, or emotional state) or when the child has been engaged in one activity for a prolonged period of time. Breaks may involve a temporary pause from or cessation of an ongoing activity, with no specific demands being made for the child to attend or participate during the break. Breaks may also involve redirection to motivating and organizing activities. Breaks may either occur in the child's current location or may involve a change of location.

IS1.8 Facilitates reengagement in interactions and activities following breaks

Criterion: Partner facilitates reengagement in interactions and activities following break times when the child is demonstrating appropriate level and emotional state to participate fully in ongoing activities.

| 2 Partner fosters initiation |

IS2.1 Offers choices nonverbally or verbally

Criterion: The partner offers choices to the child nonverbally or verbally, dependent on arousal state. For example, if the child is in a very high state of arousal, a choice is offered nonverbally; however, when the child is in a well-regulated state, choices are offered verbally. Choices may include what to eat, what to wear, what activity to participate in, what objects to use in an activity, and so forth.

IS2.2 Waits for and encourages initiations

Criterion: The partner waits for the child to initiate using verbal signals and looks expectantly at the child to encourage initiation. For example, in activities in which choice-making opportunities are provided or needs are created for the child to communicate (e.g., objects needed to complete tasks are out of reach), the child is allowed sufficient time to initiate a signal to a partner. The partner provides opportunities in conversational discourse for the child to take a turn. For example, the partner provides leading statements such as, "I saw the second Harry Potter movie, too," to elicit the child's request for information, "What was your favorite part?" The partner does not intervene unless it becomes clear the child is not going to initiate and that the child needs additional support. Initiations are encouraged regardless of whether they are nonverbal or verbal; however, there should be an increasing bias to facilitate the use of verbal initiation.

IS2.3 Provides a balance of initiated and respondent turns

Criterion: The partner does not ask too many questions or give too many commands (either of which limits a child to primarily a respondent mode) and provides a balance of taking turns in relation to the child's initiations and responses.

IS2.4 Allows child to initiate and terminate activities

Criterion: The partner shares control with the child over when to initiate and terminate activities when appropriate. For example, the child may indicate that he or she is done with an activity nonverbally (e.g., walking away when finished, pushing away materials) or verbally (saying or signing, "I'm done with this"). If the child is engaged in a must-do activity (e.g., dressing, washing, homework) or if the activity is very close to successful completion, the partner verbally acknowledges the child's communicative bid to end the activity (and may indicate steps to completion), even if it is not possible for the activity to be terminated immediately. Initiations and terminations are encouraged regardless of whether they are nonverbal or verbal; however, there should be an increasing bias to facilitate the use of symbolic strategies or the child's most sophisticated means to be used in initiations and terminations.

3
Partner
respects child's
independence

IS3.1   Allows child to take breaks to move about as needed
Criterion: The partner allows the child to take breaks from activities when appropriate for the context to move about as needed (e.g., after participating for some time, particularly in activities that require sitting and focusing attention).

IS3.2   Provides time for child to solve problems or complete activities at own pace
Criterion: The partner gives the child adequate time to actively solve problems and to finish activities at the child's pace in most activities. For example, the partner refrains from rushing the child or providing premature prompting and physical assistance as long as the child is progressing in an activity and does not need additional support.

IS3.3   Interprets problem behavior as communicative and/or regulatory
Criterion: The partner recognizes, interprets, and responds to problem behavior as serving a communicative purpose. For example, if the child pushes or hits to protest, the partner acknowledges the child's intent and may model a more socially acceptable means for the child (if appropriate). Likewise, if a child is talking loudly in an effort to block out disorganizing environmental sounds, the partner recognizes this and encourages the use of other regulatory strategies.

IS3.4   Honors protests, rejections, or refusals when appropriate
Criterion: The partner honors the child's signals to protest, reject, or refuse an object or activity when appropriate for the context. For example, in situations in which the child clearly does not wish to accept offered items or engage in activities, the partner does not continue to demand that the child do so under appropriate circumstances (e.g., during nonessential activities, when other choices of foods or activities are available).

4
Partner sets stage
for engagement

IS4.1   Secures child's attention before communicating
Criterion: The partner secures the child's attention nonverbally or verbally before communicating with the child. For example, the partner calls the child's name or touches the child before directing communicative signals to the child.

IS4.2   Uses appropriate proximity and nonverbal behavior to encourage interaction
Criterion: The partner uses appropriate proximity (closeness and orientation to the child) and enticing nonverbal behavior (facial expression, gesture, intonation) to invite and encourage interaction. For example, rather than attempting to engage the child from a distance (e.g., calling to child from across the room), the partner comes close to the child and uses clear gestures and animated facial expression to engage the child. Similarly, when looking at books, the partner may use a face-to-face orientation to

promote gaze shifting and sharing of attention. When engaged in conversation, the partner uses gestures and/or facial expression paired with explicit verbal expressions to minimize communicative breakdowns.

IS4.3 Uses appropriate words and intonation to support optimal arousal level and engagement

Criterion: The partner uses appropriate words and intonation to support the child's optimal arousal level and engagement. For example, the partner either uses a more exaggerated speaking style for an alerting effect or quieter, subdued verbalizations for a calming effect, as appropriate.

IS4.4 Shares emotions, internal states, and mental plans with child

Criterion: The partner shares his or her own emotions, internal states, and mental plans with the child by talking about what he or she is feeling, is thinking, and/or is planning to do.

5
Partner provides developmental support

IS5.1 Provides guidance for success in interaction with peers

Criterion: The partner encourages the child to interact with peers by drawing peers to the child, helping the child to respond to bids from peers, helping child initiate bids for interaction directed to peers, and mediating successful interactions with peers. The partner may use verbal and/or nonverbal means to encourage interaction.

IS5.2 Attempts to repair breakdowns verbally or nonverbally

Criterion: The partner attempts to repair *communication breakdowns* (i.e., situations in which the partner does not understand the child's signal or the child does not understand the partner's message) either verbally or nonverbally by clarifying the meaning of the signal. For example, the partner may repeat the verbal or nonverbal signal or may modify the signal by adding words or gestures.

IS5.3 Provides guidance and feedback as needed for success in activities

Criterion: The partner provides support, guidance, and feedback as needed in activities so that the child maintains a well-regulated state and experiences success. For example, the partner provides social praise or uses appropriate guided participation strategies (i.e., additional cues or prompts), without excessively prompting or directing the child.

IS5.4 Provides guidance on expressing emotions and understanding the cause of emotions

Criterion: The partner provides support, guidance, and feedback as needed in activities so that the child expresses appropriate emotions and is helped to understand the cause of his or her emotions. For example, if the child looks fearful in a busy mall, the partner notes that the child can say that he is afraid, which is understandable because being near so many people and so much noise can be overwhelming.

IS5.5 Provides guidance for interpreting others' feelings and opinions

Criterion: The partner provides support, guidance, and feedback as needed in activities so that the child can interpret the feelings and opinions of other people. For example, if another child becomes upset because he is losing in a board game, the partner labels that child's emotion and explains why he is upset.

**6
Partner adjusts
language input**

IS6.1   Uses nonverbal cues to support understanding
Criterion: When talking to the child, the partner uses clear and appropriate nonverbal cues (gestures, facial expressions, intonation) to support the child's understanding of the message. Words are not used in isolation as the only means to communicate.

IS6.2   Adjusts complexity of language input to child's developmental level
Criterion: When talking to the child, the partner adjusts the complexity of the language so that it is appropriate for the child's developmental level. For example, if the child understands different simple sentence types such as questions and commands but not complex sentences such as conditional utterances (marked by "if"), the partner uses simple sentences appropriate to the child's level of comprehension but not complex conditional statements when talking to the child (e.g., partner says, "First we finish lunch. After lunch, we have recess," but not "We go to recess if we finish lunch")

IS6.3   Adjusts quality of language input to child's arousal level
Criterion: When talking to the child, the partner adjusts the quality of the language, which may include the content, complexity, or intonation, to support the child's arousal level. For example, the partner uses a soothing vocal tone, less exaggerated intonation, and simplified language structures when the child is highly aroused or more exaggerated vocal tone and volume when child is underaroused.

**7
Partner models
appropriate
behaviors**

**IS7.1   Models appropriate nonverbal communication and emotional
            expressions**
Criterion: The partner provides clear and appropriate models of nonverbal communication (e.g., gestures) and emotional expressions (e.g., smiling and laughing to indicate pleasure).

IS7.2   Models a range of communicative functions
Criterion: The partner models a range of communicative functions verbally and nonverbally, for the following:

a.   *behavioral regulation:* For example, the partner provides a verbal model by saying, "I want to keep playing ball," to request continuation of kickball; the partner models a pushing-away gesture while stating, "I'm all done," to protest or refuse an object; or the partner models reaching paired with, "Pass the cookies, please," to request a desired object.

b.   *social interaction:* For example, the partner models saying, "Hi, Tommy," or "Bye, Tommy," to greet on arrival or departure; the partner models asking, "Can I go outside?" to request permission; the partner models saying, "I really like the way you finished your work," to praise; or the partner models saying, "I can see that you look really sad. Something bad must have happened to you," to express empathy.

c.   *joint attention:* For example, the partner models commenting in conversation by talking about a movie he saw; the partner models requesting information by asking the child if he saw the movie; or the partner models anticipated outcomes by stating, "It is getting darker outside. I think it is going to rain soon. I am going to get my umbrella."

IS7.3 Models appropriate dramatic play and recreation

Criterion: The partner models appropriate dramatic play and recreation for the child's developmental level and provides a variety of experiences with play and recreation activities. For example, with a duplicate set of play materials, the partner models dramatic play, such as cleaning and bandaging a pretend wound on a stuffed animal at the vet's office. Opportunities for dramatic play and recreation are provided on a regular basis.

IS7.4 Models appropriate behavior when child uses inappropriate behavior

Criterion: In situations in which the child displays inappropriate behavior but is regulated enough to benefit from models, the partner models appropriate behavior. For example, the partner models making a pushing-away gesture and saying, "I don't want carrots," if the child screams to reject a food item that is offered or models the use of a picture symbol, word, and/or sign for "all done" if the child is forcefully attempting to escape from an activity. Likewise, for a child who is chewing on his clothing and biting others in an effort to regulate arousal, appropriate mouthing and biting activities are modeled and provided (e.g., provision of a cup or toys).

IS7.5 Models "child-perspective" language and use of self-talk

Criterion: The partner models language from the perspective of the child and considers the child's intentions and developmental level. For example, if the child is reaching for a ball that is out of reach, the partner provides a model that matches the child's intention and developmental level, such as "I want to play kickball now." If the child produces an angry vocalization directed to the partner, the partner models saying "mad," "Billy's mad," or "I am mad because Samantha touched my paper." If the child is distracted from doing his work, the partner models. "Let's get our work done so that we have time to go to the park."

LEARNING SUPPORT

1

Partner structures activity for active participation

LS1.1 Defines clear beginning and ending to activity

Criterion: The partner structures the activity so that the beginning and ending are clearly defined for the child. Natural or planned rituals are used. For example, a swinging activity begins with saying, "Ready, set, go" and ends with saying, "It's time to stop," or the beginning of an activity is marked with taking out toys and the end of the activity is marked with the words, "We are all done." Supports such as visual timers may be used for this purpose.

LS1.2 Creates turn-taking opportunities and leaves spaces for child to fill in

Criterion: The partner structures the activity by creating turn-taking opportunities and leaving spaces for the child to fill in a turn. The child's turn should be verbal. For example, when initiating an activity, the partner models "Who wants a push?" and allows the child to say, "I do"; the partner sings songs with the child to music and pauses for the child to fill in phrases from the song; spaces are left for the child to fill in during reciprocal book reading routines; the partner provides leading statements (e.g., "I love PlayStation 2") to elicit a conversational response from the child.

LS1.3 Provides predictable sequence to activity

Criterion: The partner provides a predictable sequence to the activity by the nature of the activity itself, through repetition so that the steps become familiar or the use of other support to make the activity predictable to the child. For example, the partner presents a cooking activity requiring a fixed sequence of steps to completion, or the partner refers to a picture sequence or written recipe to indicate progress in an activity and steps to completion.

LS1.4 Offers repeated learning opportunities

Criterion: The partner consistently and predictably repeats aspects of activities across contexts throughout the child's day (e.g., choice-making opportunities at snack, in small-group work, and lunch) or repeats similar activities over time (e.g., pretend play with a feeding set one day and a grooming set another day) to provide predictable learning opportunities for the child. Similar activities may also involve rule-based group recreation activities, classroom jobs, play with peers, and so forth. Predictable repetition is in contrast to introducing too many novel activities within a time frame.

LS1.5 Offers varied learning opportunities

Criterion: Within the context of repetition and familiar routines, the partner varies an aspect of the activity, which provides novelty for the child to learn from. For example, once the child is familiar with a circle time activity (e.g., calendar), the partner may vary this routine by providing an opportunity for the child to take over parts of the routine. The partner may vary a predictable activity to elicit comments (e.g., by intentionally saying the wrong day of the week).

**2
Partner uses augmentative communication support to foster development**

LS2.1 Uses augmentative communication support to enhance child's communication and expressive language

Criterion: The partner makes available and encourages the child to use an augmentative communication support (i.e., nonspeech communication, e.g., gestures, signs, objects, pictures, photographs, picture symbols, written words) to enhance the child's ability to communicate using one or a variety of nonspeech modalities.

LS2.2 Uses augmentative communication support to enhance child's understanding of language and behavior

Criterion: The partner uses and refers to an augmentative communication support (i.e., nonspeech communication, e.g., gestures, signs, objects, photographs, picture symbols, written words) to enhance the child's ability to understand language and behavior. For example, during a snack routine, a partner may show a picture symbol sequence of the agent + action + object combination "Andrew eat pretzels" while the child is eating.

LS2.3 Uses augmentative communication support to enhance child's expression and understanding of emotion

Criterion: The partner makes available and encourages the child to use an augmentative communication support (i.e., nonspeech communication, e.g., gestures, signs, picture symbols, written words) to enhance his or her ability to express emotions and understand the emotions of others through use of word combinations.

LS2.4 Uses augmentative communication support to enhance child's emotional regulation

Criterion: The partner makes available and encourages the child to use an augmentative communication support (i.e., nonspeech communication, e.g., gestures, signs, objects, photographs, picture symbols, written words) to enhance the child's ability to request mutual regulation, such as requesting an organizing activity, a break from an activity, or assistance during an activity, through nonspeech means.

3 Partner uses visual and organizational support

Visual support is a way of presenting information using visual aids, including individual or sequences of objects, photographs, logos, picture symbols, or written words to enhance the child's active participation and understanding. ***Organizational support*** is a way of organizing materials or physical space or marking time concepts to enhance the child's organization.

LS3.1   Uses support to define steps within a task
Criterion: The partner uses visual and organizational support to define the goals or steps within a task or activity. For example, the partner refers to a within-activity picture sequence to define steps (e.g., in a scavenger hunt, partner may provide a visual map of all of the items that the child is seeking; in an art activity, partner may provide a visual or written listing of three steps, including 1) cut paper, 2) glue paper, and 3) color paper). Sophistication of the list or schedule is commensurate with the child's developmental level.

LS3.2   Uses support to define steps and time for completion of activities
Criterion: The partner uses visual and organizational support to define the steps and the time for completion of activities. For example, a visual timer may provide visual depiction of the time remaining, or a countdown strip with pull-off Velcro numbers may indicate the steps remaining in an activity.

LS3.3   Uses visual support to enhance smooth transitions between activities
Criterion: The partner uses visual support so that transitions from one activity to another are smooth and the child maintains a well-regulated state. For example, the partner uses a now–next visual sequence or refers to a written schedule to indicate what is coming next. Likewise, the partner may use a visual timer to emphasize that a transition is about to occur.

LS3.4   Uses support to organize segments of time across the day
Criterion: The partner uses visual and organizational support to organize segments of time across the day. For example, the partner refers to a written word schedule to review upcoming activities as well as completed activities over a longer time than single transitions.

LS3.5   Uses visual support to enhance attention in group activities
Criterion: The partner uses visual support to enhance the child's attention to the activity and to peers in group activities. For example, the partner uses photographs or picture symbols to cue the child to direct attention to the activity, by using copies of visual support used by the activity leader in circle time. Also, partners use writing on a wipe-off board to augment the verbal conversation.

LS3.6   Uses visual support to foster active involvement in group activities
Criterion: The partner uses visual support to foster the child's initiation and active participation in group activities. For example, the partner uses visual support (e.g., a spinner with children's pictures on segments of the spinner, a turn card) to offer choices within activities, including choices of songs, materials, and play partners and/or to signal turns in activities.

**4
Partner modifies
goals, activities,
and learning
environment**

LS4.1   Adjusts social complexity to support organization and interaction
Criterion: The partner provides a smaller group setting or one-to-one support as
needed to support the child's organization and success in interaction. The partner appropriately judges when to provide more or less social complexity.

LS4.2   Adjusts task difficulty for child success
Criterion: The partner adjusts the task difficulty as needed to foster the child's success
and to help the child maintain an optimal level of arousal. For example, the partner reduces the number of steps or simplifies steps in an activity when the child is becoming agitated.

LS4.3   Modifies sensory properties of learning environment
Criterion: The partner modifies the sensory properties of the learning environment as
needed to help the child maintain an optimal level of arousal. For example, the partner adjusts lighting and controls for noise level and visual distraction.

LS4.4   Arranges learning environment to enhance attention
Criterion: The partner modifies the arrangement of the learning environment as
needed to help the child focus attention. For example, the partner may use a preferred
seating arrangement or semicircular tables for small-group instructions or may cover
visual stimuli on a bulletin board near the child's desk if the child is distracted.

LS4.5   Arranges learning environment to promote child initiation
Criterion: The partner modifies the arrangement of the learning environment as
needed to help the child initiate interactions. For example, the partner organizes materials out of reach or sight to promote initiation of requests throughout daily routines
rather than providing all materials in specified activities.

LS4.6   Designs and modifies activities to be developmentally appropriate
Criterion: The partner designs activities to be developmentally appropriate for the
child's ability levels. For example, activities are designed with appropriate expectations
for communication, attention, and active participation for the child, taking into account language, motor, and attentional requirements.

LS4.7.   Infuses motivating materials and topics in activities
Criterion: The partner infuses materials and topics that are interesting and motivating
to the child in activities. For example, materials and topics are chosen based on the
child's preferences and learning strengths (e.g., favorite characters from stories, gross
motor play). The partner recognizes that the child's intrinsic motivation to communicate is fostered in these contexts in contrast to activities that are selected by the adult
and imposed on the child regardless of the child's interest.

LS4.8   Provides activities to promote initiation and extended interaction
Criterion: The partner provides activities in which the child has the opportunity to initiate communication and participate in extended interactions. For example, the partner captures the child's interest in toys or activities that require another's assistance
(e.g., bubbles, wind-up toys, paint bottles with tight lids); the partner places a few of
the child's preferred or desired objects out of reach (e.g., placing motivating toys or objects on a high shelf or in a sealed but see-through container that will require assistance
to open); or the partner adds repeated turns or new steps to the activity to maintain and
extend interaction.

LS4.9 Alternates between movement and sedentary activities as needed

Criterion: The partner alternates between activities in which the child has the opportunity to engage in organizing movement activities with those in which the child is expected to be sedentary or still. The frequency and types of movement activities are selected with respect to the child's arousal bias.

LS4.10 "Ups the ante" or increases expectations appropriately

Criterion: The partner "ups the ante" or increases expectations for active participation, communication, and/or problem solving when the child is being successful and is at a more optimal level of arousal. This may occur through "sabotage," or holding out for more sophisticated communication or problem solving, with modeling or prompting as needed.

References

American Psychiatric Association (APA). (2000). *Diagnostic and statistical manual of mental disorders (Text rev.).* Washington, DC: Author.

Anzalone, M.E., & Williamson, G.G. (2000). Sensory processing and motor performance in autism spectrum disorders. In S.F. Warren & J. Reichle (Series Eds.) & A.M. Wetherby & B.M. Prizant (Vol. Eds.), *Communication and language intervention series: Vol. 9. Autism spectrum disorders: A transactional developmental perspective* (pp. 143–166). Baltimore: Paul H. Brookes Publishing Co.

Attwood, T. (1998). *Asperger's syndrome: A guide for parents and professionals.* London: Jessica Kingsley.

Baron-Cohen, S., Leslie, A.M., & Frith, U. (1985). Does the autistic child have a theory of mind? *Cognition, 21,* 37–46.

Bates, E. (1976). *Language and context: The acquisition of pragmatics.* San Diego: Academic Press.

Bates, E. (1979). *The emergence of symbols: Cognition and communication in infancy.* San Diego: Academic Press.

Bates, E., Bretherton, I., & Snyder, L. (1988). *From first words to grammar: Individual, differences and dissociable mechanisms.* Cambridge, England: Cambridge University Press.

Bates, E., O'Connell, B., & Shore, C. (1987). Language and communication in infancy. In J. Osofsky (Ed.), *Handbook of infant development* (pp. 149–203). New York: Wiley.

Beukelman, D.R., & Mirenda, P. (2005). *Augmentative and alternative communication: Supporting children and adults with complex communication needs* (3rd ed.). Baltimore: Paul H. Brookes Publishing Co.

Biklen, D. (1990). Communication unbound: Autism and praxis. *Harvard Educational Review, 60,* 291–314.

Bloom, L. (1993). *The transition from infancy to language.* New York: Cambridge University Press.

Brazelton, B., & Cramer, B. (1991). *The earliest relationship.* New York: Addison Wesley.

Bristol, M., & Schopler, E. (1984). A developmental perspective on stress and coping in families of autistic children. In J. Blacher (Ed.), *Families of severely handicapped children.* San Diego: Academic Press.

Brown, F., & Bambara, L. (1999). *Intervention for young children with autism* [Special issue]. *Journal of The Association for Persons with Severe Handicaps, 24*(3).

Bruner, J. (1981). The social context of language acquisition. *Language and Communication, 1,* 155–178.

Bryson, S. (1996). Epidemiology of autism: Overview and issues outstanding. In D. Cohen & F.R. Volkmar (Eds.), *Handbook of autism and pervasive developmental disorders* (2nd ed., pp. 41–46). New York: Wiley.

Carpenter, M., & Tomasello, M. (2000). Joint attention, cultural learning, and language acquisition. In S.F. Warren & J. Reichle (Series Eds.) & A.M. Wetherby & B.M. Prizant (Vol. Eds.), *Communication and language intervention series: Vol. 9. Autism spectrum disorders: A transactional, developmental perspective* (pp. 31–54), Baltimore: Paul H. Brookes Publishing Co.

Carpenter, R., Mastergeorge, A., & Coggins, T. (1983). The acquisition of communicative intentions in infants eight to fifteen months of age. *Language and Speech, 26,* 101–116.

Cicchetti, D., Ganiban, J., & Barnett, D. (1991). Contributions from the study of high-risk populations to understanding the development of emotion regulation. In J. Garber & K. Dodge (Eds.), *The development of emotion regulation and dysregulation* (pp. 15–48). Cambridge, England: Cambridge University Press.

Cohen, S. (1999). Zeroing in on autism in young children. *Journal of The Association for Persons with Severe Handicaps, 24,* 209–212.

Crais, E. (1995). Expanding the repertoire of tools and techniques for assessing the communication skills of infants and toddlers. *American Journal of Speech-Language Pathology, 4,* 47–59.

Csikszentmihalyi, M. (1990). *Flow: The psychology of optimal experience.* New York: HarperCollins.

Damico, J. (1985). Clinical discourse analysis: A functional language assessment technique. In C. Simon (Ed.), Communication skills and classroom success: *Assessment of language-learning disabled students* (pp. 165–204). San Diego: College-Hill Press.

Dawson, G., & Adams, A. (1984). Imitation and social responsiveness in autistic children. *Journal of Abnormal Child Psychology, 12,* 209–226.

Dawson, G., Hill, D., Spencer, A., Galpert, L., & Watson, L. (1990). Affective exchanges between young autistic children and their mothers. *Journal of Abnormal Child Psychology, 18,* 335–345.

Dawson, G., & Lewy, H. (1989). Arousal, attention and socioemotional impairments of individuals with autism. In G. Dawson (Ed.), *Autism: Nature, diagnosis, and treatment* (pp. 49–74). New York: The Guilford Press.

Dawson, G., & Osterling, J. (1997). Early intervention in autism. In M.J. Guralnick (Ed.), *The effectiveness of early intervention* (pp. 307–326). Baltimore: Paul H. Brookes Publishing Co.

DeGangi, G. (2000). *Pediatric disorders of regulation in affect and behavior: A therapist's guide to assessment and treatment.* San Diego: Academic Press.

Domingue, B., Cutler, B., & McTarnaghan, J. (2000). The experience of autism in the lives of families. In S.F. Warren & J. Reichle (Series Eds.) & A.M. Wetherby & B.M. Prizant (Vol. Eds.), *Communication and language intervention series: Vol. 9. Autism spectrum disorders: A transactional developmental perspective* (pp. 369–393). Baltimore: Paul H. Brookes Publishing Co.

Early Intervention Programs for Infants and Toddlers with Disabilities, 34 C.F.R. § 300 (2004).

Education Sciences Reform Act of 2002, PL 107-279, 20 U.S.C. §§ 9501 *et seq.*

Fenson, L., Dale, P.S., Reznick, J.S., Bates, E., Thal, D., & Pethick, S.J. (1994). Variability in early communicative development. *Monographs of the Society for Research in Child Development, 59,* 1–173.

Fewell, R.R., & Kaminski, R. (1988). Play skills development and instruction for young children with handicaps. In S.L. Odom & M.B. Karnes (Eds.), *Early intervention for infants and children with handicaps* (pp. 145–158). Baltimore: Paul H. Brookes Publishing Co.

Filipek, P., Prizant, B.M., et al. (1999). The screening and diagnosis of autistic spectrum disorders. *Journal of autism and developmental disorders, 29,* 439–484.

Filipek, P., Prizant, B.M., et al. (2000). Practice parameter: Screening and diagnosis of autism. *Neurology, 55,* 468–479.

First Signs (Executive Producer). (2001). *On the spectrum: Children and autism* [Videotape]. Merrimac, MA: First Signs.

Fox, L., Dunlap, G., & Buschbacher, P. (2000). Understanding and intervening with children's problem behavior: A comprehensive approach. In S.F. Warren & J. Reichle (Series Eds.) & A.M. Wetherby & B.M. Prizant (Vol. Eds.), *Communication and language intervention series: Vol. 9. Autism spectrum disorders: A transactional developmental perspective* (pp. 307–331). Baltimore: Paul H. Brookes Publishing Co.

Frith, U. (1971). Spontaneous patterns produced by autistic, normal, and subnormal children. In M. Rutter (Ed.), *Infantile autism: Concepts, characteristics, and treatment* (pp. 113–133). London: Churchill Livingstone.

Frost, L., & Bondy, A. (1994). *PECS: The Picture Exchange Communication System training manual.* Cherry Hill, NJ: Pyramid Educational Consultants.

Garfin, D., & Lord, C. (1986). Communication as a social problem in autism. In E. Schopler & G. Mesibov (Eds.), *Social behavior in autism* (pp. 237–261). New York: Kluwer Academic/Plenum.

Grandin, T. (1995). *Thinking in pictures.* New York: Bantam Books.

Gray, C. (1994). *The new Social Story book.* Arlington, TX: Future Horizons.

Greenspan, S.I. (1992). *Infancy and early childhood: The practice of clinical assessment and intervention with emotional and developmental challenges.* Madison, CT: International Universities Press.

Greenspan, S.I., & Wieder, S. (1997). Developmental patterns and outcomes in infants and children with disorders in relating and communicating: A chart review of 200 cases of children with autistic spectrum diagnoses. *Journal of Developmental and Learning Disorders, 1,* 87–141.

Greenspan, S.I., & Wieder, S. (1998). *The child with special needs: encouraging intellectual and emotional growth.* New York: Addison-Wesley.

Greenspan, S.I., & Wieder, S. (2000). A developmental approach to difficulties in relating and communicating in autism spectrum disorders and related syndromes. In S.F. Warren & J. Reichle (Series Eds.) & A.M. Wetherby & B.M. Prizant (Vol. Eds.), *Communication and language intervention series: Vol. 9. Autism spectrum disorders: A developmental transactional perspective* (pp. 279–306). Baltimore: Paul H. Brookes Publishing Co.

Grice, H.P. (1975). Logic and conversation. In R. Cole & J. Morgan (Eds.), *Syntax and semantics: Speech acts* (pp. 85–102). San Diego: Academic Press.

Groden, J., & LeVasseur, P. (1995). Cognitive picture rehearsal: A system to teach self-control. In K. Quill (Ed.), *Teaching children with autism: Strategies to enhance communication and socialization* (pp. 286–306). Albany, NY: Delmar.

Gutstein, S. (2000). *Autism Aspergers: Solving the relationship puzzle.* Arlington, TX: Future Horizons.

Heflin, J., & Simpson, R. (1998). Interventions for children and youth with autism. *Focus on Autism and Other Developmental Disabilities, 13,* 194–221.

Hermelin, B. (1976). Coding and the sense modalities. In L. Wing (Ed.), *Early childhood autism.* London: Pergamon.

Hermelin, B., & O'Connor, N. (1970). *Psychological experiments with autistic children.* Oxford: Pergamon Press.

Individuals with Disabilities Education Act Amendments of 1997, PL 105-17, 20 U.S.C. §§ 1400 *et seq.*

Kanner, L. (1943). Autistic disturbances of affective contact. *The Nervous Child, 2,* 217–250.

Kientz, M., & Dunn, W. (1997). A comparison of the performance of children with and without autism on the sensory profile. *The American Journal of Occupational Therapy, 51,* 530–537.

Koegel, R.L., & Koegel, L.K. (Eds.). (1995). *Teaching children with autism: Strategies for initiating positive interactions and improving learning opportunities.* Baltimore: Paul H. Brookes Publishing Co.

Koegel, L., Koegel, R., Shoshan, Y., & McNerney, E. (1999). Pivotal response intervention, II: Preliminary long-term outcome data. *Journal of The Association for Persons with Severe Handicaps, 24,* 186–198.

Koenig, K., Rubin, E., Klin, A., & Volkmar, F. (2000). Autism and the pervasive developmental disorders. In C.H. Zeanah (Ed.), *Handbook of infant mental health* (2nd ed., pp. 298–310). New York: The Guilford Press.

Leonard, L. (1991). New trends in the study of early language acquisition. *Asha, 33,* 43–44.

Lester, B.M., Freier, K., & LaGasse, L. (1995). Prenatal cocaine exposure and child outcome: What do we really know. In M. Lewis & M. Bendersky (Eds.), *Mothers, babies, and cocaine: The role of toxins in development* (pp. 19–40). Mahwah, NJ: Lawrence Erlbaum Associates.

Lifter, K., & Bloom, L. (1998). Intentionality and the role of play in the transition to language. In S.F. Warren & J. Reichle (Series Eds.) & A.M. Wetherby, S.F. Warren, & J. Reichle (Vol. Eds.), *Communication and language intervention series: Vol. 7. Transitions in prelinguistic communication* (pp. 161–195). Baltimore: Paul H. Brookes Publishing Co.

Lonigan, C., Elbert, J., & Johnson, S. (1998). Empirically supported psychosocial interventions for children: An overview. *Journal of Clinical Child Psychology, 27,* 138–145.

Lord, C., & Paul, R. (1997). Language and communication in autism. In D. Cohen & F.R. Volkmar (Eds.), *Handbook of autism and pervasive developmental disorders* (2nd ed., pp. 195–225). New York: Wiley.

Lovaas, O.I. (1981). *Teaching developmentally disabled children: The ME book.* Baltimore: University Park Press.

Lucyshyn, J.M., Dunlap, G., & Albin, R.W. (2002). *Families and positive behavior support: Addressing problem behavior in family contexts.* Baltimore: Paul H. Brookes Publishing Co.

Lynch, E.W., Hanson, M.J. (Eds.). (2004). *Developing cross-cultural competence: A guide for working with children and their families* (3rd ed.). Baltimore: Paul H. Brookes Publishing Co.

Mahoney, G., & Perales, F. (2005). Relationship-focused early intervention with children with pervasive developmental disorders and other disabilities: A comparative study. *Journal of Developmental and Behavioral Pediatrics, 26,* 77–85.

Marfo, K. (1990). Maternal directiveness in interactions with mentally handicapped children: An analytical commentary.

Journal of Child Psychology and Psychiatry and Allied Disciplines, 31, 531–549.

McCune-Nicolich, L., & Carroll, S. (1981). Development of symbolic play: Implications for the language specialist. *Topics in Language Disorders, 2,* 1–15.

McEachin, J.J., Smith, T., & Lovaas, O.I. (1993). Long-term outcome for children with autism who received early intensive behavioral treatment. *American Journal on Mental Retardation, 97,* 359–372.

McGee, G. (2001). The Walden Preschool. In S. Harris & J. Handleman (Eds.), *Preschool education programs for children with autism* (2nd ed). Austin, TX: PRO-ED.

McGee, G., Morrier, M., & Daly, T. (1999). An incidental teaching approach to early intervention for toddlers with autism. *Journal of The Association for Persons with Severe Handicaps, 24,* 133–146.

McLean, J., & Snyder-McLean, L. (1978). *A transactional approach to early language training: Derivation of a model system.* Columbus, OH: Charles Merrill.

McLean, L.K.S. (1990). Communication development in the first two years of life: A transactional process. *Zero to Three, 11*(1), 13–19.

Meisels, S.J. (1996). Charting the continuum of assessment and intervention. In S.J. Meisels & E. Fenichel (Eds.), *New visions for the developmental assessment of infants and young children* (pp. 27–52). Washington, DC: ZERO TO THREE: National Center for Infants, Toddlers and Families.

Miller, A., & Miller, E. (1989). *From ritual to repertoire: A cognitive-developmental systems approach with behavior disordered children.* New York: Wiley.

Mirenda, P., & Donnellan, A. (1986). Effects of adult interactional style on conversation behavior of students with severe communication problems. *Language, Speech and Hearing Services in Schools, 17,* 126–141.

Mirenda, P., & Erickson, K. (2000). Augmentative communication and literacy. In S.F. Warren & J. Reichle (Series Eds.) & A.M. Wetherby & B.M. Prizant (Vol. Eds.), *Communication and language intervention series: Vol. 9. Autism spectrum disorders: A transactional developmental perspective.* Baltimore: Paul H. Brookes Publishing Co.

Mundy, P., & Stella, J. (2000). Joint attention, social orienting, and communication in autism. In S.F. Warren & J. Reichle (Series Eds.) & A.M. Wetherby & B.M. Prizant (Vol. Eds.), *Communication and language intervention series: Vol. 9. Autism spectrum disorders: A transactional developmental perspective* (pp. 55–77). Baltimore: Paul H. Brookes Publishing Co.

National Research Council, Division of Behavioral and Social Sciences and Education, Committee on Educational Interventions for Children with Autism (NRC). (2001). *Educating children with autism.* Washington, DC: National Academies Press.

Neisworth, J.T., & Bagnato, S.J. (2004). The mismeasure of young children: The authentic assessment alternative. *Infants and Young Children, 17,* 198–212.

Ornitz, E., & Ritvo, E. (1968). Perceptual inconstancy in early infantile autism. *Archives of General Psychiatry, 18,* 76–98.

Owens, R. (2000). *Language development.* Columbus, OH: Charles Merrill.

Peck, C. (1985). Increasing opportunities for social control by children with autism and severe handicaps: Effects on student behavior and perceived classroom climate. *Journal of The Association for Persons with Severe Handicaps, 4,* 183–193.

Pert, C. (1997). *The molecules of emotion.* New York: Basic Books.

Peters, A. (1983). *The units of language acquisition.* Cambridge, England: Cambridge University Press.

Piaget, J. (1971). *The language and thought of the child.* New York: World Publishing Co.

Prior, M. (1979). Cognitive abilities and disabilities in autism: A review. *Journal of Abnormal Child Psychology, 2,* 357–380.

Prizant, B.M. (1982). Speech-Language pathologists and autistic children: What is our role? Part I. Assessment and intervention considerations. *ASHA Journal, 24,* 463–468.

Prizant, B.M. (1983a). Echolalia in autism: Assessment and intervention. *Seminars in Speech and Language, 4,* 63–77.

Prizant, B.M. (1983b). Language acquisition and communicative behavior in autism: Toward an understanding of the "whole" of it. *Journal of Speech and Hearing Disorders, 48,* 296–307.

Prizant, B.M., & Duchan, J.F. (1981). The functions of immediate echolalia in autistic children. *Journal of Speech and Hearing Disorders, 46,* 241–249.

Prizant, B.M., & Meyer, E.C. (1993). Socioemotional aspects of communication disorders in young children and their families. *American Journal of Speech-Language Pathology, 2,* 56–71.

Prizant, B.M., & Rubin, E. (1999). Contemporary issues in interventions for autism spectrum disorders: A commentary. *Journal of The Association for Persons with Severe Handicaps, 24,* 199–217.

Prizant, B.M., & Rydell, P.J. (1984). Analysis of the functions of delayed echolalia in autistic children. *Journal of Speech and Hearing Research, 27,* 183–192.

Prizant, B.M., & Rydell, P.J. (1993). Assessment and intervention strategies for unconventional verbal behavior. In S.F. Warren & J. Reichle (Series Eds.) & J. Reichle & D. Wacker (Vol. Eds.), *Communication and language intervention series: Vol. 3. Communicative approaches to challenging behavior: Integrating functional assessment and intervention strategies* (pp. 263–297). Baltimore: Paul H. Brookes Publishing Co.

Prizant, B.M., Schuler, A.L. Wetherby, A.M., & Rydell, P.J. (1997). Enhancing language and communication: Language approaches. In D. Cohen & F.R. Volkmar (Eds.), *Handbook of autism and pervasive developmental disorders* (2nd ed., pp. 572–605). New York: Wiley.

Prizant, B.M., & Wetherby, A.M. (1987). Communicative intent: A framework for understanding social-communicative behavior in autism. *Journal of the American Academy of Child Psychiatry, 26,* 472–479.

Prizant, B., & Wetherby, A. (1989). Enhancing language and communication in autism: From theory to practice. In G. Dawson (Ed.), *Autism: Nature, diagnosis, and treatment* (pp. 282–309). New York: The Guilford Press.

Prizant, B.M., & Wetherby, A.M. (1990). Toward an integrated view of early language and communication development and socioemotional development. *Topics in Language Disorders, 10,* 1–16.

Prizant, B.M., & Wetherby, A.M. (1993). Communication in preschool autistic children. In E. Schopler, M. van Bourgondien, & M. Bristol (Eds.), *Preschool issues in autism* (pp. 95–128). New York: Kluwer Academic/Plenum.

Prizant, B.M., & Wetherby, A.M. (1998). Understanding the continuum of discrete-trial traditional behavioral to social-pragmatic developmental approaches in communication enhancement for young children with autism/PDD. *Seminars in Speech and Language, 19*(4), 329–353.

Prizant, B.M., Wetherby, A.M., & Rydell, P.J. (2000). Communication intervention issues for children with autism spectrum disorders. In S.F. Warren & J. Reichle (Series Eds.) & A.M.

Wetherby & B.M. Prizant (Vol. Eds.), *Communication and language intervention series: Vol. 9. Autism spectrum disorders: A transactional developmental perspective* (pp. 193–224). Baltimore: Paul Brookes Publishing Co.

Prizant, B.M., Wetherby, A.M., Rubin, E., & Laurent, A.C. (2003). The SCERTS Model: A family-centered, transactional approach to enhancing communication and socioemotional abilities of young children with ASD. *Infants and Young Children, 16,* 296–316.

Prizant, B.M., Wetherby, A.M., Rubin, E., Rydell, P.J., & Laurent, A.C. (2003). The SCERTS Model: Enhancing communication and socioemotional abilities of young children with ASD. *Jenison Autism Journal, 14,* 2–19.

Quill, K. (1998). Instructional considerations for young children with autism: The rationale for visually cued instruction. *Journal of Autism and Developmental Disorders, 27,* 697–714.

Quinn, J. (2003). The SCERTS Model: Our family's experience. *Jenison Autism Journal, 14,* 27–32.

Rogers, S.L., & Bennetto, L. (2000). Intersubjectivity in autism: The roles of imitation and executive function. In S.F. Warren & J. Reichle (Series Eds.) & A.M. Wetherby & B.M. Prizant (Vol. Eds.), *Communication and language intervention series: Vol. 9. Autism spectrum disorders: A transactional developmental perspective* (pp. 79–107). Baltimore: Paul H. Brookes Publishing Co.

Rydell, P.J., & Mirenda, P. (1991). The effects of two levels of linguistic constraint on echolalia and generative language production in children with autism. *Journal of Autism and Developmental Disorders, 24,* 719–735.

Rydell, P.J., & Prizant, B. (1995). Assessment and intervention strategies for children who use echolalia. In K. Quill (Ed.), *Teaching children with autism: Strategies to enhance communication and socialization* (pp. 105–129). Albany, NY: Delmar.

Sameroff, A. (1987). The social context of development. In N. Eisenburg (Ed.), *Contemporary topics in development* (pp. 273–291). New York: Wiley.

Sameroff, A., & Fiese, B. (1990). Transactional regulation and early intervention. In S. Meisels & J. Shonkoff (Eds.), *Handbook of early childhood intervention* (pp. 119–149). Cambridge, England: Cambridge University Press.

Sherrer, K.R. (1984). On the nature and function of emotion. A component process approach. In K.R. Sherrer & P. Ekman (Eds.), *Approaches to emotion* (pp. 293–317). Mahwah, NJ: Lawrence Erlbaum Associates.

Schopler, E., Mesibov, G., & Hearsey, K. (1995). Structured Teaching in the TEACCH curriculum. In E. Schopler & G. Mesibov (Eds.), *Learning and cognition in autism* (pp. 243–268). New York: Kluwer Academic/Plenum.

Schuler, A. (1995). Thinking in autism: Differences in learning and development. In K. Quill (Ed.), *Teaching children with autism: Strategies to enhance communication and socialization* (pp. 11–32). Albany, NY: Delmar.

Schuler, A.L., & Wolfberg, P.J. (2000). Promoting peer play and socialization: The art of scaffolding. In S.F. Warren & J. Reichle (Series Eds.) & A.M. Wetherby & B.M. Prizant (Vol. Eds.), *Communication and language intervention series: Vol. 9. Autism spectrum disorders: A transactional developmental perspective* (pp. 251–277). Baltimore: Paul H. Brookes Publishing Co.

Schuler, A.L., & Prizant, B.M. (1985). Echolalia in autism. In E. Schopler & G. Mesibov (Eds.), *Communication problems in autism.* New York: Kluwer Academic/Plenum.

Schuler, A.L., Wetherby, A.M., & Prizant, B.M. (1997). Enhancing language and communication: Prelanguage approaches. In

D. Cohen & F.R. Volkmar (Eds.), *Handbook of autism and pervasive developmental disorders* (2nd ed., pp. 539–571).

Shonkoff, J. (1996, March). *Some thoughts on the effectiveness of early intervention.* Paper presented at the Emerson College Symposium on Autism and PDD, Boston.

Shonkoff, J.P., & Phillips, D.A. (Eds.). (2000). *From neurons to neighborhoods: The science of early childhood development.* Washington, DC: National Academies Press.

Shore, S. (2001). *Beyond the wall.* Shawnee, KS: Autism Asperger's Publishing Co.

Stern, D. (1985). *The interpersonal world of the infant.* New York: Basic Books.

Stone, W.L., & Caro-Martinez, L.M. (1990). Naturalistic observations of spontaneous communication in autistic children. *Journal of Autism and Developmental Disorders, 20,* 437–453.

Strain, P., & Kohler, F. (1998). Peer mediated social intervention for children with autism. *Seminars in Speech and Language, 19,* 391–405.

Strain, P.S., McGee, G.G., & Kohler, F.W. (2001). Inclusion of children with autism in early intervention environments: An examination of rationale, myths, and procedures. In M.J. Guralnick (Ed.), *Early childhood inclusion: Focus on change* (pp. 337–363). Baltimore: Paul H. Brookes Publishing Co.

Sundberg, M.L., & Partington, J.W. (1998). *Teaching language to children with autism or other developmental disabilities.* Pleasant Hill, CA: Behavior Analysts.

Tiegerman, E., & Primavera, L. (1984). Imitating the autistic child: Facilitating communicative gaze behavior. *Journal of Autism and Developmental Disorders, 14,* 27–38.

Tomasello, M. (1992). *First verbs: A case study of early grammatical development.* New York: Cambridge University Press.

Tomasello, M. (1999). *The cultural origins of human cognition.* Cambridge, MA: Harvard University Press.

Tomasello, M. (2003). *Constructing a language: A usage-based theory of language acquisition.* Cambridge, MA: Harvard University Press.

Tomasello, M., Kruger, A.C., & Ratner, H.H. (1993). Cultural learning. *Behavioral and Brain Sciences, 16,* 495–552.

Trevarthen, C., Aitken, K., Papoudi, D., & Robarts, J. (1998). *Children with autism: Diagnosis and interventions to meet their needs* (2nd ed.). Philadelphia: Jessica Kingsley Publishers.

Trevarthen, C., & Hubley, P. (1978). Secondary intersubjectivity: Confidence, confiding and acts of meaning in the first year. In A. Lock (Ed.), *Action, gesture and symbols: The emergence of language* (pp. 183–229). San Diego: Academic Press.

Tronick, E. (1989). Emotions and emotional communication in infancy. *American Psychologist, 44,* 112–119.

U.S. Department of Education, Office of Special Education and Rehabilitative Services, Office of Special Education Programs. (n.d.). *OSEP Technical Assistance Center on Positive Behavioral Interventions and Supports.* Retrieved May 12, 2005, from http://www.pbis.org/main.htm

Venter, A., Lord, C., & Schopler, E. (1992). A follow-up study of high-functioning autistic children. *Journal of Child Psychology and Psychiatry and Allied Disciplines, 33,* 489–507.

Volkmar, F., Klin, A., Schultz, R., Rubin, E., & Bronen, R. (2000). Clinical case conference: Asperger's disorder. *American Journal of Psychiatry, 157*(2), 262–267.

Vygotsky, L. (1978). *Mind in society: The development of higher psychological processes.* Cambridge, MA: Harvard University Press.

Warren, S.F. (1993). Early communication and language intervention: Challenges for the 1990s and beyond. In A.P. Kaiser &

D.B. Gray (Eds.), *Enhancing children's communication: Research foundations for intervention* (pp. 375–395). Baltimore: Paul H. Brookes Publishing Co.

Westby, C. (1988). Children's play: Reflections of social competence. *Seminars in Speech and Language, 9,* 1–13.

Wetherby, A.M. (1986). The ontogeny of communicative functions in autism. *Journal of Autism and Developmental Disorders, 16,* 295–316.

Wetherby, A.M., & Prizant, B.M. (1989). The expression of communicative intent: Assessment guidelines. *Seminars in Speech and Language, 10,* 77–91.

Wetherby, A.M., & Prizant, B.M. (1992). Profiling young children's communicative competence. In S.F. Warren & J. Reichle (Series & Vol. Eds.), *Communication and language intervention series: Vol. 1. Causes and effects in communication and language intervention* (pp. 217–253). Baltimore: Paul H. Brookes Publishing Co.

Wetherby, A.M., & Prizant, B.M. (1993a). *CSBS^{TM} manual: Communication and Symbolic Behavior Scales^{TM} (Normed Ed.).* Baltimore: Paul H. Brookes Publishing Co.

Wetherby, A., & Prizant, B. (1993b). Profiling communication and symbolic abilities in young children. *Journal of Childhood Communication Disorders, 15,* 23–32.

Wetherby, A.M., & Prizant, B.M. (1999). Enhancing language and communication development in autism: Assessment and intervention guidelines. In D. Berkell Zager (Ed.), *Autism: Identification, education, and treatment* (2nd ed., pp. 141–174). Mahwah, NJ: Lawrence Erlbaum Associates.

Wetherby, A.M., & Prizant, B.M. (2002). *Communication and Symbolic Behavior Scales Developmental Profile (CSBS DP™)* (1st normed ed.). Baltimore: Paul H. Brookes Publishing Co.

Wetherby, A.M., Prizant, B.M., & Hutchinson, T. (1998). Communicative, social/affective, and symbolic profiles of young children with autism and pervasive developmental disorders. *American Journal of Speech-Language Pathology, 7,* 79–91.

Wetherby, A.M., Prizant, B.M., & Schuler, A.L. (1997). Enhancing language and communication: Theoretical foundations. In D. Cohen & F.R. Volkmar (Eds.), *Handbook of autism and pervasive developmental disorders* (2nd ed., pp. 513–538). New York: Wiley.

Wetherby, A.M., Prizant, B.M., & Schuler, A.L. (2000). Understanding the nature of communication and language impairments. In S.F. Warren & J. Reichle (Series Eds.) & A.M. Wetherby & B.M. Prizant (Vol. Eds.), *Communication and language intervention series: Vol. 9. Autism spectrum disorders: A transactional developmental perspective* (pp. 109–141). Baltimore: Paul H. Brookes Publishing Co.

Wetherby, A., & Prutting, C. (1984). Profiles of communicative and cognitive-social abilities in autistic children. *Journal of Speech and Hearing Research, 27,* 364–377.

Wetherby, A.M., Reichle, J., & Pierce, P.L. (1998). The transition to symbolic communication. In S.F. Warren & J. Reichle (Series Eds.) & A.M. Wetherby, S.F. Warren, & J. Reichle (Vol. Eds.), *Communication and language intervention series: Vol. 7. Transitions in prelinguistic communication: Preintentional to intentional and presymbolic to symbolic* (pp. 197–230). Baltimore: Paul H. Brookes Publishing Co.

Wetherby, A., & Rodriguez, G. (1992). Measurement of communicative intentions in normal children during structured and unstructured contexts. *Journal of Speech and Hearing Research, 35,* 130–138.

Wetherby, A.M., Warren, S.F., & Reichle, J. (Vol. Eds.). (1998). *Communication and language intervention series: Vol. 7. Transitions in prelinguistic communication.* Baltimore: Paul H. Brookes Publishing Co.

Williams, D. (1992). *Nobody nowhere: The extraordinary autobiography of an autistic.* New York: Times Books.

Zeidner, M., Boekaerts, M., & Pintrich, P. (2000). Self-regulation: Directions and challenges for future research. In M. Boekaerts, P. Pintrich, & M. Zeidner (Eds.), *Handbook of self-regulation.* San Diego: Academic Press.

Appendix A

SCERTS Assessment Process Forms

This appendix contains photocopiable blank forms (listed below) for use in the SCERTS Assessment Process (SAP). (See the release on page iv for the specific conditions in which photocopying is permitted.) Chapter 7 of Volume I overviews the steps of the SAP. Extended "spotlight" case studies in Chapters 5–7 of Volume II describe the implementation of the assessment process with children at the Social Partner, Language Partner, and Conversational Partner stages. Those chapters contain sample filled-in versions of some of the SAP forms.

Worksheet for Determining Communication Stage
SAP-Report Form (Social Partner stage)
SAP-Report Form (Language Partner stage)
SAP-Report Form (Conversational Partner stage)
SAP Map for Planning the SAP-Observation
SAP-Observation Form (Social Partner stage)
    Expression of Intentions and Emotions Worksheet
SAP-Observation Form (Language Partner stage)
    Expression of Intentions and Emotions Worksheet
    Word Meanings Worksheet
    Relational Meanings in Word Combinations Worksheet
SAP-Observation Form (Conversational Partner stage)
    Intentions, Presuppositions, and Conversational Rules Worksheet
    Expression and Understanding of Emotions Worksheet
    Language Elements Worksheet
    Sentence Constructions Worksheet
SAP Summary Form (Social Partner Stage)
SAP Summary Form (Language Partner Stage)
SAP Summary Form (Conversational Partner Stage)
SAP Daily Tracking Log (version 1)
SAP Daily Tracking Log (version 2)
SAP Weekly Tracking Log
SAP Activity Planning Form

Worksheet for Determining Communication Stage

Child's name: _____ Date: _____

1. Does the child use **ALL** of the following?

    1a. Does the child use **at least 3 different words or phrases** (spoken, signed, pictures, written words, or other symbolic system)? ❑

    1b. Does the child use at least 3 words or phrases **referentially** (i.e., to refer to specific objects, people, or activities)? ❑

    1c. Does the child used at least 3 words or phrases **with communicative intent** (i.e., by coordinating the words or phrases with gestures or gaze for a communicative purpose)? ❑

    1d. Does the child use at least 3 words or phrases **regularly** (i.e., often, not just on a rare occasion)? ❑

    ❑ **No:**
    Use Social Partner stage forms.

    ❑ **Yes:** Go to Question 2.

2. Does the child use **ALL** of the following?

    2a. Does the child use **at least 100 different words or phrases** (spoken, signed, pictures, written words, or other symbolic system)? ❑

    2b. Does the child use at least 100 words or phrases **referentially** (i.e., to refer to specific objects, people, or activities)? ❑

    2c. Does the child use at least 100 words or phrases **with communicative intent** (i.e., by coordinating the words or phrases with gestures or gaze for a communicative purpose)? ❑

    2d. Does the child use at least 100 words or phrases **regularly** (i.e., often)? ❑

    2e. Does the child use **at least 20 different word combinations that are creative** (i.e., not just exact imitations of phrases)? ❑

    ❑ **No:**
    Use Language Partner stage forms.

    ❑ **Yes:**
    Use Conversational Partner stage forms.

The SCERTS™ Model: A Comprehensive Educational Approach for Children with Autism Spectrum Disorders
by Barry M. Prizant, Amy M. Wetherby, Emily Rubin, Amy C. Laurent, & Patrick J. Rydell
Copyright © 2006 by Paul H. Brookes Publishing Co. All rights reserved.

SAP-REPORT FORM: Social Partner Stage

Child's name: _____ Age: _____ Date filled out: _____

Filled out by: _____ Relationship to child: _____

This questionnaire is designed to be completed by a parent, teacher, or other person who interacts with this child on a daily or regular basis. Please answer the following questions about this child's **social communication** (understanding and use of nonverbal and verbal communication in social interaction), **emotional regulation** (capacity to regulate attention, arousal, and emotional state), and **transactional support** (ways that partners and learning activities support development). We would like you to complete this when you can observe the child, or immediately after you observe the child, and notice the behaviors listed. Please provide examples.

SOCIAL COMMUNICATION

1. Describe how the child interacts with others. For example, does the child respond to bids for interaction? Initiate interaction? Take a few turns? Take many turns that follow a shared attentional focus?

2. Describe the child's use of eye gaze during interactions. For example, does the child look at people rarely or often? When playing with toys, does the child look up to see if you are watching and then look back at the object?

3. Which of the following means does the child use regularly to communicate? Check all that apply.

___ Give objects   ___ Push away objects   ___ Pull your hand to an object

___ Reach/touch   ___ Show objects   ___ Point/touch

___ Wave   ___ Clap   ___ Head shake (for rejecting or refusing)

___ Reach at a distance   ___ Point at a distance

___ Vocalizations; list sounds the child makes: _____

___ Words (or word attempts); list words the child tries to say: _____

___ Problem behaviors; give examples: _____

4. Which of the following reasons does the child communicate for? Check all that apply and give examples.

___ To request a desired object _____

___ To protest something he or she does not like _____

___ To request help _____

___ To request a social game (e.g., Peek-a-boo; chase or tickling games) _____

___ To request comfort _____

___ To greet _____

___ To draw your attention to something that he or she wants you to notice _____

5. How often does the child initiate communication when interacting . . .

	seldom or not at all	sometimes	often
. . . with a familiar person?	_____	_____	_____
. . . with an unfamiliar person?	_____	_____	_____
. . . in small groups?	_____	_____	_____

6. What happens if you can't figure out what the child is asking for? What does the child do?

7. What are the child's favorite toys? How does he or she play with them?

8. How does the child respond if a familiar adult joins in play? If a familiar peer or sibling joins?

9. How does the child respond to actions and sounds modeled by others?

	seldom or not at all	sometimes	often
Does the child take a turn?	_____	_____	_____
Does the child imitate familiar actions or sounds?	_____	_____	_____
Does the child imitate new actions or sounds?	_____	_____	_____

10. Which of the following instructions or cues does the child understand? Check all that apply.

___ Gestures other than pointing   ___ Pointing   ___ Photographs or pictures

___ Facial expressions   ___ Intonation   ___ Child's name

___ Words in social games; give examples: _____

___ Names of familiar people and objects; give examples: _____

___ Phrases in routines; give examples: _____

___ Sentences; give examples: _____

EMOTIONAL REGULATION

1. How does the child respond to people and things in his or her environment? For example, does the child show interest in a variety of situations, show intense interest in a few things, express different emotions, keep to him- or herself, respond to bids for interaction, and/or seek interaction?

2. What activities or situations are the most fun or interesting to the child?

3. What activities or situations create the most distress or are boring to the child?

4. Does the child use strategies to stay focused, interested, calm, or engaged during familiar activities (e.g., sucking on a pacifier, rubbing a blanket, rocking, toe walking)? If so, please describe.

5. Does the child use strategies to stay focused, interested, calm, or engaged during new and changing situations or situations that are otherwise challenging? If so, please describe.

6. Does the child express the following emotions? If so, how?

Happiness _____

Sadness _____

Anger _____

Fear_____

7. Does the child respond to comfort when offered by others? If so, how?

8. Does the child respond to choices offered by others? If so, how?

9. What strategies do you use to help the child stay focused, interested, calm, and engaged?

10. How do you know when the child is overwhelmed or upset? What signs does the child show?

11. How do you know when the child is bored or uninterested? What signals does the child show?

12. When the child is extremely upset or distressed,

    . . . how does the child recover by him- or herself? How long does this usually take?

    . . . how does the child recover with support from partners? How long does this usually take?

TRANSACTIONAL SUPPORT

1. What people does the child interact with or see on a regular basis (i.e., daily or weekly)?

2. What places does the child go to on a regular basis (i.e., daily or weekly)?

3. Which of the following are easy for you to read, follow, and respond to? Rate all that apply using the following key: 0, *can read or respond rarely or not at all*; 1, *can read and respond some of the time*; 2, *can read and respond most of the time.*

    ___ The child's focus of attention   ___ What the child is trying to communicate

    ___ How the child is feeling   ___ The child's preferred pace (fast or slow)

    ___ When the child needs a break   ___ Whether the child is interested

    ___ Whether the child is frustrated   ___ Whether the child is overwhelmed

4. What strategies are the most helpful to encourage the child to initiate communication (e.g., offering choices, waiting and looking at the child, taking a turn and then waiting)?

5. How do you usually react if the child uses problem behaviors, such as hitting, screaming, or biting? Is this reaction effective?

6. What strategies are the most helpful to secure the child's attention (e.g., getting down on the child's level, moving closer to or farther from the child, matching the child's emotion, waiting and following the child)?

7. What strategies are the most helpful to keep interactions going with the child (e.g., allowing the child to initiate interactions, allowing the child to take breaks and move about, following the child's interest)?

8. How do you usually communicate to the child to ensure that your message is understood?

9. Do you use visual supports to help the child communicate, understand language, express emotion, and/or flow with the day better? If so, which supports do you use (e.g., defining steps of a task with pictures, transition objects, picture choices, and/or signs)?

10. What features of the physical or social environment help the child stay engaged (e.g., limiting the number of people the child interacts with, limiting the amount of background noise and/or visual clutter, adding more opportunities for movement and rhythm, using specific places consistently for specific activities)?

11. What features of the physical or social environment help the child communicate better (e.g., using motivating toys or activities that the child prefers, placing enticing or desired objects slightly out of reach)?

ADDITIONAL COMMENTS

1. List the top strengths or assets you observe in the child.

2. List your major concerns about the child's development.

3. What information would be most useful to you in planning or updating the child's program?

4. Is there anything else about the child that you think is important to share with us?

5. Do you have any questions for us?

6. What is the best time and way to contact you?

The SCERTS™ Model: A Comprehensive Educational Approach for Children with Autism Spectrum Disorders
by Barry M. Prizant, Amy M. Wetherby, Emily Rubin, Amy C. Laurent, & Patrick J. Rydell

SAP-REPORT FORM: Language Partner Stage

Child's name: _____ Age: _____ Date filled out: _____

Filled out by: _____ Relationship to child: _____

This questionnaire is designed to be completed by a parent, teacher, or other person who interacts with this child on a daily or regular basis. Please answer the following questions about this child's **social communication** (understanding and use of nonverbal and verbal communication in social interaction), **emotional regulation** (capacity to regulate attention, arousal, and emotional state), and **transactional support** (ways that partners and learning activities support development). We would like you to complete this when you can observe the child, or immediately after you observe the child, and notice the behaviors listed. Please provide examples.

SOCIAL COMMUNICATION

1. Describe how the child interacts with others. For example, does the child respond to bids for interaction? Initiate interaction? Take a few turns? Take many turns that follow a shared attentional focus?

2. Describe the child's use of eye gaze during interactions. For example, does the child look at people rarely or often? When playing with toys, does the child look up to see if you are watching and then look back at the object?

3. Which of the following gestures does the child use regularly to communicate? Check all that apply.

    ___ Show objects   ___ Wave   ___ Point at a distance   ___ Clap

    ___ Head shake (for rejecting or refusing)   ___ Head nod (for accepting or indicating yes)

4. Which of the following types of words (spoken, signed, pictures, written words, or other symbolic system) does the child use regularly to communicate? Check all that apply and give examples.

    ___ Names of things (e.g., toys, food items, body parts) _____

    ___ Names of people or pets _____

    ___ Way to indicate "more" or "another" _____

    ___ Way to indicate "no" or "gone" _____

    ___ Greeting words (e.g., "hi," "bye," "see you later") _____

    ___ Action words (e.g., "eat," "run," "go") _____

    ___ Modifiers or words that describe things (e.g., "hot," "big," "stuck") _____

    ___ Spontaneous word combinations (e.g., "go outside," "cookie gone") _____

5. Which of the following reasons does the child communicate for? Check all that apply and give examples.

    ___ To request a desired object or help_____

    ___ To protest something he or she does not like _____

    ___ To greet _____

    ___ To request permission _____

    ___ To draw your attention to something that he or she wants you to notice _____

    ___ To request information about things of interest _____

6. How often does the child initiate communication when interacting . . .

	seldom or not at all	sometimes	often
. . . with a familiar person?	_____	_____	_____
. . . with an unfamiliar person?	_____	_____	_____
. . . in small groups?	_____	_____	_____

7. What happens if you can't figure out what the child is asking for? What does the child do?

8. What are the child's favorite toys? How does he or she play with them?

9. How does the child respond if a familiar adult joins in play? If a familiar peer or sibling joins?

10. How does the child respond to actions and sounds modeled by others?

	seldom or not at all	sometimes	often
Does the child imitate familiar actions or sounds?	_____	_____	_____
Does the child imitate new actions or sounds?	_____	_____	_____
Does the child imitate behaviors in new situations?	_____	_____	_____

11. Which of the following instructions or cues does the child understand? Check all that apply.

___ Gestures other than pointing   ___ Pointing   ___ Photographs or pictures   ___ Written words

___ Facial expressions   ___ Intonation   ___ Child's name

___ Words or phrases in familiar contexts; give examples: _____

___ Names of people and objects, without contextual cues; give examples: _____

___ Action word or modifiers, without contextual cues; give examples: _____

___ Phrases or sentences without contextual cues; give examples: _____

EMOTIONAL REGULATION

1. How does the child respond to people and things in his or her environment? For example, does the child show interest in a variety of situations, show intense interest in a few things, express different emotions, keep to him- or herself, respond to bids for interaction, and/or seek interaction?

2. What activities or situations are the most fun or interesting to the child?

3. What activities or situations create the most distress or are boring to the child?

4. Does the child use strategies to stay focused, interested, calm, or engaged during familiar activities (e.g., squeezing hands; rubbing a blanket; rocking; saying, "Finish work, then go outside")? If so, please describe.

5. Does the child use strategies to stay focused, interested, calm, or engaged during new and changing situations or situations that are otherwise challenging (e.g., singing a familiar song when changing activities; saying, "Don't worry," when scared)? If so, please describe.

6. Does the child express positive and negative emotions? If so, how?

Positive emotions	Negative emotions
Happiness _____	Sadness _____
Contentment _____	Anger or frustration _____
Silliness _____	Fear _____

7. Does the child respond to comfort when offered by others? If so, how?

8. Does the child respond to choices offered by others? If so, how?

9. What strategies do you use to help the child stay focused, interested, calm, and engaged?

10. How do you know when the child is overwhelmed or upset? What signs does the child show?

11. How do you know when the child is bored or uninterested? What signals does the child show?

12. When the child is extremely upset or distressed,

    . . . how does the child recover by him- or herself? How long does this usually take?

    . . . how does the child recover with support from partners? How long does this usually take?

TRANSACTIONAL SUPPORT

1. What people does the child interact with or see on a regular basis (i.e., daily or weekly)?

2. What places does the child go to on a regular basis (i.e., daily or weekly)?

3. Which of the following are easy for you to read, follow, and respond to? Rate all that apply using the following key: 0, *can read or respond rarely or not at all;* 1, *can read and respond some of the time;* 2, *can read and respond most of the time.*

___ The child's focus of attention	___ What the child is trying to communicate
___ How the child is feeling	___ The child's preferred pace (fast or slow)
___ When the child needs a break	___ Whether the child is interested
___ Whether the child is frustrated	___ Whether the child is overwhelmed

4. What strategies are the most helpful to encourage the child to initiate communication and take turns in interaction (e.g., offering choices, waiting and looking at the child, taking a turn and then waiting)?

5. How do you usually react if the child uses problem behaviors, such as hitting, screaming, or biting? Is this reaction effective?

6. What strategies are the most helpful to secure the child's attention (e.g., getting down on the child's level, moving closer to or farther from the child, matching the child's emotion, waiting and following the child)?

7. What strategies are the most helpful to keep interactions going with the child (e.g., allowing the child to initiate interactions, allowing the child to take breaks and move about, following the child's interest)?

8. How do you usually communicate to the child to ensure that your message is understood?

9. Do you use visual supports to help the child communicate, understand language, express emotion, and/or flow with the day better? If so, which supports do you use (e.g., defining steps of a task with pictures, transition objects, picture choices, and/or signs)?

10. What features of the physical or social environment help the child stay engaged (e.g., limiting the number of people the child interacts with, limiting the amount of background noise and/or visual clutter, adding more opportunities for movement and rhythm, using specific places consistently for specific activities)?

11. What features of the physical or social environment help the child communicate better (e.g., using motivating toys or activities that the child prefers, placing enticing or desired objects slightly out of reach)?

ADDITIONAL COMMENTS

1. List the top strengths or assets you observe in the child.

2. List your major concerns about the child's development.

3. What information would be most useful to you in planning or updating the child's program?

4. Is there anything else about the child that you think is important to share with us?

5. Do you have any questions for us?

6. What is the best time and way to contact you?

The SCERTS™ Model: A Comprehensive Educational Approach for Children with Autism Spectrum Disorders
by Barry M. Prizant, Amy M. Wetherby, Emily Rubin, Amy C. Laurent, & Patrick J. Rydell
Copyright © 2006 by Paul H. Brookes Publishing Co. All rights reserved.

SAP-REPORT FORM: Conversational Partner Stage

Child's name: _____ Age: _____ Date filled out: _____

Filled out by: _____ Relationship to child: _____

This questionnaire is designed to be completed by a parent, teacher, or other person who interacts with this child on a daily or regular basis. Please answer the following questions about this child's *social communication* (understanding and use of nonverbal and verbal communication in social interaction), *emotional regulation* (capacity to regulate attention, arousal, and emotional state), and *transactional support* (ways that partners and learning activities support development). We would like you to complete this when you can observe the child, or immediately after you observe the child, and notice the behaviors listed. Please provide examples.

SOCIAL COMMUNICATION

1. Describe how the child interacts with others. For example, does the child monitor what a partner is attending to? Get a partner's attention before talking? Take many turns that follow a shared attentional focus?

2. Which of the following reasons does the child communicate for in conversation? Check all that apply and give examples.

    ___ To request desired objects or help _____

    ___ To request a break _____

    ___ To protest/refuse an undesired activity _____

    ___ To greet_____

    ___ To request permission _____

    ___ To express empathy _____

    ___ To comment on immediate and past events _____

    ___ To request information about immediate and past events _____

    ___ To express feelings and opinions _____

    ___ To plan ahead and discuss what will happen _____

3. What happens if you can't figure out what the child is asking for or talking about? What does the child do?

4. Which of the following types of words does the child use regularly in sentences? Check all that apply and give examples.

    ___ *Wh-* words (e.g., *what, where, who*) _____

    ___ Words describing time (e.g., *before, now, later, when*) _____

    ___ Words describing size or number (e.g., *small, many*) _____

    ___ Words describing location (e.g., next to, between, under) _____

    ___ Pronouns (e.g., *I/you, he/she, we/they*) _____

    ___ Verbs (e.g., past, present, or future tense [e.g., *ate, ran, will go*]) _____

    ___ Conjunctions that link (e.g., *and, or*) _____

    ___ Conjunctions that imply cause (e.g., *but, so, because, if*) _____

5. Which of the following "rules" of conversation does the child follow regularly? Check all that apply and give examples.

___ Initiates a variety of topics _____

___ Initiates topics frequently _____

___ Talks about things of interest to others _____

___ Takes turns as a speaker and listener appropriately _____

___ Provides needed information based on what others know _____

___ Requests relevant information _____

___ Adjusts length of turn based on partner's behavior _____

___ Shifts topics smoothly _____

___ Ends conversations politely _____

6. Which of the following nonverbal behaviors does the child use appropriately during conversation? Check all that apply.

___ Facial expression   ___ Gestures   ___ Body posture   ___ Proximity or physical distance to partner

___ Volume or loudness of voice   ___ Intonation or melody of voice

7. What are the child's favorite toys, games, or recreational activities? How does he or she play or have fun?

8. Who are the child's favorite friends? What kinds of things do they do like to do together or talk about?

9. How does the child learn in group situations?

	seldom or not at all	sometimes	often
Does the child imitate behaviors in new situations?	_____	_____	_____
Does the child learn rules modeled by adults?	_____	_____	_____
Does the child collaborate and negotiate with peers?	_____	_____	_____

10. Which of the following meanings or nonverbal cues does the child consistently understand? Check all that apply.

___ Nonverbal cues of turn taking   ___ Nonverbal cues of emotion   ___ Humor

___ Figures of speech   ___ Teasing   ___ Sarcasm   ___ Deception

EMOTIONAL REGULATION

1. How does the child respond to people and things in his or her environment? For example, does the child show interest in a variety of situations, show intense interest in a few things, express different emotions, keep to him- or herself, respond to and seek interaction, inhibit actions and behaviors, and/or persist during tasks appropriate for his or her abilities?

2. What activities or situations are the most fun or interesting to the child?

3. What activities or situations create the most distress or are boring to the child?

4. Does the child use strategies to stay focused, interested, calm, or engaged during familiar activities (e.g., mouthing or chewing on clothing or other items, fidgeting, rocking, verbally repeating schedule sequences, using checklists to monitor task progress)? If so, please describe.

5. Does the child use strategies to stay focused, interested, calm, or engaged during new and changing situations, or situations that are otherwise challenging (e.g., saying, "I'm finished with writing," and checking schedule to see what's next; expressing emotion or asking for information to ease stress when having to wait)? If so, please describe.

6. Does the child express positive and negative emotions verbally or nonverbally? If so, how?

Positive emotions	Negative emotions
Happiness _____	Sadness _____
Contentment _____	Anger or frustration _____
Silliness _____	Fear _____
Excitement _____	Sickness or tiredness _____
Interest _____	Anxiety, stress, or worry _____
Pride _____	Boredom _____
Hope _____	Embarrassment _____

7. Does the child respond to feedback and guidance offered by others about regulating emotion? If so, how?

8. What strategies do you use to help the child stay focused, interested, calm, and engaged?

9. How do you know when the child is overwhelmed or upset? What signs does the child show?

10. How do you know when the child is bored or uninterested? What signals does the child show?

11. When the child is extremely upset or distressed,

. . . how does the child recover by him- or herself? How long does this usually take?

. . . how does the child recover with support from partners? How long does this usually take?

TRANSACTIONAL SUPPORT

1. What people does the child interact with or see on a regular basis (i.e., daily or weekly)?

2. What places does the child go to on a regular basis (i.e., daily or weekly)?

3. Which of the following are easy for you to read, follow, and respond to? Rate all that apply using the following key: 0, *can read or respond rarely or not at all;* 1, *can read and respond some of the time;* 2, *can read and respond most of the time.*

____ The child's focus of attention   ____ What the child is trying to communicate

____ How the child is feeling   ____ The child's preferred pace (fast or slow)

____ When the child needs a break   ____ Whether the child is interested

____ Whether the child is frustrated   ____ Whether the child is overwhelmed

4. What strategies are the most helpful to encourage the child to initiate and stay on topics in conversation (e.g., offering choices, waiting and encouraging initiations, following the child's topic, requesting information)?

5. How do you usually react if the child uses problem behaviors when very stressed, such as screaming, bolting, or incessantly reciting certain phrases? Is this reaction effective?

6. What strategies are the most helpful to secure the child's attention (e.g., moving closer to or farther from the child, calling the child's name, introduce motivating topics into conversation)?

7. What strategies are the most helpful to keep interactions going with the child (e.g., allowing the child to initiate interactions, allowing the child to take breaks and move about, following the child's interest)?

8. How do you usually communicate to the child to ensure that your message is understood?

9. Do you use visual supports to help the child communicate, understand language, express emotion, and/or flow with the day better? If so, which supports do you use (e.g., pairing language and written cues; defining steps of a task with pictures or written words, schedules, or calendars; using video modeling; using a feelings diary)?

10. What features of the physical or social environment help the child stay engaged (e.g., limiting the number of people the child interacts with, limiting the amount of background noise and/or visual stimulation, adding more opportunities for movement and rhythm, using specific places consistently for specific activities)?

11. What features of the physical or social environment help the child communicate better (e.g., smaller group size, motivating topics or activities that the child prefers, practicing social activities prior to an event)?

ADDITIONAL COMMENTS

1. List the top strengths or assets you observe in the child.

2. List your major concerns about the child's development.

3. What information would be most useful to you in planning or updating the child's program?

4. Is there anything else about the child that you think is important to share with us?

5. Do you have any questions for us?

6. What is the best time and way to contact you?

The SCERTS™ Model: A Comprehensive Educational Approach for Children with Autism Spectrum Disorders by Barry M. Prizant, Amy M. Wetherby, Emily Rubin, Amy C. Laurent, & Patrick J. Rydell

SAP Map for Planning the SAP-Observation

Child's name: _____ Date: _____ Page #: _____

Observation #: _____	Observation #: _____
Location	Location

At least two natural contexts (e.g., home, learning center or school, community)

Date and time	Date and time
Length	Length

Total observation time of at least 2 hours for Social Partner and Language Partner stages and at least 3–4 hours for Conversational Partner stage

Team members	Team members
Partners and group size	Partners and group size

At least two group sizes (one to one, small group, large group) at all stages if appropriate;
familiar and unfamiliar partners for Language and Conversational Partner stages

Activities	Variables	Activities	Variables

At least 4 activities that vary along at least four variables

Key for activity variables:
1a) Structured	1b) Unstructured	2a) Must do	2b) Fun
3a) Adult directed	3b) Child directed	4a) Motor based	4b) Sedentary
5a) Familiar	5b) Unfamiliar	6a) Preferred	6b) Nonpreferred
7a) Easy	7b) Difficult	8a) Language based	8b) Non–language based
9a) Social	9b) Solitary	10a) Busy	10b) Calm

Transitions	Transitions

At least three transitions involving a significant change of activity, setting, location, or partner

The SCERTS™ Model: A Comprehensive Educational Approach for Children with Autism Spectrum Disorders
by Barry M. Prizant, Amy M. Wetherby, Emily Rubin, Amy C. Laurent, & Patrick J. Rydell

SCERTS™

SAP-OBSERVATION FORM: Social Partner Stage

Child's name: _____   **Date of birth:** _____

Background information:

Team members:

Documentation of assessment context

Group size:
☐ One to one   ☐ Small group   ☐ Large group

Partner:
☐ Familiar adults   ☐ Familiar peers/siblings   ☐ Unfamiliar adults   ☐ Unfamiliar peers

Natural contexts:
☐ Home   ☐ Learning center/school   ☐ Community

Activity variables:

1. Structured/Unstructured	3. Adult directed/Child directed	5. Familiar/Unfamiliar	7. Easy/Difficult	9. Social/Solitary
2. Must do/Fun	4. Motor based/Sedentary	6. Preferred/Nonpreferred	8. Language based/ Non-language based	10. Busy/Calm

Transitions: 1: _____   2: _____   3: _____

Date of observation		Qtr 1	Qtr 2	Qtr 3	Qtr 4
Qtr 1 start date:	Length of total observation:				
Qtr 2 start date:	Length of total observation:				
Qtr 3 start date:	Length of total observation:				
Qtr 4 start date:	Length of total observation:				

SCERTS Profile Summary	Qtr 1	Qtr 2	Qtr 3	Qtr 4
Social Communication				
Joint Attention	/54	/54	/54	/54
Symbol Use	/62	/62	/62	/62
Emotional Regulation				
Mutual Regulation	/38	/38	/38	/38
Self-Regulation	/40	/40	/40	/40
Transactional Support				
Interpersonal Support	/66	/66	/66	/66

Social-Emotional Growth Indicators Profile	Qtr 1	Qtr 2	Qtr 3	Qtr 4
Happiness	/10	/10	/10	/10
Sense of Self	/10	/10	/10	/10
Sense of Other	/10	/10	/10	/10
Active Learning and Organization	/10	/10	/10	/10
Flexibility and Resilience	/10	/10	/10	/10
Cooperation and Appropriateness of Behavior	/10	/10	/10	/10
Independence	/10	/10	/10	/10
Social Membership and Friendships	/10	/10	/10	/10

SCORING KEY:

2 = criterion met consistently with at least two partners in at least two contexts

1 = criterion met inconsistently, in one activity, or with assistance

0 = criterion not met based on observed or reported information or would not be expected

Child's name: _____

Qtr 1	Qtr 2	Qtr 3	Qtr 4	JOINT ATTENTION
				1 Engages in reciprocal interaction
				JA1.1 Responds to bids for interaction (= MR2.3)
				JA1.2 Initiates bids for interaction (= SR1.4)
				JA1.3 Engages in brief reciprocal interaction (= SR1.5)
				JA1.4 Engages in extended reciprocal interaction (= SR1.6)
				2 Shares attention
				JA2.1 Looks toward people
				JA2.2 Shifts gaze between people and objects
				JA2.3 Follows contact point (= SU2.4)
				JA2.4 Follows distal point (= SU2.5)
				3 Shares emotion
				JA3.1 Shares negative emotion using facial expressions or vocalizations (≈ MR3.1)
				JA3.2 Shares positive emotion using facial expressions or vocalizations (≈ MR3.2)
				JA3.3 Responds to changes in partners' expression of emotion (= MR2.4, SU2.7)
				JA3.4 Attunes to changes in partners' expression of emotion (= MR2.5)
				4 Shares intentions to regulate the behavior of others (↔ JA7.2, JA7.3, SU4–SU5)
				JA4.1 Requests desired food or objects (≈ MR2.6)
				JA4.2 Protests/refuses undesired food or objects (≈ MR3.4)
				JA4.3 Requests help or other actions (≈ MR3.3)
				JA4.4 Protests undesired actions or activities (≈ MR3.4)
				5 Shares intentions for social interaction (↔ JA7.2, JA7.3, SU4–SU5)
				JA5.1 Requests comfort (≈ MR3.1)
				JA5.2 Requests social game
				JA5.3 Takes turns
				JA5.4 Greets
				JA5.5 Calls
				JA5.6 Shows off
				6 Shares intentions for joint attention (↔ JA7.2, JA7.3, SU4–SU5)
				JA6.1 Comments on object
				JA6.2 Comments on action or event
				7 Persists and repairs communication breakdowns
				JA7.1 Uses appropriate rate of communication for context
				JA7.2 Repeats communication to repair breakdowns (↔ JA4–JA6)
				JA7.3 Modifies communication to repair breakdowns (↔ JA4–JA6)

SCORING KEY: 2, criterion met consistently (across two partners in two contexts);
1, criterion met inconsistently or with assistance; **0,** criterion not met

Child's name: _____

Qtr 1	Qtr 2	Qtr 3	Qtr 4	SYMBOL USE
				1 Learns by imitation of familiar actions and sounds
				SU1.1 Takes turns by repeating own actions or sounds
				SU1.2 Imitates familiar actions or sounds when elicited immediately after a model
				SU1.3 Spontaneously imitates familiar actions or sounds immediately after a model
				SU1.4 Spontaneously imitates familiar actions or sounds at a later time
				2 Understands nonverbal cues in familiar activities
				SU2.1 Anticipates another person's actions in familiar routines (= SR3.1)
				SU2.2 Follows situational cues in familiar activities
				SU2.3 Follows gestural cues other than a point
				SU2.4 Follows a contact point (= JA2.3)
				SU2.5 Follows a distal point (= JA2.4)
				SU2.6 Responds to visual cues (photographs or pictures)
				SU2.7 Responds to facial expression and intonation cues (≈ JA3.3)
				3 Uses familiar objects conventionally in play
				SU3.1 Uses exploratory actions on objects (↔ SR2.1)
				SU3.2 Uses familiar objects in constructive play
				SU3.3 Uses familiar objects conventionally toward self
				SU3.4 Uses familiar objects conventionally toward other
				4 Uses gestures and nonverbal means to share intentions (↔ JA4–JA6, MR1, MR3.3, MR3.4)
				SU4.1 Uses proximity
				SU4.2 Uses facial expressions
				SU4.3 Uses simple motor actions
				SU4.4 Uses conventional contact gestures ☐ give ☐ push away ☐ show ☐ reach/touch ☐ point/touch
				SU4.5 Uses conventional distal gestures ☐ wave ☐ distal reach ☐ distal point ☐ clap ☐ head shake ☐ head nod
				SU4.6 Uses reenactment or symbolic distal gestures
				SU4.7 Uses sequence of gestures or nonverbal means
				SU4.8 Coordinates gestures and gaze
				5 Uses vocalizations to share intentions (↔ JA4–JA6, MR1, MR3.3, MR3.4)
				SU5.1 Uses differentiated vocalizations (↔ MR1)
				SU5.2 Uses a variety of consonant + vowel combinations
				SU5.3 Uses words bound to routines
				SU5.4 Coordinates vocalizations with gaze and gestures
				6 Understands a few familiar words
				SU6.1 Responds to own name
				SU6.2 Responds to a few words in familiar social games
				SU6.3 Responds to a few familiar person, body part, or object names
				SU6.4 Responds to a few frequently used phrases in familiar routines

SCORING KEY: 2, criterion met consistently (across two partners in two contexts);
1, criterion met inconsistently or with assistance; **0,** criterion not met

Child's name: _____

Qtr 1	Qtr 2	Qtr 3	Qtr 4	**MUTUAL REGULATION**
				1 Expresses range of emotions (↔ SU4–SU5)
				MR1.1 Expresses happiness
				MR1.2 Expresses sadness
				MR1.3 Expresses anger
				MR1.4 Expresses fear
				2 Responds to assistance offered by partners
				MR2.1 Soothes when comforted by partners
				MR2.2 Engages when alerted by partners
				MR2.3 Responds to bids for interaction (= JA1.1)
				MR2.4 Responds to changes in partners' expression of emotion (= JA3.3)
				MR2.5 Attunes to changes in partners' expression of emotion (= JA3.4)
				MR2.6 Makes choices when offered by partners (≈ JA4.1)
				3 Requests partners' assistance to regulate state
				MR3.1 Shares negative emotion to seek comfort (≈ JA3.1; ↔ JA5.1)
				MR3.2 Shares positive emotion to seek interaction (≈ JA3.2)
				MR3.3 Requests help when frustrated (≈ JA4.3; ↔ SU4–SU5)
				MR3.4 Protests when distressed (≈ JA4.2, JA4.4; ↔ SU4–SU5)
				4 Recovers from extreme dysregulation with support from partners
				MR4.1 Responds to partners' efforts to assist with recovery by moving away from activity
				MR4.2 Responds to partners' use of behavioral strategies
				MR4.3 Responds to partners' attempts to reengage in interaction or activity
				MR4.4 Decreases amount of time to recover from extreme dysregulation due to support from partners
				MR4.5 Decreases intensity of dysregulated state due to support from partners

SCORING KEY: 2, criterion met consistently (across two partners in two contexts);
1, criterion met inconsistently or with assistance; **0,** criterion not met

Child's name: _____

Qtr 1	Qtr 2	Qtr 3	Qtr 4	SELF-REGULATION
				1 Demonstrates availability for learning and interacting
				SR1.1 Notices people and things in the environment
				SR1.2 Shows interest in a variety of sensory and social experiences
				SR1.3 Seeks and tolerates a variety of sensory experiences
				SR1.4 Initiates bids for interaction (= JA1.2)
				SR1.5 Engages in brief reciprocal interaction (= JA1.3)
				SR1.6 Engages in extended reciprocal interaction (= JA1.4)
				SR1.7 Responds to sensory and social experiences with differentiated emotions
				2 Uses behavioral strategies to regulate arousal level during familiar activities
				SR2.1 Uses behavioral strategies to regulate arousal level during solitary activities (↔ SU3.1)
				SR2.2 Uses behavioral strategies to regulate arousal level during social interactions
				SR2.3 Uses behavioral strategies modeled by partners to regulate arousal level
				SR2.4 Uses behavioral strategies to engage productively in an extended activity
				3 Regulates emotion in new and changing situations
				SR3.1 Anticipates another person's actions in familiar routines (= SU2.1)
				SR3.2 Participates in new and changing situations
				SR3.3 Uses behavioral strategies to regulate arousal level in new and changing situations
				SR3.4 Uses behavioral strategies to regulate arousal level during transitions
				4 Recovers from extreme dysregulation by self
				SR4.1 Removes self from overstimulating or undesired activity
				SR4.2 Uses behavioral strategies to recover from extreme dysregulation
				SR4.3 Reengages in interaction or activity after recovery from extreme dysregulation
				SR4.4 Decreases amount of time to recover from extreme dysregulation
				SR4.5 Decreases intensity of dysregulated state

SCORING KEY: 2, criterion met consistently (across two partners in two contexts);
1, criterion met inconsistently or with assistance; **0,** criterion not met

Child's name: _____

Qtr 1	Qtr 2	Qtr 3	Qtr 4	INTERPERSONAL SUPPORT
				1 Partner is responsive to child
				IS1.1 Follows child's focus of attention
				IS1.2 Attunes to child's emotion and pace
				IS1.3 Responds appropriately to child's signals to foster a sense of communicative competence
				IS1.4 Recognizes and supports child's behavioral strategies to regulate arousal level
				IS1.5 Recognizes signs of dysregulation and offers support
				IS1.6 Imitates child
				IS1.7 Offers breaks from interaction or activity as needed
				IS1.8 Facilitates reengagement in interactions and activities following breaks
				2 Partner fosters initiation
				IS2.1 Offers choices nonverbally or verbally
				IS2.2 Waits for and encourages initiations
				IS2.3 Provides a balance of initiated and respondent turns
				IS2.4 Allows child to initiate and terminate activities
				3 Partner respects child's independence
				IS3.1 Allows child to take breaks to move about as needed
				IS3.2 Provides time for child to solve problems or complete activities at own pace
				IS3.3 Interprets problem behavior as communicative and/or regulatory
				IS3.4 Honors protests, rejections, or refusals when appropriate
				4 Partner sets stage for engagement
				IS4.1 Gets down on child's level when communicating
				IS4.2 Secures child's attention before communicating
				IS4.3 Uses appropriate proximity and nonverbal behavior to encourage interaction
				IS4.4 Uses appropriate words and intonation to support optimal arousal level and engagement
				5 Partner provides developmental support
				IS5.1 Encourages imitation
				IS5.2 Encourages interaction with peers
				IS5.3 Attempts to repair breakdowns verbally or nonverbally
				IS5.4 Provides guidance and feedback as needed for success in activities
				IS5.5 Expands on child's play and nonverbal communication
				6 Partner adjusts language input
				IS6.1 Uses nonverbal cues to support understanding
				IS6.2 Adjusts complexity of language input to child's developmental level
				IS6.3 Adjusts quality of language input to child's arousal level
				7 Partner models appropriate behaviors
				IS7.1 Models appropriate nonverbal communication and emotional expressions
				IS7.2 Models a range of communicative functions ☐ a. behavior regulation ☐ b. social interaction ☐ c. joint attention
				IS7.3 Models appropriate play
				IS7.4 Models appropriate behavior when child uses inappropriate behavior
				IS7.5 Models "child-perspective" language

SCORING KEY: 2, criterion met consistently (across two partners in two contexts);
1, criterion met inconsistently or with assistance; **0,** criterion not met

Child's name: _____

Qtr 1	Qtr 2	Qtr 3	Qtr 4	LEARNING SUPPORT
				1 Partner structures activity for active participation
				LS1.1 Defines clear beginning and ending to activity
				LS1.2 Creates turn-taking opportunities and leaves spaces for child to fill in
				LS1.3 Provides predictable sequence to activity
				LS1.4 Offers repeated learning opportunities
				LS1.5 Offers varied learning opportunities
				2 Partner uses augmentative communication support to foster development
				LS2.1 Uses augmentative communication support to enhance child's communication and expressive language
				LS2.2 Uses augmentative communication support to enhance child's understanding of language and behavior
				LS2.3 Uses augmentative communication support to enhance child's expression and understanding of emotion
				LS2.4 Uses augmentative communication support to enhance child's emotional regulation
				3 Partner uses visual and organizational support
				LS3.1 Uses support to define steps within a task
				LS3.2 Uses support to define steps and time for completion of activities
				LS3.3 Uses visual support to enhance smooth transitions between activities
				LS3.4 Uses support to organize segments of time across the day
				LS3.5 Uses visual support to enhance attention in group activities
				LS3.6 Uses visual support to foster active involvement in group activities
				4 Partner modifies goals, activities, and learning environment
				LS4.1 Adjusts social complexity to support organization and interaction
				LS4.2 Adjusts task difficulty for child success
				LS4.3 Modifies sensory properties of learning environment
				LS4.4 Arranges learning environment to enhance attention
				LS4.5 Arranges learning environment to promote child initiation
				LS4.6 Designs and modifies activities to be developmentally appropriate
				LS4.7 Infuses motivating materials and topics in activities
				LS4.8 Provides activities to promote initiation and extended interaction
				LS4.9 Alternates between movement and sedentary activities as needed
				LS4.10 "Ups the ante" or increases expectations appropriately

SCORING KEY: 2, criterion met consistently (across two partners in two contexts);
1, criterion met inconsistently or with assistance; **0,** criterion not met

Social Partner Stage
Expression of Intentions and Emotions Worksheet

Child's name: _____ Date: _____

Context/activity: _____ Partners: _____

	COMMUNICATIVE MEANS		
	Presymbolic means		**Symbolic means**

COMMUNICATIVE INTENTIONS	Proximity	Eye gaze (shifting)	Facial expressions	Simple motor actions	Crying/whining	Tantrum	Aggression	Self-injury	Giving	Reaching	Pushing away	Pointing	Showing	Waving	Head shake	Head nod	Reenactments	Differentiated vocalizations	Variety of consonants and vowels	Other:	Immediate echolalia	Delayed echolalia	Single words (spoken)	Creative word combinations	Sign language	Picture system	Other:
Behavior regulation																											
JA4.1 Requests desired food or objects																											
JA4.2 Protests/refuses undesired food or objects																											
JA4.3 Requests help or other actions																											
JA4.4 Protests undesired actions or activities																											
Social interaction																											
JA5.1 Requests comfort																											
JA5.2 Requests social game																											
JA5.3 Takes turns																											
JA5.4 Greets																											
JA5.5 Calls																											
JA5.6 Shows off																											
Joint attention																											
JA6.1 Comments on object																											
JA6.2 Comments on action or event																											
EXPRESSION OF EMOTIONS																											
MR1.1 Expresses happiness																											
MR1.2 Expresses sadness																											
MR1.3 Expresses anger																											
MR1.4 Expresses fear																											

Child's name: _____   **Date of birth:** _____

Background information:

Team members:

Documentation of assessment context

Group size:
- ☐ One to one
- ☐ Small group
- ☐ Large group

Partner:
- ☐ Familiar adults
- ☐ Familiar peers/siblings
- ☐ Unfamiliar adults
- ☐ Unfamiliar peers

Natural contexts:
- ☐ Home
- ☐ Learning center/school
- ☐ Community

Activity variables:

1. Structured/Unstructured
2. Must do/Fun
3. Adult directed/Child directed
4. Motor based/Sedentary
5. Familiar/Unfamiliar
6. Preferred/Nonpreferred
7. Easy/Difficult
8. Language based/ Non-language based
9. Social/Solitary
10. Busy/Calm

Transitions: 1:   2:   3:

Date of observation		Qtr 1	Qtr 2	Qtr 3	Qtr 4
Qtr 1 start date:	Length of total observation:				
Qtr 2 start date:	Length of total observation:				
Qtr 3 start date:	Length of total observation:				
Qtr 4 start date:	Length of total observation:				

SCERTS Profile Summary	Qtr 1	Qtr 2	Qtr 3	Qtr 4
Social Communication				
Joint Attention	/62	/62	/62	/62
Symbol Use	/50	/50	/50	/50
Emotional Regulation				
Mutual Regulation	/46	/46	/46	/46
Self-Regulation	/56	/56	/56	/56
Transactional Support				
Interpersonal Support	/66	/66	/66	/66

Social-Emotional Growth Indicators Profile	Qtr 1	Qtr 2	Qtr 3	Qtr 4
Happiness	/10	/10	/10	/10
Sense of Self	/10	/10	/10	/10
Sense of Other	/10	/10	/10	/10
Active Learning and Organization	/10	/10	/10	/10
Flexibility and Resilience	/10	/10	/10	/10
Cooperation and Appropriateness of Behavior	/10	/10	/10	/10
Independence	/10	/10	/10	/10
Social Membership and Friendships	/10	/10	/10	/10

SCORING KEY:

2 = criterion met consistently with at least three partners in at least two contexts

1 = criterion met inconsistently, in one activity, or with assistance

0 = criterion not met based on observed or reported information or would not be expected

Child's name: _____

Qtr 1	Qtr 2	Qtr 3	Qtr 4	**JOINT ATTENTION**
				1 Engages in reciprocal interaction
				JA1.1 Initiates bids for interaction (= SR1.1)
				JA1.2 Engages in brief reciprocal interaction (= SR1.2)
				JA1.3 Engages in extended reciprocal interaction (= SR1.3)
				2 Shares attention
				JA2.1 Shifts gaze between people and objects
				JA2.2 Follows contact and distal point (= SU2.2)
				JA2.3 Monitors attentional focus of a social partner
				JA2.4 Secures attention to oneself prior to expressing intentions (≈ JA5.5)
				3 Shares emotion
				JA3.1 Shares negative and positive emotion (= MR1.1; ≈ MR3.1, MR3.2)
				JA3.2 Understands and uses symbols to express a range of emotions (≈ MR1.2, SR3.5)
				JA3.3 Attunes to changes in partners' expression of emotion (≈ SU2.4; = MR2.5)
				JA3.4 Describes the emotional state of another person (↔ SU5.6)
				4 Shares intentions to regulate the behavior of others (↔ JA7.2, JA8.2, SU4–SU5, MR3.7)
				JA4.1 Requests desired food or objects (≈ MR2.6)
				JA4.2 Protests/refuses undesired food or objects (≈ MR3.4)
				JA4.3 Requests help or other actions (≈ MR3.3)
				JA4.4 Protests undesired actions or activities (≈ MR3.4)
				5 Shares intentions for social interaction (↔ JA7.2, JA8.2, SU4–SU5)
				JA5.1 Requests comfort (≈ MR3.1)
				JA5.2 Requests social game
				JA5.3 Takes turns
				JA5.4 Greets
				JA5.5 Calls (≈ JA2.4)
				JA5.6 Shows off
				JA5.7 Requests permission
				6 Shares intentions for joint attention (↔ JA7.2, JA8.2, SU4–SU5)
				JA6.1 Comments on object
				JA6.2 Comments on action or event
				JA6.3 Requests information about things of interest
				7 Persists and repairs communication breakdowns
				JA7.1 Uses appropriate rate of communication for context
				JA7.2 Repeats and modifies communication to repair (↔ JA4–JA6)
				JA7.3 Recognizes breakdowns in communication
				8 Shares experiences in reciprocal interaction
				JA8.1 Coordinates attention, emotion, and intentions to share experiences
				JA8.2 Shows reciprocity in speaker and listener roles to share experiences (↔ JA4–JA6)
				JA8.3 Initiates interaction and shares experiences with a friend

SCORING KEY: 2, criterion met consistently (across three partners in two contexts);
1, criterion met inconsistently or with assistance; **0,** criterion not met

Child's name: _____

Qtr 1	Qtr 2	Qtr 3	Qtr 4	SYMBOL USE
				1 Learns by observation and imitation of familiar and unfamiliar actions and words
				SU1.1 Spontaneously imitates familiar actions or words immediately after a model
				SU1.2 Spontaneously imitates unfamiliar actions or words immediately after a model
				SU1.3 Spontaneously imitates actions or words and adds a different behavior
				SU1.4 Spontaneously imitates a variety of behaviors later in a different context
				2 Understands nonverbal cues in familiar and unfamiliar activities
				SU2.1 Follows situational and gestural cues in familiar and unfamiliar activities (= SR4.2)
				SU2.2 Follows contact and distal point (= JA2.2)
				SU2.3 Follows instructions with visual cues (photographs or pictures)
				SU2.4 Responds to facial expression and intonation cues (≈ JA3.3)
				3 Uses familiar objects conventionally in play
				SU3.1 Uses a variety of objects in constructive play
				SU3.2 Uses a variety of familiar objects conventionally toward self
				SU3.3 Uses a variety of familiar objects conventionally toward other
				SU3.4 Combines a variety of actions with objects in play
				4 Uses gestures and nonverbal means to share intentions (↔ JA4–JA6, MR3.3, MR3.4)
				SU4.1 Uses a variety of conventional and symbolic gestures ☐ a. show ☐ d. clap ☐ f. head nod ☐ b. wave ☐ e. head shake ☐ g. other _____ ☐ c. distal reach/point
				SU4.2 Uses sequence of gestures or nonverbal means in coordination with gaze
				5 Uses words and word combinations to express meanings (↔ JA4–JA6, MR3.3, MR3.4)
				SU5.1 Coordinates sounds/words with gaze and gestures
				SU5.2 Uses at least 5–10 words or echolalic phrases as symbols
				SU5.3 Uses early relational words ☐ a. existence ☐ b. nonexistence/disappearance ☐ c. recurrence ☐ d. rejection
				SU5.4 Uses variety of names for objects, body parts, and agents
				SU5.5 Uses variety of advanced relational words ☐ a. personal-social ☐ b. action ☐ c. modifier ☐ d. *wh-* word
				SU5.6 Uses variety of relational meanings in word combinations (↔ JA3.4) ☐ a. modifier + object ☐ b. negation + object ☐ c. agent + action + object
				6 Understands a variety of words and word combinations without contextual cues
				SU6.1 Responds to own name
				SU6.2 Responds to a variety of familiar words and phrases (= SR1.6)
				SU6.3 Understands a variety of names without contextual cues
				SU6.4 Understands a variety of relational words without contextual cues ☐ a. action ☐ b. modifier ☐ c. *wh-* word
				SU6.5 Understands a variety of relational meanings in word combinations without contextual cues ☐ a. modifier + object ☐ b. negation + object ☐ c. agent + action + object

SCORING KEY: 2, criterion met consistently (across three partners in two contexts);
1, criterion met inconsistently or with assistance; **0,** criterion not met

Child's name: _____

Qtr 1	Qtr 2	Qtr 3	Qtr 4	**MUTUAL REGULATION**
				1 Expresses range of emotions (↔ SU4–SU5)
				MR1.1 Shares negative and positive emotion (= JA3.1)
				MR1.2 Understands and uses symbols to express a range of emotions (≈ JA3.2; = SR3.5)
				MR1.3 Changes emotional expression in familiar activities based on partners' feedback
				2 Responds to assistance offered by partners
				MR2.1 Soothes when comforted by partners
				MR2.2 Engages when alerted by partners
				MR2.3 Responds to bids for interaction
				MR2.4 Responds to changes in partners' expression of emotion
				MR2.5 Attunes to changes in partners' expression of emotion (= JA3.3)
				MR2.6 Makes choices when offered by partners
				MR2.7 Changes regulatory strategies based on partners' feedback in familiar activities
				3 Requests partners' assistance to regulate state
				MR3.1 Shares negative emotion to seek comfort (≈ JA3.1; ↔ JA5.1)
				MR3.2 Shares positive emotion to seek interaction (≈ JA3.1)
				MR3.3 Requests help when frustrated (≈ JA4.3; ↔ SU4–SU5)
				MR3.4 Protests when distressed (≈ JA4.2, JA4.4; ↔ SU4–SU5)
				MR3.5 Uses language strategies to request a break
				MR3.6 Uses language strategies to request regulating activity or input
				MR3.7 Uses language strategies to exert social control (↔ JA4)
				4 Recovers from extreme dysregulation with support from partners
				MR4.1 Responds to partners' efforts to assist with recovery by moving away from activity
				MR4.2 Responds to partners' use of behavioral strategies
				MR4.3 Responds to partners' use of language strategies
				MR4.4 Responds to partners' attempts to reengage in interaction or activity
				MR4.5 Decreases amount of time to recover from extreme dysregulation due to support from partners
				MR4.6 Decreases intensity of dysregulated state due to support from partners

SCORING KEY: 2, criterion met consistently (across three partners in two contexts);
1, criterion met inconsistently or with assistance; **0,** criterion not met

Child's name: _____

Qtr 1	Qtr 2	Qtr 3	Qtr 4	SELF-REGULATION
				1 Demonstrates availability for learning and interacting
				SR1.1 Initiates bids for interaction (= JA1.1)
				SR1.2 Engages in brief reciprocal interaction (= JA1.2)
				SR1.3 Engages in extended reciprocal interaction (= JA1.3)
				SR1.4 Responds to sensory and social experiences with differentiated emotions
				SR1.5 Demonstrates ability to inhibit actions and behaviors
				SR1.6 Responds to a variety of familiar words and phrases (= SU6.2)
				SR1.7 Persists during tasks with reasonable demands
				SR1.8 Demonstrates emotional expression appropriate to context
				2 Uses behavioral strategies to regulate arousal level during familiar activities
				SR2.1 Uses behavioral strategies to regulate arousal level during solitary and social activities
				SR2.2 Uses behavioral strategies modeled by partners to regulate arousal level
				SR2.3 Uses behavioral strategies to engage productively in an extended activity
				3 Uses language strategies to regulate arousal level during familiar activities
				SR3.1 Uses language strategies to regulate arousal level during solitary activities
				SR3.2 Uses language strategies to regulate arousal level during social interactions
				SR3.3 Uses language strategies modeled by partners to regulate arousal level
				SR3.4 Uses language strategies to engage productively in an extended activity
				SR3.5 Uses symbols to express a range of emotions ($\approx$ JA3.2; = MR1.2)
				4 Regulates emotion during new and changing situations
				SR4.1 Participates in new and changing situations
				SR4.2 Follows situational and gestural cues in unfamiliar activities (= SU2.1)
				SR4.3 Uses behavioral strategies to regulate arousal level in new and changing situations
				SR4.4 Uses language strategies to regulate arousal level in new and changing situations
				SR4.5 Uses behavioral strategies to regulate arousal level during transitions
				SR4.6 Uses language strategies to regulate arousal level during transitions
				5 Recovers from extreme dysregulation by self
				SR5.1 Removes self from overstimulating or undesired activity
				SR5.2 Uses behavioral strategies to recover from extreme dysregulation
				SR5.3 Uses language strategies to recover from extreme dysregulation
				SR5.4 Reengages in interaction or activity after recovery from extreme dysregulation
				SR5.5 Decreases amount of time to recover from extreme dysregulation
				SR5.6 Decreases intensity of dysregulated state

SCORING KEY: 2, criterion met consistently (across three partners in two contexts);
1, criterion met inconsistently or with assistance; **0,** criterion not met

Child's name: _____

Qtr 1	Qtr 2	Qtr 3	Qtr 4	**INTERPERSONAL SUPPORT**
				1 Partner is responsive to child
				IS1.1 Follows child's focus of attention
				IS1.2 Attunes to child's emotion and pace
				IS1.3 Responds appropriately to child's signals to foster a sense of communicative competence
				IS1.4 Recognizes and supports child's behavioral and language strategies to regulate arousal level
				IS1.5 Recognizes signs of dysregulation and offers support
				IS1.6 Imitates child
				IS1.7 Offers breaks from interaction or activity as needed
				IS1.8 Facilitates reengagement in interactions and activities following breaks
				2 Partner fosters initiation
				IS2.1 Offers choices nonverbally or verbally
				IS2.2 Waits for and encourages initiations
				IS2.3 Provides a balance of initiated and respondent turns
				IS2.4 Allows child to initiate and terminate activities
				3 Partner respects child's independence
				IS3.1 Allows child to take breaks to move about as needed
				IS3.2 Provides time for child to solve problems or complete activities at own pace
				IS3.3 Interprets problem behavior as communicative and/or regulatory
				IS3.4 Honors protests, rejections, or refusals when appropriate
				4 Partner sets stage for engagement
				IS4.1 Gets down on child's level when communicating
				IS4.2 Secures child's attention before communicating
				IS4.3 Uses appropriate proximity and nonverbal behavior to encourage interaction
				IS4.4 Uses appropriate words and intonation to support optimal arousal level and engagement
				5 Partner provides developmental support
				IS5.1 Encourages imitation
				IS5.2 Encourages interaction with peers
				IS5.3 Attempts to repair breakdowns verbally or nonverbally
				IS5.4 Provides guidance and feedback as needed for success in activities
				IS5.5 Provides guidance on expressing emotions and understanding the cause of emotions
				6 Partner adjusts language input
				IS6.1 Uses nonverbal cues to support understanding
				IS6.2 Adjusts complexity of language input to child's developmental level
				IS6.3 Adjusts quality of language input to child's arousal level
				7 Partner models appropriate behaviors
				IS7.1 Models appropriate nonverbal communication and emotional expressions
				IS7.2 Models a range of communicative functions ☐ a. behavior regulation ☐ b. social interaction ☐ c. joint attention
				IS7.3 Models appropriate constructive and symbolic play
				IS7.4 Models appropriate behavior when child uses inappropriate behavior
				IS7.5 Models "child-perspective" language

SCORING KEY: 2, criterion met consistently (across three partners in two contexts);
1, criterion met inconsistently or with assistance; **0,** criterion not met

Child's name: _____

Qtr 1	Qtr 2	Qtr 3	Qtr 4	LEARNING SUPPORT
				1 Partner structures activity for active participation
				LS1.1 Defines clear beginning and ending to activity
				LS1.2 Creates turn-taking opportunities and leaves spaces for child to fill in
				LS1.3 Provides predictable sequence to activity
				LS1.4 Offers repeated learning opportunities
				LS1.5 Offers varied learning opportunities
				2 Partner uses augmentative communication support to foster development
				LS2.1 Uses augmentative communication support to enhance child's communication and expressive language
				LS2.2 Uses augmentative communication support to enhance child's understanding of language and behavior
				LS2.3 Uses augmentative communication support to enhance child's expression and understanding of emotion
				LS2.4 Uses augmentative communication support to enhance child's emotional regulation
				3 Partner uses visual and organizational support
				LS3.1 Uses support to define steps within a task
				LS3.2 Uses support to define steps and time for completion of activities
				LS3.3 Uses visual support to enhance smooth transitions between activities
				LS3.4 Uses support to organize segments of time across the day
				LS3.5 Uses visual support to enhance attention in group activities
				LS3.6 Uses visual support to foster active involvement in group activities
				4 Partner modifies goals, activities, and learning environment
				LS4.1 Adjusts social complexity to support organization and interaction
				LS4.2 Adjusts task difficulty for child success
				LS4.3 Modifies sensory properties of learning environment
				LS4.4 Arranges learning environment to enhance attention
				LS4.5 Arranges learning environment to promote child initiation
				LS4.6 Designs and modifies activities to be developmentally appropriate
				LS4.7 Infuses motivating materials and topics in activities
				LS4.8 Provides activities to promote initiation and extended interaction
				LS4.9 Alternates between movement and sedentary activities as needed
				LS4.10 "Ups the ante" or increases expectations appropriately

SCORING KEY: 2, criterion met consistently (across three partners in two contexts);
1, criterion met inconsistently or with assistance; **0,** criterion not met

Language Partner Stage
Expression of Intentions and Emotions Worksheet

Child's name: _____ Date: _____

Context/activity: _____ Partners: _____

	COMMUNICATIVE MEANS																									
	Presymbolic means																			Symbolic means						
	Proximity	Eye gaze (shifting)	Facial expressions	Simple motor actions	Crying/whining	Tantrum	Aggression	Self-injury	Giving	Reaching	Pushing away	Pointing	Showing	Waving	Head shake	Head nod	Reenactments	Differentiated vocalizations	Variety of consonants and vowels	Other:	Immediate echolalia	Delayed echolalia	Single words (spoken)	Creative word combinations	Sign language	Picture system	Other:
COMMUNICATIVE INTENTIONS																											
Behavior regulation																											
JA4.1 Requests desired food or objects																											
JA4.2 Protests/refuses undesired food or objects																											
JA4.3 Requests help or other actions																											
JA4.4 Protests undesired actions or activities																											
Social interaction																											
JA5.1 Requests comfort																											
JA5.2 Requests social game																											
JA5.3 Takes turns																											
JA5.4 Greets																											
JA5.5 Calls																											
JA5.6 Shows off																											
JA5.7 Requests permission																											
Joint attention																											
JA6.1 Comments on object																											
JA6.2 Comments on action or event																											
JA6.3 Requests information about things of interest																											
EXPRESSION OF EMOTIONS																											
Expresses happiness																											
Expresses sadness																											
Expresses anger																											
Expresses fear																											

Language Partner Stage
Word Meanings Worksheet

Child's name: _____ Date: _____

Context/activity: _____ Partners: _____

Observed (Uses)	Type	Definitions and examples	Observed (Understands)
	EARLY RELATIONAL WORDS		
☐	**existence**	Notes the existence of something or directs attention to it (e.g., *this, that, here, what's that?*)	☐
☐	**nonexistence/ disappearance**	Notes that something is not there when expected or that something was there and has disappeared (e.g., *no, gone, all gone, bye-bye*)	☐
☐	**recurrence**	Requests an object to replace an absent object or notes that an object appears after having been gone (e.g., *more, again, another*)	☐
☐	**rejection**	Refuses something that is offered (e.g., *no, bye-bye, stop*)	☐
	NAMES FOR THINGS OR PERSONS		
☐☐☐☐☐	**object**	Entity or thing that is the recipient of an action (e.g., *milk, juice, water, cookie, cup, bottle, ball, car, hat, shoe*)	☐☐☐☐☐
☐☐	**body part**	Part of the body (e.g., *eye, nose, hand, tummy*)	☐☐☐
☐☐	**agent**	Person or animal that can be the source of an action (e.g., *mommy, daddy, baby, doggie, kitty*)	☐☐☐
	ADVANCED RELATIONAL WORDS		
☐☐	**personal-social**	Acknowledges someone (e.g., *hi, bye-bye, please, thank you*)	☐☐
☐☐☐	**action**	Describes actions that can be general or specific and may or may not involve objects General-purpose action words that do not refer to any specific action (e.g., *do, put, make, get, want, give, go bye-bye*) Deictic action words to direct the listener's attention (e.g., *lookit, see*) Object-related action words referring to specific actions (e.g., *push, open, eat, drink, throw, kiss, jump*) Intransitive action words that do not involve objects (e.g., *walk, run, sleep, laugh*)	☐☐☐☐
☐☐☐☐	**modifier**	Describes states, qualities, or relationships of things Attribute: Describes characteristics of or differences between things (e.g., *hot, big, stinky, dirty*) Possession: Notes that an agent possesses something (e.g., *mine, Mommy*) Location: Denotes direction or spatial relationship of two objects (early location words function as action words, such as *up, out,* and *off,* and are referred to as *locatives*) (e.g., *up, on, off, in, out, under*) Denial: Denies the existence of something (e.g., *no, not*)	☐☐☐☐☐
☐	**wh- word**	Poses questions about the name or location of things (early questions may be with a rising intonation) (e.g., *what, where*)	☐

The SCERTS™ Model: A Comprehensive Educational Approach for Children with Autism Spectrum Disorders
Copyright © 2006 by Paul H. Brookes Publishing Co. All rights reserved.

Language Partner Stage
Relational Meanings in Word Combinations Worksheet

Child's name: _____ Date: _____

Context/activity: _____ Partners: _____

Observed (Uses)	Relational meanings	Examples	Observed (Understands)
☐☐☐☐☐	**modifier + object**		☐☐☐☐☐
	recurrence + object	*more cookie, 'nuther jump*	
	attribute + object	*big shoe, dirty diaper, one baby, nice kitty*	
	possessor + possession	*Mommy shoe, Daddy hair, my cup*	
	demonstrative + object	*this cup, that ball*	
	location + object	*on table, in box*	
☐☐☐☐☐	**negation + object**		☐☐☐☐☐
	nonexistence	*no juice, water gone*	
	disappearance	*bubbles bye-bye, milk gone*	
	rejection	*no night-night*	
	denial	*no baby, not shoe*	
☐☐☐☐☐	**agent + action + object**		☐☐☐☐☐
	action + object	*eat cookie, throw ball, drink juice, lookit that, get me, put table, shirt off*	
	agent + action	*Mommy go bye-bye, baby sleep, Daddy throw, doggie sit*	
	agent + object	*Daddy cookie, Mommy bottle, doggie ball, dolly chair*	
	agent + action + object	*Daddy throw ball, Daddy push car, Mommy kiss baby, Mommy get bottle*	

Source: Owens, 2000.

SAP-OBSERVATION FORM: Conversational Partner Stage

(page 1)

Child's name: _____

Date of birth: _____

Background information:

Team members:

Documentation of assessment context

Group size: ☐ One to one ☐ Small group ☐ Large group

Partner: ☐ Familiar adults ☐ Familiar peers/siblings ☐ Unfamiliar adults ☐ Unfamiliar peers

Natural contexts: ☐ Home ☐ Learning center/school ☐ Community

Activity variables:

1. Structured/Unstructured
2. Must do/Fun
3. Adult directed/Child directed
4. Motor based/Sedentary
5. Familiar/Unfamiliar
6. Preferred/Nonpreferred
7. Easy/Difficult
8. Language based/Non-language based
9. Social/Solitary
10. Busy/Calm

Transitions:

1:

2:

3:

Date of observation		Qtr 1	Qtr 2	Qtr 3	Qtr 4
Qtr 1 start date:	Length of total observation:				
Qtr 2 start date:	Length of total observation:				
Qtr 3 start date:	Length of total observation:				
Qtr 4 start date:	Length of total observation:				

SCERTS Profile Summary	Qtr 1	Qtr 2	Qtr 3	Qtr 4
Social Communication				
Joint Attention	/58	/58	/58	/58
Symbol Use	/58	/58	/58	/58
Emotional Regulation				
Mutual Regulation	/56	/56	/56	/56
Self-Regulation	/64	/64	/64	/64
Transactional Support				
Interpersonal Support	/66	/66	/66	/66
Learning Support	/50	/50	/50	/50

Social-Emotional Growth Indicators Profile	Qtr 1	Qtr 2	Qtr 3	Qtr 4
Happiness	/10	/10	/10	/10
Sense of Self	/10	/10	/10	/10
Sense of Other	/10	/10	/10	/10
Active Learning and Organization	/10	/10	/10	/10
Flexibility and Resilience	/10	/10	/10	/10
Cooperation and Appropriateness of Behavior	/10	/10	/10	/10
Independence	/10	/10	/10	/10
Social Membership and Friendships	/10	/10	/10	/10

SCORING KEY:

2 = criterion met consistently with at least three partners in at least two contexts

1 = criterion met inconsistently, in one activity, or with assistance

0 = criterion not met based on observed or reported information or would not be expected

Child's name: _____

Qtr 1	Qtr 2	Qtr 3	Qtr 4	**JOINT ATTENTION**
				1 Shares attention
				JA1.1 Monitors attentional focus of a social partner (= SR1.2)
				JA1.2 Secures attention to oneself prior to expressing intentions
				JA1.3 Understands nonverbal cues of shifts in attentional focus
				JA1.4 Modifies language based on what partners have seen or heard
				JA1.5 Shares internal thoughts or mental plans with partners
				2 Shares emotion
				JA2.1 Understands and uses early emotion words (= MR1.1, SR3.1)
				JA2.2 Describes others' emotional states with early emotion words
				JA2.3 Understands and uses advanced emotion words (= MR1.2, SR3.2)
				JA2.4 Describes others' emotional states with advanced emotion words
				JA2.5 Understands and uses graded emotions (= MR1.3, SR3.3)
				JA2.6 Understands nonverbal cues of emotional expression (= SU2.2)
				JA2.7 Describes plausible causal factors for emotions of self and others
				3 Shares intentions for a variety of purposes (↔ JA5.2, SU4–SU5)
				JA3.1 Shares intentions to regulate the behavior of others (= MR4.3) ☐ a. requests desired objects and activities ☐ c. requests a break ☐ b. requests help ☐ d. protests/refuses undesired objects or activities
				JA3.2 Shares intentions for social interaction (= MR4.4) ☐ a. greets ☐ d. regulates turns ☐ g. expresses empathy ☐ b. calls ☐ e. requests permission ☐ h. shares secrets ☐ c. requests comfort ☐ f. praises partner
				JA3.3 Shares intentions for joint attention (= MR4.5) ☐ a. comments on immediate, past, and imagined events ☐ b. provides requested information about immediate and past events ☐ c. requests information about immediate, past, and future events ☐ d. expresses feelings and opinions ☐ e. anticipates and plans outcomes
				4 Shares experiences in reciprocal interaction
				JA4.1 Shows reciprocity in speaker and listener roles to share experiences (= SR1.3)
				JA4.2 Initiates a variety of conversational topics
				JA4.3 Initiates and maintains conversations that relate to partners' interests
				JA4.4 Maintains interaction by requesting or providing relevant information
				JA4.5 Provides needed information based on partners' knowledge of topic
				JA4.6 Gauges length and content of conversational turn based on partners
				JA4.7 Prefers to be engaged with partners
				JA4.8 Has friendships with partners who share interests
				5 Persists and repairs communication breakdowns
				JA5.1 Uses appropriate rate of communication for context
				JA5.2 Repeats and modifies communication to repair breakdowns (↔JA3)
				JA5.3 Recognizes breakdowns in communication and requests clarification
				JA5.4 Modifies language and behavior based on partners' change in agenda
				JA5.5 Modifies language and behavior based on partners' emotional reaction
				JA5.6 Expresses feelings of success and confidence during interactions

SCORING KEY: 2, criterion met consistently (across three partners in two contexts);
1, criterion met inconsistently or with assistance; **0,** criterion not met

The SCERTS™ Model: A Comprehensive Educational Approach for Children with Autism Spectrum Disorders
Copyright © 2006 by Paul H. Brookes Publishing Co. All rights reserved.

Child's name: _____

Qtr 1	Qtr 2	Qtr 3	Qtr 4	SYMBOL USE
				1 Learns by imitation, observation, instruction, and collaboration
				SU1.1 Spontaneously imitates a variety of behaviors later in a different context
				SU1.2 Uses behaviors modeled by partners to guide social behavior (= MR3.3)
				SU1.3 Uses internalized rules modeled by adult instruction to guide behavior (= SR4.1)
				SU1.4 Uses self-monitoring and self-talk to guide behavior (= SR4.3)
				SU1.5 Collaborates and negotiates with peers in problem solving (= MR3.4)
				2 Understands nonverbal cues and nonliteral meanings in reciprocal interactions
				SU2.1 Understands nonverbal cues of turn taking and topic change
				SU2.2 Understands nonverbal cues of emotional expression (= JA2.6)
				SU2.3 Understands nonverbal cues and nonliteral meanings of humor and figures of speech
				SU2.4 Understands nonverbal cues and nonliteral meanings of teasing, sarcasm, and deception
				3 Participates conventionally in dramatic play and recreation
				SU3.1 Uses logical sequences of actions in play about familiar events
				SU3.2 Uses miniature or abstract objects as props
				SU3.3 Uses logical sequences of actions in play about less familiar events
				SU3.4 Takes on a role and engages in dramatic play
				SU3.5 Plays in a common activity with other children
				SU3.6 Takes on a role and cooperates with peers in dramatic play
				SU3.7 Participates in rule-based group recreation
				4 Uses appropriate gestures and nonverbal behavior for the context (↔ JA3, MR1)
				SU4.1 Uses appropriate facial expressions for the context and partner
				SU4.2 Uses appropriate gestures for the context and partner
				SU4.3 Uses appropriate body posture and proximity for the context and partner
				SU4.4 Uses appropriate volume and intonation for the context and partner
				5 Understands and uses generative language to express meanings (↔ JA3, MR1)
				SU5.1 Understands and uses a variety of advanced relational words □ a. *wh-* words □ c. physical □ e. location □ g. causal □ b. temporal □ d. numerical □ f. kinship
				SU5.2 Understands and uses reference to things □ a. subject pronouns □ b. other pronouns □ c. determiners □ d. plurals
				SU5.3 Understands and uses a variety of verb phrases □ a. main verbs □ c. helping verbs □ e. negation □ b. tense markers □ d. modals
				SU5.4 Understands and uses a variety of sentence constructions □ a. declarative □ c. negative □ e. embedding □ b. imperative □ d. interrogative □ f. conjoining
				SU5.5 Understands and uses connected sentences in oral and written discourse
				6 Follows rules of conversation
				SU6.1 Follows conventions for initiating conversation and taking turns
				SU6.2 Follows conventions for shifting topics in conversation
				SU6.3 Follows conventions for ending conversation
				SU6.4 Follows conventions of politeness and register

SCORING KEY: 2, criterion met consistently (across three partners in two contexts);
1, criterion met inconsistently or with assistance; **0,** criterion not met

Child's name: _____

Qtr 1	Qtr 2	Qtr 3	Qtr 4	**MUTUAL REGULATION**
				1 Expresses range of emotions (↔ SU4–SU5)
				MR1.1 Understands and uses early emotion words (= JA2.1, SR3.1)
				MR1.2 Understands and uses advanced emotion words (= JA2.3, SR3.2)
				MR1.3 Understands and uses graded emotions (= JA2.5, SR3.3)
				MR1.4 Changes emotional expression based on partners' feedback
				MR1.5 Uses nonverbal cues of emotional expression
				2 Responds to assistance offered by partners
				MR2.1 Soothes when comforted by partners
				MR2.2 Engages when alerted by partners
				MR2.3 Responds to bids for interaction
				MR2.4 Responds to changes in partners' expression of emotion
				MR2.5 Attunes to changes in partners' expression of emotion
				MR2.6 Responds to information or strategies offered by partners
				3 Responds to feedback and guidance regarding behavior
				MR3.1 Responds to feedback regarding the appropriateness of emotional display
				MR3.2 Responds to feedback regarding the appropriateness of regulatory strategies
				MR3.3 Uses behaviors modeled by partners to guide behavior (= SU1.2)
				MR3.4 Collaborates and negotiates with peers in problem solving (= SU1.5)
				MR3.5 Accepts ideas from partners during negotiation to reach compromise
				4 Requests partners' assistance to regulate state
				MR4.1 Shares negative emotion to seek comfort
				MR4.2 Shares positive emotion to seek interaction
				MR4.3 Shares intentions to regulate the behavior of others (= JA3.1) ☐ a. requests desired objects and activities ☐ b. requests help ☐ c. requests a break ☐ d. protests/refuses undesired objects or activities
				MR4.4 Shares intentions for social interaction (= JA3.2) ☐ a. greets ☐ c. requests comfort ☐ e. requests permission ☐ g. expresses empathy ☐ b. calls ☐ d. regulates turns ☐ f. praises partner ☐ h. shares secrets
				MR4.5 Shares intentions for joint attention (= JA3.3) ☐ a. comments on immediate, past, and imagined events ☐ b. provides requested information about immediate and past events ☐ c. requests information about immediate, past, and future events ☐ d. expresses feelings and opinions ☐ e. anticipates and plans outcomes
				MR4.6 Requests assistance to resolve conflict and problem-solve situations
				5 Recovers from extreme dysregulation with support from partners
				MR5.1 Responds to partners' efforts to assist with recovery by moving away from activity
				MR5.2 Responds to partners' use of behavioral strategies
				MR5.3 Responds to partners' use of language strategies
				MR5.4 Responds to partners' attempts to reengage in interaction or activity
				MR5.5 Decreases amount of time to recover from extreme dysregulation due to support from partners
				MR5.6 Decreases intensity of dysregulated state due to support from partners

SCORING KEY: 2, criterion met consistently (across three partners in two contexts);
1, criterion met inconsistently or with assistance; **0,** criterion not met

The SCERTS™ Model: A Comprehensive Educational Approach for Children with Autism Spectrum Disorders
Copyright © 2006 by Paul H. Brookes Publishing Co. All rights reserved.

Child's name: _____

Qtr 1	Qtr 2	Qtr 3	Qtr 4	SELF-REGULATION
				1 Demonstrates availability for learning and interacting
				SR1.1 Responds to sensory and social experiences with differentiated emotions
				SR1.2 Monitors attentional focus of a social partner (= JA1.1)
				SR1.3 Shows reciprocity in speaker and listener roles to share experiences (= JA4.1)
				SR1.4 Demonstrates ability to inhibit actions and behaviors
				SR1.5 Persists during tasks with reasonable demands
				SR1.6 Demonstrates emotional expression appropriate to context
				2 Uses behavioral strategies to regulate arousal level during familiar activities
				SR2.1 Uses behavioral strategies to regulate arousal level in solitary and social activities
				SR2.2 Uses behavioral strategies modeled by partners to regulate arousal level
				SR2.3 Uses behavioral strategies to engage productively in an extended activity
				3 Uses language strategies to regulate arousal level during familiar activities
				SR3.1 Understands and uses early emotion words (= JA2.1, MR1.1)
				SR3.2 Understands and uses advanced emotion words (= JA2.3, MR1.2)
				SR3.3 Understands and uses graded emotions (= JA2.5, MR1.3)
				SR3.4 Uses language strategies to regulate arousal level during solitary and social activities
				SR3.5 Uses language strategies modeled by partners to regulate arousal level
				SR3.6 Uses language strategies to engage productively in an extended activity
				4 Uses metacognitive strategies to regulate arousal level during familiar activities
				SR4.1 Uses internalized rules modeled by adult instruction to guide behavior (SU1.3)
				SR4.2 Uses metacognitive strategies to plan and complete activities
				SR4.3 Uses self-monitoring and self-talk to guide behavior (SU1.4)
				SR4.4 Uses emotional memory to assist with emotional regulation
				SR4.5 Identifies and reflects on strategies to support regulation
				5 Regulates emotion during new and changing situations
				SR5.1 Uses behavioral strategies to regulate arousal level during new and changing situations
				SR5.2 Uses language strategies to regulate arousal level in new and changing situations
				SR5.3 Uses metacognitive strategies to regulate arousal level in new and changing situations
				SR5.4 Uses behavioral strategies to regulate arousal level during transitions
				SR5.5 Uses language strategies to regulate arousal level during transitions
				SR5.6 Uses metacognitive strategies to regulate arousal level during transitions
				6 Recovers from extreme dysregulation by self
				SR6.1 Removes self from overstimulating or undesired activity
				SR6.2 Uses behavioral strategies to recover from extreme dysregulation
				SR6.3 Uses language strategies to recover from extreme dysregulation
				SR6.4 Reengages in interaction or activity after recovery from extreme dysregulation
				SR6.5 Decreases amount of time to recover from extreme dysregulation
				SR6.6 Decreases intensity of dysregulated state

SCORING KEY: 2, criterion met consistently (across three partners in two contexts);
1, criterion met inconsistently or with assistance; **0,** criterion not met

Child's name: _____

Qtr 1	Qtr 2	Qtr 3	Qtr 4	INTERPERSONAL SUPPORT
				1 Partner is responsive to child
				IS1.1 Follows child's focus of attention
				IS1.2 Attunes to child's emotion and pace
				IS1.3 Responds appropriately to child's signals to foster a sense of communicative competence
				IS1.4 Recognizes and supports child's behavioral, language, and metacognitive strategies to regulate arousal level
				IS1.5 Recognizes signs of dysregulation and offers support
				IS1.6 Provides information or assistance to regulate state
				IS1.7 Offers breaks from interaction or activity as needed
				IS1.8 Facilitates reengagement in interactions and activities following breaks
				2 Partner fosters initiation
				IS2.1 Offers choices nonverbally or verbally
				IS2.2 Waits for and encourages initiations
				IS2.3 Provides a balance of initiated and respondent turns
				IS2.4 Allows child to initiate and terminate activities
				3 Partner respects child's independence
				IS3.1 Allows child to take breaks to move about as needed
				IS3.2 Provides time for child to solve problems or complete activities at own pace
				IS3.3 Interprets problem behavior as communicative and/or regulatory
				IS3.4 Honors protests, rejections, or refusals when appropriate
				4 Partner sets stage for engagement
				IS4.1 Secures child's attention before communicating
				IS4.2 Uses appropriate proximity and nonverbal behavior to encourage interaction
				IS4.3 Uses appropriate words and intonation to support optimal arousal level and engagement
				IS4.4 Shares emotions, internal states, and mental plans with child
				5 Partner provides developmental support
				IS5.1 Provides guidance for success in interaction with peers
				IS5.2 Attempts to repair breakdowns verbally or nonverbally
				IS5.3 Provides guidance and feedback as needed for success in activities
				IS5.4 Provides guidance on expressing emotions and understanding the cause of emotions
				IS5.5 Provides guidance for interpreting others' feelings and opinions
				6 Partner adjusts language input
				IS6.1 Uses nonverbal cues to support understanding
				IS6.2 Adjusts complexity of language input to child's developmental level
				IS6.3 Adjusts quality of language input to child's arousal level
				7 Partner models appropriate behaviors
				IS7.1 Models appropriate nonverbal communication and emotional expressions
				IS7.2 Models a range of communicative functions ☐ a. behavior regulation ☐ b. social interaction ☐ c. joint attention
				IS7.3 Models appropriate dramatic play and recreation
				IS7.4 Models appropriate behavior when child uses inappropriate behavior
				IS7.5 Models "child-perspective" language and use of self-talk

SCORING KEY: 2, criterion met consistently (across three partners in two contexts);
1, criterion met inconsistently or with assistance; **0,** criterion not met

The SCERTS™ Model: A Comprehensive Educational Approach for Children with Autism Spectrum Disorders
Copyright © 2006 by Paul H. Brookes Publishing Co. All rights reserved.

Child's name: _____

Qtr 1	Qtr 2	Qtr 3	Qtr 4	LEARNING SUPPORT
				1 Partner structures activity for active participation
				LS1.1 Defines clear beginning and ending to activity
				LS1.2 Creates turn-taking opportunities and leaves spaces for child to fill in
				LS1.3 Provides predictable sequence to activity
				LS1.4 Offers repeated learning opportunities
				LS1.5 Offers varied learning opportunities
				2 Partner uses augmentative communication support to foster development
				LS2.1 Uses augmentative communication support to enhance child's communication and expressive language
				LS2.2 Uses augmentative communication support to enhance child's understanding of language and behavior
				LS2.3 Uses augmentative communication support to enhance child's expression and understanding of emotion
				LS2.4 Uses augmentative communication support to enhance child's emotional regulation
				3 Partner uses visual and organizational support
				LS3.1 Uses support to define steps within a task
				LS3.2 Uses support to define steps and time for completion of activities
				LS3.3 Uses visual support to enhance smooth transitions between activities
				LS3.4 Uses support to organize segments of time across the day
				LS3.5 Uses visual support to enhance attention in group activities
				LS3.6 Uses visual support to foster active involvement in group activities
				4 Partner modifies goals, activities, and learning environment
				LS4.1 Adjusts social complexity to support organization and interaction
				LS4.2 Adjusts task difficulty for child success
				LS4.3 Modifies sensory properties of learning environment
				LS4.4 Arranges learning environment to enhance attention
				LS4.5 Arranges learning environment to promote child initiation
				LS4.6 Designs and modifies activities to be developmentally appropriate
				LS4.7 Infuses motivating materials and topics in activities
				LS4.8 Provides activities to promote initiation and extended interaction
				LS4.9 Alternates between movement and sedentary activities as needed
				LS4.10 "Ups the ante" or increases expectations appropriately

SCORING KEY: 2, criterion met consistently (across three partners in two contexts);
1, criterion met inconsistently or with assistance; **0,** criterion not met

Conversational Partner Stage
Intentions, Presuppositions, and Conversational Rules Worksheet

Child's name: _____   Date: _____

Contexts/activities: _____   Partners: _____

Contexts		Partners			
1	2	1	2	3	**COMMUNICATIVE INTENTIONS: KNOWING HOW TO EXPRESS IDEAS**
					Shares intentions to regulate the behavior of others
					JA3.1a Requests desired objects and activities
					JA3.1b Requests help
					JA3.1c Requests a break
					JA3.1d Protests/refuses undesired objects or activities
					Shares intentions for social interaction
					JA3.2a Greets
					JA3.2b Calls
					JA3.2c Requests comfort
					JA3.2d Regulates turns
					JA3.2e Requests permission
					JA3.2f Praises partner
					JA3.2g Expresses empathy
					JA3.2h Shares secrets
					Shares intentions for joint attention
					JA3.3a Comments on immediate, past, and imagined events
					JA3.3b Provides requested information about immediate and past events
					JA3.3c Requests information about immediate, past, and future events
					JA3.3d Expresses feelings and opinions
					JA3.3e Anticipates and plans outcomes
					PRESUPPOSITION: KNOWING WHAT KNOWLEDGE IS SHARED
					JA1.4 Modifies language based on what partners have seen or heard
					JA1.5 Shares internal thoughts or mental plans with partners
					JA4.5 Provides needed information based on partners' knowledge of topic
					Gauges content of conversational turn based on partners
					CONVERSATIONAL RULES: KNOWING HOW TO PLAY THE GAME
					Reciprocity: Flow and relevance of information
					JA4.1 Shows reciprocity in speaker and listener roles to share experiences
					JA4.2 Initiates a variety of conversational topics
					JA4.3 Initiates and maintains conversations that relate to partners' interests
					JA4.4 Maintains interaction by requesting or providing relevant information
					Gauges length of conversational turn based on partners
					Repair strategies: Keeping it going
					JA5.2 Repeats and modifies communication to repair breakdowns
					JA5.3 Recognizes breakdowns in communication and requests clarification
					JA5.4 Modifies language and behavior based on partners' change in agenda
					JA5.5 Modifies language and behavior based on partners' emotional reaction
					JA5.6 Expresses feelings of success and confidence during interactions
					Conventions: How to deliver
					SU4.1 Uses appropriate facial expressions for the context and partner
					SU4.2 Uses appropriate gestures for the context and partner
					SU4.3 Uses appropriate body posture and proximity for the context and partner
					SU4.4 Uses appropriate volume and intonation for the context and partner
					SU6.1 Follows conventions for initiating conversation and taking turns
					SU6.2 Follows conventions for shifting topics in conversation
					SU6.3 Follows conventions for ending conversation
					SU6.4 Follows conventions of politeness and register

Conversational Partner Stage
Expression and Understanding of Emotions Worksheet

Child's name: _____   Date: _____

Contexts/activities: _____   Partners: _____

Contexts		Partners				Understands emotion words	Uses emotion words	Describes others' emotional states	Uses nonverbal cues of emotional expression	Understands and uses graded emotion	Understands nonverbal cues of emotional expression	Describes plausible causal factors for emotions of self and others
1	2	1	2	3	**EARLY EMOTION WORDS**							
					Positive							
					happy							
					silly							
					funny							
					good							
					Negative							
					mad							
					angry							
					sad							
					sick							
					tired							
					ADVANCED EMOTION WORDS							
					Positive							
					content							
					hopeful							
					excited							
					proud							
					delighted							
					interested							
					Negative							
					frustrated							
					scared							
					worried							
					bored							
					stressed							
					terrified							
					embarrassed							
					guilty							
					jealous							

Conversational Partner Stage
Language Elements Worksheet

Child's name: _____ Date: _____

Context/activity: _____ Partners: _____

Observed (Uses)	Type	Examples

ADVANCED RELATIONAL MEANING

☐☐☐☐☐	*wh-* words	*what, where, who, whose, which, when, how, why*
☐☐☐☐☐	**temporal relations**	*now, later, before, after, since, then, until, in a minute, in a day, in a week, while*
☐☐☐☐☐	**physical relations**	*colors, shapes, hard/soft, big/little, heavy/light, tall/short, thick/thin*
☐☐☐☐☐	**numerical relations**	*numbers, few, some, many, more/less*
☐☐☐☐☐	**location terms**	*in, on, under, next to, behind, in back of, in front of, above, below, left/right*
☐☐☐☐☐	**kinship terms**	*mother, father, sister, brother, son, daughter, grandmother, grandfather, aunt, uncle, cousin, niece, nephew*
☐☐☐☐☐	**causal terms**	*but, so, because, if, or*

REFERENCE TO THINGS: Helping to locate the intended reference

☐☐☐☐☐	**subject pronouns**	*I/you, he/she, it, we/they*
☐☐☐☐☐	**other pronouns**	
	object	*me/you, him/her, it, us, them*
	possessive	*your/my, yours/mine, his/her, our, their*
	indefinite	*some, any, none, all, every, many, lots, something, nothing, anything, everything*
	demonstrative	*this, that, these, those*
☐☐	**determiners (articles)**	*the, a/an*
☐☐☐☐☐	**plurals**	*cats, cookies, cows, sheep*

VERB PHRASES: Helping to ground the event in time and attitude

☐☐☐☐☐	**main verbs**	
	change of state	*open, break, stop, find, fall down, die*
	activity	*run, smile, jump, lick, draw, see, catch*
	enduring states	*to be, have, love,*
	mental states	*think, know, guess, remember, wish, bet, hope, feel*
☐☐☐☐☐	**tense markers**	
	present progressive	*is walking, am going, are running*
	third person	*barks, hits, runs, goes, does, has*
	past tense	*dropped, spilled, broke, came, brought, was, were, been, had, did*
	future tense	*will, can, may, should, wanna, gonna, hafta,*
☐☐☐☐☐	**helping verbs**	*has, have, had, do, does, did, am, is, are, was, were, been*
☐☐☐☐☐	**modal verbs**	
	early	*wanna, gonna, hafta, needta*
	advanced	*may, might, can, could, shall, should, will, would, must*
☐☐☐☐☐	**negation**	*no, not, won't can't, don't, doesn't, wasn't, wouldn't*

Source: Owens, 2000; Tomasello, 2003.

Conversational Partner Stage
Sentence Constructions Worksheet

Child's name: _____ Date: _____

Context/activity: _____ Partners: _____

Observed (Uses)	Sentence type	Examples
▢▢▢▢▢	**declarative**	*I need a break.* *The boy is riding a bike.* *He has a brand new car.*
▢▢▢▢▢	**imperative**	*Go outside now.* *Pick up your toys.* *Take this home to your mom.*
▢▢▢▢▢	**negative**	*I don't know.* *I don't want any peas.* *I can't do that.*
▢▢▢▢▢	**interrogative** yes/no questions *wh-* questions	 *Can you help?* *Will you open this?* *Did John kick the ball?* *Who is in the house?* *What do you think?* *Which one is right?* *When are we done?* *Why did you go home?*
▢▢▢▢▢	**embedding** prepositional phrases infinitive phrases object noun phrases subject noun phrases	 *The bird is in the cage.* *The dog is on the bed.* *I wanna go outside.* *I gotta go to the bathroom.* *I think I should go first.* *I see you have some too.* *Here's the toy that spins.* *The boy who lived next door came over for dinner.* *The man selling balloons gave one to the boy.*
▢▢▢▢▢	**conjoining**	*There is a little boy and he is running home.* *The boy is crying because he fell down.* *If I eat all my dinner, then I get dessert.* *But you said I could, so I hafta have some.* *When I am done with my work, I get to go outside.*

Source: Owens, 2000.

The SCERTS™ Model: A Comprehensive Educational Approach for Children with Autism Spectrum Disorders
Copyright © 2006 by Paul H. Brookes Publishing Co. All rights reserved.

SAP Summary Form
Social Partner Stage

Child's name:_____

Quarterly start date of observation: _____ Child's age:_____

SCERTS Profile

SOCIAL COMMUNICATION

Joint Attention

JA1 Engages in reciprocal interaction

JA2 Shares attention

JA3 Shares emotion

JA4 Shares intentions to regulate the behavior of others

JA5 Shares intentions for social interaction

JA6 Shares intentions for joint attention

JA7 Persists and repairs communication breakdowns

Symbol Use

SU1 Learns by imitation of familiar actions and sounds

SU2 Understands nonverbal cues in familiar activities

SU3 Uses familiar objects conventionally in play

SU4 Uses gestures and nonverbal means to share intentions

SU5 Uses vocalizations to share intentions

SU6 Understands a few familiar words

EMOTIONAL REGULATION

Mutual Regulation

MR1 Expresses range of emotions

MR2 Responds to assistance offered by partners

MR3 Requests partners' assistance to regulate state

MR4 Recovers from extreme dysregulation with support from partners

Self-Regulation

SR1 Demonstrates availability for learning and interacting

SR2 Uses behavioral strategies to regulate arousal level during familiar activities

SR3 Regulates emotion during new and changing situations

SR4 Recovers from extreme dysregulation by self

SCERTS Profile (continued)

TRANSACTIONAL SUPPORT

Interpersonal Support

IS1 Partner is responsive to child

IS2 Partner fosters initiation

IS3 Partner respects child's independence

IS4 Partner sets stage for engagement

IS5 Partner provides developmental support

IS6 Partner adjusts language input

IS7 Partner models appropriate behaviors

Learning Support

LS1 Partner structures activity for active participation

LS2 Partner uses augmentative communication support to foster development

LS3 Partner uses visual and organizational support

LS4 Partner modifies goals, activities, and learning environment

Social-Emotional Growth Indicators Profile

1. Happiness
2. Sense of Self
3. Sense of Other
4. Active Learning and Organization
5. Flexibility and Resilience
6. Cooperation and Appropriateness of Behavior
7. Independence
8. Social Membership and Friendships

Family Perception and Priorities

Is this profile an accurate picture of your child? If not, explain.

Is there any additional information that is needed to develop your child's educational plan?

If you were to focus your energies on one thing for your child, what would that be?

What skills would you like your child to learn in the next 3 months?

Prioritize Weekly SCERTS Objectives

Child Social Communication and Emotional Regulation objectives

1.

2.

3.

4.

5.

6.

7.

8.

Partner Transactional Support objectives

1.

2.

3.

4.

5.

6.

7.

8.

Further Assessment—Key Results or Additional Recommendations

SAP Activity Planning

Identify key activities using the SAP Activity Planning Form for

❑ Morning schedule   ❑ Afternoon schedule

SCERTS Family Support Plan

Educational Support		Emotional Support	
Activity	How often	Activity	How often

SCERTS Support Plan for Professionals and Service Providers

Educational Support		Emotional Support	
Activity	How often	Activity	How often

SAP Summary Form
Language Partner Stage

Child's name:_____

Quarterly start date of observation: _____ Child's age:_____

SCERTS Profile

SOCIAL COMMUNICATION

Joint Attention

JA1 Engages in reciprocal interaction

JA2 Shares attention

JA3 Shares emotion

JA4 Shares intentions to regulate the behavior of others

JA5 Shares intentions for social interaction

JA6 Shares intentions for joint attention

JA7 Persists and repairs communication breakdowns

JA8 Shares experiences in reciprocal interaction

Symbol Use

SU1 Learns by observation and imitation of actions and words

SU2 Understands nonverbal cues in familiar and unfamiliar activities

SU3 Uses familiar objects conventionally in play

SU4 Uses gestures and nonverbal means to share intentions

SU5 Uses words and word combinations to express meanings

SU6 Understands a variety of words and word combinations without contextual cues

EMOTIONAL REGULATION

Mutual Regulation

MR1 Expresses range of emotions

MR2 Responds to assistance offered by partners

MR3 Requests partners' assistance to regulate state

MR4 Recovers from extreme dysregulation with support from partners

Self-Regulation

SR1 Demonstrates availability for learning and interacting

SR2 Uses behavioral strategies to regulate arousal level during familiar activities

SR3 Uses language strategies to regulate arousal level during familiar activities

SR4 Regulates emotion during new and changing situations

SR5 Recovers from extreme dysregulation by self

TRANSACTIONAL SUPPORT

Interpersonal Support

IS1 Partner is responsive to child

IS2 Partner fosters initiation

IS3 Partner respects child's independence

IS4 Partner sets stage for engagement

IS5 Partner provides developmental support

IS6 Partner adjusts language input

IS7 Partner models appropriate behaviors

Learning Support

LS1 Partner structures activity for active participation

LS2 Partner uses augmentative communication support to foster development

LS3 Partner uses visual and organizational support

LS4 Partner modifies goals, activities, and learning environment

Social-Emotional Growth Indicators Profile

1. Happiness

2. Sense of Self

3. Sense of Other

4. Active Learning and Organization

5. Flexibility and Resilience

6. Cooperation and Appropriateness of Behavior

7. Independence

8. Social Membership and Friendships

Family Perception and Priorities

Is this profile an accurate picture of your child? If not, explain.

Is there any additional information that is needed to develop your child's educational plan?

If you were to focus your energies on one thing for your child, what would that be?

What skills would you like your child to learn in the next 3 months?

Prioritize Weekly SCERTS Objectives

Child Social Communication and Emotional Regulation objectives	Partner Transactional Support objectives
1.	1.
2.	2.
3.	3.
4.	4.
5.	5.
6.	6.
7.	7.
8.	8.

Further Assessment—Key Results or Additional Recommendations

SAP Activity Planning

Identify key activities using the SAP Activity Planning Form for

❑ Morning schedule   ❑ Afternoon schedule

SCERTS Family Support Plan

Educational Support		Emotional Support	
Activity	How often	Activity	How often

SCERTS Support Plan for Professionals and Service Providers

Educational Support		Emotional Support	
Activity	How often	Activity	How often

Child's name:_____

Quarterly start date of observation: _____ Child's age:_____

SCERTS Profile

SOCIAL COMMUNICATION

Joint Attention

JA1 Shares attention

JA2 Shares emotion

JA3 Shares intentions for a variety of purposes

JA4 Shares experiences in reciprocal interaction

JA5 Persists and repairs communication breakdowns

Symbol Use

SU1 Learns by imitation, observation, instruction, and collaboration

SU2 Understands nonverbal cues and nonliteral meanings in reciprocal interactions

SU3 Participates conventionally in dramatic play and recreation

SU4 Uses appropriate gestures and nonverbal behavior for the context

SU5 Understands and uses generative language to express meaning

SU6 Follows rules of conversation

EMOTIONAL REGULATION

Mutual Regulation

MR1 Expresses range of emotions

MR2 Responds to assistance offered by partners

MR3 Responds to feedback and guidance regarding behavior

MR4 Requests partners' assistance to regulate state

MR5 Recovers from extreme dysregulation with support from partners

Self-Regulation

SR1 Demonstrates availability for learning and interacting

SR2 Uses behavioral strategies to regulate arousal level during familiar activities

SR3 Uses language strategies to regulate arousal level during familiar activities

SR4 Uses metacognitive strategies to regulate arousal level during familiar activities

SR5 Regulates emotion during new and changing situations

SR6 Recovers from extreme dysregulation by self

TRANSACTIONAL SUPPORT

Interpersonal Support

IS1 Partner is responsive to child

IS2 Partner fosters initiation

IS3 Partner respects child's independence

IS4 Partner sets stage for engagement

IS5 Partner provides developmental support

IS6 Partner adjusts language input

IS7 Partner models appropriate behaviors

Learning Support

LS1 Partner structures activity for active participation

LS2 Partner uses augmentative system to foster development

LS3 Partner uses visual and organizational support

LS4 Partner modifies goals, activities, and learning environment

Social-Emotional Growth Indicators Profile

1. Happiness

2. Sense of Self

3. Sense of Other

4. Active Learning and Organization

5. Flexibility and Resilience

6. Cooperation and Appropriateness of Behavior

7. Independence

8. Social Membership and Friendships

Family Perception and Priorities

Is this profile an accurate picture of your child? If not, explain.

Is there any additional information that is needed to develop your child's educational plan?

If you were to focus your energies on one thing for your child, what would that be?

What skills would you like your child to learn in the next 3 months?

Prioritize Weekly SCERTS Objectives

Child Social Communication and Emotional Regulation objectives	Partner Transactional Support objectives
1.	1.
2.	2.
3.	3.
4.	4.
5.	5.
6.	6.
7.	7.
8.	8.

Further Assessment—Key Results or Additional Recommendations

SAP Activity Planning

Identify key activities using the SAP Activity Planning Form for

❏ Morning schedule ❏ Afternoon schedule

SCERTS Family Support Plan

Educational Support		Emotional Support	
Activity	How often	Activity	How often

SCERTS Support Plan for Professionals and Service Providers

Educational Support		Emotional Support	
Activity	How often	Activity	How often

SAP Daily Tracking Log

Child's name: _____ Communication stage: _____ Date: _____

Child Social Communication and Emotional Regulation objectives

	Activity: Notes:
	Activity: Notes:
	Activity: Notes:
	Activity: Notes:
	Activity: Notes:

Partner Transactional Support objectives

	Activity: Notes:
	Activity: Notes:
	Activity: Notes:
	Activity: Notes:
	Activity: Notes:

Activity: Describe the activity to characterize the group size, partner, context, and activity variables.
Notes: Document the child's or partner's performance (e.g., number of initiations, number of correct trials), or describe the child's or partner's best behavior during that activity.

The SCERTS™ Model: A Comprehensive Educational Approach for Children with Autism Spectrum Disorders
by Barry M. Prizant, Amy M. Wetherby, Emily Rubin, Amy C. Laurent, & Patrick J. Rydell
Copyright © 2006 by Paul H. Brookes Publishing Co. All rights reserved.

SAP Daily Tracking Log

Child's name: _____ Communication stage: _____ Date: _____

Child Social Communication and Emotional Regulation objectives

	Activity: Notes:	Activity: Notes:
	Activity: Notes:	Activity: Notes:
	Activity: Notes:	Activity: Notes:
	Activity: Notes:	Activity: Notes:
	Activity: Notes:	Activity: Notes:

Partner Transactional Support objectives

	Activity: Notes:	Activity: Notes:
	Activity: Notes:	Activity: Notes:
	Activity: Notes:	Activity: Notes:
	Activity: Notes:	Activity: Notes:
	Activity: Notes:	Activity: Notes:

Activity: Describe the activity to characterize the group size, partner, context, and activity variables.
Notes: Document the child's or partner's performance (e.g., number of initiations, number of correct trials), or describe the child's or partner's best behavior during that activity.

The SCERTS™ Model: A Comprehensive Educational Approach for Children with Autism Spectrum Disorders
by Barry M. Prizant, Amy M. Wetherby, Emily Rubin, Amy C. Laurent, & Patrick J. Rydell

SAP Weekly Tracking Log

Child's name: _____ Communication stage: _____ Date: _____

Child Social Communication and Emotional Regulation objectives	Weeks											
	1	2	3	4	5	6	7	8	9	10	11	12

Partner Transactional Support objectives

Social Partner stage scoring key: 2, criterion met consistently (across two partners in two contexts); **1,** criterion met inconsistently or with assistance; **0,** criterion not met

Language Partner and Conversational Partner stages scoring key: 2, criterion met consistently (across two partners in two contexts); **1,** criterion met inconsistently or with assistance; **0,** criterion not met

SAP Activity Planning Form

Child's name: _____   Communication stage: _____   Date: _____   Page #: _____

Activity/time	Social complexity	Group size	Team members and partners	Weekly child objectives	Weekly partner objectives	Team members and partners	Sample transactional supports

Instructions: Write the weekly Social Communication and Emotional Regulation objectives for the child and the Transactional Support objectives for the partner in the vertical boxes across the top. In the far right vertical box at the upper right-hand corner, list the team members and the child's partners and numbers or initials for each team member or partner. In each row below the column headings, write a

Appendix B

Glossary

AAC *See* augmentative and alternative communication.

ABI Activity-based intervention. *See* activity-based learning approaches.

active learning A child's capacity to initiate efforts to engage others for learning, to seek information, to problem solve, to relate new experiences to previous experiences, and to remain organized and engaged in activities in a manner that contributes to learning. Active learning also involves the ability to engage in goal-directed behavior, maintain attention, and remain emotionally well regulated and focused in planning and carrying out activities across settings.

activity-based learning approaches Instructional approaches that focus on using logical and meaningful activities to teach skills and social understanding and to support generalization of skills. This approach is in contrast to skill-based approaches, which may focus on training skills primarily outside of the context of meaningful activities. *Also called* activity-based intervention (ABI). *See also* skill-based approaches.

arousal bias A person's bias or tendency to experience particular arousal states, either low or high arousal. Individuals may vary in their arousal states from low arousal to high arousal. Arousal has been defined as a continuum of physiological or biobehavioral states ranging from deep sleep to wakeful and alert to highly agitated (Lester, Freier, & LaGasse, 1995).

arousal state Physiological state controlled by the autonomic nervous system, measured along a continuum of deep sleep, to underaroused but conscious, to quiet and actively alert, to extremely overaroused (agitated). Physiological arousal is closely related to emotional experience. *See also* high state of arousal; low state of arousal.

augmentative and alternative communication (AAC) Nonspeech strategies and communication aids used in addition to or as an alternative to the development and use of speech for communication. AAC means may include the use of specific aids such as photographs or picture symbols or may be unaided as in the use of sign language and/or natural gestures as means of communication.

availability for learning A state in which a child is most available for learning and is best able to attend to the most relevant information; remain socially engaged with others; process verbal and nonverbal information; initiate interactions using higher level communication abilities, including language; respond to others in reciprocal interaction; and actively participate in everyday activities. Availability is determined by arousal, motivation, and an appropriate match between the child's abilities and the demands of the activity and social demands.

behavior regulation A category of communicative functions or intentions that appears relatively early for children with autism spectrum disorders (ASD). Communicative acts are used to regulate the behavior of another person to obtain or restrict environmental needs (e.g., requesting or protesting, rejecting or refusing an object or action). The motivation is to meet immediate needs and is relatively nonsocial, as compared with the more social functions of social interaction or joint attention.

behavioral strategies *Also called* sensory-motor strategies. Sensory and/or motor means used to support emotional regulation (i.e., to increase or decrease emotional arousal to allow a child to remain alert and well regulated). Examples include vocalizing or focusing attention on oneself for self-soothing or distraction; looking at one's hands; seeking oral sensory input; and engaging in repetitive motor actions, such as rocking or finger tapping. The purpose of such activity may be to shift attention away from dysregulating events to neutral or more organizing events or to provide sensory or motor input that in and of itself has a regulating effect.

challenging behavior *See* problem behavior.

changing situations Situations that have variation in key features (e.g., sensory stimulation, activity level, activity sequence, task difficulty) or unexpected features (e.g., unpredictable events such as changes in the place or sequence of common routines or premature termination of activities).

classroom structure A high degree of predictability and consistency in a classroom, employed to minimize the dysregulating effect of uncertainty. Structure may pertain to aspects of the physical environment, such as the use of activity centers, or to temporal aspects, such as the daily schedule.

cognitive appraisal The ability to reflect on one's own emotional experience, as well as to read and understand social-emotional cues from others such as facial expression, body posture, and vocal tone to support social understanding and emotional regulation

communication breakdown A lack of success in communication between partners due to problems in understanding a child or a partner's attempt to communicate. Factors that may contribute to breakdowns include unclear or unintelligible speech or nonverbal signals, use of unconventional speech or gestures, or environmental factors such as auditory or visual distraction. Thus, the desired goal is not achieved. Following a breakdown, it is most desirable for a child or partner to attempt to repair the breakdown by repeating or modifying the signal. *See also* repair strategies.

communicative competence Knowledge of how to communicate effectively and the ability to communicate for a variety of purposes across partners and settings in a socially appropriate manner.

communicative exchange *See* exchange (social or communicative).

communicative function   The effect of a child's communicative act on the listener, which can be readily observed in most cases.

communicative intention   The communicative goal of a child or a partner, which cannot be directly observed and may only be inferred from the person's behavior within the social context.

communicative means   The behaviors used to communicate (i.e., how children communicate), involving 1) *presymbolic means,* including gestures or use of objects, and 2) *symbolic means,* including sign language, picture symbol systems, and/or speech.

communicative repair   Following a communication breakdown, a turn in which the child or partner repeats or substantially modifies all or part of the communicative signal to fix the breakdown.

contingent response   A partner's immediate response that maintains the focus of attention or topic.

conventional communicative means   Verbal and/or nonverbal signals that are easily understood by others due to a shared system of meanings among the partners.

conversational discourse   Social conversation abilities that include 1) understanding and using higher level grammar and syntax to be more efficient in conveying meaning and to clarify differences in meaning; 2) interpreting and using nonverbal information (e.g., gaze, facial expressions, body orientation, proximity, prosodic patterns) and nonliteral meanings (e.g., idioms, puns) as they relate to social conventions and clarification of meaning; 3) adhering to the conversational conventions of initiating interactions, exchanging turns in interactions, demarcating topic shifts, and terminating interactions; and 4) adhering to the social requirements of different social settings.

Conversational Partner stage   The third and most sophisticated stage in the SCERTS Model, preceded by the Social Partner and Language Partner stages. In general, children at the Conversational Partner stage are communicating through more complex and grammatical combinations of spoken words, signs, and/or pictures or picture symbols, typically with at least some emerging ability to participate beyond single turns in communicative exchange. *See also* Language Partner stage; Social Partner stage.

cooperative turn-taking games   Activities in which the primary goal is the success of social reciprocity, turn taking, and mutual enjoyment of participants.

criterion-referenced assessment   Assessment that measures a child's level of performance, degree of mastery on a specific tasks, or expected developmental skills within a domain. Often developmental progressions are used as guidelines for standards of the domains assessed. *See also* curriculum-based assessment.

curriculum modification and adaptation   Changes to a curriculum, teaching strategies, learning materials, and their presentation to assist a child to better understand the content and expectations and to support success in learning.

curriculum-based assessment   A criterion-referenced assessment that is linked to a curriculum. For example, the SCERTS Assessment Process–Observation (SAP-O) is a curriculum-based assessment, with many of the items based on developmental progressions documented in research on the development of children with and without disabilities. *See also* criterion-referenced assessment.

delayed echolalia   *See* echolalia.

directive teaching approaches   Highly repetitive and adult-selected and -directed instruction (often involving drills), with the primary focus being on teaching children compliance with requests and/or production of "correct" responses relative to a predetermined program. *See also* facilitative teaching approaches.

dysregulation   Abnormally high or low state of emotional arousal leading to increased difficulties in organization, social engagement, attention, and processing.

echolalia   A child's repetition of speech produced by others. When the repetition occurs immediately following the model, it is referred to as *immediate echolalia.* When the repetition occurs at a later time, it is referred to as *delayed echolalia.* Immediate or delayed echolalia may be produced with or without communicative intent and with or without comprehension of the utterance that is echoed. *Mitigated echolalia* is immediate or delayed echolalia that is produced with a change in wording, or intonation and is usually indicative of a higher degree of comprehension of the utterance that is echoed. *See also* unconventional verbal behavior.

ecologically valid measures   Measurement involving baseline information or measured changes in a child's developmental abilities and adaptive functioning within natural environments and across partners, which are deemed to be truly representative of a child's behavior.

educational support   An aspect of the support to families component of Transactional Support, involving sharing of helpful information and resources or direct instruction in facilitating a child's social communication, emotional regulation, and daily living skills and in implementing learning supports.

emotional arousal   Mild to extreme states of heightened or reduced emotional reactions caused by anxiety, fear, distress, or even dysregulating positive emotional states of elation and giddiness. *Overarousal* may be due to excessive sensory stimulation, too much excitement, or stressful events. Underarousal may be due to fatigue, boredom, or lack of organizing stimulation and may result in lack of attention or nonresponsiveness.

emotional memory   The affective component of memory, involving such aspects as feelings experienced with a person (e.g., joy, stress), a place (e.g., familiarity and safety, unfamiliarity and threat), or an activity or experience (e.g., fun and of interest, unexciting and boring).

emotional regulation   A core developmental process underlying attention, arousal, and the establishment of social relationships.

Emotional Regulation   The domain of the SCERTS Model that deals with a child's emotional regulatory capacities. The domain is divided into two components: Mutual Regulation and Self-Regulation. Recovery from extreme dysregualtion is addressed under each of these components.

emotional support   An aspect of the support to families component of Transactional Support, involving support designed to enhance a family's skills for coping and adaptation to the challenges of raising a child with autism spectrum disorder (ASD).

engineered activities and settings   Activities and settings that may not occur naturally in a child's life but that are designed and scheduled to provide consistent familiar and predictable formats for learning.

environmental arrangement   The ways typical settings and activities are set up or modified to foster social communication and emotional regulation.

exchange (social or communicative)   A turn from the child and a turn from the partner.

executive functioning   Higher cortical function dependent on a cluster of cognitive skills that include the ability to set goals, plan, sequence, organize, and execute goal-directed behavior; inhibit responses to irrelevant stimuli; and respond flexibly and adaptively, allowing a child to be better able to remain organized and achieve goals.

expression of emotion   The communicative component of emotional regulation that involves observable expression of internal feeling states (*also called* affect displays), which provides information about a partner's specific emotions and the intensity of those emotions.

extreme dysregulation   A very high or low state of emotional arousal leading to extreme difficulties in organization, attention, and processing.

facilitative teaching approaches   Teaching practices that primarily follow a child's preferences and motivations and accept the child's behavioral responses through imitation or positive emotional reactions. An adult partner provides minimal structure or direction. *See also* directive teaching approaches.

fight-or-flight reactions   Primitive reactive responses to threatening circumstances. When a child exhibits these reactions, he or she may be described as aggressive, noncompliant, or intentionally manipulative, when in fact the responses may be attempts at coping or survival reactions. For instance, children who are hyperreactive to visual and auditory stimulation may attempt to escape from overly stimulating environments or activities. Children who are confused by a situation or who are hyperreactive to touch may flail or strike out at others attempting to hold them in an activity. Due to misinterpretations, these reactions may be treated as problem behavior.

formal supports   Emotional support provided by professionals who are trained to respond to a family's as well as a child's needs. *See also* emotional support; informal supports.

functional skills   Practical and useful skills that can be directly applied in naturalistic contexts and everyday activities to foster independence and self-determination.

functional spontaneous communication   Practical and useful verbal and/or nonverbal communication skills that are self-initiated and directly applied in naturalistic contexts to foster independence and self-determination.

gaze shift   Social referencing that occurs when a child is looking at a person, shifts gaze to an object, and then immediately shifts back to the person) (two-point gaze shift) or looks at an object, shifts gaze to a person, then to a second person, and then immediately shifts back to the object (three-point gaze shift). Such patterns are indicative of a child's social awareness and joint attention abilities.

goal-directed activities   Activities that have a clear sequence of steps with a clearly perceived end goal.

high state of arousal   An arousal state in which a child is at the mercy of overwhelming reactions such as anxiety, fear, distress, or even dysregulating positive emotional states of elation and giddiness. A child in a high state of arousal may withdraw or shut down in an attempt to cope with disorganizing or overly stimulating experiences. *See also* arousal state; low state of arousal.

homeostasis   The inner drive to attain and maintain a steady, internal state (i.e., emotional and physiological stability), which promotes adaptive functioning, learning, and active social engagement.

immediate echolalia   *See* echolalia.

incessant questioning   Repeated verbal inquiries that are directed toward the communicative partner and are produced with communicative intent with an expectation for a response. The questioning may persist either immediatley following a response or after a short respite even though a response may have been provided. *Also called* repetitive questioning. *See also* unconventional verbal behavior.

individual differences   The unique profiles of abilities in social communication, emotional regulation, and learning observed across children. Assessment efforts and educational programming address such differences in the SCERTS Model.

informal supports   Social and emotional support provided incidentally by nonprofessionals such as relatives, neighbors, and/or members of a religious community who may help to mitigate the stresses and daily challenges of raising a child with autism spectrum disorder (ASD). *See also* emotional support; formal supports.

initiated communicative behavior   An intentional communicative act that is not a response to another person's behavior.

initiated mutual regulation   The ability to initiate requests for regulatory support as a child becomes more aware and better able to intentionally communicate needs (e.g., for assistance, for comfort) to caregivers through verbal and/or nonverbal means. *See also* mutual regulation; respondent mutual regulation.

intentional communication   The direction of vocal, gestural, nonverbal, or verbal behavior to others for a specific purpose or function. The means used to communicate may be conventional or unconventional and may vary in social acceptability, such as screaming to protest in contrast to saying "no" to protest.

Interpersonal Support   The component of the Transactional Support domain of the SCERTS Model that deals with partners' use of interpersonal supports.

interpersonal supports   Adjustments made by adult and peer communicative partners in language use, emotional expression and interactive style that are effective in helping a child process language, participate in social interaction, experience social activities as emotionally satisfying, and maintain a well-regulated state.

joint attention   The capacity to maintain a common focus with another person on an event in the immediate environment, or on a topic through language. *Joint attention communication* occurs when signals are used to direct another's attention to an object or event for purposes of sharing observations or experiences (e.g., commenting on an object or event, requesting information).

Joint Attention   The component of the Social Communication domain of the SCERTS Model that deals with a child's capacity for joint attention.

Language Partner stage   The second stage of development in the SCERTS Model, preceded by the Social Partner stage and followed by the Conversational Partner stage. In general, children at the Language Partner stage are communicating through symbolic means, which may include single or simple combinations of spoken words, signs, and/or pictures or picture symbols. *See also* Conversational Partner stage; Social Partner stage.

language strategies   Emotional regulatory strategies that are symbolically based (i.e., language and conceptual) and therefore that are more sophisticated, varied, and flexible than behavioral strategies. Examples include using audible self-talk to organize one's actions or to calm oneself when too highly aroused, thinking in language (i.e., inner language) for similar purposes as for self-talk, and self-monitoring emotional states (i.e., reflecting on how one is feeling).

learning and playing with peers (LAPP)   Activities, involving learning and playing with peers, that address Interpersonal Support goals (for peer support) in the SCERTS Model.

learning style   The individualized manner in which a child uses his or her cognitive, social, communicative, and sensory strengths to process and use information.

Learning Support   The component of Transactional Support in the SCERTS Model that deals with partners' use of learning supports.

learning supports Transactional supports used to clarify expectations, support understanding of activities (e.g., the sequence of steps and end goal of an activity), support emotional regulation, and create natural and motivating opportunities for participation and communication. Learning supports may involve use of aids such as visual and augmentative communication supports, as well as the strategies for implementation of these supports in instruction by partners.

low state of arousal An arousal state in which a child has difficulty attending to the salient features of the environment and sustaining attention for social interactions and educational activities. Children in a low state of arousal often appear passive, disengaged, and inattentive. *See also* arousal state; high state of arousal.

MA & PA approach The use of meaningful and purposeful activities in the SCERTS Model, to emphasize the priority on children learning functional skills within an activity-based approach.

meaningful activities Intrinsically motivating activities that are the most conducive to learning and preferred contexts in which to promote natural interactions among partners.

metacognitive skills The ability to reflect on and talk about thoughts and plans by sharing internal thoughts or mental plans with a partner.

mitigated echolalia *See* echolalia.

modified natural activities and settings Natural activities and settings that are already part of a child's life routines and that are modified to support optimal participation and engagement, through the addition of supports for social communication and emotional regulation.

modulation of arousal The unconscious process of increasing or decreasing arousal state controlled by the autonomic nervous system based on perception of internal sensation and external stimulation.

motor planning difficulties Limitations in the coordination and execution of motor skills that underlie limitations in speech intelligibility as well as problems in more general skilled, purposeful movements.

multimodal communication Use of a combination of means to communicate, including vocal, verbal, gestural, sign language, and visual systems.

multisensory teaching Approaches that use a combination of sensory modalities, strategies, and techniques to assist in a child's learning (e.g., visual, auditory, tactile, kinesthetic).

mutual regulation Emotional regulation that occurs in the context of social interaction such as when a child seeks assistance and/or responds to others' attempts to provide support for emotional regulation when faced with stressful, overly stimulating or emotionally dysregulating circumstances. *See also* initiated mutual regulation; respondent mutual regulation.

Mutual Regulation The component of the Emotional Regulation domain of the SCERTS Model that addresses a child's mutual regulation skills.

naturally occuring activities and settings Learning opportunities that occur within settings and activities that already are present in the life of a child and his or her family.

negative emotional display A clearly observable vocal or facial expression of distress or frustration that may be accompanied by a gesture or change in body posture.

new situations Activities or features of activities that are unfamiliar to a child (e.g., an activity that the child has not participated in; a new person joining a familiar activity). Often, such situations place a child with autism spectrum disorder (ASD) at greater risk for experiencing dysregulation.

nonverbal communication Forms of communication that do not involve speech or other language-based means (e.g., gestures, body proximity, communicative gaze, nonspeech vocalizations).

optimal arousal A state of arousal in which the child is most available for learning and engaging relative to the demands of an activity or setting. In such a state, the child is not experiencing predominant patterns of arousal of being too high or too low with regard to the demands of the social and physical environment.

organizational supports Ways of organizing materials, physical space, or marking time concepts to enhance the child's organization as part of the Learning Support component of Transactional Support in the SCERTS Model.

overarousal *See* emotional arousal; high state of arousal.

partners People with whom a child engages in social exchange in which there exists mutual influence among the partners.

PBS *See* positive behavior support.

peer support One category of interpersonal support in the SCERTS Model in which support is provided to a child by similar-age children in activities that serve to promote peer-related competencies. These competencies include the ability to initiate and maintain successful social-communicative interactions across partners, settings, and circumstances, which ultimately contributes to the development of friendships and long-term positive relationships.

perseverative speech Persistenat repetition of a speech pattern that is produced in a cyclical, recurring manner, with or without evidence of communicative intent or expectation of a response from the partner. *See also* unconventional verbal behavior.

physiological arousal *See* arousal state.

physiological aspects of emotion Arousal state changes that occur and are correlated with emotional experience, which allow a person to feel emotions in the body.

planned activity routines Learning routines that target the instruction of specific skills through multiple learning opportunities for learning a specific skill or set of skills. The routines involve a relatively high level of adult facilitation and support. The skills are only targeted if they directly support other routines occuring in other parts of the day.

positive behavior support (PBS) Contemporary applied behavior analysis (ABA) approaches to address problem behaviors based on a functional behavioral assessment, such as teaching communicative replacements, functional equivalents, and related strategies.

positive emotional display A clear facial expression of pleasure or excitement, which may or may not be accompanied by a vocalization such as laughing or squealing, or signals observed in body language indicative of positive emotional experience.

prescriptive approaches Structured and systematic teaching practices that follow a specific sequence of teaching steps, with little room for variation, flexibility, or spontaneity on the part of the instructor or the child.

problem behavior Behavior that is considered problematic because it is socially undesirable, is harmful to oneself or others, or interferes with learning and/or social engagement. Whether a behavior is or is not considered a problem behavior may be based on a child's age, cultural norms and values, and/or attributions made about the behavior. Therefore, this judgment often is subjective. For example, a repetitive motor behavior such as hand flapping may be considered a problem behavior by a professional but not by the child's parents. *Also called* challenging behavior.

reciprocity Ongoing social-emotional exchange between two or more partners that are mutual, responsive, and contingent on the partners' previous actions.

recovery from dysregulation The ability to regain a well-regulated state after extreme dysregulation.

regulation of emotional and mood states The ability to regulate emotional reactions and to adjust or modify one's emotional response relative to constitutional (internal) variables and environmental and social demands. This regulation also involves the ability to recover from extreme emotional reactions and dysregulating experiences and to maintain active engagement in goal-directed activities.

relaxation techniques Procedures that are designed to regulate and organize bodily systems to a state of calmness.

repair strategies A partner's nonverbal and or verbal attempts to communicate more successfully following a communication breakdown, which may involve repeating or modifying the signal. *See also* communication breakdown.

respondent mutual regulation Emotional regulation that occurs when a partner reads a child's signals of dysregulation and responds in a manner to help the child achieve a well-regulated state and/or prevent further dysregulation. *See also* initiated mutual regulation; mutual regulation.

SAP *See* SCERTS Assessment Process.

SAP-O *See* SCERTS Assessment Process–Observation.

SAP-Q *See* SCERTS Assessment Process–Quality Indicators.

SAP-R *See* SCERTS Assessment Process–Report.

SCERTS Assessment Process (SAP) A comprehensive system for profiling a child's strengths and needs, as well as partners' abilities supporting the child to develop and comprehensive SCERTS educational plan for a child.

SCERTS Assessment Process–Observation (SAP-O) The observational component of the SCERTS Assessment Process (SAP) that provides crucial information about a child's abilities in social communication and emotional regulation, as well as partners' abilities in providing transactional supports. Such abilities are documented in the SCERTS curriculum-based assessment.

SCERTS Assessment Process–Quality Indicators (SAP-Q) Quality indicator checklists that allow for an external or self-assessment of an agency or school program relative to the critical features of the SCERTS Model.

SCERTS Assessment Process–Report (SAP-R) Questionnaire filled out by a child's parents and other caregivers as part of the SCERTS Assessment Process (SAP), used to capture the most accurate picture of a child's abilities.

SCERTS Model A comprehensive, multidisciplinary approach to enhancing the communication and social-emotional abilities of children with ASD and related disabilities. The model prioritizes social communication, emotional regulation, and transactional support as the primary developmental domains that must be addressed in a comprehensive educational program.

self-determination The capacity to live one's life in a manner that allows for regular and frequent opportunities for active decision making regarding personal choices and preferences, independent of external influences.

self-regulation The independent use of emotional regulatory capacities and skills to remain organized and well regulated in the face of potentially stressful circumstances.

Self-Regulation The component of Emotional Regulation in the SCERTS Model that addresses a child's self-regulation capacities.

sensory processing disturbances Impairments in the ability to register and or integrate multimodal sensory stimulation from the environment or one's own body in order to stay well regulated and respond adaptively in everyday activities.

sensory-motor strategies *See* behavioral strategies.

sentence grammar The rule-governed linguistic system concerned with the acquisition of the fundamentals of morphology and syntax (word and sentence organization).

setting events Within a positive behavior support (PBS) approach, setting events are identified as those factors that do not directly cause problem behaviors but that make it more likely that a child will engage in problem behavior. For example, difficult task demands may be a setting event for problem behavior.

shared control An arrangement in which two or more partners have opportunities for turn taking and choice making, with the ultimate goal of each partner developing the capacity to follow the other partner's agenda in a flexible manner.

shutdown A state of extreme emotional dysregulation characterized by disengagement and unavailability, typically resulting from the inability to cope with levels of sensory or social input.

signals of dysregulation Observable physical signs or behaviors that indicate a child's state of dysregulation, which may reflect high or low emotional arousal; these signs or behaviors may or may not be conventional or easily recognizable. For example, conventional signals include facial expressions or vocalizations clearly indicative of distress or anxiety that are easily understood as such by a variety of partners. Unconventional signals may include more subtle or difficult-to-read signals, such as bodily postures or idiosyncratic vocalizations that are only understood by the child's parents or those who know the child well.

situation-specific learning Skill acquisition that remains specific to a learning context, teacher or partner, and teaching materials. Due to a lack of generalization, skills learned in this manner are often prompt dependent, inflexible, and not functional.

skill-based approaches Educational approaches that focus on teaching skills, often using a highly repetitive drill format outside the context of meaningful activities. *See also* activity-based learning approaches.

social communication A child's ability to understand social events, and to participate and communicate as a competent, confident, and active participant in social activities using both verbal and/or nonverbal skills.

Social Communication The first major domain of the SCERTS Model, which pertains to a child's social communication abilities. This domain is divided into two components: Joint Attention and Symbol Use.

social control The ability to express one's opinions and direct others in a manner that best meets one's needs for self-determination. Problem behaviors often are an attempt at exerting social control using less socially desirable means to communicate.

social interaction A category of communicative function involving signals that are used to attract and maintain another's attention to oneself (e.g., requesting a social game or continuation of a game, requesting comfort, greeting, calling, showing off).

social motivation The drive and desire to be with, relate to, and learn from family members, other children, and partners.

social exchange *See* exchange (social or communicative).

Social Partner stage The first and earliest stage in the SCERTS Model, followed by the Language Partner and Conversational Partner stages. In general, children at the Social Partner stage are presymbolic and are communicating primarily through gestures and/or vocalizations. *See also* Language Partner stage; Social Partner stage.

Social Stories   Strategies developed by Carol Gray (1994) to support the development of social understanding. Social Stories may involve rehearsed visual and/or written scripts that provide social-communicative rules and conventions for understanding of and successful participation in everyday activities, taking into account the perspectives of partners.

social understanding   The ability to process how interpersonal actions, cues, and contextual variables influence participants in social activities.

Social-Emotional Growth Indicators   A composite of a child's growth in social and emotional development, which affects a child's engagement with the environment and people and capacity to learn. The indicators are based on a child's scores on selected SCERTS Assessment Process-Observation (SAP-O) objectives that are combined to measure progress in the areas of 1) Happiness, 2) Sense of Self, 3) Sense of Other, 4) Active Learning and Organization, 5) Flexibility and Resilience, 6) Cooperation and Appropriateness of Behavior, 7) Independence, and 8) Social Membership and Friendships.

socialization   The process of shaping a child's social behavior, determined by how others react to the child's emotional expression and whether such expression is viewed as socially acceptable relative to culturally determined standards of behavior.

structure   Consistency, predictability, and familiarity within activities and routines fostered by environmental, instructional, and interpersonal features and supports.

support among professionals   One component of Transactional Support in the SCERTS Model, involving direct and explicit recognition of professionals' challenges (educational and emotional) and a plan to mitigate these challenges so that the professionals may be as effective as possible in supporting children and families.

support to families   One component of Transactional Support in the SCERTS Model, involving direct and explicit recognition of families' challenges (educational and emotional) and a plan to mitigate these challenges so that families may be as effective as possible in supporting their children and the educational process.

symbol use   The ability for a child to make one thing stand for or represent something else and to hold and manipulate that symbol in his or her mind. This ability underlies language and imaginative play abilities.

Symbol Use   The component of the Social Communication domain in the SCERTS Model that deals with a child's symbol use.

teachable moments   Spontaneous episodes of instruction of skills within meaningful, purposeful, and intrinsically motivating activities that take advantage of naturally occurring cues and opportunities.

theme-oriented activities   Activities that are organized around and have multiple embedded components related to functional skills in daily routines or imaginary events.

three-point gaze shift   *See* gaze shift.

transactional model of development   One of the most influential models in the study of child development, first introduced by psychologist Arnold Sameroff (1987) in the 1970s and expanded on since then. It is the source of a number of defining characteristics of the SCERTS Model: 1) A child is viewed as an active learner; 2) all aspects of development are seen as interrelated rather than as separate strands; 3) interactions with children who provide good social and language models are viewed as an essential part of supporting communication and emotional regulation; and 4) when professionals and paraprofessionals begin to work with a child, they enter into dynamic relationships with the family.

transactional support   The support that is available to a child and his or her family and among professionals that work with the child that enable the child to function and develop optimally.

Transactional Support   The third major domain of the SCERTS Model that delineates a child's needs in interpersonal support and learning support, as well as support to be provided to families and among professionals. The concept of Transactional Support recognizes that there is an ongoing mutual influence between two or more partners in social exchange and that all partners bear some responsibility to make it successful.

two-point gaze shift   *See* gaze shift.

unconventional verbal behavior   Vocal production that is composed of recognizable speech but that violates, to some degree, socially accepted conventions of linguistic communication. This category of behavior includes classes of speech behavior that have been referred to as echolalia (immediate or delayed), incessant questioning, and perseverative speech. *See also specific classes of speech behavior.*

underarousal   *See* emotional arousal; low state of arousal.

visual supports   Ways of presenting information using visual aids, including individual or sequences of objects, photographs, logos, picture symbols, and written language to enhance a child's active participation and understanding.

REFERENCE

Lester, B.M., Freier, K., & LaGasse, L. (1995). Prenatal cocaine exposure and child outcome: What do we really know. In M. Lewis & M. Bendersky (Eds.), *Mothers, babies, and cocaine: The role of toxins in development* (pp. 19-40). Mahwah, NJ: Lawrence Erlbaum Associates.

Index
Volumes I and II

This index serves both volumes of *The SCERTS™ Model: A Comprehensive Educational Approach for Children with Autism Spectrum Disorders.* I and II indicate Volumes I and II, respectively. Page numbers followed by *t* and *f* indicate tables and figures, respectively.